China's foreign policy in the Arab world, 1955-75

China's foreign policy in the Arab world, 1955-75

Three case studies

Hashim S. H. Behbehani

KPI

London, Boston, Melbourne and Henley

First published in 1981 by KPI Limited
14 Leicester Square, London WC2H 7PH, England
Published in paperback in 1985

Distributed by
Routledge & Kegan Paul plc
14 Leicester Square, London WC2H 7PH, England

Routledge & Kegan Paul Inc
9 Park Street, Boston, Mass. 02108, USA

Routledge & Kegan Paul
464 St Kilda Road, Melbourne,
Victoria 3004, Australia and

Routledge & Kegan Paul plc
Broadway House, Newtown Road,
Henley-on-Thames, Oxon RG9 1EN, England

Printed in Great Britain by
Redwood Burn Limited, Trowbridge, Wiltshire

ISBN 0-7103-0125-1

To my mother (1928–80)
And the revolutionary spirit and soul of
Abu Khalid (GEORGE SHAFĪḲ)

Contents

Contents

Contents

Illustrations

Abbreviations

AAPSO	Afro-Asian People's Solidarity Organisation
AASC	Afro-Asian Solidarity Committee
AAWB	Afro-Asian Writers' Bureau
A-CFLAC	All-China Federation of Literature and Art Circles
A-CSF	All-China Student Federation
ALPO	Arab Labour Party of Oman
ANM	Arab Nationalist Movement
ARY	Arab Republic of Yemen
ASLP	Arab Socialist Labour Party
AWP	Arab Workers' Party
CCAAS	Chinese Committee for Afro-Asian Solidarity
CCP	Chinese Communist Party
CIA	Chinese Islamic Association
CPAFFC	Chinese People's Association for Friendship with Foreign Countries
CPCCRFC	Chinese People's Committee for Cultural Relations with Foreign Countries
CPIFA	Chinese People's Institute for Foreign Affairs
CPSU	Communist Party of the Soviet Union
DCA	Dhofar Charitable Association
DLF	Dhofar Liberation Front
DSO	Dhofar Soldiers' Organisation
Fataḥ	National Liberation Movement of Palestine
FLN	Front de Liberation Nationale
MEN	Middle East News
NCNA	New China News Agency (Hsin hua)
NDFLOAG	National Democratic Front for the Liberation of Oman and the Arabian Gulf
NFLP	National Front for the Liberation of Palestine
OAP	Organisation of Arab Palestine

OLF	Oman Liberation Front
OLS	Organisation of Lebanese Socialists
OPEC	Organisation of Petroleum Exporting Countries
PDFLP	Popular Democratic Front for the Liberation of Palestine
PDRY	People's Democratic Republic of Yemen (South Yemen)
PFLO	Popular Front for the Liberation of Oman
PFLOAG	Popular Front for the Liberation of Occupied Arabian Gulf
PFLOAG	Popular Front for the Liberation of Oman and the Arabian Gulf
PFLP	Popular Front for the Liberation of Palestine
PFLP-GC	Popular Front for the Liberation of Palestine-General Command
PLA	Palestine Liberation Army
PLF	Palestine Liberation Front
PLO	Palestine Liberation Organisation
PLO-NC	Palestine Liberation Organisation — National Council
PRC	People's Republic of China
PRM	Palestine Resistance Movement
PRMOAG	Popular Revolutionary Movement of Oman and Arabian Gulf
SAF	Sultan's Armed Forces
SCMM	Selection of China Mainland Magazine
SCMP	Survey of China Mainland Press
SCMS	South China Morning Star
UDF	Union Defence Force
UNEF	United Nations Emergency Force
YAR	Yemen Arab Republic (North Yemen)

Note on transliteration and sources

The transliteration of Arabic is according to the *Encyclopaedia of Islam* (New Edition, 1965). The standard Wade-Giles transliteration is employed for Chinese terms. In the Bibliography, essential sources are indicated with an asterisk.

Names of places and states are according to official standards.

Chapter 1

China and the Arab world

China's foreign policy towards the Arab world is here dealt with in three separate, distinct, but complementary phases (1955-66; 1967-70; 1970-5). The first deals with issues of foreign policy which emerged after independence in 1949 until the early 1960s, although by 1959 Chinese leaders had set a course for a foreign policy independent of that of the USSR, whose role and prestige in the communist bloc had previously dominated all communist bloc foreign policies. Immediately after the establishment of the People's Republic of China (PRC), the new regime was confronted with one of the most serious military operations in the history of the emerging state. The Korean War, in 1950, though it was by no means wanted by China, actually enhanced the People's Republic's prestige in the world as a whole, and particularly within the communist bloc. Security in Manchuria, as its most important heavy industrial area, was essential to China. Since North Korea had a common border with Manchuria, it was important that the North Korean regime be sympathetic to, and preferably under the influence of, the Chinese regime. Thus China had to face directly the most formidable nation in the world, and its troops found themselves in direct confrontation with American forces on the battlefield. China's ability to withstand American might was very important to the survival of the regime. Moreover, it is important to remember that although the USSR supplied a limited quantity of arms to its allies, the Soviet role in the conflict was only secondary. This confirmed China's fears concerning the limited extent to which the Soviet leadership was willing to intervene actively on the side of its communist allies.

After the stalemate in Korea, and once China's borders were secure in that area, attention was diverted to Indo-China, where France was facing insurmountable difficulties, particularly in Vietnam. The Geneva Peace Conference from 27 April to 15 June 1954[1] had originally been convened to discuss the unification of Korea; but it failed to accomplish this task and, taking place shortly after the Viet Minh victory at Dien Bien Phu, only succeeded in temporarily halting the war in Indo-China. Shortly after this, China once again got involved in a problem which was considered central to its basic foreign policy objectives: in September 1954, it shelled Quemoy, an island off the coast of China held by the Republic of China (Taiwan). Though China failed to liberate Taiwan, this had apparently not been its immediate objective. Rather, the whole affair had been aimed at following a 'tit for tat' policy against 'US imperialism', and brought about two developments. On the one hand, Taiwan signed a Mutual Defence Treaty with the USA, thus adding a new element to the USA's intensification of the cold war policy of containing China. On the other hand, the USSR consistently kept a low profile in the whole affair, thus increasing Chinese disappointment.

The Bandung Conference and its aftermath

The Bandung Conference in 1955 opened a new phase in China's diplomatic thrust in the Arab world. China had had diplomatic relations with Arab states since 1936 during the Republican era. Trade relations between the USSR and Saudi Arabia had started in 1927 when two Soviet trade delegations visited Saudi Arabia (the USSR was the first foreign power to recognise the rule of Ibn Sa'ud), but no substantial gains were achieved because of British influence. However on 2 August 1931 an agreement was signed between the two parties 'which provided for a Soviet shipment to Saudi Arabia of 100,000 crates of petrol and kerosene. Prince Faisal (subsequent ruler of Saudi Arabia), a son of Ibn Sa'ud, served as a sort of Minister of Foreign Affairs and visited the USSR in May 1932'.[2] Through the efforts of the USSR attempts were made to establish diplomatic relations between the Republic of China and the Arab World, and China appointed its first consul to Jidda in 1939.[3] Relations with other Arab states followed: Iraq, which signed a Sino-Iraqi Treaty of Amity on 16 March 1942, received Li Tieh-tseng as the first Chinese Minister to Egypt on 7 September 1943; and on 14 November 1944 the Chinese Ministry of Foreign Affairs announced the Chinese government's decision to extend recognition to both Lebanon and Syria.[4] When the PRC was established in 1949 all the independent Arab states extended recognition to the Republic of China (Taiwan), leaving Peking in a disadvantageous position.

Up to the beginning of the Cultural Revolution China's definition of the Third World was quite different from what it became in the 1970s, and the Arab World was of course included in it. Chu Jung-fu succinctly outlined China's foreign policy in the world and set out Chinese priorities, in October 1954. According to him, the countries of the world in their relations with China 'may be divided into four' categories, each of which is different:

To the first category belong the Socialist Soviet Union and the people's democracies in Europe and Asia. . . .

To the second category belong the countries of Asia, Africa and Latin America. These colonial and semi-colonial states have either won national independence or are engaged in the struggle for national independence. Both the Chinese people and the people of these countries have for a long time been subjected to the oppression and exploitation of imperialism and have suffered long enough . . . the people's war of liberation had been attended by victory, they became widely jubilant, and the governments of many Asian countries announced their recognition of the People's Government of China. *There are quite many other countries where the people desire the recognition of People's China, but their governments, under pressure from the United States, have not dared to do so.* [Emphasis added]

To the third category belong all the Western countries other than the United States. All these countries had enjoyed special privileges in old China, and among them there are some colonial powers. These enfeebled old colonial powers naturally do not welcome the movement for national liberation in the colonies and semi-colonies. . . .

To the fourth category belongs the United States . . . The United States not only refuses itself to recognise the Government of the Chinese people, but also applies all kinds of pressure to force other countries into non-recognition. The United States furthermore controls the voting machinery of the United Nations and deprives the People's Republic of China of its legal status and rights in the United Nations. . . .

The peaceful foreign policy of People's China is based on the strengthening of its unity, mutual aid, and cooperation with the Soviet Union and the People's Democracies. The great Soviet Union is the strong bastion of world peace, and the most reliable friend of the Chinese people.[5]

To counter the US policy of containing China, Chu proposed first that 'unity and cooperation' between China and the Socialist bloc, led by the Soviet Union, be strengthened. Secondly, although co-operation with the Asian, African and Latin American states was impeded because of the USA's 'aggressive' policies towards China, 'differences in social and political systems do not constitute obstacles to the establishment of such peaceful and cooperative relations'.[6] More significant to Chinese understanding of these areas, the 'liberation' of any of these countries meant above all 'liberation from colonialism and imperialism' and *not necessarily* the support of liberation movements at the expense of a moderate government in any of these states. Priority was given to reducing American influence in this area, and relations with such countries should be based on 'the principles of mutual respect for territorial sovereignty, mutual non-aggression, mutual non-interference with internal affairs, equality and mutual benefit, and peaceful co-existence'.[7] The Five Principles of Peaceful Co-existence were first formally expressed in a statement signed between China and India in June 1954. Thirdly, relations with western countries other than the USA must be based on 'equality and respect [for] the territorial sovereignty of new China',[8] and China is 'desirous' to develop trade relations with this bloc. Lastly, to break the USA containment policy, China must 'oppose resolutely such aggressive policies'[9] throughout the world.

When Chou-En-lai went to the Bandung Conference in April 1955, China was given an opportunity that it could not neglect; the Chinese delegation was most impressive and Chou went out of his way to dispel fears among the participants of China's 'aggressive communist designs' by advocating strongly its adherence to the Five Principles of Peaceful Co-existence. Of the 26 states which participated at the Bandung Conference, 18 had not recognised China and the overwhelming majority were tied, in one way or another, to the USA in direct or indirect military pacts. Bandung was most rewarding to China's diplomatic thrust in the Arab world for, after the conference, Egypt, Syria and Yemen recognised and established diplomatic relations with China in 1956 and Egypt was, in the same year, the first Arab recipient of Chinese foreign aid. Later in 1956 the Suez crisis erupted, and China was a strong political supporter of the Egyptian cause throughout the crisis. Chou, moreover, recognising the different composition and the importance of this bloc, was more than keen to make certain distinctions between the political development of the participating states.

It was

At Bandung, and for two years afterwards, the Chinese avoided
the term 'national liberation' using instead more neutral phrases
such as 'the struggle against colonialism and for independence and
freedom'. Only Mao, interestingly, referred to 'the national
independence and liberation movement' (in his opening address
to the Eighth Party Congress [September 1956]), thus confirming
that the words were not synonymous. A nation could win
independence [emphasis in original] from the colonial power,
whether the revolution was led by the proletariat or by the
national bourgeoisie. The term *liberation* [emphasis in original]
suggested a social dimension to the anti-colonial revolution. China
had been liberated. India had achieved national independence.[10]

Until 1967, when China's militant stand was exemplified by support
for national liberation movements, Sino-Arab relations were of minor
importance to internal developments in the Arab world, except Algeria,
where China played a significant role in both military and political aid
to the Front de Liberation Nationale (FLN). [From 1958 to 1962
Sino-Arab relations reflected the influence of the Soviet Union on
Chinese internal affairs.[11]] China turned towards Iraq when the revolution of 14 July 1958 took place under the leadership of 'Abd al-Karim
Ḳasim and 'Abd al-Salam 'Araf. The Iraqi Communist Party was found
to have influence in the Iraqi state apparatus, at a time when most
Syrian communists were in prison or in exile, and there were hardly
any communists left in Egypt because of Naṣir's campaign against
them. The success of the coup d'etat in Iraq gave hope of a change
from a traditionally pro-western monarchy to a popular pro-socialist
bloc tendency, although the success of the Iraqi progressives' take-over
was viewed by Naṣir with reservations because it threatened Arab
nationalism in general and, in particular, was a threat to the Union
of Syria and Egypt (led by Naṣir). China clearly intended to develop
relations with Iraq, for the latter not only achieved political independence but also had a sizeable and growing Communist Movement which
was also favoured by the Soviet Union. Naṣir, in December 1958,
started his criticism – and subsequent persecution – of local communists who were attempting to undermine the Union of Egypt and Syria.
China's response to Naṣir's persecution of local communists and attacks
on Ḳasim's Iraq, was strong. It condemned these actions, and launched
attacks, even personal ones, against Naṣir in March–April 1959. These
attacks were reciprocated by the United Arab Republic's (UAR's)

(Egypt and Syria) propaganda campaign against China and the Soviet Union. In an obvious rebuff to Naṣir, China invited the outlawed Secretary-General of the Syrian Communist Party, Khalid Bakdash, to the celebrations of the 10th anniversary of the PRC's foundation, and gave him the warmest reception. (He spoke at the ceremonies in the presence of Mao, Liu-Shao-Chi, Chou En-lai and world communist leaders, and strongly attacked Naṣir and his policies.)

In October 1962, when the Sino-Indian border clashes occurred, Egypt claimed to follow a policy of neutrality on the dispute, but was officially sympathetic to the Indian side. Naṣir however played a significant role in temporarily reconciling the two sides and Nehru expressed gratitude to Naṣir's obvious pro-Indian stand at the Colombo Conference in Ceylon in December 1962. Though the Colombo Conference succeeded in achieving a cessation of hostilities between the antagonists, Sino-Indian relations did not improve.

Radicalisation of China's foreign policy

The 1960–70 period of the Cultural Revolution had an important impact on China's foreign policies in the Arab world. Starting with the exchange of polemics at the Bucharest meeting of the Third Congress of the Communist Party of Rumania in June 1960, relations between China and the USSR deteriorated, and in August of the same year all Soviet experts were withdrawn from China and aid terminated. The polemics between the two states remained concealed until 1963, and their final deterioration in 1967. Until then China's relations with the Third World concentrated on the 'national independence' gains of these countries and few statements were made on the viability of the 'people's war' theory. National independence, as indicated earlier, had two implications: a given developing country must gain political independence; the corollary is the 'struggle to achieve economic independence'. Nan Han-chen, addressing the Afro-Asian Economic Seminar in Algiers on 23 February 1965 argued these points at length.[12] In his attempt to analyse the subject he presented two main questions and one proposition.

1 What is the root cause of poverty and backwardness in the economy of the Afro-Asian countries at the present time?
2 Why is it that the development of an independent national economy is the basic way to achieve economic independence?[13]
3 Self reliance and mutual assistance.

In answering the first question he presented six points that had to be noted:

1 Under various forms and in various degrees the imperialists and old and new colonialists still maintain various kinds of privileges which encroach upon the sovereignty and independence of many countries. Militarily, for instance, the imperialists headed by the United States have the privilege of establishing military bases and stationing troops in many countries; politically they enjoy extra-territoriality and economically the so-called rights of land concessions, prospecting and exploiting mines, customs administration, issuance of paper money.

2 The imperialists and old and new colonialists still control the major branches of production and economic lifelines of many countries. . . About four-fifths of the total output of 22 kinds of important raw materials in Asia, Africa and Latin America are under the control of the monopoly capital of these imperialist countries. . . What merits special mention is the exploitation of the oil resources by the imperialists in Asian and African countries.

3 The imperialists also control the international market, manipulate world prices, arbitrarily lower the prices of primary products and raise the prices of manufactured goods, they buy cheap and sell dear, practising non-equivalent exchange and causing great losses to the Afro-Asian countries.

4 The imperialists also practise usury in various forms exacting high rates of interest and seriously impairing the normal development of the national economy of the debtor nations.

5 The so-called 'economic aid' provided by the imperialists, particularly by the US imperialists, is a typical instrument through which the neo-colonialists attempt to extend their control and exploitation, even to interfere in the internal affairs of or to subvert the recipient countries.

6 The imperialists also control and monopolise maritime shipping and insurance business[14] and exploit the Afro-Asian countries through invisible trade.

These elements were basic in Chinese arguments, but Nan went on to illustrate the means by which these countries could achieve their ultimate objective of political independence:

From their own experience in the struggle, the Afro-Asian peoples have come to understand that the achievement of

> political independence is but the first step towards complete
> national liberation, because political independence and economic
> independence are inseparable . . . . Therefore the fundamental
> way for the Afro-Asian peoples to realise these aspirations is to
> develop an independent national economy on the basis of self-
> reliance and through assistance to each other based on equality
> and mutual benefit.[15]

According to Nan the model for these countries was China's political and economic development, to achieve which he proposed the policy of 'self-reliance'.

> The starting point of our aid to foreign countries is: in accordance
> with the spirit of proletarian internationalism, first to support
> the fraternal countries of the socialist camp to carry out their
> socialist construction so as to increase the might of the whole
> socialist camp; secondly to support the newly independent
> countries in developing their national economies through their
> own efforts so as to strengthen the forces of the peoples of the
> world in their united struggle against imperialism and, thirdly,
> to support those countries[16] which are not yet independent in
> winning their independence.

Although this recommendation may be desirable for many developing countries, its implementation poses quite insurmountable obstacles in this difficult period of national development. The Chinese case, unlike that of other developing countries, is different through the sheer presence and historical development of the Chinese Communist Party, an experience which was unique. Secondly, for any of these countries to attain political, let alone economic independence, is almost impossible given the basic dependence on the international markets of their economic structures. Thirdly, throughout the discussion on foreign aid, priority was given to aid to the socialist countries but the USSR was omitted and no longer recognised as a 'leader of the socialist bloc'.

With the emergence of the Cultural Revolution, Lin Piao published the famous article 'Long Live the Victory of People's War' in September 1965. Both these Liberation Movements under study here (Nan's and Lin Piao's) adhered to the idea of a people's war and members of both fronts started studying the Chinese experience in this field, but Lin singled out Palestine in the Arab world where armed struggle was growing. Lin's general assumption was rather simplistic: North America and Western Europe constitute the 'cities of the world' while Asia, Africa and Latin America are 'the rural areas of the world'; the liberation movements, Lin argued from Chinese experience, can succeed *only* through the countryside which provides 'the broad areas in which the revolutionaries can manoeuvre freely'.

The process of liberation and revolution, according to Lin, must be 'led by the proletariat and the genuinely revolutionary party armed with Marxism–Leninism', and by no other class or party; the revolution must embrace other strata besides the worker-peasants and the urban petty bourgeoisie like the 'national bourgeoisie and other patriotic and anti-imperialist democrats; which implies that the revolution is directed against imperialism, feudalism and bureaucrat-capitalism', and finally socialism will be achieved. One of the most remarkable features of Lin's argument was the omission of any reference to the USSR's role in enhancing 'world revolution' and the assertion that the Chinese experience alone sufficed as an example to Afro-Asian-Latin American conditions. This omission became more marked during the upheavals of the Cultural Revolution. On one map put out in 1968[17] the world was interpreted by China in such a way that the emphases of world politics were put on the possibilities of armed struggle, the internal 'severe crises' in the western system, and the USSR's policy of 'capitulation and betrayal abroad', and seen to divide the world into spheres of domination by the USA. Omissions from this map are also of interest: for example, in the case of the Arab world, developments in Dhofar were omitted just at a time, in 1968, when China was actively interested in the war; only Palestine and the People's Democratic Republic of Yemen are noted to represent the 'excellent world situation' in this area.

Until 1971, however, China's foreign policy priorities revolved around the support for national liberation movements based on the principles of armed struggle, at the expense of China's existing diplomatic relations with foreign countries. China opposed 'Soviet revisionism' and 'US imperialism' and gave importance to the militant role played by 'the progressive forces' in the industrial states.

The contradictions of China's Three Worlds theory 1971–5

Discussion of the different aspects of the division of the world is abundantly scattered throughout Chinese literature from 1971 to 1975, and particular attention is given to the USSR which is said to share the superpower privilege with the USA.[18] One of the most valuable Chinese studies of their world outlook was published in 1977 by the *People's*

Daily.[19] Mao, we are told, had a theory dividing the international political situation on a 'scientific Marxist assessment' which included three divisions:

1. The first world comprising the United States and the Soviet Union.
2. The second world including industrialised Europe, Japan and Canada.
3. The third world encompasses the rest of the countries, and China is a forerunner in this bloc.

This differentiation 'is based on the analysis of the development of the fundamental contradictions of the contemporary world and the changes in them in accordance with Lenin's thesis that our era is the era of imperialism and proletarian revolution'.[20] It is, we are told, based intrinsically on 'present-day class struggle on a world scale'. Thus 'in waging the struggle on the international arena, the proletariat must unite with all those who can be united in the light of what is imperative and feasible in different historical periods, so as to *develop the progressive forces, win over the middle forces and isolate the diehards.*[21] [emphasis in original] It is within this Chinese logic that the imperative of uniting with whoever necessary in the 'different historical periods' is the most crucial element in the argument; its basic implication is that a nation's alignment must be evaluated and readjusted according to its *national interest* at different historical periods, and that it must act according to what it perceives to serve best its international objectives. This is not to say that the Chinese division lacks inherent internal cohesion, i.e. the theory could be realised and applied within a certain world situation, particularly in the case of the Third World; but the arguments presented by Chinese advocates of Mao's theory must be viewed with certain reservations because its potential implementation lacks credibility.

Since the Second World War, the *People's Daily* argues, the international political situation was initially characterised by the emergence of US imperialism which 'raised an incessant anti-Soviet clamour'. But 'contradictions' among western imperialist powers resulted in a conflict of interests among them, and the Suez canal crisis of 1956 was only an example of this. Mao had argued at the time that:

From this incident we can pin-point the focus of struggle in the world today. The contradiction between the imperialist countries and the socialist countries is certainly most acute. But the

10

> *imperialist countries are now contending with each other for*
> *the control of different areas in the name of opposing commun-*
> *ism. . . . In the Middle East, two kinds of contradiction and three*
> *kinds of force are in conflict. The two kinds of contradiction are:*
> *first those between different imperialist powers, that is between*
> *the United States and Britain and between the United States and*
> *France, and second, those between the imperialist powers and the*
> *oppressed nations. The three kinds of force are: one the United*
> *States, the biggest imperialist power, two, Britain and France,*
> *second-rate imperialist powers, and three, the oppressed nations.*[22]
> [emphasis in original]

During this period, according to the argument, several Third World countries gained their national independence and the socialist camp marked the division between the imperialist one and the Third World. But during the 1960s and 'after a succession of grave events' the world was faced with a 'new historical situation' due mainly to the USSR's 'betrayal of socialism': it had itself become a superpower contending with the US for 'world hegemony'. With the weakening of the USA as a result of its involvement in wars, we are told that the USSR

> strove to develop its own strength, narrowed the gap in economic
> development between itself and the United States and immensely
> expanded its military power. It has caught up with the United
> States in nuclear armament and surpassed it in conventional
> weaponry. As its military and economic power increases, Soviet
> Social-imperialism becomes more and more flagrant in its attempt
> to expand and penetrate all parts of the world.[23]

The USSR, thus the main contender for superpower hegemony, had surpassed the USA militarily: its deployment of troops in Europe, the main zone of contention for military supremacy, is an obvious example. Moreover, while the US 'exercises control over the economy and politics of many countries through its trans-national corporations and other instruments of aggression . . . [at] present the Soviet Union is carrying on such activities mainly within the "socialist community"'.[24] The USSR also exercises its control abroad through selling arms 'in order to extract huge profits' and also terminates 'supplies of needed parts and accessories and dunning them for payment' when it feels this is necessary.

Lastly, according to the Chinese argument, of the two superpowers the USSR is the more dangerous source of world war because it is a latecomer to imperialism, and thus seeks speedy expansion, and it is easier for the Soviet leadership since it has transformed 'a highly centralised socialist state-owned economy into a state monopoly capitalist economy without its equal in any other country and has transformed a state under the dictatorship of the proletariat into a state under fascist dictatorship'.[25] It is also more dangerous because it is comparatively inferior to the US economically and therefore has to resort to military expansion and threats of war; and finally it originated as a result 'of the degeneration of the first socialist country in the world'. Thus it 'exploits Lenin's prestige and flaunts the banner of "socialism" to bluff and deceive people everywhere'.

The Second World, which includes Europe, Japan and Canada, is, to China, a force that could be 'united with in the struggle against hegemonism'. From the Second World War changes occurred which altered the Second World's role in 'international political and economic relations': they sought independence from US domination by establishing, for example, the Common Market; their relations with the Third World have altered, for they

> no longer constitute the main force dominating and oppressing
> these countries. In certain cases their own interests even compel
> them to make certain concessions to the Third World countries
> or to give some support to the Third World's struggle against
> hegemonism or to remain neutral.[26]

The Third World, however, in Chinese terms, 'constitutes the main force in the worldwide struggle against the hegemonism of the two superpowers and against imperialism and colonialism', and it is in this region that the more interesting questions arise. Before examining China's interpretation, a few points must be made, including some which are acknowledged in the Chinese arguments themselves only to be lightly dismissed, i.e., recognised but not considered as serious impediments for ultimate Third World unity. First, the Third World shares a wide range of common attitudes towards the former colonialists: nationalism, anti-colonialism, non-alignment and 'socialism'. Of these factors only nationalism remains a strong force. Anti-colonialism has fulfilled its role and is not a strong unifying force. Socialism has no accepted definition and its application to the Third World has encountered obstacles. Non-alignment has lost its importance not only because of these countries' need for help from industrialised countries, but also because the 'non-aligned bloc' manifests the same divisions as the rest of the world, including an anti-Soviet drive generated by the bloc's pro-US states like Saudi Arabia, and pro-Chinese states, like the Sudan. Second, the differences within the states of this bloc are enormous: different political structures, different cultural backgrounds, different levels of economic development, per capita income, and different historical experiences. Third, the term Third World is not clearly defined and politically aims at forming a bloc against the industrialised countries, but is *not* directly against either the USA or the USSR. It is merely an association for furthering its interests and attempting to obtain more economic gains and some compromises from the industrialised world. All these states are weak, insecure and poor by comparison with the industrialised world. Last, only a handful of these states, at best, share the Chinese understanding of the three-world division. The developing countries have complex and demanding problems of their own, and have little time for Chinese notions about 'unifying' a bloc to counter 'superpower hegemony'. The obstacles they face, particularly at the economic level, have widened the gap between the industrialised and the developing countries.[27]

What and who, according to the Chinese, is the Third World? The *People's Daily* points out that since the Second World War, 'the revolutionary people of Asia, Africa and Latin America have waged one revolutionary armed struggle after another and scored a series of magnificent victories that have changed the face of the world'.[28] The Third World includes over 3,000 million people — i.e. 70 per cent of the world population — 'enslaved people' who are or were 'freeing themselves from the fetters of colonialism'. In a few of these countries Communist Parties have been built and the proletariat has waged antiimperialist struggles, but there never existed a 'worldwide movement embracing all areas' in the process of liberation for the people of the colonies. Now the transition is different:

> will the countries of Asia, Africa and Latin America which have
> won independence continue to be the main force in the struggle
> against imperialism for a fairly long historical period? Our answer
> is yes. It must be realised that though they have declared their
> independence they are still faced with the grave task of winning
> complete political and economic independence.[29]

And the struggle must be waged 'above all against the expansionist activities of the superpowers'. This is the primary task of Asian, African and Latin-American countries. Moreover the conditions set for Chinese aid to any liberation movement — i.e. based on armed struggle — are that it should openly and clearly oppose the USSR's 'hegemonistic' international role and, to a lesser extent, it should be opposed to the USA. The point here which the Chinese do not appear to be aware of is that a national liberation movement in Asia, Africa or Latin America does not operate in an internal vacuum: its armed struggle is primarily aimed at the ruling élite in its own country. Once this is accomplished, imperialism, represented by the USA in particular, will be abolished from their country. One may justifiably ask how Pinochet of Chile, the Shah of Iran, or for that matter Sultan Ḳabus of Oman, could be said to have achieved national independence in the political sense, when all they aspired to was the suppression of certain internal political movements, while they were closely linked to the USA internationally, and displayed elements of anti-Sovietism.

The Chinese argument is that 'political awareness' in the Third World states has enhanced its unity: examples are the Latin-American alliance 'against superpower maritime hegemony', and the actions of the Arab members of OPEC (Organisation of Petroleum Exporting Countries). Moreover, the anti-imperialist revolutionary forces of the Third World 'gain a favourable position because of the superpowers' clash of interests in the Third World'. These states, we are told, entertain hopes of support from segments of the Second World; but such support is deemed unlikely by the Chinese:

> The workers' movements in the countries of the first and second
> worlds and the anti-imperialist struggles of the third world support
> each other. The working class and revolutionary masses of the
> developed capitalist countries have scored many signal victories
> in their heroic struggles, dealing imperialism and social-imperialism
> telling blows and rendering powerful support to the people of the
> world in their fight against imperialism and hegemonism . . . .
> But generally speaking and for the time being, as a result of the
> Soviet ruling clique's betrayal, the spread of revisionist ideology
> and the splits in the ranks of the working class, the workers'
> revolutionary movement in the developed capitalist countries
> *cannot but remain at the stage of regrouping and accumulating
> strength*[30] [emphasis added] .

Yet China, we are told, *does* differentiate between the social, political and economic development among Third World countries, and the ruling élite of these countries do adopt

> different attitudes towards imperialism and the superpowers and
> towards their own people . . . certain disputes have arisen and even
> armed conflicts have occurred between some of them. But taken

as a whole, the majority of these countries are for struggle against imperialism and hegemonism.[31]

Since, as it claims most vehemently, China belongs to the Third World, some examination of its role in the area, and its means of accomplishing its stated objectives, is needed. One way to approach this is through China's foreign aid and trade with the Third World.

Several writers argue that China's economic aid to the Third World countries is a 'sacrifice' since China ranks as one of the poorest countries in the Third World. Why then the sacrifice? We will not concentrate here on the 'origins' of Chinese foreign aid, the historical similarities between China's development and that of the Third World, Mao's vision of the international scene, or other similar problems, but will confine discussion to the general approaches, trends and above all the limitations of such aid to Third World countries. It is worth pointing out here that the needy Arab states are an important element in China's foreign aid programme; of course China constantly advocates Arab unity and looks at the various Arab states as a single political entity, but this is not reflected in international trade figures.

The importance of the Arab world, in China's view, centres around two main strategic points: geographical location and oil potential. From 1956 to 1973 China's foreign aid programmes to the Arab world (see Table 1.1) require certain comments. First, aid was granted and given directly after an Arab state gained independence: the first Chinese aid to the Arab world went to Egypt in 1956. Second, aid is used as a basis for competition with the USSR: after the June 1967 war Egypt and Algeria ranked highest in China's aid programme after Pakistan. As we will see later this aid had purely political objectives as it was given after the disastrous Arab, particularly Egyptian, defeat by Israel. Third, Sino-Soviet rivalry in aid was favourable to the USSR; the states where Chinese aid surpassed that of the USSR were Sudan, Tunisia and the People's Democratic Republic of Yemen (PDRY). The balance throughout the Arab world was in favour of the Soviet Union, who gave most of its aid to Egypt, Iraq and Algeria.[32] Fourth, 1970–2 were the years of greatest rivalry, during which Chinese aid surpassed that of the USSR. Then the Arab world, seen as one political entity, ranked highest from 1956 to 1973 in Chinese economic loans to the Third World.[33] But the majority of Chinese economic loans to the Third World went to Africa.

In granting aid, China has put forward a number of principles which rival the USSR in its approach to foreign aid. The Chinese press considers aid to be a part of 'Third World solidarity' given the unenviable

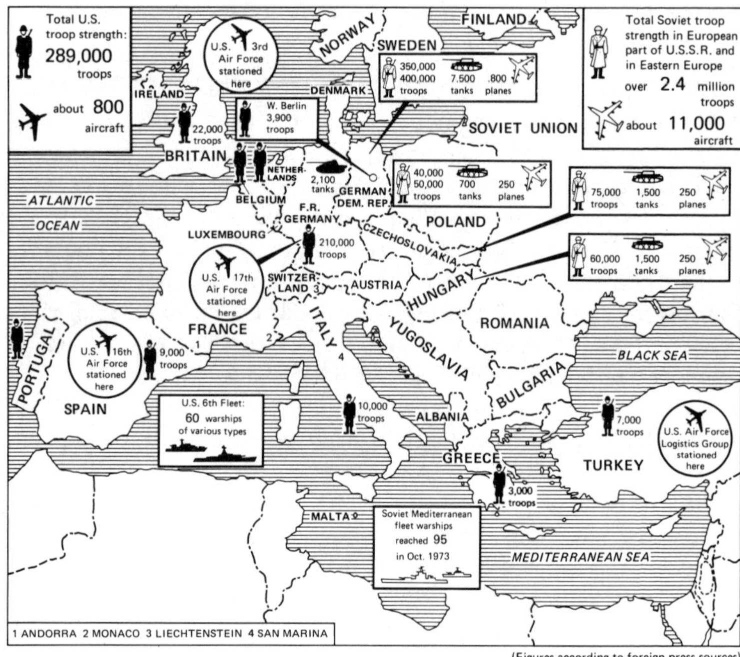

Map 1.1 Soviet and U.S. Military Deployment in Europe

Source: *Peking Review*, 'World in great disorder: excellent situation', vol. 17, no. 3, (8 January 1974), p. 8.

economic circumstances and conditions suffered by these countries in their search for foreign aid. Chinese aid is of three types, donations, interest-free loans and low interest loans. Since China is one of the poorest states in the world, why then does it embark on such a highly unprofitable economic programme? Political objectives are primary. The limitation of such aid must be considered since it is supposed to be primarily aimed at helping needy Third World countries. This must however be viewed with caution and reservations since an accurate evaluation would require knowledge of the utility of such aid for the public sector of Third World economies. China's 'transfer of technology' to Pakistan, Zaire and Ethiopia was not beneficial.[34] Given the uncertain economic development patterns of Third World countries, seen here from 1955-75, the issue is that of the long-term effect and limitation of Chinese aid in such economies. Finally, the ruling élites of these countries, be they military, traditional or other, most often had no clear notion of how to bring forward their development; by contrast the case is the opposite in the states which adhere either to the capitalist or the socialist form of development.

Table 1.1 *The foreign aid of the People's Republic of China to less developed countries (in million US$)*

	1956	1957	1958	1959	1960	1961	1962	1963	1964	1965	1966	1967	1968	1969	1970	1971	1972	1973	Total	at an interest of 2.5%	free of interest	Donation	still unused in Dec '73 (estimate)
Asia	35.1	25.6	35.5		32.6	128	20.5		4.2	260	20	40	42		219.3	128.2	68.2	30	1,089.2	69.7	711.9	257.6	
1 Burma		4.2				88.2													92.4	4.2	84	4.2	25
2 Cambodia	22.4	5.6			11.4													30[1]	69.1			69.4	25
3 Indonesia			25			30				200									255	55	150		229
4 Laos							10												10		6[1]	4	
5 Nepal	12.7				21.2	9.8					20						35[1]		98		55	437	13
6 Pakistan										60		40	42		210	93.7			335		335.7	110	110
7 Sri Lanka		15.8	10.5				10.5		4.2						9.3	34.5	33.2		118	10.5	81.2	26.3	20
Africa			4.9		25	39.2		74	119.2	21.1	15	29.8	6	45	460	323.5	282	199	1,643.7	0.5	1,612.6	30.6	
1 Algeria			4.9					51		2		2				40			99.9		93	6.9	20
2 Burundi																	20		20		20		15
3 Cameroon																	20[1]	10[1]	30		30		20
4 Central Africa									4.1										4.1		4.1		
5 Chad																		12	12		12		10
6 Congo (Brazz.)									25.4				1				30[1]		56.4		56.4		20
7 Dahomey																	46		46		46		35
8 Equatorial Guinea																10[1]			10		10		5
9 Ethiopia																80			80		80		40
10 Ghana						19.6			22.4										42		42		15
11 Guinea					25									45			30[1]		100		100		25
12 Kenya									18										18		15	3	12
13 Malagasy																		12	12		12		11
14 Mali						19.6			7.9		3		5[1]		20			10[1]	65.5		53.4	8.1	15
15 Mauritania											4					23.5			27.5		27.5		15
16 Mauritius																	32		32		32		25
17 Nigeria																	3		3		3		1
18 Ruanda																	20		20		20		15
19 Senegal																		20[1]	20		20		18
20 Sierra Leone																	20[1]		20		20		15
21 Somalia								23								110			133		130	3	70
22 Sudan															35	40			75		75		25
23 Tanzania									45.5		12				270				327.5	0.5	320.4	6.6	80
24 Togo																	45		45		45		35
25 Tunisia																	36		36		36		25
26 Uganda										15									15		12	3	10
27 Upper Volta																		10[1]	10		10		8
28 Zaire																		115	115		115		110
29 Zambia												23.8			135			10	168.8		168.8		60

Near Middle East	4		16	0.1			4.8	16.4	108.2	27.5		10	9.6	
1 Afghanistan										27.5				
2 Egypt	4								80			10		
3 Iraq														
4 South Yemen													9.6	
5 Syria								16.4						
6 Yemen			16	0.1			4.8		28.2					
Latin America														
1 Chile														
2 Guyana														
3 Peru														
Europe														
1 Malta														
Total	39.1	25.6	56.4	0.1	57.6	167.2	25.3	90.4	231.6	308.6	35	79.8	57.6	45

Near Middle East	43.2	72	138.1		449.9		428.9	21	
1 Afghanistan			49		76.5		69.5	7	35
2 Egypt					94		80	14	80
3 Iraq		36			36		36		23
4 South Yemen	43.2		20[1]		72.8		72.8		35
5 Syria		36	47		99.4		99.4		45
6 Yemen			22.1		71.2		71.2		25
Latin America	42		117		159		159		
1 Chile			65		65		65		65
2 Guyana			52		52		52		45
3 Peru	42				42		42		30
Europe					42.6				
1 Malta			42.6		42.6		42.6		35
Total	722.5	565.7	647.9	229	3,384.4	70.2	2,993.4	309.2	1589

[1] Estimate

Source: W. Bartke, *China's economic aid*, New York, 1975, pp. 10–11.

Chapter 2

Sino-Palestinian relations 1955–66

The initial phase: 1955–63

A number of important political realities must be taken into account in examining China's relations and attitudes towards the Palestinian question in this early phase of foreign policy. At that time there were no movements, independent Palestinian fronts or organisations which claimed to represent Palestinian goals and aspirations and which were considered viable forces in Arab and international politics. In these circumstances China – like the USSR – thought that the Arab-Israeli conflict could be solved through 'peaceful means and non-intervention by outside forces' (i.e. the USA). Further, in its attempt to obtain international recognition as the sole legitimate Chinese state, China initially paid lip service to the cause of Palestinian refugees in order to obtain recognition from Arab regimes. This support was shown in two ways: on the one hand through direct diplomatic contacts with Arab governments, and on the other at the Bandung Conference, in which China played an important role. Finally, though it viewed Israel as a base for 'western imperialism', China hoped that any change taking place within Israel would, in the long run, weaken the position of the USA in perpetuating the existence of a pro-western regime in Israel. Consequently, because of its belief in the same political theory, the Israeli Communist Party (Maki) was considered by China to be the only viable force which could change conditions from within, and thus create a political force which would help rid Israel of its western alliance and solve the problem of Palestinian refugees. China's position was in no way different from the Soviet Union's at that time.

Relations mediated through Arab governments: Bandung and its aftermath

The Conference of Afro-Asian States which took place between 18 and

24 April 1955 in Bandung in Indonesia marked a new stage in China's diplomatic thrust into the Arab world, since the Arab and Islamic blocs constituted a sizeable proportion of participants.[1] There were four stated basic objectives for the conference and the third one was crucial in soliciting and obtaining aid for the Palestinian cause. It stated that the Conference ought 'to consider problems of special interest to Asian and African peoples, for example, problems affecting national sovereignty, racialism and colonialism'.[2] Most participating states did not hesitate to indulge in vituperative attacks against the 'colonial heritage' and as a corollary to this, a fundamental aspect of their belief was their assertion of political independence, particularly in foreign policy decisions. The Arab bloc was determined to further the Palestinian cause at the conference and Naṣir played a key role in doing so.[3] This was an essential element in their basic political aspiration to extricate themselves from the bi-polar world of the cold war: they saw the conference as an opportunity to disentangle themselves from it, and perceived that Bandung gave them an opportunity to carry out an active independent policy in world affairs, outside the limits of the cold war. Throughout its proceedings, the conference witnessed a new upsurge of Arab nationalism.

It was at Bandung that Chou En-lai first met 'Aḥmad al-<u>Sh</u>uḳairy and Naṣir. For the first time, at Naṣir's prompting, he became aware of the numerical strength which the Arab bloc brought to bear on the Palestinian question. <u>Sh</u>uḳairy relates in his memoirs[4] that reports, said to emanate from Syrian embassies in Indonesia and India, circulated at the conference, to the effect that 'certain' Arab states planned to oppose any discussion of the Palestinian issue. Egypt and Syria resolved to defeat such attempts. <u>Sh</u>uḳairy joined the Syrian delegation in order to be able to participate fully in the effort to put the Palestinian question to the conference. This gave all participants the opportunity to observe the masterly technique displayed by Chou in easing tensions among disputing states. <u>Sh</u>uḳairy took advantage of one of the meetings arranged by Chou with the head of the Syrian delegation to raise the Syrian and Palestinian problems. <u>Sh</u>uḳairy states that he explained the history of the Palestinian problem to Chou; in return Chou 'promised' that in future he would support both Arab aims in general and the Arab position on the Palestinian question in particular. The immediate outcome was that Chou strongly supported the discussion by the conference of a resolution on Palestine. However, the inclusion of the Palestinian question was taken to be a Human Rights issue under the United Nations Charter. Chou's strong support for the Palestinian cause came as a surprise to Arab delegates, who were dismayed by the lack of support and the reservations of India's Nehru and Burma's U Nu. Chou announced at the conference's Political Committee that he 'was prepared to support a resolution expressing Arab demands for territorial revisions and recognition of the right of Arab refugees'.[5] Although the Arab block successfully obtained support for the Palestinian issue as an issue of Human Rights, the question of self-determination of the Palestinians was left unresolved. Chou's speech at the closing session[6] of the conference was repeated in detail later on, in his report to the Standing Committee of the National People's Congress on 13 May 1955.[7]

It was at Bandung also that Sino-Egyptian relations were developed, resulting in the first Sino-Arab trade agreement.[8] This agreement was signed before Egypt recognised the People's Republic of China on 16 May 1956. This development of relations sparked off an allegation that China was on the verge of supplying Egypt with armaments, an allegation refuted by China.[9] Nevertheless, Chou's 'strong effort' to support the Palestinian refugees prompted the Syrian delegation at the conference to 'thank China officially for its efforts on behalf of Palestine in its introduction of strong work for the resolution on Palestine . . . .' [In] explaining this strong Chinese attitude on the Palestine Question, the Chinese Premier stated that 'there was a parallel between the problems of Palestine and Formosa, neither could be solved peacefully unless intervention by outside forces was excluded'.[10]

In the final analysis, in China's view, no deep issue of principle was at stake; rather, Chou En-lai's diplomatic achievements at the Bandung Conference, particularly those with the Arabs, all have the characteristics of tactical manoeuvres. His 19 April speech was carefully calculated to dispel the fears of the states represented at the conference, being aimed precisely at countering each of their possible causes for anxiety. First he stressed the feasibility of peaceful co-existence between states with differing ideologies, pointing out that all of them shared the condition of being 'backward economically and culturally'. Then he went on to assure the participants, who had manifested fear of communist attitudes to religion, that safeguarding religious beliefs was in fact one of the tasks of the communist regime in China, and he was careful to include Chinese Muslims, Buddhists and Christians. Finally he assured the heads of state that China did not intend to carry out subversive actions nor would it attempt to propagate communism in other countries.[11] Chou's second remark was obviously aimed at the many states present at the Conference whose citizens were Muslim.

To emphasise this the Chinese delegation even included an Imam. Meanwhile China's propaganda apparatus in Peking was aimed at ensuring that this message was transmitted to the Muslim world.[12] After this first attempt at bringing Palestine to the attention of the Third World, the various Arab regimes furthered their diplomatic initiatives on the Palestinian question at all subsequent conferences of what were thereafter called the Non-Aligned States.[13]

Between the Bandung Conference and the end of 1963, Sino-Palestinian relations, though slow in developing, were basically mediated by Sino-Arab government relations. At the beginning, China viewed the Arab-Israeli conflict as a war by proxy with the USA, and did not mention the plight of the Palestinians. Tsui Chi, writing in the *People's Daily* argued that the

> United States consistently carried out a policy of setting Israel
> and Arab States against one another . . . . [And] recently, the
> United States has more and more come out in the open to sow
> discord between Israel and Egypt. By using Israel, it is trying to
> force Egypt into submission, so as to interfere in Egypt's
> independence and sovereignty.[14]

Further, *Ta Kung Pao* suggested that a solution to the conflict could be found, declaring that

> the constant conflict on the Israel-Egypt border impairs the
> interests and security of the two countries and at the same time
> affects peace in the Middle East and elsewhere. . . . [A] solution
> of the problems as between Israel and the Arab states through
> peaceful consultation is possible only if United States inter-
> vention is eliminated.[15]

Finally China foresaw, in peaceful negotiations on the issue, a corner-stone for ending the plight of the Palestinians. The *People's Daily*'s 'Observer', for example, noted that

> for peace in the Middle East . . . it is necessary that consultations
> be held among the countries concerned on the basis of the United
> Nations principles and the wishes of all countries in the Near
> East. . . . [It] is necessary to avoid military conflict. All those who
> are interested in peace in the Near East believe that if efforts are
> made along these lines, the Palestine question can be peacefully
> settled.[16]

This theme in China's view of Israel as a bridge for 'western imperialism' was most evident during the Suez crisis, in October-November 1956. Although China supported Egypt's nationalisation of the Suez Canal, both through mass demonstrations and international protests against Britain and France, it stopped short of condemning Israel as one of the real aggressors. When it became clear by 7 November 1956 that Soviet and American pressures (basically the former's threat to intervene) were having their effect, China declared that:

> The Chinese Government and people, in response to the appeal
> of the Egyptian Government, are willing to adopt all effective
> measures within our ability, including the supply of material aid,
> to support Egypt's struggle and oppose the British and French
> aggression.[17]

It is worth pointing out here that this Chinese stand was in total agreement with the USSR's position on Israel's stand during the Suez affair. Bulganin's note to Eden, Prime Minister of Britain, on 5 November 1959, expressed this position more accurately:

> The Soviet Government considers it necessary to draw your
> attention to the fact that the aggressive war engineered by
> Britain and France against the Egyptian State, in which Israel
> played the role of an instigator, is fraught with very dangerous
> consequences for universal peace.[18]

However, China's involvement in the Palestinian issue was cautiously developed before reaching its climax of active support a few years later. The Afro-Asian People's Solidarity Organisation (AAPSO) convened a conference in Cairo on 26 December 1957. China was active in preparatory meetings and discussions of the issues to be agreed upon, but 'the Chinese representative on the Secretariat, Yang Shuo, arrived in Cairo, evidently, with a large staff, in late April. The Chinese undoubtedly made their weight felt within the Secretariat, but theirs was, relatively speaking, still a subordinate role'.[19]

The Palestinian issue was raised by Arab delegates at the conference under the leadership of Egypt. China was particularly interested in furthering the question of colonialism for historical reasons and, more significantly, because of the composition of the representation at the conference. The Arab bloc, through the Palestine Sub-Committee of the Political Commission, put the issue forward by exposing

> the imperialist role in undermining the Middle East area and the
> establishment of the state of Israel to replace the Arabs who

were forcibly driven from their homes. The Committee submitted
a report stressing the danger of the Zionist movement in helping
Israel and providing her with financial, military and moral aid.
The report, which will be submitted to the Conference, says that
the existence of Israel endangers the peace and security of the
peoples of the Middle East and world peace as well. The Committee
asked the Secretariat of the Conference to organise a visit to the
refugee camps to inspect conditions there. [And] it was decided
that a sub-committee should be formed to prepare a draft
resolution on the matter, to be composed of Sayed Moḥammad
'Aḥmad Maḥdjub (Sudan), Sayed Salvea (India), Sayed Abdel
Aziz Sadek (Ēgypt), Mr Liu Lyam (China), Sayed 'Aḥmad
Rashad 'Alī (Zanzibar) and Sayed Nahad al-Ṣhadrī (Syria).[20]

Thus China began its direct acknowledgement of the plight of the
Palestinians, and, more significantly, awareness of the complexity of
the question at hand. However, China's direct support to Palestinian
refugees came about three years later.

During the intervening period Sino-Egyptian relations witnessed
a certain coolness, due largely to three major factors: Naṣir's campaign
of persecution of Egyptian and Syrian communists (especially the
so-called Bakdaṣh incident), his attacks on Ḳasim's Iraq, and his attacks
on the Soviet Union. Relations were however normalised at the beginning of 1960 and the first Chinese acknowledgement and direct support
of Palestinian refugees took place in late 1960. At the invitation of
UAR's Marshal 'Abdal-Ḥakim 'Amar, a Chinese military delegation
arrived in Cairo on 23 September 1960. In October 1960 a Chinese

military goodwill mission headed by Chang Tsung-hsun, Deputy
Chief of General Staff of the Chinese People's Liberation Army,
has donated thirty thousand Syrian pounds to the Palestinian
refugees camp in Damascus. Members of the Chinese mission
visited the Palestinian refugees camp in Damascus on 3 October
and were warmly welcomed there.[21]

There was one particular development which helped markedly to
increase Chinese support for the Palestinians: with the open eruption
of the Sino-Soviet dispute, China sought to assert its presence and
status in the widest possible diplomatic terms. Africa was one of its
main targets; consequently Chou En-lai's high-ranking and elaborate
delegation's tour of ten African states, including five Arab ones

(Somalia had not yet been admitted to the Arab League) lasted from 14 December 1963 to 14 February 1964. The Cairo stop was the first visit by a high Chinese official since the establishment of diplomatic relations in 1956. Chou declared in his lengthy speech at the State banquet on 14 December that:

> The Chinese Government and people have always supported the UAR people and the other Arab peoples in their just struggle against imperialism and the old and new colonialism, and supported the Arab people of Palestine in their struggle to restore their due rights.[22]

This declaration on Palestine was rather mild and reserved and Naşir expected more, given China's eagerness to make concessions in order to discredit the Soviet Union. Three days later Chou announced at a press conference that 'the Chinese people have always stood firmly behind the Arabs in Palestine in their just struggle for their legitimate rights. Our diplomatic actions have testified to this'.[23] None the less, by the end of the talks the Chinese premier had been prompted to declare China's stand on the issue even more clearly, and the joint communiqué, issued the following day, stated that 'the Chinese side declared its full support to the people of Palestine in restoring their legitimate rights *and in returning to their homeland*'[24] [emphasis added]. Chou's next stop was at Algiers; the two countries had a cordial and strong relationship throughout Algeria's war of independence against France; Algeria however had always refrained from publicly taking sides in the Sino-Soviet dispute. Unlike Egypt, Algeria was never involved in polemical disputes with China either on the internal role of communists or on inter-Arab rivalries which would affect its relations with China. More significantly, Algeria emerged from its war as the champion of liberation movements, to which China's contribution was notable. Consequently, Chou En-lai's latest position on Palestine was emphatically reaffirmed both at a press conference[25] and in the joint communiqué which stated that 'the Chinese and Algerian Governments reaffirm their support *without reservation* [emphasis added] for the people of Palestine for the restoration of their legitimate rights. . .'[26]

Sino-Israeli relations: contacts and attitudes

This is one of the most intriguing, complex and short-lived episodes in China's relations with the Arab world. In tracing the methods and constraints of China's attempt to establish formal relations with Israel, one can separate its policies into two distinct categories, both of them implemented with great caution: first, formal relationships carried out by diplomats and second, China's general political support for the Israeli Communist Party.

Just at the time when Chou En-lai was extending diplomatic support to the Arabs on the Palestinian question at Bandung, Israel's diplomatic relations were developing. Prior to this conference only two Israeli delegations had made official visits to China, an Israeli Women's Delegation in 1954 and a trade delegation in 1955.[27] Following Bandung, the only exception to the general ban was an official invitation extended by the Chinese to a delegation of Israeli Communist representatives,[28] and in that case, the Chinese could explain, with ideological justifications, that there were special circumstances behind the invitation.[29]

When Israel established diplomatic relations with Burma in 1953 a new phase was opened in Israel's relations with China, although events were to prove that this phase would not be lasting. Throughout the 1950s Israel's growing awareness of the diplomatic importance of East Asia took the form of a concerted effort to secure recognition from as broad a range of governments as possible.[30] A typical and important example of the leap-frogging technique is shown in the way the Israeli trade delegation's trip to China was arranged by Israel's Ambassador to Burma, David Hacohen.

According to Hacohen, the Chinese Ambassador in Rangoon arranged a meeting between Chou En-lai and himself on the former's return from the 1954 Geneva conference. In the course of their meeting Chou En-lai 'revealed interest' in the possibility of a visit by an Israeli delegation to China. Consequently, an official Israeli trade delegation was despatched to Peking: it was headed by Hacohen and 'comprised of Levin and de Shalit of the Foreign Ministry, Joseph Zarchin, Head of the Export Department of the Ministry of Commerce and Industry, and Moshe Bejarano, an industrialist who has served as Commercial Attaché in Moscow'.[31] Obviously the composition of the Israeli delegation hardly matched its title, as the overwhelming majority of its members were from the diplomatic section of the Israeli Government. The delegation toured China for two weeks and the 'formal outcome' was a five-point protocol signed on 18 February:

1 Both sides desired trade relations on the basis of equality and mutual benefit.
2 Both sides presented the foreign problems of their countries, studied the lists of commodities available for foreign trade, and examined other questions relating to commerce.

3 Both sides agreed that the mutual talks and exchanges of
   information had laid the foundation for the development of
   closer ties between the two countries.
4 Both sides agreed to present reports to their governments on
   the atmosphere prevailing during the Peking talks and to
   continue through existing channels and others to be formed
   in the future, to develop the commercial ties between the two
   countries.
5 On behalf of the government of Israel, the Israeli delegation
   expressed the hope that the government of the People's Republic
   of China would send a trade delegation to visit Israel as the
   official guests of the Israeli Government.[32]

The 'agreement', however, was loosely formulated in that it left
none of the parties involved bound by any economic, political or legal
obligation. In retrospect, the only concrete and hopeful result, from the
Israeli point of view, was the last point, and it subsequently failed to
materialise. It is worthy of note that the trade protocol was signed only
two months before the Bandung Conference. But for Israel trade was
only an excuse. The most crucial issue remained the question of full
diplomatic representation as Israel had been the first Middle Eastern
government to grant China formal recognition at a time when 'most
of the Arab regimes in the Middle East were under western influences
and the main Arab League members, Egypt, Syria, Iraq and Lebanon
had decided to recognise Taiwan as China's legal government.'[33] The
question of recognition will be dealt with below.

China's attitude towards indigenous developments in Israel had
several aspects. In the absence of any viable Palestinian force or movement in the area, and for ideological reasons, China looked to and gave
political support, like the USSR, to the Israeli Communist Party (Maki)
as a counterweight to the existing pro-western regime. Maki, before its
split in August 1965, played a significant role in espousing the cause
of the Palestinian Arabs and demanding that they be given rights
within Israeli society, and consequently had sizeable support from the
local Arab inhabitants. Jacob Landau points out three reasons for
Maki's success among the Arabs in Israel:

1 The communists began political activities among the Arabs
   earlier than any other party. During the period of British rule
   communist nuclei operated among the Palestinian Arabs, both
   openly and clandestinely. . .
2 In their propaganda, the communists were the sole party which

could point out that their ideology was not Zionist. Therefore
it claimed the communists alone had the real interests of the
Israeli Arabs at heart and could be trusted to guard these
interests against the nefarious intentions of the Government. . .
3 The party's composition reflects its political approach. It is
the sole party in Israel during the whole period of Israel's
existence that has included both Jewish and Arab members.[34]

China, during the 1955–63 period, gave it support on the three main
issues of Israeli's internal political situation. First, and most important,
was the identification of Maki as a genuine political force although it
was small in size and had little effectiveness in Israeli politics; China
continued to report Maki's stand on several vital questions. The close
link between the State of Israel and 'Western imperialism', according
to the Chinese press, was one of the main obstacles to peaceful co-
existence of Arabs and Jews in Israel. Quoting the General Secretary
of Maki, Shmir el Mikunis, on the occasion of the 21st Congress of the
Communist Party of the Soviet Union, *NCNA* stated that:

> The Soviet Union was assisting and would continue to assist the
> people of the Middle East in their struggle against imperialism
> and military pacts and for peace and national independence. . . .
> [It] was obvious, Mikunis said, Israel could also win the friendly
> support of the Soviet Union if only Israel took the road of
> independence, ceased to serve the interests of imperialism,
> carried out a policy of peace and cooperated with the Arab
> people in the struggle against imperialism. . . . Mikunis pointed
> out that one of the main obstacles to the establishment of peace
> was the Ben-Gurion Government's refusal to recognise the right
> of the Arab refugees to return to their home place.[35]

Moreover, relying on Soviet coverage of Israeli political developments,
Chinese press reports pointed out several of what it considered to be
'negative aspects' of Israeli society. When, for example, Ben Gurion
paid an official visit to the USA in March 1960, *Pravda* claimed,
according to *NCNA*, that 'Israeli rulers were again acting as a tool of
the western quarters which refused to abandon their colonialist designs
in the Middle East . . . . Ben Gurion had advised Washington to make
use of Israel's ties with the Asian and African countries which had
newly achieved independence. . .'[36]

Such amicable Israeli relations and mutual interest with the west
were further criticised, especially by China, when Israel sought to buy

armaments from West Germany;[37] it was then stated that 'Adenauer represented the Government which is responsible for the resurgence of fascism and anti-semitism in West Germany'.[38] The Chinese press consistently blamed the Israeli Government for most evils, quoting Maki's position on the issues, such as discrimination against local Arab inhabitants,[39] strikes by airline crews,[40] teachers' demands for higher wages,[41] workers' opposition to mounting taxes,[42] Israel as a link and base for 'US imperialism' penetrating Africa,[43] discrimination against Sephardi (Eastern) Jews,[44] and 'solidarity with the struggle of Jewish intelligentsia against the dictatorship of Ben-Gurion'.[45]

Second, the Chinese press paid lip service to moral condemnation of Nazism and the fear of its resurgence in West Germany. When the trial of Adolf Eichmann, which subsequently resulted in his execution in June, began in April 1961, *NCNA* cautioned that

> it has been disclosed that influential circles in Israel are colluding
> with West Germany and making every effort to prevent the
> Eichmann trial from becoming a trial of fascism and, in particular,
> to prevent the publication of testimony on the past of a number
> of Nazi criminals who now hold high government posts in Bonn.[46]

China's attitude was not unique, for it followed the mainstream of the USSR and its bloc at the time. On the 16th anniversary of the victory over fascism, *NCNA* informed its readership that 'ten thousand Israelis' attended the celebration in the Israeli sector of Jerusalem, and that this meeting 'which was organised by the Israeli-USSR Friendship Movement was addressed by Chairman of the Israeli Association of Democratic Women, Ruth Lubitsch, who expressed the Israeli people's gratitude to the Soviet people for defeating fascism. It was also addressed by the Soviet Ambassador to Israel, M. F. Bodrov. The Cuban Ambassador to Israel was present at the meeting.'[47]

Finally China paid tribute to Maki and its publication *Kol Haam*, for its support for China's stand on international and internal policies. The conclusion of both the Sino-Burmese[48] and the Sino-Nepalese[49] boundary agreements received support from Maki, whose spokesmen claimed that such improvements of relations had 'dealt a blow to the anti-Chinese slanderers who tried to represent this great Asian socialist power as an "aggressor"' and moreover, it was a 'further proof that the Chinese People's Republic had completely peaceful intentions towards all of its neighbours. China was not only a great power but a power standing guard over peace'. Maki's praises of China's internal developments also received welcome attention from Peking. *Kol Haam* referred to China's famous Great Leap Forward, as *NCNA* informs us, as a significant development in the construction of socialism; it added that the 'achievements of the Chinese people in the Great Leap were especially important for the Afro-Asian countries whose economies were, on the whole, poorly developed'.[50]

In spite of these overtures and attitudes one can justifiably ask why China had not recognised Israel, given that the mentor of the communist world, the USSR, had done so immediately after the creation of the state. It has been claimed that this was due to both ideology and pragmatism. However, it is one of the basic contentions of this study that in China's foreign policy, ideology *per se* is of secondary significance.

When the People's Republic of China was proclaimed in 1949, only one non-communist state, India, recognised it; the other states which recognised it were the USSR and the communist bloc, Albania, Yugoslavia, Burma, North Korea; altogether 13 states. Between 1950 and 1955 another 13 states extended recognition, most of them from Western Europe. Between 1956 and 1965, another 23 states followed, bringing the total to 49 states. By 1965 only 8 Arab states had recognised China: they were, in 1956 Syria, Egypt and Yemen; in 1958 Iraq (which resumed relations after its revolution), Morocco and Sudan; in 1962 Algeria (China was the first non-Arab government to recognise the Algerian Provisional Revolutionary Government) and in 1964 Tunisia. Thus the main aim of China's diplomatic offensive was to establish relations and break its isolation as effectively as possible, particularly as by the mid-1960s, China was not only faced with two hostile powers, the USA and the USSR, but had entered a phase of internal upheaval following the Cultural Revolution. The only Arab state which recognised China during the Cultural Revolution was the People's Democratic Republic of Yemen (South Yemen) and that decision was taken regardless of China's position on Palestine. By contrast it is to be noticed that as China re-emerged from the Cultural Revolution, the number of states which extended recognition to it and established diplomatic relations between 1971 and 1975 was 52.[51]

To give recognition to Palestinian rights, on however limited a scale at this early stage, not only won China favour with whoever spoke for the Palestinians, but, more significantly, opened the gates of the Arab world on an issue that was of vital Arab national interest. Moreover, the Arab world had an added dimension, its geographical position and resources, extending from South West Asia to North Africa, which constituted a significant geo-political element, and the Chinese were aware of this. All Palestinian sources and leaders constantly gave credit to the role which ideology – i.e. support for national liberation movements – played in Sino-Palestinian relations. It is in this field, the argument goes, that one of the greatest attributes of Chinese consistent support lies; this element will be discussed fully in the following analysis of Sino-Palestinian relations. Nevertheless it ought to be recognised that ideology in China's relations with the Palestinian Resistance Movement (PRM) was only a catalyst for a long-term strategy.

First direct Sino-Palestinian contacts: 1964–5

Following the establishment of the state of Israel and the subsequent dispersal of the Palestinians within and outside the Arab world, the Palestinian question remained at first under the jurisdiction of Arab regimes, with the Arab League acting as a diplomatic means to further the cause. The problem of saving the Arab world from Zionism remained one of the tasks confronting Arab regimes. It was within the dispersed Palestinian population that new trends began to develop to find a way out of this dilemma; it is important to note that one of the kernel ideas in Palestinian political thought at the time was that the 'road to Palestine must be preceded by Arab unity'. Palestinians were consequently actively immersed in several Arab nationalist movements. In 1958 Egypt and Syria announced their unity in the United Arab Republic (UAR) and most Palestinians, particularly intellectuals, conceived it to be a move towards total Arab unity, and thus a step towards the liberation of Palestine.

Within this search for Palestinian identity, there emerged two trends: one sponsored and operated through the willingness of Arab regimes, while the other sought a totally independent course. Palestinians in the Gaza Strip formed the first active student group and secretly developed plans for an eventually independent movement. In 1959 a low circulation monthly magazine called *Our Palestine* (Filisṭunynā) started publication in Beirut. Although some of the ideas of its founders were considered reactionary, such as the call for revenge (al-tha'r) against Jews living in Palestine, its basic principles were behind the foundation of Ḥarakat al-Taḥrīr al-Waṭanī al-Filisṭīnī (Fataḥ, the National Liberation Movement of Palestine).

Fataḥ was based on the simple political realities of the situation; its founders advocated that Palestinians must have an identity of their own to carry on the task of liberating Palestine, that Palestinians will gain nothing from taking sides in inter-Arab disputes because such an approach would divert them from the main issue, and that the only solution for the Palestinian problem was the creation of a guerrilla (Feda'īn) movement. The strategy for the liberation of Palestine seemed to be in contradiction with the idea of total Arab unity. But this is where the originality of Fataḥ lies, because its founders believed that the liberation of Palestine would lead in the long run to Arab unity, rather than the reverse.

Yasir 'Arafat ('Abū 'Amar) and other prominent members like Ṣalaḥ Khalaf ('Abū'Iyad), Khalīl al-Wazīr ('Abū Djhad) and Khalid al-Hassan started the movement from the Arabian Gulf, particularly Kuwait, where they were working, West Germany and the Gaza Strip, and after a while concentrated on the potential of the refugee camps. At first, recruitment was slow and hampered by Naṣir's charismatic appeal in the Arab world as a rallying point for Arab nationalism. However with the collapse of Egyptian-Syrian unity in 1961 all hopes for a unified Arab world that would eventually lift the burden of Zionism disappeared. As a result many organisations sprang up to carry on the task of liberation, but they lacked sufficient broad popular support to convert this thought and trend into a viable political force. The success of the Algerian revolution in 1962 gave the Palestinians, especially Fataḥ, faith in the idea of creating an independent political force based on the concept of armed struggle; so Fataḥ established its military wing al-'Aṣifa. However this was contained as a result of the political and military limitations of Fataḥ itself and because Arab governments actively suppressed any independent Palestinian movement. Fataḥ at that time was the only Palestinian organisation which advocated an armed struggle to achieve its ultimate goal.[52] On 1 January 1965 al Fataḥ's first communiqué announced the beginning of military activity in the occupied territories.

In their long search to apply the concepts of 'people's war', Fataḥ leaders were much influenced by the Algerian and, to a lesser extent, by the Vietnamese experiences, and they looked towards China for lessons and support. It was through their Algiers office that the idea of visiting China was first aired and, as a result, Yasir 'Arafat (Abū 'Amar) and Khalīl al-Wazīr (Abū Djhad) were despatched on an official visit to China.[53] The decision of Fataḥ leaders was to send Yasir 'Arafat and Khalīl al-Wazīr to solicit political support in China, Vietnam and Pakistan; the idea of military support was not considered because Fataḥ, except for its clandestine operations, was still at a formative stage. The reasons for this visit were determined by the realities of the conditions in which it was operating; needless to say, the founders of

Fataḥ were far from having any leftist, let alone Marxist, inclinations; on the contrary. As one Palestinian leader put it, Fataḥ during

> the period of its infancy, sought to solicit support from every corner of the world, regardless of ideological conviction. China, moreover, had acquired at the time a reputation as the leading nation with long experience in a people's war. More significantly, China did not recognise and had no diplomatic relations with Israel. At the time [1960s] China's knowledge of the Palestinian cause was limited, though there had been a number of contacts at Algiers between Fataḥ and the Chinese embassy in order to communicate Palestinian aims, desires and requirements for the launching of a people's war. Finally, Fataḥ was then on the verge of preparing for a wide military build up; this issue was taken into consideration when the delegation was dispatched. However the primary aim of the visit was to exchange views and possibilities for future assistance; contacts therefore were confined to the Chinese Communist Party, for it is the main decision-making body in China. Then relations were promoted to the Foreign Ministry apparatus.[54]

Abū 'Amar and Abu Djhad left Algiers under the pseudonyms Muḥammad Rifa'at and Muḥammad Khalil.[55]

At the invitation of the Chinese Committee for Afro-Asian Solidarity (CCAAS), the delegation arrived in Peking on 17 March 1964. There they met with Liao Ch'eng-chih, the famous Chinese Communist Party figure, who had attended the Bandung Conference as the senior Chinese delegate after Chou En-lai. According to Muḥammad Rifa'at, in a later press conference he declared to the delegation that 'we shall not recognise Israel for a minute, for a day, or even for the next hundred years'.[56] On 20 March a public rally was held in Peking in honour of the delegation and speeches were made. According to the *New China News Agency* (*NCNA*) a wide range of Chinese and Arab personalities were present at the occasion:

> Liao Cheng-chih, Chairman of the Chinese Committee for Afro-Asian Solidarity, and leaders of seven other organisations that sponsored the rally . . . Diplomatic envoys of Morocco, the United Arab Republic and Syria . . . Chang Chieh, Vice-President of the Chinese Islamic Association (CIA) . . . Mao Tun, Vice-Chairman of the Chinese Committee for Afro-Asian Solidarity . . . and Tseng Yung-chuan, Vice-Foreign Minister, Tsai Ting-Kai,

Vice-Chairman of the Revolutionary Committee of the Kuomintang
and Li-Teh-Chuan, Vice-Chairman of the Chinese Committee for
Afro-Asian Solidarity.[57]

An official message was published in which the Chinese viewed the
Palestinian problem with an Arab-Israeli perspective, reiterated Chou
En-lai's previous declarations and communiqué signed in Egypt a
month earlier (see above) and declared 'may the Palestinian people's
justified demands for regaining their legitimate rights and returning
to their homeland to be justified at an early stage'.[58] Muḥammad
Rifa'at, who spoke at the rally on behalf of Fataḥ, presented the
historical background of the Palestinian plight and touched on a wide
range of issues, such as China's right to a seat at the United Nations and
the USA's policy in the Arab world and its support for Israel; and
coined the Palestinian motto in China that 'Palestine will be liberated
from Zionism and Colonialism'.

On 21 March CCAAS held a banquet in the delegation's honour, at
which Muḥammad Rifa'at announced 'that for the Palestinian people,
the support of the Chinese people was a mighty force which would
contribute to the struggle of the Palestinian people against imperialism
and Zionism'.[59] China's stand on Fataḥ's cause must have been promising, at least at the political level, although no public declaration was
made on the issue of the 'liberation of Palestine'. Two days later,
NCNA reported from Damascus that:

> The Syrian Foreign Minister Ḥassan Maryoud today received the
> Chinese Ambassador to Syria, Hsu Yi-shin. On behalf of the Syrian
> Government, Minister Maryoud expressed ardent and sincere
> gratitude to the Chinese people for their rally held recently in
> Peking in support of the Palestinian and Arab peoples' struggle
> against imperialism. He said 'the Syrian Government was moved
> by the friendly Chinese support'.[60]

It is most probable that concrete military aid was not discussed
or explicitly asked for by the delegation, for Fataḥ at this period had
no military bases in the Arab world, and, had they wanted it, Algeria
could easily have received it, as it did later on, and transmitted it to
Fataḥ. But political relations were widely discussed and it was agreed
that Fataḥ would send a non-official Palestinian representative as a
liaison officer.[61]

This agreement concluded, Muḥammad Khalil went to North Vietnam[62] while Muḥammad Rifa'at proceeded to Pakistan[63] to solicit

further support. Fataḥ's representative, Abū al-'Abid, arrived in Peking in August 1964 and remained there until July 1965.[64] His main task was to transmit and negotiate with Chinese officials on behalf of Fataḥ; officially he was a translator of Arabic – e.g. correcting final drafts of Arabic texts – at *NCNA*.

The next Fataḥ delegation to Peking happened almost by accident. Fataḥ had sent two of its members, 'Alī al-Ḥassan ('Abū al-'Amīn) and 'Amīn al-Sharīf, to attend a meeting in North Korea. They left for Korea after Abū 'Amar and Abū Djhad completed their visit to Peking, and on their return from Korea via China the Chinese authorities inquired whether they could extend their stay. 'Abū al-'Amīn remained for one month while 'Amīn al-Sharīf returned home. He had audiences with Chinese Communist Party (CCP) members, Foreign Ministry personnel and CCAAS. As 'Abū al'Amīn recounted, discussions evolved around the following:

> Most of the meetings were held with CCAAS representatives. Ideologically, I presented Fatah's stand during that period, that is a national liberation movement which entails that all strata of the society are involved in the process of liberation regardless of ideological belief. Before the actual declaration of the establishment of Fatah, we studied several experiences in this field. Chinese experience was strikingly similar to ours in its nationalist approach and most appropriate to our conditions, and Fatah published a study on the Chinese experience [see Appendix 1]. Our major aim from our relations with China at this initial phase was to study that rich experience. We were mostly interested in their methodology for national liberation, and one striking idea was that of Mao's article 'On Contradiction' which meant, in a nut-shell, that secondary contradictions must be avoided for the ultimate success of the primary one and when the latter is accomplished, attention will be shifted to the secondary one. In our case, this meant that all Palestinians must unite under the idea of a national force for liberation and avoid minor contradictions, like polemics of class struggle, adherence to one defined political line, etc. . . . We could not afford to indulge in metaphysical questions. The Chinese, for their part, agreed with Fatah's nationalist approach, but at the same time hinted at the necessity of establishing a communist party.

At the practical level, Fatah sought relations with China because the Chinese experience in people's war was recent. Moreover, China, by the early 1960s, had not yet indulged in global power struggle, and it retained certain ideological clarity and principles in its dealings with liberation movements. We disagreed, however, on one issue. Fatah at the time was of the opinion that the USSR's attitude to Palestine was rather antagonistic, the Chinese were not entirely in agreement.[65]

Fataḥ's first official delegation was undoubtedly successful. Fataḥ was surprised at China's willingness to accept and recognise as important a few unknown persons with no ideological background, given the limited aim of the visit and Fataḥ's own status in the Arab world. But contrary to Abū al-'Abid's assumption, it is likely that China's perception of the Palestinian question must have involved an awareness of the significance not only of the Arab world but, more importantly, of the emergence of a unique chance that the Palestinians might in future be able to sustain an independent movement which would one day have its own impact. None the less China kept its options open and waited for the creation of a stronger organisation. This happened almost a year later when the Palestine Liberation Organisation (PLO) was established.

The creation of the Palestine Liberation Organisation (PLO) and its relations with China

The first steps towards the creation of the PLO acted as a catalyst to Israel's plan to divert the waters of the Jordan river,[66] in response to which Naṣir called for the convening of an Arab Summit Conference despite inter-Arab rivalry which was increasing at the time.[67] The Arab Summit Conference opened on 13 January 1964 in Cairo and decided that 'one way of repelling the threatening Zionist danger was through the organisation of the Palestinian people, thus enabling them to play their part in liberating Palestine and in determining its future'.[68]

'Aḥmad al-Shuḳairy who, since 15 September 1963, had been responsible for presenting Palestine at the Arab League and was a protégé of Naṣir, was given the task of consulting and organising Palestinians in the Arab world. He was to lay the foundation for an eventual gathering of Palestinians in a single organisation recognised by Arab regimes and other states sympathetic to the Palestian cause. The Summit Conference was the first occasion where the slogan 'liberation of Palestine' was coined, as previously the Arab states had called for the 'application of the United Nations resolutions on Palestine'.

After touring the Arab world, al-Shuḳairy called a meeting of Palestinians in Jerusalem in May 1964. The first Palestine National

Council (invariably referred to as Congress) met and laid down the infrastructure of the PLO. al-Shuḳairy's project was received with reservations by other Palestinian organisations. It was viewed as a by-product of Arab regimes and did not support the idea of armed struggle, but instead based its military strategy on conventional armed forces; also it was tightly controlled by Naṣir. In May, for example, a unified statement by the Political Bureau of United Action of the Revolutionary Palestinian Forces declared that it did not oppose the PLO's tentative proposal for a Palestinian entity, but expressed caution about joining the PLO's Council on the grounds that it followed the conventional policies of Arab states, was linked to them, and offered no effective new suggestions for the liberation of Palestine. This group 'consisted of a variety of Palestinian organisations: the Palestine Liberation Front (PLF), the Revolutionary Front for the Liberation of Palestine, the Palestine National Liberation Movement (Fataḥ), the Bloc of Palestinian Commandos, the Arab Front for the Liberation of Palestine and the National Front for Liberation.'[69] Despite this, al-Shuḳairy was elected Chairman and at the end of May was able to establish the infrastructure and general goals of the PLO.[70] He then diverted his energy to Arab and international diplomatic lobbying on behalf of the newly created organisation: China was more than willing to co-operate with this.

China's attitude towards the Palestinian issue enhanced its image within the Palestine Resistance Movement (PRM) at the time of the PLO's formation. On the day before the opening of the PLO National Council (PLO-NC) of 28 May to 2 June, the CCAAS sent a message of greetings, declaring its 'firm support' for the Palestinian cause and expressing 'the conviction that the opening of the Palestine National Congress would contribute to the implementation of the resolutions of the Arab Summit Conference on opposing imperialism and restoring the rights of the Palestinian people, the strengthening of the unity of the Arab countries'.[71] The first PLO-NC, for its part, acknowledged the importance of separating the two giant socialist states in its tributes: 'The Conference notes with appreciation the stand taken by the socialist states [on general Arab problems and Palestine in particular] in particular the USSR and the PRC on these issues'.[72] The inclusion of the USSR in this resolution was a reflection of its role in influencing Arab regimes rather than on its stand on Palestine as a separate question, and was an expression of the delegates' hope for future co-operation. A few days after the convening of the PLO-NC, Krushchev paid an official visit to Egypt: the joint communiqué which resulted from it was cautiously worded, and Palestine was still referred to in terms of United Nations resolutions:

> The Soviet Union expresses full support for the struggle of the Arab states against the aggressive intrigues of the imperialist forces which are striving to use the Palestine issue in order to increase tension in the Middle East and which are obstructing a settlement to this problem that is in keeping with the United Nations decisions and takes due account of the lawful and inalienable rights of the Palestine Arabs. The Soviet side expressed support for the stand of the Arab states on the question of the utilisation of the waters of the River Jordan.[73]

The *People's Daily*, commenting on the conclusion of the PLO-NC, had a different tone. It argued that:

> the so-called Palestine question was artificially created by the US and British imperialists. And in their attempt to control Palestine and the Middle East countries and strangle the national liberation movement there, they have taken reactionary Zionism under their wings, fomented national disputes between the Arabs and Jews, built a bridgehead for aggression in Palestine and created tension in the Middle East . . . . In the common struggle against imperialism, the Chinese and Arab peoples have forged a deep bond of friendship. The Chinese people will always support the Palestine Arabs' struggle for recovering their legitimate rights and for returning to their homeland, and will likewise back up the struggle of the peoples of the Arab countries against imperialism, colonialism and neo-colonialism and for national independence.[74]

Before Aḥmad al-Shuḳairy's visit to China as head of the PLO, a delegation of the General Union of Palestinian Students, led by Taiysīr Ḳuba'h, was invited to Peking by the All-China Student Federation[75] at the end of August 1964. At a rally held for the delegation Ḳuba'h declared that 'to achieve victory . . . one must rely on the armed struggle of the masses'.[76] China's willingness to support the Palestinian cause manifested itself on several occasions: when a Lebanese Parliamentary delegation, led by Kamal Djunblaṭ, visited Peking in late February 1965, Chou En-lai conveyed to the delegation China's readiness 'to extend every possible aid to the Arabs, including volunteers, munitions and money' in their struggle for Palestine, and reasserted that China would never recognise Israel.[77]

Aḥmad al Shuḳairy's visit to China as head of the PLO produced positive results which are still noticeable today in Sino-Palestinian relations, though his account of the whole affair is a mixture of exaggeration and misleading historical self-glorification. In his memoirs,[78] al-Shuḳairy relates that although he had had no direct contacts with Chinese leaders and representatives since his last meeting with Chou En-lai in Bandung in 1955 he, none the less, proceeded [in 1965], for 'the first time' to the Chinese embassy in Cairo, inquiring whether it would be possible to visit China. According to *NCNA* this is inaccurate as on 7 February 1964, exactly a year earlier, it reported that:

'Aḥmad al-Shuḳairy, Palestine representative to the Arab League, called on Chinese ambassador to the UAR Egypt, Chen Chia-kang, today and expressed the gratitude of the Palestine people to Chinese Premier Chou En-Lai for his support for the Palestine cause in his recent statement made in Somalia. After meeting the Chinese ambassador, Shuḳairy stated that People's China has always supported the Palestine people in their just struggle for the liberation of their country.[79]

Four days after this second visit, al-Shuḳairy relates, the Chinese ambassador informed him that Chou En-lai had extended both a personal and an official invitation; whereas, according to *NCNA*, the invitation was officially extended by the Chinese People's Institute of Foreign Affairs.[80] He then formed a PLO delegation from its three main branches: the Executive Committee, the National Council and the Palestine Liberation Army.

Arriving in Canton on 16 March 1965, the delegation was received with a rousing popular demonstration. On 17 March, they landed at Peking where, as al-Shuḳairy relates, the welcoming party was beyond their expectations. Besides Arab envoys at Peking, there were:

Vice-Premier Chen Yi; Kao Chung-min, Vice-Chairman of the National Committee of the Chinese People's Political Consultative Conference; Chang Hsi-jo, President, and Li Yi-mang, Vice-President of the Chinese People's Institute of Foreign Affairs; Liao Ch'eng-chih, Chairman of the Chinese Committee for Afro-Asian Solidarity; and Chiao Kuan-hua, Vice-Foreign Minister . . [Also] on hand to welcome the Palestine guests at the airport were Lieutenant General Hsiao Hsiang-jung, Director of the General Office of the Ministry of National Defence; Yueh Sung-Sheng, Vice Mayor of Peking; [and] Ḥadj Yūsuf Sha Meng-pi, Vice-President of the China Islamic Association.[81]

The following day al-Shuḳairy met Chou En-lai, when he faced the most difficult decisions in furthering the Palestinian cause, though he thought of them as 'triumphs'. According to al-Shuḳairy, his meeting with Chou En-lai was conducted in total privacy with no other person present. This would have been highly unusual: Chou always had minutes made of such meetings. The following is al-Shuḳairy's account of the talks:

Chou:	Now that you have explained your cause, what exactly do you want from us?
al-Shuḳairy:	In addition to political support, we want military aid.
Chou:	And what do you want explicitly?
al-Shuḳairy:	We need small and medium arms. We also need to send a mission of our officers to train in guerrilla warfare. You have a wealth of experience in this matter.
Chou.	You know we are always ready to support any liberation movement in the world as much as we can. Our responsibilities towards our people are great; we are not rich. But we feel we have a duty towards the liberation movements in the world in support of the oppressed nations to fight American imperialism. We will not delay in helping you as much as we can.
al-Shuḳairy:	Our demands are not great. I leave up to you the amount of aid that you can give us.
Chou:	We are not like everybody else who offers aid and expects payment with interest. This is political payoff. It is not our method.
al-Shuḳairy:	We do not want planes or tanks. We need the arms that are appropriate for guerrilla warfare.
Chou:	And where do you want the arms to arrive? Have you agreed with any of the Arab governments? Have you talked with President Nasser on the subject?
al-Shuḳairy:	Actually, I did not discuss the subject with anybody, but I believe Cairo will not object to that. We would like the arms to be shipped to the port of Alexandria.
Chou:	We are ready to do this, and we can send you the arms free. We will ship them on our ships directly to Alexandria. We do not trust other ships for the American fleet is closely watching. State what you want. We are not afraid of the Americans, but we do fear the Americans for you.

al-<u>Sh</u>uḳairy:	I cannot find the appropriate words to express my great gratitude. Since your ships are going to Alexandria, will it not be possible for us to send our officers on them too, to begin their training with you?
Chou:	Of course that is possible. It is better if you keep in close touch with our Embassy in Cairo to make all necessary arrangements for the arms and officers.
al-<u>Sh</u>uḳairy:	I will never forget this favour.
Chou:	This is our duty. There is no reason to thank us. You want to fight for your land. We cannot abandon you and we cannot abandon the Afro-Asian nations. . . . Did the Russians give you anything?
al-<u>Sh</u>uḳairy:	Nothing received till now from Moscow.
Chou:	What aid have you requested from Moscow?
al-<u>Sh</u>uḳairy:	We have asked for military and cultural aid, but nothing has been received till now.
Chou:	I know you are a close friend of the Soviet leaders.
al-<u>Sh</u>uḳairy:	The friendship is there, but the aid is not.
Chou:	But from us, friendship and aid. I would like to emphasise that we will be very pleased if the Russians offer you any aid. We do not want our friendship to be at the expense of your friendship with Moscow. If they offer you any aid, we will be very happy. What concerns us is that you win your independence and freedom.
al-<u>Sh</u>uḳairy:	This is the revolutionary spirit.
Chou:	Continue your efforts with the Soviet Union, although I think you will get nothing from them. No political or cultural aid. Moscow recognised Israel and has economic relations with it. In addition the Soviet Union agreed with America to the Partition of Palestine and the creation of Israel.
al-<u>Sh</u>uḳairy:	That is true. The Arab world remembers this stand. Would you allow us to open an office in Peking?
Chou:	Tomorrow morning. We will give you the office space, recognise the PLO and will grant your office diplomatic immunity. We will treat you like any other friendly embassy. We are with you, and we are ready to do whatever we can.
al-<u>Sh</u>uḳairy:	We came to Peking as a twelve-man delegation representing the Palestinian people, now we leave

> as seven hundred millions. It is the beginning of
> victory, no matter how long it takes.[82]

From the discussion, one can see that Chou's understanding of the limits and complexities under which the PLO operated exceeded that of al-Shuḳairy. First, Chou admitted China's limited military and economic capacities; China was still unable to fulfil all the demands of a liberation movement which wanted to conduct classical warfare. Second, and more significantly, there was Chou's implicit hint of the PLO's military limitations; for any Palestinian guerrilla organisation is strategically land-locked. The Palestinians have no defined land from which they could carry out independent and uninterrupted military operations. Third, linked with the above, there is the political dimension for receiving arms: i.e. were China to supply arms to the PLO, the latter would always be at the mercy of the 'host' Arab government which acts as a transition area. In one instance, for example, when the Algerians sent heavy arms of Chinese origin to Fataḥ in July 1971, the Syrian Government refused to allow Fataḥ to take delivery of them.[83] Furthermore, Chou's explicit mention of Nasser's role in either approving or disapproving of the PLO's will to operate independently is significant. al-Shuḳairy was to face this problem on his return. Fourth, Sino-Soviet rivalry and Chou's apparent criticism of the USSR's role in creating and establishing relations with Israel, a factor that even current Palestinian sources regard with indignation, is an obvious attempt to gain influence with the PLO on this basis;[84] al-Shuḳairy stated in his memoirs that for two years, 1963–5, he unsuccessfully tried to obtain Soviet support.[85] It is noteworthy here that Chou, in pointing out the Soviet role in the partition plan, failed to mention Taiwan's role in the UN; for when the plan was put to a roll call at the General Assembly on 29 November 1947, Taiwan remained 'neutral' by abstaining on the resolution.[86] Moreover, the Chinese, while they condemned Soviet support for the implementation of the Partition Plan and recognition of Israel, never mentioned the part played by Stalin in those important decisions. Lastly, China, by granting the PLO full diplomatic privileges, became the first non-Arab state to do so and thus gained a political advantage in the Arab world which is acknowledged today by all in the Palestine Resistance Movement. The combination of all these factors contributed to China's penetration of the Arab world at a time when it was most needed.

al-Shuḳairy, obviously elated by his unexpected success, cabled Naṣir immediately,[87] and on that afternoon the whole delegation had an audience with Chou En-lai.[88] The next morning the delegation split into two parties: the civilians went sight-seeing and the military group proceeded to the Ministry of Defence. There, al-Shukairy, who relates this with reservations, and Wadjih al-Madani, head of the Palestine Liberation Army, for the first time encountered Chinese views on the methodology the PLO would have to use in conducting its war of liberation effectively. A detailed map of Palestine was hung on the wall, and al-Shukairy was asked to present the military aspects of the Palestinian problem. We are informed that he proceeded to elaborate on the 'historical expansion of Israel and the topography of Palestine'. Then Lieutenant-General Hsiao Hsiang-jung, Director of the General Office of the Ministry of National Defence, presented the Chinese point of view, making three main points. He said:

> The presence of PLA in the West Bank is essential for the battle of liberation. The West Bank, if effectively utilised, has destructive strategic positions for attacking Israel. . . . Thus we understand why American imperialism forbids concentration of your own army in the West Bank [the West Bank being under Jordanian rule]. Our information has it that the Jordanian army is well trained and its units have high combat capabilities, but the problem is that its destiny is not in the people's hands, therefore it cannot fulfil its role in a people's war. . . . [The] Palestinian liberation war must have a base outside Israel; operations from outside might irritate Israel a bit, but it does not produce genuine results. . . . [pointing to the al-Djatil area he continued] These mountains must be your base; it has a great military advantage for it is close to vital Israeli positions and surmounted by Syria and Lebanon, so they will be your rear bases.
>
> Liberation does not need a large army. Your army should be organised in small units, trained specially to carry out courageous and speedy operations to inflict heaviest casualties on the enemy. Avoid fighting the enemy in open battles. The real weapon is the well-trained soldier who knows how to exploit his military capabilities in a battle.[89]

Hsiao then conferred with Wadjih al-Madani on the composition, organisation and training of PLA units. Neither al-Shukairy nor his followers, who had founded the PLO for conventional military warfare, believed in the feasibility of guerrilla warfare against a superior enemy, although China was a prime example of its possibilities. In retrospect it seems that all al-Shukairy aspired to obtain from the Chinese were political gains, and perhaps a few light arms to justify that end.

The delegation then proceeded to a meeting with Chou En-lai and later went for prayers to a mosque. Al-Shukairy, however, deleted one meeting from his memoirs of this day. This may have been in deference to subsequent events in China itself. *NCNA* reported that

> Liu Shao-chi, Chairman of the People's Republic of China, received and had a cordial, friendly talk here this evening with 'Aḥmad Shukairy, President of the Palestine Liberation Organisation, and the members of the delegation of the Palestine Liberation Organisation he is leading. Among those present were Chang Hsi-jo, President, and Hu Yu-chih, Vice-President of the Chinese People's Institute of Foreign Affairs; and Chiao Kuan-hua, Vice Foreign Minister.[90]

It is most likely that, since he published his memoirs in 1971, after the Cultural Revolution and Liu Shao-chi's disgrace, he avoided mentioning this meeting to keep in line with current Chinese positions. However in the joint communiqué, which was translated into Arabic in the memoirs, there was a reference to a meeting with Liu Shao-chi.[91]

The delegation's itinerary included visits to factories, schools, etc. It attended a mass rally in their honour on 21 March and a reception by Arab envoys to China. On 22 March Chou and al-Shukairy signed the first Sino-Palestinian 'agreement' as al-Shukairy calls it, which the *NCNA* described as a joint communiqué. Its most significant phrase was:

> The two parties agreed that the Palestine Liberation Organisation shall set up a mission in Peking to strengthen mutual cooperation. The Chinese people will make every effort to support the Arab people of Palestine in their struggle to return to their homeland by all means, political and otherwise.[92]

After leaving Peking the delegation stopped at Wuhan where they visited a military academy, which puzzled al-Shukairy, who mistakenly guessed that this show of artillery was aimed at PLO units as Chou had promised earlier.[93] *NCNA*, however, reports the visit in a different light:

> Founded by Chairman Mao Tse-tung, the great leader of the Chinese people, the thirty year old academy has trained tens of thousands of commanders for the Chinese PLA. It made tremendous contributions to the cause of China's liberation. . . . Ahmed Shukairy praised the cadets for their superb skills. He said that Chairman Mao Tse-tung was the creator of an independent

military theory. His army, built up from nothing, had become
a mighty revolutionary army. Going along the same path, the
Palestine Liberation Army would be founded.[94]

In the afternoon, to the delegation's surprise, they met Mao.[95] During
their conversation, Mao emphasised four points on 'the theory of war':

> Firstly: strike whenever you are sure of victory, retreat whenever
> you are weak.
> Secondly: attack the enemy in stages . . . . You cannot cut your
> enemy's hand with your teeth, but you can cut his fingers one
> by one.
> Thirdly: fight according to your own method and conditions;
> never copy blindly.
> Fourthly: military academies do not produce accomplished
> commanders. It is necessary to found military academies so that
> students could spend six months studying theoretical matters,
> like atomic science, but war is the most important university
> for graduating successful soldiers.[96]

Mao finally revealed that in 1949, after the CCP's victory, Israel had
offered to recognise the new nation, but China refused this recognition,
because 'we knew that all the Arab world was against Israel . . . and we,
on our part, cannot recognise Israel because it is a base for American,
British, French and West German imperialisms'.[97] For the second time
al-Shuḳairy was confronted by the fact that he could not conceive of
the PLO being based and organised on a Chinese model of warfare, nor
did he have assurances that it would last in surrounding Arab conditions,
though he alluded to such a possibility on his return to Cairo.[98]

Back in Cairo al-Shuḳairy faced his first test as leader of an 'independent' decision-making PLO. Egypt's total silence on his visit to China
puzzled him. He never obtained a precise explanation of this, for
Naṣir refused to see him or even to hear of the delegation's achievements. He suspected four reasons for Naṣir's attitude, and this time he
was right. First, Naṣir saw the PLO's success in Peking as *political*, and
regarded Chinese military aid as unthinkable because the Palestinians
had neither an independent government nor conditions favourable for
waging war. Second, the PLO's success in China annoyed the Soviets
who were then engaging in polemical confrontation with China at the
highest level. Third, for Naṣir the USSR was more valuable than China
in the world balance of power. Last, the agreement concluded with
Chou on shipping Chinese arms to Alexandria was reached without any
consultation with Naṣir and without his explicit permission.[99]

This early phase of China's direct involvement in Palestinian affairs achieved several limited political ends and helped the Chinese to bridge the gap in Sino-Arab relations. The first PLO representative to arrive in Peking was Rashīd Djarbu' whom the Chinese received with enthusiasm in May 1965.[100]

In 1964–5 China supported two fronts with the same aspirations and emerging at the same time. This support was given notwithstanding the fact that during the 1960s the Sino-Indian border dispute erupted, and that Arab communist parties were all pro-Soviet. Both Fataḥ and the PLO were in the formative stages; there were no guarantees that China would receive any advantage from supporting them, since every indication was that they lacked any popular or governmental support (though here the PLO had a certain advantage). China's choice was to keep its options open. While al-Shuḳairy was appointed by Arab governments at the Summit Conference in January 1964, it was only two months later, in March, that China received the first Fataḥ delegation. Exactly a year later, when al-Shuḳairy went to Peking, the Chinese reception indicated more power and willingness. China's recognition of the PLO added a new dimension to its position vis-a-vis the USSR. China's contribution to the Palestinian cause in this period, whatever its aims may have been, undoubtedly gave it a foothold in the PRM and, to a much lesser extent, among Arab states.

After al-Shuḳairy's visit, China seized every opportunity to voice support for the Palestinian cause, condemning the establishment of Israeli-West German diplomatic relations,[101] taking a strong stand at AAPSO conferences,[102] the CCAAS sending various messages of support,[103] and sponsoring celebrations of Palestine Day in Peking,[104] concerning which *Ta Kung Pao*, for example, declared that:

> We firmly support the struggle of the Palestinian people to recover their legitimate rights and return to their homeland and the common struggle of the Arab peoples to oppose US imperialism and its aggressive tool Israel, to oppose West German militarism and to win and safeguard national independence. This solemn stand of the Chinese people is consistent and unequivocal. We regard it as our internationalist duty to support the just struggle of the peoples of Palestine and the Arab countries whose struggle is also a support to us.[105]

Such attitudes were reinforced by Chinese spokesmen and leaders whenever an opportunity arose. Chou En-lai, in an interview in Cairo with *al-Muṣawar* stated that 'we are ready to give you all you ask for.

Whenever you are ready, say the word and you will find us ready. We are willing to give you anything and everything for we support the Arab claim to Palestine unreservedly'.[106] The Chinese press even went a step further in siding with the Palestinian cause in inter-Arab relations, for it condemned Tunisia's Bourguiba for his call for peaceful co-existence and direct negotiations with Israel.[107]

Such unequivocal support for Palestine was to be intensified as Sino-Palestinian relations coincided with the initial radicalisation of China's foreign policy as a result of the Cultural Revolution. Rashīd Djarbu', deputy head of the PLO mission in Peking, was promoted to become head of the mission to both China and North Korea,[108] and became the most active PLO representative in a non-Arab capital. One manifestation of cordiality was China's agreement to celebrate 15 May as in the Arab world, and calling it Palestine Day, when demonstrations and speeches took place. The *People's Daily* noted this occasion in an editorial claiming that the PLO advocated 'armed struggle as the only way to liberate Palestine', condemned 'US imperialism' and added a new vituperative attack on the USSR:

> It must be pointed out that the revisionist leading group of the
> Soviet Union is a partner of the US in the latter's criminal plan
> against the Arabs. It is a well-known fact that the Soviet revisionists
> are linked with the Israeli Zionists. Recently the newspapers and
> other publications in the Soviet Union have enthusiastically called
> for the 'solution of conflicts' in the various regions in the 'Tashkent
> Spirit'. *New Times* in Moscow openly advocated the application
> of the 'Tashkent Spirit' to the settlement of the Israel-Arab dispute.
> Obviously a conspiracy is afoot in which the Soviet revisionist
> leading groups work hand in glove with the US imperialists in
> betraying the Palestinian and Arab people's interests and their
> anti-imperialist struggle.[109]

The 'Tashkent Spirit' is a reference to the USSR's effort to reach an agreement between India and Pakistan for peaceful co-existence and reconciliation between the two bordering states. China believed that this approach, though officially denied by the Soviet side,[110] did not apply to the Arab-Israeli conflict. Nevertheless, during the talks between al-Shuḳairy and Kosygin in Cairo on 18 May 1966, the former asked for USSR permission to open a PLO office in Moscow, for Soviet Jewry immigration to the occupied area to be halted and for Soviet recognition of Israel to be withdrawn.[111] Obviously the Soviet response was negative, thus giving China added favour within the

PRM. At the end of Kosygin's visit to Cairo, China held rallies commemorating Palestine Day in Peking on 20 May 1966, which were sponsored by the Chinese Ministry of National Defence[112] and CCAAS.[113] It is noteworthy that the PLO's National Council was holding its third session, 20–24 May, in Gaza, on the day when the rallies were held in Peking, and the PLO's appreciation of Chinese support was marked by the invitation to two *NCNA* correspondents to attend the meetings.[114] At the meetings it was declared that China had accepted the PLO's request for the observation in Peking of 'a week of support to the Palestine cause'.[115]

PLO-NC's political resolutions reflected the prevailing mood of pro-Chinese sympathy and gratitude; they accorded China prominence, acknowledging China's support as the first non-Arab state, before North Korea and the USSR and its communist bloc. Resolution 12 of the Council referring to China stated unequivocally that:

A Because the Chinese Government had extended thankfully all practical assistance to enable the Palestinian people's struggle against colonialism with its base Israel, thus the National Council salutes the Chinese people and expresses its appreciation for the Chinese Government's policy which is based on the principle of self-reliance. The council also reaffirms its support for the Chinese people's struggle against American colonialism and for the liberation of Taiwan from the Chiang Kai-shek clique.

B Since Arab governments have decided that their stand on foreign states should be based in accordance with these governments' stand towards the Palestine cause, the Conference demands that Arab governments which have not yet recognised China should do so in appreciation of China's stand on the Palestinian cause and the PLO.[116]

Such forceful recognition and appreciation was undoubtedly a political success for China in the Arab world. But its limits were obvious, for the PLO, being born through Arab governmental efforts, had no meaningful power whatsoever to dictate decisions, and the number of Arab states recognising China did not increase. Although the Palestinian issue had no practical effect on Sino-Arab government relations, it influenced major political trends among PRM leaders and thinkers on the process of liberation (see Appendix 1).

The Palestine question in China's foreign policy also affected the mounting Sino-Soviet conflict. It was seen most vividly in organisations where both parties sought influence: AAPSO's Afro-Asian Writers'

Bureau (AAWB) was one example. The pro-Soviet faction in AAPSO held a meeting in Cairo in late June 1966 under the chairmanship of Yūsuf al-Siba'ī, AAPSO's General Secretary, and was attended by delegates from Egypt, USSR, Ceylon, India, Sudan and the Cameroons; while China and three other members, Ghana, Indonesia, and Japan were not invited. China, obviously indignant at the move, reacted by convening a rival AAWB meeting to be held in Peking, 7 June to 9 July 1966. At the Peking meeting 'the Cairo conference was condemned, the new Secretary-General elected by the Cairo meeting was denounced and AAWB headquarters were transferred from Ceylon to Peking'.[117] The 'special resolution' of the Peking meeting on Palestine was uncompromising in its support for the Palestinian cause, championed by the PLO. It pointed out, among other things, to AAWB that 'it considers Zionism to be intrinsically a colonialist movement, aggressive in its aims, founded on racism, and fascist in its means; it considers so-called Israel as a base for colonialism. .; condemns the Zionist movement and Israeli presence in occupied Palestine; considers that the Palestinian people's right to liberate their homeland is a natural extension of self-defence and self-determination; demands that all political, economic and cultural relations be severed with Israel . . .; condemns strongly continuous Jewish immigration into Palestine.'[118]

By the end of 1966, Syrian-Israeli border skirmishes intensified and China's reaction was characteristic. The *People's Daily*, for example, followed the events, adding that Arabs can always draw their fighting methodology from Chinese experience in the field:

> According to the experience of the Chinese revolution, one must
> give imperialism and all reactionaries tit for tat and fight for
> every inch of land.[119]

China's stand on the Palestinian question went beyond political support. al-Shuḳairy declared at a press conference on 4 November 1966 in Algiers that 'China has put military training bases at the disposal of the PLO and it is also sending light arms'.[120] Furthermore when the PLO formed the Palestine Writers' Union, Kuo Mo-jo, chairman of the All-China Federation of Literature and Art Circles, greeted the new union with a hint of future co-operation:

> At the Afro-Asian Writers' emergency meeting attended by
> representatives of 53 Afro-Asian countries or regions, the
> Chinese writers had the honour of cooperating with the
> representatives of 9 Arab countries. . . . We are convinced
> that at the Third Afro-Asian Writers' Conference which will be

held in China next year, the representatives from the Arab countries will play a greater part in supporting the national liberation struggles of the Afro-Asian peoples.[121]

In turn the Palestine Writers' Union Conference which met in Gaza between 30 November and 3 December paid tribute only to China among non-Arab states, as a 'special supporter, materially or otherwise' of the Palestinian cause.[122]

To conclude, it can be said that between 1955 and 1964 the Palestine question was politically and militarily viewed as an 'Arab question', and therefore all decisions concerning it were handled by Arab governments, particularly by Naṣir's in Egypt. Because of this, Sino-Palestinian relations were primarily determined by the state of relations between China and the Arab states.

The side issue of Sino-Israeli relations is very interesting. Why did China not recognise Israel when all other members of the Soviet bloc did at the time of its independence? When China became independent in 1949 the Israelis offered to recognise it. This offer was rejected. A number of possible explanations for the rejection may be hypothesised. First by the summer of 1950 the Korean War had started and Israel immediately aligned itself with the USA in this conflict. Second the Chinese may have been aware of the dimensions of the Arab-Israeli conflict and looked at it with greater foresight than other Communist states. (Non-recognition of Israel gave China a pragmatic advantage in later years in the Arab world.) Finally, ideological motives may have had some part in so far as China considered Israel to be a base for US imperialism in the area.

After 1964 Sino-Palestinian relations could become direct since there were then Palestinian organisations speaking independently of Arab regimes. China, once again, played it safe by supporting both organisations, though at this early stage it showed a preference for the PLO. Although Fataḥ was in contact with the Chinese earlier than the PLO, the support it received was political; military issues were apparently not discussed at this stage. But on the very first visit of the PLO military matters had been discussed. China's willingness to support the PLO politically and militarily had one significant implication: because the PLO was created and dominated by Arab governments, support for it meant support for the general aims of Arab governments. China's willingness to give the PLO military aid gave it an advantage over the USSR, which refused even to recognise the PLO, and China hoped this would help it break the diplomatic blockade against it, in the Arab world at least.

Chapter 3

The 1967 June War and its aftermath: developments in the Palestine Resistance Movement

The 1967 June war was a turning point in Arab history. In a well-planned move, Israel within a few days shocked the Arab regular armies by inflicting devastating military defeats on the Egyptian, Syrian and Jordanian fronts. The political repercussions were immense: 'Nasserism' vanished, the Arab regimes' claimed ability to defeat Israel in a conventional war lost credibility. The PLO under al-Shukairy's leadership witnessed the initiation of grass-root changes. Fataḥ emerged as the dominant movement within the PRM. The intellectual search for other world experience in 'people's war' flourished within the PRM. The familiar slogan that Arab unity was the road to the liberation of Palestine was reversed. The USA's political bargaining power, by its siding with the victor and appeasing powerful Arab oil producers at the same time, was enhanced. The USSR, faced by this unprecedented defeat of its clients, cut off diplomatic relations with Israel but did not halt Jewish immigration or trade contacts. We will be mostly concerned here, for the sake of brevity, with the general tendencies of the PRM until the end of 1969.

Within the PRM two significant forces emerged which rapidly gained control of the whole movement and became the dominant voice of the Palestinian cause in particular and the Arab one in general: they were Fataḥ and the various splinter groups of the Arab Nationalist Movement (ANM).

Fataḥ, militarily and politically superior, had followed a policy of training, and execution of military activities, on a broader and more effective level than any other Palestinian organisation.

The ANM's various emerging groups and organisations had a different fate. The ANM originated among students at the American University of Beirut in the late 1940s and early 1950s. Following the June 1967 war it shifted to the left: the unforeseen result was the rupture of the ANM's apparatus. One of its prominent founders, Dr George Ḥabash, and other members, established, with the agreement of the movement, a new branch called the National Front for the Liberation of Palestine at the Movement's National Conference in May 1964. The NFLP's strategy

> unlike that of Fatah was not based on the idea of mobilising Palestinians to wage independently a 'war of Liberation'. The major political and military objective of the NFLP was to act merely as a catalyst which would detonate a conventional war between the Arab states, led by the UAR, and Israel.[1]

The June War defeat put an end to this approach. In September, at the ANM's Palestine Regional Conference, Habash condemned their previous strategy and put forward a military line similar to Fatah's. By December Habash and his followers had announced the creation of the Popular Front for the Liberation of Palestine (PFLP). However, the newly founded front, which was originally formed by the merging of three Palestinian organisations – the Heroes of Return, the Palestine Liberation Front headed by Ahmad Djbril and the NFLP – witnessed a new split masterminded personally by Djbril, who formed the PFLP – General Command.

For its part, Fatah was progressing in building its organisation so that it would soon be able to play a meaningful role. This aim was to be enhanced at the Battle of al-Karamah, an East Bank Jordanian town, on 21 March 1968, where Fatah derived great capital from its victory (with the assistance of the Jordanian army) over a heavy Israeli attack; al-Karamah boosted Fatah's position as a symbol of Palestinian resistance, and resulted in hundreds of recruits flocking to its ranks. Militarily Fatah recruits were initially trained in Palestinian camps, a few were sent to Arab countries, while specialists were despatched to China and, to a lesser extent, North Vietnam.[2] Al-Karamah had repercussions on the PRM as it began to 'assert itself in the Arab world, obliged Israel to take account of its existence, began to mobilise the Palestinian movement, and set up the beginnings of an administrative infrastructure'.[3] With the progress of its military build-up, Fatah concentrated heavily on establishing a strong political foothold, especially in Jordan, where it was claimed at the time that it constituted a 'state within a state', having its own hospitals, tax collectors, social security, and an army composed of militia and regular combatants.

At the same time Fatah started to consolidate its leadership over the PLO as it saw the latter's obvious potential in the Arab context, and began to lay down plans for total domination of the organisation. This

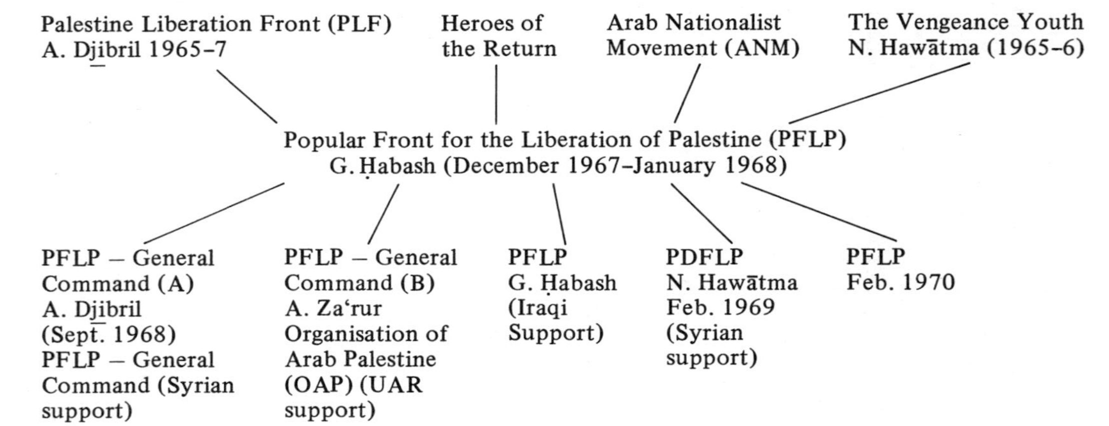

Fig. 3.1 Precursors and Offshoots of the Popular Front for the Liberation of Palestine

Source: William B. Quandt, Faud Jabber and Ann Mosely Leach, *The Politics of Palestinian Nationalism*, Berkeley and Los Angeles, 1973, p. 61.

was accomplished gradually through three National Council (NC) meetings. After the June 1967 war, al-Shuḳairy submitted his resignation, following a bitter confrontation in the Executive Committee which actually demanded it. Yaḥya Ḥamidī, earlier President of the Jordanian Lawyers' Association and expelled from Jordan under the pretext that he was a communist, was appointed Acting President until a final decision was reached. Ḥamidī supported guerrilla warfare and a PLO which adhered to such principles, and consequently, one which played a more active role than supporters of the conventional approach to the liberation of Palestine. The fifth NC meeting in Cairo, 1–4 February 1969, whose primary task was to elect a new Executive Committee, elected Yasir 'Arafat, who officially held 33 of the 105 seats, as Chairman. Thus the commando wing came to dominate the PLO's political and military structures. However, almost two weeks after the convening of the NC's fifth meeting, the PFLP suffered a further split when armed clashes occurred within its ranks and a new front under the leadership of Na'īf Ḥawātma was formed under the name of the Popular Democratic Front for the Liberation of Palestine (PDFLP) on 24 February 1969. Thus by early 1970, the original ANM had developed into clearly defined groups (see Figure 3.1, page 54).

With the changes which took place at the PLO-NC's Sixth meeting in Cairo 1-6 September 1969, where the basis for representation was changed,[4] Fataḥ achieved total control of the PLO under 'Arafat's leadership. At the end of the meeting 'Arafat announced the PLO's endorsement of, and adherence to, the principle of establishing a 'democratic state in Palestine' which meant that Jews, Christians and Muslims must live harmoniously and equally in 'liberated Palestine'. Among the PRM's leadership and cadres this is not merely a 'progressive' idea; it is taken seriously and its implementation in the course of the war of liberation is an integral part of the strategy.

China's attitudes and involvement in the Arab-Israeli conflict 1967–9

Several factors in the events which surrounded the June 1967 war influenced China's position. China's attitudes then developed around certain themes, as a result of the radicalisation of China's foreign policy which took place at the height of the Cultural Revolution: condemnation of the USA's and the USSR's roles in the Middle East, emphasising the latter's wrongs; expressing strong political support to Arab governments; extending political and military aid to Fataḥ in particular; promoting a 'people's war' as the only means to achieve Palestinian and Arab aspirations. The combination of these factors had a gradual impact on shaping the military and political orientations of the Palestine Resistance Movement.

In early 1967 preparations for renewed war started on both sides. On 18 May 1967 Egypt asked for the removal of the United Nations Emergency Force (UNEF), the PLO was put under an Arab Military Command two days later, Egypt closed the Straits of Tiran on the 23rd and Aqaba on the following day. Israel announced national mobilisation of its armed forces, and at the end of the month, Egypt and Jordan signed a mutual defence pact. China's reaction was swift and loud.

Ten thousand Chinese held a rally on 25 May at the Great Hall of the People in Peking in a show of solidarity with the Palestinian and Arab cause. Present on the occasion were Rashid Djarbu', other Arab diplomatic envoys and the sponsors of the rally, Kuo Mo-jo and Liu Ning-yi, respectively Vice Chairman of the National People's Congress Standing Committee and Vice Chairman of the Afro-Asian Solidarity Committee. After the rally a declaration was issued expressing the support of 700 million Chinese for the Arab cause; condemning 'US and British imperialists' for creating Israel through the UN machinery in order to hinder Arab unity and dominate the Arab world, and the Soviet 'revisionist clique' for their collaboration with the US in the whole scheme; and stating that 'the Chinese people firmly support the armed struggle of the Palestinian people to liberate and return to their homeland'.[5]

Through sundry diplomatic officials in Arab capitals, China conveyed messages of support which were reciprocated: Yu Chun, chargé d'affaires ad interim in Damascus, expressed his country's staunch support to the Syrian Vice-Premier and Foreign Minister;[6] Chen Yi, Vice Premier and Foreign Minister, informed Egypt's ambassador in Peking that the 'Chinese people will always remain faithful and reliable comrades-in-arms of the Arab people'.[7] On the same day, 27 May, Egypt's Foreign Minister met Huang Hua, China's ambassador, and, in the course of the discussions, the former 'conveyed President Nasser's thanks to Premier Chou En-lai for the support given by the Chinese Government and people to the UAR Government and people in their struggle against imperialism and Zionism';[8] Arab acknowledgement of China's support came from various quarters, such as Yemen,[9] the Kuwait National Assembly (the Kuwait Government had not then recognised China),[10] and President 'Arif of Iraq.[11] The Chinese

Government issued a statement denouncing Israel and attacked the US for 'hatching a big plot of aggression against Syria, the United Arab Republic and other Arab states [viz. Jordan] by making use of Israel', condemned 'the Soviet revisionist leading clique . . . the number one accomplice of US imperialism' and expressed unreserved support for the Arabs.[12] Throughout the initial crisis period, the Chinese press followed the same themes whenever an opportunity arose,[13] and the Soviet press counter-attacked[14] these positions, for 'such moves have clearly worried Russia and their Ambassador had urgent talks with Naṣir on Thursday — the day after the first Chinese wheat shipment of 26,000 tons reached Alexandria'[15] as a gesture of support.

The war, which lasted from 5 to 10 June presented China with a unique opportunity to voice strong political support for the Arab cause, although it made only minor contributions in aid because of its limited resources and its inability to replace Soviet military aid sufficiently to satisfy Syrian and Egyptian demands for conventional weapons. Its strength and emphasis rested on the viability of a people's war as the only choice for eventual victory against a superior enemy, and thus it steadily and gradually increased its support for Fataḥ. Nevertheless, China was selective in its initial reactions in denouncing Israel, the USA, Britain and their 'collaborator' the USSR while it expressed support for the Arab states involved in the fighting. A *People's Daily* editorial on the second day of the war stated that 'on June 5 Israel, a running dog of US imperialism, flagrantly launched a war of aggression against the Arab countries by mounting massive air and ground attacks on the UAR, Syria and other countries', i.e. Jordan, and cautiously advised the Arabs in a phrase that was quoted earlier but here received certain additions —

> Chairman Mao Tse-tung has said: 'if they [the enemy] fight we
> will wipe them out completely. This is the way things are: if they
> attack and we wipe them out, they will have that satisfaction;
> wipe out some, some satisfaction; wipe out more, more satisfaction;
> wipe out the whole lot, complete satisfaction'. This is the way for
> the Arab people to deal with imperialism and its lackey.[16]

China's official stand on the war was first stated to Syria and then to Egypt. One day after the eruption of war, Chou En-lai sent, on behalf of Mao Tse-tung and Vice Chairman Lin Piao, a message of support to Nur al-Dīn al-'Atāsī of Syria, affirming China's support for the Arabs,[17] and on 8 June he met Egypt's ambassador to China, Zakaria al-'Adlī 'Imām, and conveyed the same message to him;[18] Huang Hua gave the same message to Naṣir in Cairo.[19] And for three consecutive days, 7–9 June, some one million two hundred thousand people demonstrated in Peking in solidarity with the Arab cause.[20]

China's condemnation of the USSR's role in the war was obviously an exaggeration, which served China's propaganda purposes, but it provided the Chinese with an opportunity to attack the Soviets for not intervening directly on the Arab side as a 'true ally'. During the Six-Day War, the Chinese press devoted a large number of editorials and commentaries to the Soviet 'sell-out and betrayal' of the Arabs. After the Arab states' acceptance of the UN cease-fire on 9 June, the *People's Daily* asked some rhetorical questions which suited some Chinese aims:

> Why was it that at the very time when Israel was sabre-rattlingly threatening the Arab countries with war, the ɔoviet revisionist clique was so zealous in urging the Arab people to exercise 'restraint' which helped to throw them off their guard?

> Why was it that after Israel started its surprise attack on the Arab countries, the Soviet revisionist leading clique which had made such solemn vows of supporting the Arab people watched the Arab countries falling victims to aggression without even lifting a finger to help them?

> Why was it that although it was obviously US imperialism which first directed Israel to carry out armed aggression and later took direct part in the aggression itself, the Soviet revisionist clique dared not say a single word in condemnation of US imperialism?

> Why was it that the Soviet revisionist clique voted with the United States for the 'immediate cease-fire' resolution directly after it signified opposition to 'immediate cease-fire by all sides concerned' and later on tabled a resolution of its own, calling for a cease-fire with a set of time limits?

> Why is it that the Soviet revisionist clique first made a show of denouncing Israel but when Israel took over control of the Gulf of Aqaba, a Soviet vessel was the first to pass through the Straits of Tiran and even received the salute of Israeli aggressor troops?

> Answers to all these can now be furnished in no uncertain terms.[21]

The USSR, whose role was delicate in such a volatile situation, took steps to bolster its image as an ally of the Arabs, and it

> (1) broke diplomatic relations with Israel on 10 June; (2) introduced a draft resolution (S/7951/Rev.1) which, among other

things, 'vigorously condemned' Israel's 'aggressive' activities and
violations of Security Council resolutions and demanded that Israel
halt her military operations, withdraw her forces behind the 1949
armistice lines, and respect the status of the demilitarised zones;
(3) held a meeting of Communist bloc leaders in Moscow who
issued a statement promising to aid the Arabs if 'aggression' did not
stop; (4) warned that she would re-arm the Arabs if Israel did not
withdraw from occupied Arab areas; and (5) threatened to demand
the application of sanctions if Israel failed to abide by UN decisions.
The increasing vehemence of the Russian threats caused the United
States and other Security Council Members to press Israel to halt
her advances before the Russians felt it necessary to intervene.[22]

In China, however, how the Arabs should thwart Israeli victory was
seen differently. Mao, according to Muḥammad H. Heikal, even sent
President Naṣir a military map of the fighting area urging and explaining
the means by which the Egyptian army must be divided so as to resist
the invading Israelis 'until victory'.[23] Summing up the initial shock of
the Arab regimes' defeat, the *People's Daily* noted (and here Jordan
was mentioned for the first time):

> With the large-scale armed aggression suddenly unleashed by the
> US-Israeli aggressors. . . the Governments of the United Arab
> Republic, Syria and Jordan have been compelled to announce
> their acceptance of the UN Security Council's cease-fire
> resolution . . . . The Chinese people and the peoples of the
> Arab world have stood firmly by the Arab people fully exposed
> to the US-British-Soviet big counterrevolutionary scheme and
> extended their all-out support to the Arab people in their
> struggle against aggression. . . . This is a fact which opens the
> eyes of the Arab people. It is a profound lesson enabling them
> to recognise even more clearly who is their sinister enemy and
> who their loyal, reliable comrade-in-arms.[24]

At this time, China began, for the first time, to differentiate between
the roles played by 'Arab countries and Arab people' in the Arab-
Israeli conflict. It was a signal that an alternative solution to conventional strategic warfare must be adopted in view of the Arab regimes'
inability to wage another war against Israel and, more significantly,
their persistence in continuing their unequal relations with the USA
and the USSR in particular. The *People's Daily*, in an editorial, warned
of this danger:

> The war has awakened the Arab people, educated the people.
> [It] is perfectly natural for the different countries, different
> classes and different political forces in the Arab world to have
> different views on the current Middle East situation. But one
> thing is clear: anyone who tries to direct the spearhead of struggle,
> and not recognise the mortal enemy of the Arab people and their
> partners, but rather against the friends of the Arab people — and
> anyone who tries to defend the friends of the Arab people's chief
> enemy — stands no chance at all of winning the support of the
> Arab people, but is sure to be spurned and spat upon by them.[25]

China's support for the Arabs was marked by the strengths and
weaknesses of its own position. The Chinese were unable to provide
the main Arab confrontation states, Egypt and Syria, who had been
severely defeated, with the sophisticated arms needed to tilt the military
balance in their favour. Although in June 1967 China exploded its
sixth nuclear device, this was of no immediate use either to Egypt or
Syria, for China refused to transfer such technology, which would have
entangled it in one of the most volatile and sensitive wars in modern
history. al-<u>Sh</u>ukairy hailed China's successful nuclear test, stating in
Cairo that it 'has given added confidence to the Arab people'.[26] Chou
En-lai, in an interview with the *Pakistan Times*'s Minaj Burna, stated
that:

> his country had produced atomic weapons to counter nuclear
> blackmail by the United States and Russia. . . . On the Middle
> East, Chou was quoted as saying the Afro-Asian people, including
> Arabs, should not rely on heavy weapons, but more on the ability
> to protract and sustain war.[27]

What the Chinese could provide, and gave willingly, was the 'theory and
practice' of Chinese-style 'people's war'. Yet this approach to the Arab-
Israeli conflict was beyond the comprehension of the Egyptians and
the Syrians, because its application meant restructuring whole political,
military, social, economic and other policies in a way which was totally
at variance with conventional Arab thinking. However the Chinese
model was welcome to the Palestinians who, by then, were actively
involved in an intensive study of guerrilla warfare and its applicability
to the Arab-Israeli conflict.

The most elaborate and extensive analysis of the Arab-Israeli June
War, from China's point of view, was written by a certain Chou T'ien-
ch'ih in an article entitled 'Lessons of the Arab War against Aggression',

first published in *Red Flag*, then reprinted in the *People's Daily*.[28] The article is obviously significant as it states what China saw, at the height of the Cultural Revolution, to be the primary tasks of the 'Arab people' to reverse their defeat by Israel. Chou rhetorically asks 'What are the lessons to be drawn from this war by the Arab people in particular and the revolutionary people of the world in general? In this present article we propose to put forward the following points'. The first was the 'fact that US imperialism is the sworn and number one enemy' of the Arab people; the second was that the war had exposed the 'renegade features of the Soviet revisionist ruling clique' and their collaboration with the USA in the affair. The third concerned the military dimensions of Arab war against Israel and the strategic import-ance of the theory of 'people's war', especially Mao's. Chou argued that

> This war once again tells the people that to defeat the armed
> attack of imperialism and its lackeys, the oppressed nations and
> people can only rely on the theory, strategy and tactics of
> people's war: any other strategy and tactics will not work.
>   This war against aggression proves that it will not do to rely
> on modern weapons. It will not do to rely on aircraft, tanks or
> long-range artillery. Chairman Mao says: weapons are an
> important factor in war, but not the decisive factor; it is the
> people, not things, that are decisive.[29]

He went on to present historical precedents to prove the point: China's war against Japan; China's assistance to North Korea; and the example of South Vietnam. Chou cites two related military aspects of the war that Arab regimes had neglected:

> This war against aggression also proves that to defeat the armed
> attack of imperialism, it will not do for the oppressed nations
> to adopt the strategy of war of quick decision, but they should
> use the strategic principles of protracted war.
>   This war against aggression also proves that it will not do to
> have allied forces without a main force. All allied forces in
> history which have won victories had a unified command
> and overall strategic deployment as well as a strong main
> force.[30]

The fourth point drew attention to the political nature of the Arab world and what course China thought Arab politics should follow. Chou posed the following questions:

Why did the Arab countries with 100 million people over more than ten million square kilometres of land suffer a setback in the war? What sort of road should the Arab people follow in order to achieve complete victory in the anti-imperialist struggle?

At present the Arab countries are still in the historical stage of national-democratic revolution. Neo-colonialism, headed by the United States, is still riding roughshod over the Arab people. The Arab people definitely have no wish to see their countries subjugated and to become slaves of neo-colonialism. . . . The popular masses, first and foremost the workers and peasants, are the basic motive force of the national-democratic revolution of the Arab countries.

With the exception of the bureaucrat-comprador class, the bourgeoisie in the Arab countries has a dual character. On the one hand, it suffers from imperialist oppression and has contradictions with the imperialists. In a given stage and to a certain extent it can take part in the anti-imperialist struggle. But on the other hand, being weak economically and politically, it vacillates and is prone to conciliation with the enemy.[31]

What, one may ask, are the possibilities left open in such an impasse? Chou tells us that

The ruling bourgeoisie in the Arab countries is confronted with the choice: if they persist in the anti-imperialist struggle, oppose neo-colonialism headed by the United States and safeguard national independence, they will have the support of the people; if they go against the aspirations of the people, fail to persist in the struggle against US imperialism and do not resist the deception and pressure of the Soviet revisionists, they will not only alienate themselves from the people, but will also be overthrown by the US imperialists and Soviet revisionists. . .

The peaceful solution of the Arab-Israeli conflict, mainly through United Nations channels (specifically the Security Council Resolution 242 of 22 November 1967[32]) as the basis, was considered by China, as by the PRM, as a 'product of a new US-Soviet deal'[33] and condemned by Chinese leaders at every available opportunity.[34]

The different approaches of the Chinese and the Soviets to the Arab-Israeli conflict were increasingly often stated, and underlined by the growth of the PRM. The Chinese continued advocating the familiar doctrine of protracted war, the best exponents of which were forces within the PRM; while the USSR concentrated on the 'political and peaceful solution', mainly through UN machinery, relying on major Arab governments and traditional Arab communist parties. Rivalry was often spelled out openly. John Cooley, for example, reported in an interview that a 'Palestinian close to the guerrilla leadership and who has acted as a political adviser to al-'Aṣifa, al Fataḥ's military wing, was scornful of Russian and Chinese instructors'. He said he had seen them working in Syria. 'They teach ideology, not military tactics' he said. 'In Syria they even spend time quarrelling among themselves'.[35] Chinese help contributed increasingly to the PRM's strength in the area.[36]

With the gradual subsiding of public manifestations of the Cultural Revolution in China, no demonstrations were held in Peking or in any other part of China, in any open show of solidarity with the Palestinian cause; but the Chinese press continued to mark other occasions related to the Palestinian question, such as Palestine Day on 15 May.[37] Moreover, on the first anniversary of the June War, the Chinese press presented an elaborate exposé of the occasion in the *People's Daily* and *NCNA*'s coverage. In two separate commentaries issued on the same day, *NCNA* correspondents argued[38] the theme of Soviet-US 'collaboration' at the UN in the search for a political settlement of the Middle East crisis. Referring to Security Council resolutions, to the three cease-fire resolutions, resolution 242 of 22 November 1967 and that of 27 April 1968 (the commentator gave the wrong date of 25 April) he stated that they have

several features in common:

1 They are directed primarily against the Arab national liberation movement. Again and again they deplore all violent incidents, demand 'termination of all claims of belligerency' and the prevention of 'all violent incidents'.

2 They are intended to provide legal cover for the fait accompli resulting from the Israeli aggression. These 'resolutions' fervently call for 'cease-fire' by the two sides. In fact they are coercing the Arab countries into accepting 'cease-fire' unilaterally, thus binding the hands of the 100 million Arab people from carrying on their just struggle against aggression. On the other hand, these 'resolutions' try in every possible way to protect Israel and connive at its aggression.

3 The November 1967 Security Council 'resolution' stressed the necessity for 'guaranteeing the territorial inviolability and

political independence of every state in the area'. In appearance it looks fair and impartial, but if one examines its essence behind the appearance, one can easily see that the US imperialists and the Soviet revisionists have ganged up with Israel to bring pressure to bear on the Arab countries.

4   The UN 'resolutions' also advocate a guarantee of 'freedom of navigation through international waterways in the area' and contain other clauses in favour of Israel in order to help the United States and Israel to realise the objectives which they have not been able to entirely achieve through their war of aggression.[39]

He went on to quote declarations by 'leading members' of Fataḥ that armed struggle is the only formula for 'the final liberation of Palestine'. Obviously these UN resolutions did not *solely* reflect US, Soviet and Israeli interests: voting patterns at the Security Council throughout 1968 indicate otherwise. In 1968 the Security Council passed a total of eight resolutions on the Arab-Israeli conflict. Six of them were direct condemnations of Israeli actions in violating Arab sovereignty; five of them were adopted unanimously and, much to the disappointment of China, Nationalist China (Taiwan) consistently voted on the Arab side. Algeria abstained only on one resolution (258 of 18 September which called for insistence 'on respect for the ceasefire and urging co-operation with the Secretary General's Special Representatives' by all parties concerned).[40]

The second *NCNA* article of 5 June 1968 dealt with the theme of a general uprising of the Arab people, particularly Palestinians, under the leadership of Fataḥ 'against US imperialism'. Though the initial intention of the *NCNA* correspondent was to discredit US policy in the Arab world, two related points are clearly evident throughout the article. The first is that an immediate by-product of the war was 'that the flames of the Palestinian people's armed struggle are raging ever more fiercely. This is the orientation for the struggle of the Arab people, and their hope of victory'. Furthermore, that the PRM's goals in this direction rested on Fataḥ's leadership as, through its strength, it would be able to achieve success over Israel. In its first reference to the battle of al-Karamah, on 21 March 1968, Fataḥ was given a significant role:

Israeli Premier Levi Eshkol had to admit that the Israeli troops were having a 'tougher' time with the Palestinian guerrillas than they had in the war fought last June.

The second point covered the prominence of Mao's thought among the Palestinian people —

> In the course of their struggle against the US-Israeli aggressors, more and more revolutionary Arab people pointed out that the Great Thought of Mao-Tse-tung is their beacon light, their most powerful weapon to defeat the enemy. Amidst the eager anticipation of the Arab people, the Arabic editions of Chairman Mao's brilliant works were published and distributed in the capitals of Syria, Lebanon and the United Arab Republic during the latter half of last year. Many Arab revolutionaries have been avidly studying the brilliant works of Chairman Mao; they have found in them the revolutionary truth and the correct orientation for their struggle.[41]

China's support, whether military or political, for the Palestinian cause, especially for Fataḥ, was received with spontaneous appreciation. When the PLO-NC met in Cairo between 10 and 17 July 1968, China's ambassador to Egypt, Huang Hua, attended the proceedings,[42] although this session witnessed the stormiest power struggle and Fataḥ's gradual gain of control over the organisation. At the end of the meeting, the NC passed a number of resolutions, which among other things stated that 'armed struggle is the only way for the liberation of Palestine', emphatically rejecting any form of political solution to the Palestinian problem. They also noted with appreciation China's support for the Palestinian cause and its refusal to recognise Israel, *de jure* or *de facto*. China was the *only* foreign state mentioned by name and whose support for the Palestinian cause was credited and acknowledged; the resolution stated that the two parties 'share common aims in combating international imperialism headed by the USA, and mutual duty in supporting liberation fronts in the world'.[43]

By 1969, the drive for a 'political solution' of the Arab-Israeli conflict, sponsored by the USSR and the USA, was growing stronger, though the precise form of this solution was never coherently explained. China indicated its attitude by intensifying polemical attacks against supporters of such a solution. At the same time, within the PRM some of the Palestinian fronts, such as the PFLP, were making moves towards a rapprochement with the Soviets, while China had consistently backed Fataḥ's position and undertaken the military training of its forces in China. Soviet and American attempts at finding a political solution were based on Security Council resolution 242, although there were differences since each side supported the position of one of the antagonists. China's response was that these attempts were aimed at 'controlling the strategic positions in this part of the world, looting the rich oil resources and enslaving the Arab people there'.[44] Moreover, US-USSR attempts at a political solution had the following aims, according to an *NCNA* correspondent:

One. To put down the armed struggle of the Palestinian people and deprive the Arab countries of their right to struggle against aggression and safeguard their territorial sovereignty.

Two. To sacrifice the interests of the Arab people and infringe on the territory and sovereignty of the Arab countries in order to satisfy the ambitions of Israel, a tool of US imperialism for aggression and negate altogether the rights and demands of the Palestinian people.

Three. To allow the imperialist and revisionist powers to intervene in the Middle East affairs and control the destiny of the Middle East people. Here lies the basic aim of the United States and the Soviet Union in pushing forward the 'political solution' scheme.[45]

The USSR's drive for a political solution took other forms than diplomatic channels. The 2nd International Conference for the Support of the Arab Peoples held in Cairo in January 1969 was dominated by the USSR which sought to ensure, in one way or another, Arab acceptance of such proposals; all these efforts were later denounced by the PLO. China, for one, considered this conference to be 'hatched and cooked up single-handedly by the Soviet revisionist renegade clique'.[46] Moreover, the PLO-NC meeting in Cairo between 1 and 4 February 1969 voiced the strongest opposition to 'all peaceful and capitulationist solutions' to the Palestinian problem, including the 'United Nations Security Council Resolution of 22 November 1967, the Soviet plan and other similar ones'.[47] To China this was a welcome conclusion by the Palestinians. On the day after the conclusion of the meeting, the NCNA correspondent declared, referring to the second International Conference, that:

Preparations for the Conference were started several months before, by the Soviet-controlled 'World Council of Peace' and the Afro-Asian People's Solidarity Organisation. In order to give the conference an appearance of 'world opinion' 15 'international organisations' under the aegis of the Soviet revisionists sent 'delegates' to it. . . . The main disputes arising at the Conference reflected the struggle between two lines on the Middle East issue: the line of compromise and capitulation and the line of persisting in the armed struggle.[48]

Up to this time, the USSR had refused to supply arms[49] to Fataḥ, and was cautious about giving full political support to the PRM; it viewed Fataḥ as a seeker of financial aid and arms from 'reactionary states like Kuwait and Saudi Arabia, and also from China'. Centred around the Palestinian question, Sino-Soviet rivalry in the area developed to include Syria which was disenchanted with the Soviet approach to the whole Arab-Israeli conflict. Syria's Head of State, Nur al-Dīn al-'Atāsī, was due to visit Moscow on 5 May 1969, but the visit was cancelled by Moscow, apparently annoyed at Syria's rejection of Soviet political settlement proposals. In an obvious rebuff the Syrians sent Major-General Muṣṭafa Ṭlas to lead the first Syrian military mission to Peking.

The Syrian military delegation, invited by Huang Yung-sheng, Chief of the General Staff of the Chinese People's Liberation Army,[50] arrived in Peking on 13 May 1969 and was received with much ceremony by the Chinese; it visited a naval base at Shanghai[51] and conferred with Chou En-lai before leaving for home.[52] While the delegation was in Peking, the *NCNA* correspondent in Damascus had an exclusive interview with General Ḥadīth Murad, Commander of the Syrian People's Army and Minister of Front Villages Affairs, during which the latter spoke in the warmest terms of the 'cordiality and friendship' of Sino-Syrian relations.[53] These moves prompted the Soviet Ambassador, Nourredine Mohieddinov, to confer with Syrian President al-'Atāsī for 45 minutes. Syrian newspapers and broadcasts deleted the anti-Soviet remarks from their accounts of General Ṭlas's Peking visit. He was believed to be buying offensive arms which Moscow had denied Syria, including ground-to-ground rockets.[54] The Soviet Foreign Minister, Andrei Gromyko, arrived in Cairo on 10 June 1969 to press Soviet proposals for a political settlement; the outcome, however, seemed to be favourable to the Palestinian cause, apparently thanks to Naṣir's insistence on the rights of the Palestinians and his demand for a tough line on Israel. *al-'Ahram* pointed out that the two sides had agreed on three basic principles:

First: there are two questions which the UAR considers to be subject to no discussion under any circumstances: 1 — Full withdrawal of Israel from all Arab lands occupied after 5 June 1967.
2 — The right of the Palestinian people to their nation. This

right belongs to the Palestinian people and no one can bargain on it or decide anything on behalf of this people.

Second: the Soviet Union, whether in the four-power talks in New York or the bilateral talks in Washington, can only accept what the Arabs will accept. Mr Gromyko reiterated this principle and affirmed it fully and categorically on behalf of the Soviet Union.

Third: the UAR and the Soviet Union hold that international contacts on the Middle East should continue and that these contacts perform a certain role, which interest dictates to be continued.[55]

On 3 July 1969, the Syrian Head of State, al'Atāsi, paid his post-poned visit to Moscow in order to normalise the cool relations between the two states and conclude an arms deal.[56] Meanwhile in al-Atāsi's absence, Ambassador Cheng [Tien] on July 6 began a series of calls

on Syrian leaders. He saw the Ministers of Interior, Economy and Oil and Electricity and Industrial Projects. On 8 July, while Syrian and Israeli jets fought their biggest battle since 1967, Mr Cheng was reported to be meeting Syrian leaders. That also was the day of a secret conference in the Syrian capital of armed forces chiefs of Syria, the UAR, Iraq and Jordan. Two days later, a pro-Egyptian Beirut newspaper reported that Syria had received between $10 million and $15 million in Chinese arms aid as a 'gift'. It added that they had been sent immediately to the front with Israel.[57]

The Soviet press, at last, began to note the importance of the Palestinians and their guerrilla movements' impact on the Arab scene, which at that time started to gather momentum; but the emphasis was on the role played by the PFLP.[58]

The PLO, now dominated by Fataḥ, began to give considerable thought to the necessity for future Soviet aid and backing of the PRM. Fataḥ's tactic of keeping its options open, and its hope of future co-operation, were revealed at the PLO-NC meeting 1–6 September 1969 in Cairo. In its political resolutions on international positions concerning Palestine, for the first time in the NC's history, the USSR's support was acknowledged before China's. Resolution Two cautiously pointed out that the NC 'appreciates the stand taken by the Soviet Union and other socialist states, especially Democratic Germany, on national liberation questions, the Arab-Israeli conflict and their support for people's rights of self determination, and the Council requests from the Soviet Union further cooperation and support'.[59] China and other states like Albania, North Korea, Cuba and Vietnam, were put in second place.[60]

Chinese press coverage of the Council's meeting paid more attention to Palestinian-Arab relations, expressing hope for unified action by all Arabs against Israel, and referred to the Council's rejection of any 'political solution', but mentioned briefly that the Council's final statement had 'paid tribute to all friendly peoples, states and forces of liberation and progress the world over, for their support of the Palestinian people's struggle'.[61] In late July a *NCNA* correspondent visited various Palestinian refugee and guerrilla camps in Jordan (China and Jordan had no diplomatic relations). These camps were under the control of Fatah, and the correspondent reported the significance of Mao's Thought and Writings among Palestinian fighters, cadres and refugees. The correspondent relates that this 'political education' programme was conducted by Fatah's leadership in the form of a 'mobile library' and this 'library' has neither rooms, desks nor chairs. 'All it has is one or two suitcases filled with the works of Marx, Engels, Lenin, Stalin and Mao Tse-tung and some books and periodicals about the Palestinian revolution.'[62] The correspondent's clear aim of furthering Mao's personality cult was clearly evident, but exaggerated, when he claimed that he had 'witnessed the moving scene showing how invincible Mao Tse-tung Thought has gone deep into the hearts of more and more Palestinian guerrillas daily'.[63] It is noteworthy that this article was published two months after the visit of the *NCNA* correspondent to the camps, which coincided with the end of the PLO-NC meeting, and at a time when there are signs of some Palestinian, particularly Fatah, willingness to receive Soviet aid, military or political. Fatah, however, had sought to strengthen its relations with China whenever an opportunity arose, for China remained the only effective communist, and for that matter major, foreign power to support Fatah with much-needed military aid.

At the celebrations of the 20th anniversary of the People's Republic of China, Fatah sent a delegation led by 'Abū Qassem to attend the celebrations at Peking and conclude some agreements. The delegation arrived on 27 September 1969 to an impressive Chinese reception, particularly if one considers the composition of the Fatah delegation, and was received at the airport by high-ranking Chinese personalities including Li Hsien-nien, Vice Premier of the State Council, Chiu Hui-tso, Deputy Chief of the General Staff of the Chinese People's Liberation

Army and Kuo Mo-jo, Vice Chairman of the Standing Committee of the National People's Congress.[64] The delegation's visit to China was clearly meant to further military co-operation, as the host most responsible for the delegation was the Chinese People's Liberation Army, rather than any of the usual agencies, and it sponsored a banquet in the delegation's honour;[65] the delegation went on a visit to a PLA unit in Peking.[66]

While the delegation was in China, the Chinese press carried lengthy accounts of Palestinian guerrilla activities, noting Fataḥ's role only within the PRM and paying considerable attention to the effect of Mao's personality cult on Fataḥ's leaders and fighters. An *NCNA* correspondent claimed in an article,[67] for example, that 'in the course of their just struggle against US imperialism and Israeli Zionism, the revolutionary Palestinian people have come to realise more and more profoundly that Mao Tse-tung Thought is a powerful ideological weapon guiding them to persevere in struggle and to win victory' and went on to describe how Fataḥ's cadres and fighters praised Mao's effective knowledge of guerrilla warfare and its applicability to the Palestinian cause.[68] Before its departure on 7 October 1969 the delegation had an audience with Chou En-lai in the presence of Peng Shao-hui, Deputy Chief of the General Staff of the PLA.[69]

At this point China began to express an interest, though a small one, in other Palestinian guerrilla fronts. When the 'political solution' began to surface more seriously — with the idea of 'indirect talks' between Arab governments and Israel — *NCNA* for the first time quoted the staunch rejection by PRM forces of such diplomacy and gave a list of organisations, Fataḥ, PFLP, and PDFLP.[70]

China's most militant stand in this period took place when military clashes erupted between Palestinian units in Lebanon and the Lebanese army in late October 1969. Lebanon then became the focus of power struggle in the area: the US declared in a statement issued in Beirut that its interests in the area 'exceed the interests of any other individual state'; the USSR condemned the American statement and demanded non-interference by foreign powers in Lebanon, but not once in its declaration and condemnation did it mention the role of the PRM or the Palestinians' right to self determination.[71] China viewed events in Lebanon differently. It repeatedly referred to Palestinian sources in condemning 'US and Israeli imperialism'.[72] Writing in the *People's Daily*, Chung Chien-ping stated *inter alia* that:

> The crime of US imperialism in instigating the reactionary forces
> of Arab countries to suppress the Palestinian armed forces has

met with the heroic resistance of the Palestinian armed forces and aroused the strong indignation of the Arab people . . . . Because of the heroic fighting and rapid growth of the Palestinian armed forces, US imperialism and Zionism have long wanted to remove this thorn in their flesh.

Recently US imperialism has been redoubling its efforts to increase the military strength of the Israeli aggressors on the one hand and blatantly hatching the so-called 'Rhodesia-type' negotiations on the other. This is an attempt to induce and compel the Arab countries to accept terms of national humiliation so as to bring about a 'political solution' of the Middle East problem. . . . However. . . it was firmly resisted and opposed by the Palestinian and other Arab people. The Palestine Liberation Organisation and other nationalist organisations of Palestine have declared unequivocally that they will never compromise and will never lay down their arms or stop fighting.

It was in these circumstances that US imperialism stepped up its plot of suppressing the Palestinian armed forces. Not long ago, US imperialism flagrantly declared in a statement that the United States 'would view with greatest concern any threat to that [Lebanon's territorial] integrity from any source'. The talk about 'threats' was merely a pretext created by US imperialism to attack the Palestinian armed forces. Sure enough, a few days later, the reactionary Lebanese forces called out troops and launched frenzied attacks on the Palestinian armed forces stationed in southern Lebanon. The Israeli aggressor troops also acted vigorously in coordination. This plot of US imperialism has been seen through by the Arab people and the revolutionary people through the world.[73]

Egypt, on the other hand, had under Naṣir's leadership sought to use its influence to further Soviet-Fataḥ relations. Naṣir sent a high-ranking delegation, led by 'Anwar al-Sadat, Member of the Supreme Executive Committee, as his personal representative, Foreign Minister Mahmud Riyadh, and Minister of War Muḥammad Fawzi, to Moscow for three days, 9 to 12 December 1969, to discuss bi-lateral relations and the Arab-Israeli conflict. The most significant aspect of the talks for the PRM was the apparent gradual Soviet change of attitude on the Palestinian question. The joint communiqué stated that

the withdrawal of Israeli troops from the occupied Arab territories, the elimination of the other consequences of the Israeli aggression and the establishment of a lasting peace based on respect for the legitimate rights and interests of all Arab peoples, including the Arab people of Palestine, were absolutely essential for a political settlement in the Middle East.[74]

In conclusion, we can say that this was the period of closest co-operation between the Chinese and the Palestinians. It was due to a radicalisation on both sides which brought about greater convergence of interests in the Middle East. The Arab-Israeli 1967 war vindicated Chinese military theories and confirmed that 'armed struggle' by the people was the 'only' way to liberate Palestine, just as armed struggle had led to the liberation of China. The defeat and the loss of face of the Arab regimes helped Fataḥ to gain power within the PRM and to obtain control of the PLO, thus effectively reducing to one the number of Palestinian organisations with which the Chinese were dealing.

Fataḥ had been more flexible on military strategy, and as a result of the 1967 defeat it encouraged the publicising of the Chinese experience in guerrilla warfare and other Chinese writings, including those of Mao. Thus these ideas began to gather momentum and influence in the PRM as cadres started to practise guerrilla warfare. It was also at this time that the Chinese provided Fataḥ with the maximum military aid and training, thus becoming the only non-Arab state to do so. This public support for 'Maoism', viewed from Peking, coincided with the eruption of the Cultural Revolution which resulted in the radicalisation of foreign policy. In this context the receptivity of the Palestinians increased China's tendency to give loud support to world liberation movements and to affirm the validity of Chinese ideas through Mao's personality cult.

The radicalisation of Chinese foreign policy included consistent condemnation of any 'political solution' to the Arab-Israeli conflict, coupled with particular condemnation of the USSR as one of the 'superpowers'. This phase coincided with the emergence of the Chinese theory of the 'Three Worlds' concept. This Chinese position was, of course, most welcome to the Palestinians, who considered such a 'solution' anathema.

It could thus be said that the disarray caused by the 1967 defeat in the Arab world encouraged the adoption of new concepts and the development of the PLO at the expense of the Arab states, and that this was welcome to China at a time when it was also in a stage of radicalisation and wanted to see Mao's theories applied in other countries. This convergence of interests makes it easy to see why this was the time of maximum support by China for the Palestinians.

Chapter 4

Black September and its aftermath

This third phase, 1970–5, of Sino-PRM relations is the most crucial and strained period the two sides went through after Bandung. This chapter examines the first two stages of this phase. The period saw severe tests of Sino-Palestinian relations which were based primarily on the strength of the PRM, and Fataḥ in particular, and its ability to maintain itself at the Arab and international levels.

The period started with the Civil War in Jordan in September 1970, later called Black September by the PRM, when the Jordanian army successfully curtailed the PRM's military and political presence in Jordan. This, ironically, led to the further growth of the PRM – mainly Fataḥ – presence in Lebanon. For the PRM this was a phase of 'tilting to the left'. The second factor was China's emergence from years of internal turmoil caused by the Cultural Revolution, and its thrust into world politics as it sought the leadership of the Third World, among other aims. In the case of the PRM, this took the form of intensified Sino-Soviet rivalry in the Arab world. This increased rivalry coincided with China's entry into the United Nations, Fataḥ's expanding relations with the USSR, and the Soviet Union's withdrawal from Egypt. The third factor, to be discussed in the next chapter, was the fourth Arab-Israeli war of October 1973. For China, this war presented the opportunity to involve itself in Arab politics and to have some influence, particularly on Fataḥ, despite China's limited capacity. This was implemented by China's willingness to support other PRM forces, such as the PDFLP, the PFLP and al-Sa'iqa (a Syrian-created and -backed front). However, thanks to its keen political and military judgement, its strength and its ability to re-adjust to circumstances, Fataḥ maintained its prominence in Sino-PRM relations.

Sino-Soviet rivalry in Sino-Palestinian relations

Sino-Soviet rivalry became so significant a factor in relations between the Palestinians and the Chinese that Fataḥ had to readjust its priorities in the changed circumstances. This, of course, resulted from the importance China had attached to the Palestinian cause in its foreign policy priorities in the Arab-Israeli conflict. From early 1970 both China and Fataḥ made carefully calculated diplomatic moves, for both of them were facing new developments in their own conditions. During 1970 China was perhaps the only foreign power to play a significant role in the Palestinian-Jordanian war before and after the Black September Massacre by the Jordanian army. It was the culmination of its involvement in the Palestinian struggle for survival in an Arab state, since by this time the Palestinian question had become so obviously an inter-Arab dilemma that foreign powers were necessarily getting involved.

As usual the Chinese press paid tribute to Fataḥ on the occasion of the anniversary of the initiation of guerrilla warfare, in January 1970, though this time there were no mass demonstrations, and in contrast with 1965 and 1967 the date was given no prominence.[1] Nevertheless, the USSR continued to press its formula of a 'political solution' and, in the process, was extremely hesitant in supporting the PLO, represented by Fataḥ. Until 1970 it still regarded the Palestinian plight as a problem of 'refugees'.

China's stand, on the other hand, was in accordance with main PRM views, especially those of Fataḥ before Black September, on the 'political solution'. This position also extended unreservedly to Arab regimes. When Israel attacked Egypt, and the USA announced its intention to supply weapons to Israel, while the USSR was withholding supplies of offensive weapons to Egypt, Chou En-lai met the Egyptian Ambassador to China, Ṣalaḥ al 'Abid, and gave him a letter for Naṣir in which he stated that

> The Chinese people are greatly concerned for the struggle of the
> people of the UAR, Palestine and other Arab countries, and are
> indignant at the US and Israeli clamours of aggression and their
> war provocation. . . . I would like to take this opportunity to
> reiterate to you that in the common struggle against imperialism,
> the Chinese people will forever remain the most reliable friend of
> the people of the UAR, Palestine and other Arab countries.[2]

Naṣir's reply to Chou, though cordial, failed to mention the Palestinians – possibly as a result of Soviet pressures. It merely stated that 'we have complete faith in China's constant support for the struggle of the Arab Nation and the struggle of the people of all countries for political and social freedom'.[3] It is worth noting that at the time of these exchanges, 'Arafat was in Moscow at the invitation of the Soviet Afro-Asian Solidarity Committee (AASC). 'Arafat's eleven-day stay, 10–20 February, achieved no significant or immediate Soviet promises of support for the military and political aims of the PLO. There are no reports that 'Arafat met any high ranking Soviet leaders, and his meetings were confined to the host organisation (despite PLO claims to the contrary).[4] The Soviet Union was cautious in divulging, officially, the nature and extent of its support to the PLO. The Soviet press reported the visit and talks in a restrained way and though the PLO-Soviet AASC talks stressed the latter's mild support for the 'national liberation' cause of the PLO, 'Arafat received no concrete promises of active Soviet help.

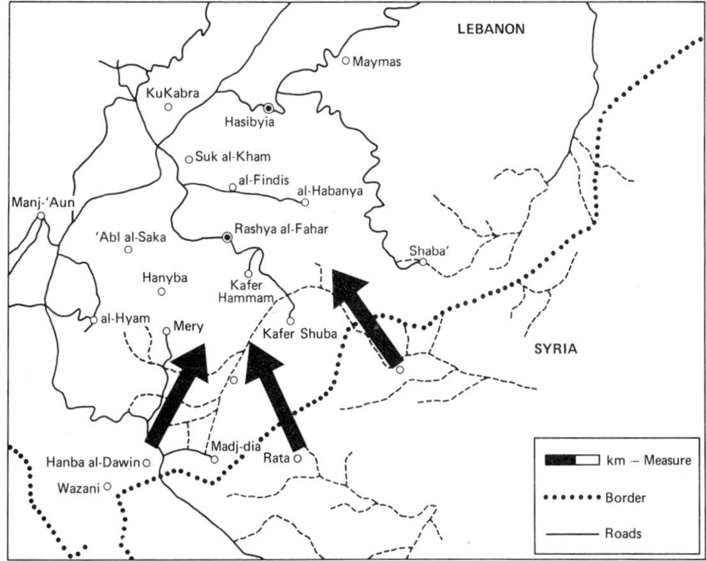

Map 4.1 The Battle of al-'Arḳūb

Source: 'Adīb 'abū-Kamel, 'Observations of a Fed'ī in the al-'Arḳūb battle' *Dirāsāt 'Arabiya*, no. 9, July 1970, p. 92.

Recognising the futility of the visit, 'Arafat travelled a month later to China, as the PLO needed military aid because of increasing tension and uncertainty about the Palestinian presence in Jordan. It was 'Arafat's first and last visit to China as Chairman of the PLO. Three days before his arrival, on 17 March 1970, Chi Peng-fei, the Chinese Vice-Foreign Minister, had a meeting with eight Arab envoys in China: those of Algeria, Syria, Egypt, North Yemen, Iraq, Morocco, South Yemen, and the Head of the PLO mission. The meeting was requested by the Arab envoys to enlist China's support against Israeli attempts to establish settlements in the Gaza Strip, and thereby annex, gradually, an important Arab territory. China's response, through Chi, was one of 'unswerving support for the Arabs', and he added that 'as long as the Palestinian people and the people of the Arab countries were united as one and persevered in their struggle, they would certainly frustrate all imperialist plots and win final victory'.[5]

In contrast to his trip to the Soviet Union, 'Arafat's visit to China was surrounded by the widest publicity, and he conferred with the highest-ranking Chinese leaders. Both are common in Sino-Palestinian relations. Arriving in Peking on 21 March, 'Arafat – invited in his capacity as official spokesman for Fataḥ and chairman of the Executive Committee of the PLO – and his delegation were met at the airport by Li Hsien-nien, Vice Premier of the State Council, Chiu Hui-tso, Deputy Chief of the General Staff of the Chinese People's Army, who throughout the entire visit was present at each occasion, Kuo Mo-jo, Vice Chairman of the Standing Committee of the National People's Congress, other Foreign Ministry and PLA personalities, and Arab envoys in Peking.[6] Speaking at a banquet given by Li Hsien-nien in honour of the delegation, 'Arafat revealed for the first time that 'the Chinese people's support for the revolutionary cause of Palestine, which is being occupied and plundered, forms an important pillar of the Palestine revolution. It is no secret if I say that "al-Fataḥ", initiator of the Palestine revolution, received aid first from Peking'.[7] During its stay the delegation visited a PLA Unit in Peking,[8] conferred with Chou En-lai,[9] Li-Hsien-nien,[10] and then proceeded to Hanoi.[11]

Military assistance was the primary objective of the visit, as was proved by subsequent events. From that date on, it became Fataḥ's standard procedure, when a delegation went in the name of Fataḥ or the PLO to Moscow, to send another to Peking, sometimes simultaneously, to keep the balance. Moreover, it became clearer that 'Arafat personally handled all negotiations with the Soviet Union, while Sino-PLO (Fataḥ) relations were entrusted to 'Abū Djihad and

'Abū Mahr and, to a lesser extent, to lower-ranking personalities, according to circumstances. Thus the Sino-Soviet dispute became a reality within the PRM, even at the intellectual level (see Appendix 1).

The importance of 'Arafat's visit to China, and its prominence within the PRM ideologically and militarily during this crucial period, underscores the PLO's desperate need for a secure source of military supplies at a time, not only of the threat presented by Israel but, more ominously, when the battle with Jordan was impending and the PLO was apprehensive about Arab complacency — justifiably, as the Iraqi army's 'neutral' stand in the subsequent events of Black September demonstrated.

Fatah's reliance on Chinese aid, especially with ammunition and training, is perhaps best illustrated by the battle of al-'Arkūb in southern Lebanon.[12] On 12 May 1970 Israeli artillery, aircraft, and infantry backed by tanks, streamed from 'Abasya, a Syrian village occupied by Israel since 1967, and Madjīdia, a village on the Lebanese border. The tactics used by the Israeli army and the counter tactics of the Palestinian guerrilla forces (mainly Fatah but aided by the PFLP General Command) were reminiscent of typical Chinese and Vietnamese experiences. An important difference was the Palestinian units' lack of ammunition. In its initial advance, the Israeli army encountered Fatah units on the Lebanese side, and compelled the temporary withdrawal of Fatah's mobile forces after sustaining some casualties. Advancing on another village, Rashya al-Fahar, the Israeli forces once again met fierce Palestinian resistance; but the Palestinian units had to retreat to rear bases, after exhausting their ammunition. The tactic of encircling the Israeli army's advance after drawing it in deep, as Mao advocated, though hampered in many instances by the lack of ammunition, was successful. After encountering hard resistance by Palestinian units, the Israeli army disengaged, and finally retreated. Israeli aims in the military operation were conventional. They hoped that the Lebanese inhabitants of the invaded area would turn against the Palestinians and put an end to their operations from that part of the border, thus giving moral support to Israeli inhabitants of newly-created settlements who were facing almost regular bombardment from Palestinian units stationed at the Lebanese border. The exercise was to be seen as a show of Israeli military strength by both populations, and as a demonstration of the Lebanese Government's inability to curtail Palestinian power in the area. Nevertheless, as 'Adib 'abū-Kamel argues the PRM's conduct of the battle was defective on the following grounds, apart from lack of ammunition:

1 Lack of co-ordination among Fedayeen organisations, and the absence of a unified plan of counter-attack.
2 Lack of planting bombs in the enemy's route of advance.
3 The Fedayeen leadership [in the battlefield] lacked experience in facing [the enemy] for the majority of the Fedayeen had training of no more than two months and then were recruited for the battle. Thus the leadership was not more experienced than the units.
4 There is a difference between guerrilla warfare and regular warfare. Though the [tactical] retreat of the Fedayeen from their bases is commendable . . . there is a difference between positive retreat and a negative one, and an organised retreat and a haphazard one.
5 The area through which the Israeli army advanced is an open one for the Fedayeen units stationed [at the villages of] Kafer Shuba, Kafer Hammam, Rashaya al Fahar; why then was the advanced area not bombarded with rockets?[13]

After the battle of al-'Arḳūb, Chou En-lai sent 'Arafat an official message in which he elaborately stated that

With the support of US imperialism, Israel not long ago brazenly despatched large numbers of troops to invade the southern part of Lebanon in a vain attempt to wipe out the Palestinian guerrillas. Together with the armymen and people of Arab countries, the Palestinian guerrillas rose in resistance and repulsed the enemy's frenzied attacks, thus smashing the enemy's ignominious designs. Your victory has greatly heightened the morale of the revolutionary people and deflated the enemy's arrogance. We highly admire you for your revolutionary spirit of fearing no sacrifice and fighting valiantly and strongly condemn the US-Israeli reactionaries for their new acts of aggression.

A new upsurge is now emerging in the struggle of the people of the world against US imperialism. The revolutionary armed struggle waged by the Indo-Chinese people against US imperialism and its lackeys is spreading rapidly and vigorously like a prairie fire, giving powerful support and encouragement to the Arab people and the people of the whole world in their struggle against imperialism. In the Middle East, tightening the noose round the neck of US imperialism, you are dealing incessant blows at the US-Israeli aggressors and in so doing you on your part are giving powerful support and encouragement to the three Indo-Chinese peoples and the people of the whole world in their struggle against imperialism. The Chinese people's Great Leader Chairman Mao has recently issued the call: 'People of the world, unite and defeat the US aggressors and all their running dogs!'

At present the revolutionary struggles of the peoples of Asia, Africa, Latin America and the rest of the world against US imperialism are all developing vigorously, and within the United States a revolutionary mass movement is also being unfolded on an unprecedented scale. All this is fiercely pounding at the reactionary rule of US imperialism. The day is not far off when US imperialism and its running dogs will be buried.

Your Excellency, your struggle is just and has the support of the revolutionary people throughout the world. The Chinese Government and people consistently and unswervingly support your struggle. We will always stand together with you. We are firmly convinced that the Palestinian and other Arab peoples tempered through anti-imperialist revolutionary struggles, persevering in unity and in protracted people's war, will surely overcome the difficulties on their road of advance, smash all plots and schemes of the enemy, defeat the aggressors and win complete victory.[14]

China's view of the Palestinian struggle, as indicated by Chou, within its complex Arab surroundings, was that it was one element of a 'unified world-wide' bloc against the USA and, to a lesser extent, 'Soviet Revisionism'; this was at the time, in 1970, of the ominous developments in Cambodia and the escalation of the Vietnamese war.

Marking the anniversary of the June war, *NCNA* carried a lengthy article[15] discussing Chou's main themes. First, the current Arab political situation, particularly that of the PRM, is favourable to 'world revolution', and most of the Arab states are included in this change:

The anti-imperialist struggles of the people the world over have always supported and encouraged each other. The Arab people's struggle against aggression is an important component part of the anti-imperialist struggles of the people the world over and enjoys their support. . .[16]

Next, in military terms, Israel, backed by the USA, had maintained military superiority over the Arab states throughout its existence, but this factor, the correspondent argues, is insignificant, for, as one of Mao's principles states, 'the people are the decisive factor' in a war; in this case the correspondent referred repeatedly to the 'Arab people':

> The Chinese people's Great Leader Chairman Mao points out in his May 20 [1970] solemn statement: 'a weak nation can defeat a strong, a small nation can defeat a big. The people of a small country can certainly defeat aggression by a big country, if only they dare to rise in struggle, dare to take up arms and grasp in their own hands the destiny of their country. This is a law of history'. The history of the Arab people's anti-imperialist struggle is advancing according to this law. In the Middle East today, who actually is powerful? Who actually can win? The development of the Arab people's struggle in the past three years has answered the questions. The US-Israeli aggressors fancy themselves strong, but actually they are very weak. Strengthening their unity and persevering in a protracted people's war, the Arab people will eventually defeat the US-Israeli gangsters. This is an inevitable and irresistible law . . . . The Palestinian guerrillas whom US imperialism has underrated have neither airplanes nor tanks, but by mobilising the people, relying on the people, daring to take up arms and fight the Israeli aggressors armed to the teeth, they have scored brilliant and magnificent military successes and have thus become the valiant shock fighters now striking at US imperialism in the Middle East . . . . What is tragic for US imperialism and its followers is that they only see the role of 'Phantom' planes and the 'strength' of so-called modern weapons, but they can never see the great strength of the people. It is precisely the great strength of the Arab people that is deciding the destiny of the Middle East and will sooner or later drive the US-Israeli aggressors into their graves.[17]

Third, unity of the PRM is a fundamental goal for which the Palestinians must strive, so as to counter hostile surrounding forces, in this case, basically, Israel and US intrigues in the area. Such 'unity', according to the correspondent, had manifested itself in the convening of the PLO-NC's seventh session in Cairo between 5 May and 4 June 1970,[18] and the second conference of Heads of State of the Arab Front Line States (Syria, Jordan, Egypt and Iraq), held in Cairo during 7–9 February 1970. Although the NC meeting had tried to develop some kind of united policy in anticipation of the coming show-down with the Jordanian army, its failure was demonstrated two months later. The other meeting failed to produce any substantial results.[19] Nevertheless the *NCNA* correspondent had some hopes:

Today the unity among the various guerrilla organisations has
been greatly strengthened. In the course of their struggle they
have set up the joint command of the Palestine Resistance
Movement, and reached agreement recently on a common
political and military programme of action and prepared to
establish unified organisations. The seventh session of the
Palestine National Council is now discussing the matter and
will make a decision . . . . The Palestinian guerrillas and the
Arab people share the common weal and woe and are brothers
fighting on the same front and in the same trench . . . . Many
Arab countries have for years given political and material
support to the Palestinian people's armed struggle and regard
this support as their bounden national duty . . .[20]

Finally, one of China's favourite ideas in foreign policy was reiterated
very cautiously, although it was difficult to apply in the Palestinian
case:

Through three years of struggle the Arab people have come to
realise that to win over the US-Israeli aggressors, it is imperative
to adopt a policy of self-reliance and hard work . . . to practise
self-reliance does not mean to rule out foreign aid. The Arab
people need aid on the basis of equality, free from strings and
privileges and genuinely disinterested. They understand that to
defeat the US-Israeli aggressors they should mainly rely on their
own struggle, not foreign aid. They must particularly guard
against the dirty tricks of infiltration under the disguise of
so-called aid.[21]

The last point was seriously considered by Fataḥ but, given its
imperative need for foreign aid, especially from the USSR and its
bloc, the point would not be taken too rigorously. On the day following publication of the above-quoted article, the *Algerian News Agency*
in Cairo asked 'Arafat about the practical results of his visits to the
USSR in February at which no agreement was reached, and to China
and Vietnam in March 1970. 'Arafat responded with a carefully
balanced statement, that

The mere fact that a delegation representing the Palestinian
revolution has visited the USSR, People's China and North
Vietnam is an expression of the unity of Arab and world struggle
against the imperialist-Zionist camp. We believe that, by receiving
a Palestinian delegation, the USSR has indirectly recognised the

Palestinian revolution and its method of struggle which goes further than methods of political struggle. We hope that this relationship will continue and that the USSR will come to acquire a clearer understanding of the dimensions of our cause and our struggle. As for the results of our visits to China and North Vietnam, we cannot but appreciate the attitudes of those countries to the cause of our people and to their armed struggle, which they unreservedly support, their support consisting both of the constant aid that China has provided to the Palestinian revolution, both before and since the June war, and which it is still providing, and of the firm relationship between the Palestinian revolution and the Vietnamese revolution through the experience provided to us by the heroic people of Vietnam and their mighty revolution.[22]

Further tributes to Chinese aid and to Mao Tse-tung's support for the PRM were voiced to *NCNA* correspondents in Arab front-line states, most notably Jordan; for example 'Abū al-Lutuf (Farūk al-Kadūmī) of Fatah, Na'īf Hawātma of PDFLP, the PLO-People's Liberation Army Command, and al-Sa'iqa members were all quoted in interviews to this effect.[23] George Habash of the PFLP went a step further by claiming that 'we PFLP buy arms in European black markets, and both the USSR and China offer us some'.[24]

Black September and China's involvement in it

The road to a final military showdown between the PRM and the Jordanian army marked a significant development in the former's history; it also highlighted a tragic miscalculation of the balance of power between the Jordanian army and the Palestinian resistance. In the summer of 1970 the possibility of overthrowing King Hussein began to look like an acceptable proposition to the PRM. This idea was based on the fundamental miscalculation that the well-equipped and well-trained Jordanian army would hesitate, or even refuse, to have an open showdown with the Resistance forces. From mid-June to mid-September the area was engulfed in local and international turbulence which was followed by the Jordanian army's onslaught on the Palestinians residing in Jordan, particularly in the camps. The confrontation eventually resulted in the termination of the PRM's presence, particularly Fatah's, in Jordan.

Encouraged by the irrational hope of overthrowing King Hussein and installing a pro-Palestinian government, the PFLP and the PDFLP forced a confrontation which was, to say the least, premature, given their real power: throughout June to August minor military clashes took place between the Jordanian Army and various roaming guerrilla units. In mid-June fighting erupted in south 'Amman, where the Jordanian army bombed the al-Hussein Refugee Camp, al-'Aṣifa units and the vicinity of central 'Amman. Conditions, however, calmed down after King Hussein announced that both Naṣir bin Jamil and Zaid bin Shakir, arch-enemies of the Palestinians, had been relieved of their military duties in the Jordanian army. Up to this point China had given strong support to the PRM. The *People's Daily*, for example, declared that:

> A grave incident of bloodshed broke out recently when the pro-American Jordanian reactionary forces, under the machination of the US Central Intelligence Agency, unleashed an armed attack on the Palestinian guerrillas and the Palestinian residents in the vicinity of Amman . . . . A month ago, US imperialism instructed Israel to send large numbers of troops to invade southern Lebanon in an attempt to eliminate the Palestinian guerrillas in the area. Having failed in this scheme, US imperialism now again directed the pro-US Jordanian reactionary forces to launch attacks on the Palestinian people, plotting to eliminate the Palestinian guerrillas through the venomous schemes of using 'Arabs to fight Arabs'.[25]

Fataḥ was dependent on Chinese arms, and therefore China had a military role in the coming civil war in Jordan. Even before Fataḥ's request for arms in late August–early September, the PLO representative in Peking declared in an interview with Fataḥ on 5 July that China considered the establishment of a 'Jewish nationalist state in Palestine as a reactionary, racist and imperialistic move' and that China's view for a solution 'for the Jewish problem is a Marxist-Leninist one' which stipulates that Jewish workers must be integrated in all countries they live in, and he praised China's stand on the Palestinian question.[26] Meanwhile, according to reports, 'Arafat negotiated with Chinese representatives in Beirut on the likelihood of delivering arms to a Syrian port rather than to 'Aqaba for fear of Jordanian or Saudi Arabian interference.[27] On the day before this meeting, 'Arafat's special envoy, Ḥusnī Yūnis, was sent to China, North Korea and North Vietnam. Yūnis arrived in Peking on 20 August and immediately held talks with Chou En-lai;[28] he then proceeded to North Korea and North Vietnam. On his return to Peking from North Vietnam on 5 September, Yūnis conferred with Li Hsien-nien, and at a banquet in honour of the delegation, Li declared that:

> While carrying out their political scheme, US imperialism and its collaborators have instigated the reactionary forces in Jordan to carry out repeated armed provocations against the Palestinian guerrillas in a vain attempt to disrupt the unity of the Arab countries and the Arab people so as to realise their scheme of making Arab fight Arab.[29]

Arms to Fataḥ could be routed through the Iraqi port of Basra on the Arabian Gulf, then shipped overland to Jordan, or alternatively shipped directly to Lebanese and Syrian ports. It is worth noting here that most PRM sources relate that George Ḥabash of PFLP paid a visit to North Korea and stopped on his way at Peking airport for talks with 'Chinese authorities', although he had not been invited by the Chinese. The latter refrained from making any promises to help the PFLP either militarily or politically.[30] The Chinese were hesitant for pragmatic reasons: the PLO, dominated by Fataḥ, was the sole legitimate representative of the Palestinians; Fataḥ was the strongest and best organised Palestinian guerrilla front; it had had relations with China since 1964; Fataḥ's relations with the USSR had never been cordial; there were no signs of change in this. However, PFLP had established closer links with the USSR and its tactics: e.g. aircraft hi-jackings hardly fitted in with China's model of a revolutionary liberation movement. Furthermore, the PFLP's overt Marxist-Leninist approach to the liberation of Palestine, though apparently supporting the Chinese model, had isolated the front in the Arab world. None the less when Ḥabash granted an interview to *Jeune Afrique* on 2 September, *NCNA* quoted his condemnation of the Rogers Plan, Zionism, and his call for PRM unity in the first direct reference to Ḥabash.[31]

As the crisis in Jordan intensified, the PLO-NC met in an emergency session in 'Amman between 27 and 28 August, only two months after its 7th Session in Cairo, as two issues needed urgent discussion. The total and unequivocal rejection of the Rogers Plan and any other 'political solution' was the first. The second, and more important, one was the unity of PRM forces: this was entrusted as a primary task to the PLO Executive Committee to ensure that the Jordanian-Palestinian area would constitute 'a unified struggling battlefield, that no other authority is permitted to mingle in our destiny and that of the wish of our people'.[32] The sense of crisis intensified when the PFLP carried out the spectacular hi-jackings of three international airliners on 6 September and subsequently blew up two of them in Jordan and the third in Cairo while the passengers were kept as hostages.

On 15 September Hussein formed a military government and, the next day, 'Arafat was given full military powers as head of all PRM forces, after negotiations with the newly-appointed Jordanian military government collapsed. Fighting broke out between the Jordanian army and the guerrillas and lasted ten days, while no Arab government gave any active support. The result was that the Palestinian side suffered heavy casualties, the PRM moved totally to the defensive, and under Naṣir's personal mediation, agreement was reached between 'Arafat and Hussein for a cease-fire on 27 September at a gathering of Arab Heads of State in Cairo. The following day Naṣir died, thus temporarily weakening the PRM's political status as it lost a valuable supporter. The PRM was surprised by the suddenness and violence of the military onslaught and the ferocity of the Jordanian army's attacks on Palestinian strongholds and camps. This left the whole resistance movement in a chaotic military and political state, and undoubtedly weakened. For the remainder of the year it tried to regroup and reorganise. Internally, polemical confrontations on the causes of its failure in Jordan intensified. The majority of the forces regrouped in Lebanon after their total elimination in Jordan.

Throughout the Civil War there were marked differences in Sino-Soviet attitudes towards the PRM and the Arab-Israeli conflict as a whole. The *Tass* statement of 19 September, for example, was cautious and non-committal:

The fratricidal conflict in Jordan is jeopardising the vital interests
of Jordan and the Palestinian resistance movement and the
interests of the national liberation struggle of the Arab nations,
and is playing into the hands of the enemies of the Arab nations,
especially as Israel is continuing her aggression. In this connection
we cannot but be alarmed by the reports of the present movement
to the Eastern Mediterranean of the US Sixth Fleet which, as is
well known, has been used on more than one occasion as a weapon
against the national liberation movement in the Arab East. Other
reports indicate that plans for foreign military intervention in
the conflict in Jordan are being hatched by definite circles in
certain countries. . . . It is believed in the Soviet Union that
foreign armed intervention in the events in Jordan would

aggravate the conflict and would hamper the struggle of the Arab nations for the removal of the consequences of Israel's aggression, for a lasting peace with justice in the Middle East and for the restoration of their violated rights and national interests.[33]

The Chinese press, on the other hand, unequivocally favoured and supported the Palestinian cause in the strongest terms and concentrated its attacks on 'US imperialism as an instigator' of the Civil War and on the Jordanian government's massacre of Palestinians.[34] The statement issued by the Chinese government on the Civil War was very important. It declared, *inter alia*, that:

> On September 17, 1970, US imperialism instigated the reactionary military government of the Kingdom of Jordan flagrantly to dispatch large numbers of troops to launch frenzied attacks unprecedented in scale against Palestinian guerrillas in a wild attempt to wipe out the revolutionary armed forces of the Palestinian people at one stroke. . . . The recent incident is another and still graver military attack launched by the reactionary Arab forces following the defeats in their continuous armed repression of the Palestinian guerrillas under the instigation of US imperialism in October last year and February and June this year. . . . The Chinese government and people strongly condemn US imperialism and its collaborators and lackeys for the recently concocted plot of a fresh military aggression in the Middle East, and strongly condemn US imperialism for instigating the reactionary Jordanian authorities to launch attacks against the Palestinian people's armed forces. . . . Should US imperialism launch a new military adventure in the Middle East, it will inevitably end up in even more tightening the noose around its neck, thereby hastening its own destruction. The Palestinian people's revolutionary struggle is *'a just cause enjoying abundant support'* [emphasis in original]. We believe that so long as the Palestinian and other Arab peoples persist in unity, persevere in armed struggle, fear no threat, and refuse to be deceived, they will certainly frustrate all military attacks and political schemes of US imperialism.[35]

China's role in this brief and stormy period for the PRM had certain characteristics that need to be noted for future comparison. First, 'Arafat paid his first visit to the USSR and returned with no substantial political or military promises, then he proceeded to China where the response was favourable. Second, Fataḥ sources claim that after Black September, China began to reconsider its support to Fataḥ alone because the latter was unable to sustain the Palestinian revolution and presence in Jordan.[36] It wanted, in a nutshell, to keep its options open within the PRM. However, despite this assumption, China's attitude to, and active support for, al Fataḥ as a leading force in PRM showed no change until July 1972. As will appear below, China preferred dealing with Fataḥ rather than with any other PRM force. Third, China's attitudes and stands on vital political issues, for example the 'political solution and Rogers Plan' was directly opposed to that of the USSR, and thus it was the only non-Arab state which followed strongly the line of the PRM on these issues. Fourth, the importance of China's role in consistently aiding Fataḥ militarily is undeniable, since it was the only foreign state which played a significant role in satisfying Fataḥ's military needs. Finally, an important consequence of Black September was China's forthright condemnation of the Jordanian monarch. As far as the operations and existence of the PRM were concerned, China had previously kept almost total silence about Arab states' attempts to suppress the advance of the PRM, mainly at the political level. In contrast to earlier incidents, such as China's condemnation of Naṣir's onslaught against local communists in his dispute with Qasim of Iraq in early 1959, China's attacks on Jordan had always been consistent.

China and the 'Political Settlement' solution

Shortly before 'Black September' an initiative for a 'political settlement' was voiced in the Rogers Plan. The so-called Rogers Plan, announced on 25 June 1970, started with letters to the Egyptian and Jordanian Foreign Ministers proposing that their respective states and Israel restore the cease-fire for a further three months, and agree to discuss, with the mediation of UN Special Envoy Ambassador Jarring, a final agreement, based on the UN Security Council Resolution 242 to achieve a 'just and lasting peace' in the Middle East. The PRM rejected this plan and warned against any Arab-Israeli co-operation in such an approach to solving the Arab-Israeli conflict.[37] The most vocal and lengthy non-Arab foreign condemnation of the Rogers Plan came in the Chinese press. *NCNA* pointed out four flaws in the Rogers political initiative:

> First it requires 'the parties to stop shooting' and 'restore the
> cease-fire'. The 'parties' are in fact the two parties: the US-Israeli

aggressors on the one side and Palestine and other Arab countries, the victims of aggression, on the other. Deliberately obliterating the distinction between the aggressor and the victims of aggression to cover up their own crimes of aggression, the US aggressors are now hypocritically 'appealing for a ceasefire'.

Second, it demands the recognition of the 'sovereignty, independence and territorial integrity of Israel'. This is an unreasonable demand which the masters of the White House have raised to the Arab countries over and over again. According to this demand, to recognise the 'sovereignty' of Israel means to admit that Israel, running dog of US imperialism, can permanently deprive the Palestinian people of their sovereignty while the Palestinian people can never recover their sacred right to their own territory.

Third, it demands protection of the 'interests of the United States'. US imperialism has been saying outright that the Middle East is 'extremely important' to it, and therefore a 'political settlement' is required to protect the interest of US imperialism. What is the US interest? Nixon has stated many a time: first petroleum and second, the strategic position.

Fourth, it wants to 'maintain the balance of power' in the Middle East. Around the time when Rogers dished up the 'political initiative' the Chieftain of US imperialism, Nixon, vociferously preached the fallacy about the so-called two 'super-powers' maintaining 'the balance of power in the Middle East'.[38]

China's attitudes in the following months centred around the basic issues which affected the PRM's future. With most Arab states by then favouring some sort of negotiated political settlement with Israel, voices within the PRM were heard to this effect. Some Palestinian leaders favoured establishing a Palestinian government-in-exile. Moreover, in hoping to overcome politically, the September débâcle, proposals were made to strengthen the unity of the PRM under PLO auspices, but these prompted disagreements on the practical steps to achieve it. Egypt tried to improve its relations with China, which had been particularly cool under Naṣir, in the hope of gaining support for its plans for a 'political solution'. A goodwill delegation, led by the President of Egypt's Arab Socialist Union, personally representing President 'Anwar al Sadat, went to China on 26 January 1971[39] to confer with Chinese leaders on the drive for a 'political solution' and in the hope of obtaining US military aid.[40] The Egyptian delegation's visit was timed to coincide with the imminent admission of China to the United Nations at the end of the year. This admission would place China in an important political position, with the power of veto in the Security Council. Further, China was considered to be the only strong foreign state which backed PLO aspirations politically and militarily, consequently it could play an important role if it accepted the 'political solution' in influencing the PLO. Finally, and most significantly, Egypt under Sadat was desperately seeking to find a way out of its heavy reliance on the USSR. Given its anti-Soviet stand, China was an alternative, though not a very serious one since it was militarily weak. The visit was probably meant as a step to show China's importance in the absence of USSR willingness to accept Egyptian policies.

During the delegation's visit Chinese leaders and press refrained from explicitly condemning the 'political solution' approach to the Arab-Israeli conflict. However, there appeared to be a noticeable Chinese emphasis on the important role played by Palestinian aspirations and the Palestinian movement in the whole conflict, in contrast to the Egyptian one. At a banquet given by Chou En-lai in honour of the delegation on 27 January 1971, Kuo Mo-jo, speaking on China's behalf, did not directly condemn the 'political solution' formula, but he pointed out that in the Middle East, the US

> 'has again instigated the Jordanian reactionary forces to carry out sanguinary suppression of the Palestinian guerrillas . . . we firmly believe that the Palestinian people, who are resolved to be masters of their own destiny, will never lay down their arms in face of the butcher knives of the enemy. . . . The Chinese people have consistently given support to the just struggle of the UAR people, the Palestinian and other Arab peoples. The Chinese people will forever remain their reliable friend in their anti-imperialist struggle'. He went on to express China's gratitude to 'the UAR Government for its consistent support for the restoration of China's legitimate rights in the United Nations'.[41]

In contrast, the Egyptian speaker mentioned the Palestine people's struggle against the US only once, in passing, and that his mission expressed:

> our love, friendship, esteem and admiration for and gratitude to the noble Chinese people and their dedicated leaders for their stand of giving full support to the just cause of the UAR people and other Arab people against the most ferocious imperialism and colonialism and against imperialist and Zionist invasion of Arab territory.[42]

The drive of the Arab states, Egypt in particular, for the political solution favoured by the USSR, included the attempt to convince the PLO, and Fataḥ in particular, of the need to establish a Palestinian government in exile, and to agree to the creation of a 'mini-Palestinian state', probably in the West Bank and Gaza Strip, as part of the over-all agreement with Israel. On 16 February 1971, Anatoly Antonov, the Soviet Ambassador to Jordan, visited 'Arafat for the second time in three days at his temporary headquarters in Jara_sh_, Jordan, to discuss these points.[43] The Soviet Ambassador received no definite promise of PLO agreement to the political solution or the position the PRM would adopt. The PLO-NC which met in Cairo between 28 February and 5 March explicitly stated that the Palestinian revolution must 'reject with determination those who advocate the establishment of such a mini-state on the part of Palestine proper, and consider the attempt to establish such a state as part of the plot to liquidate the Palestine question'.[44] On the eve of the PLO-NC meeting, the Soviet Union issued a statement declaring unequivocally that

> Every government, every responsible politician must realise that
> the alternative in the Middle East is this: a political solution or
> a military clash.[45]

China's positions on Palestine took a new upturn in the following weeks after a relatively short period of silence. An international Week of Solidarity with Palestine was called by the Arab League and the PLO to be held in the first week of May. The Chinese People's Association for Friendship with Foreign Countries (CPAFFC) and Peking Municipal Revolutionary Committee agreed to hold week-long ceremonies from 3–8 May in Peking. Since the invitation was extended to the PLO the delegation was composed of representatives of the three major fronts, Fataḥ, the PDFLP and the PFLP. It was headed by 'Abū 'Amār Sa'ad and included personalities like 'Abū Niḍal, 'Abū _Khalid_, 'Abū 'Alī, and others. On their arrival on 2 May they were met at Peking airport by Wang Hsin-ting, Deputy Chief of the General Staff of the PLA, Chi Peng-fei, Acting Minister of Foreign Affairs, and other Chinese officials and Arab diplomatic envoys.[46] On the same day the first batch of Arab journalists invited to cover the events arrived, followed on 5 May by others who brought the total to 15 Arab correspondents, many of them highly distinguished, from 12 Arab states and the PLO.

On 3 May the celebrations started with long articles in the Chinese press on the Middle East and the role played by the PRM in the region and globally. A rally, attended by 10,000 Chinese, Li Hsien-nien and

Kuo Mo-jo, sent a message of support to 'Arafat.[47] 'Abū 'Amār Sa'ad spoke at length on the historical development of the Palestine problem; Kuo Mo-jo's speech, though strongly supportive of the PRM, failed to mention the 'political solution';[48] Syrian ambassador Yūsuf Shakrh[49] spoke on behalf of Arab diplomatic envoys in China. The rally was opened with a speech by Liu Hsi-chang, Member of the Standing Committee of the Peking Municipal Revolutionary Committee and a leading member of the Conference of Representatives of Peking Revolutionary Workers.[50] The most elaborate commentaries on Palestine appeared in *NCNA* and the *People's Daily*, who published simultaneous articles, both referring to the 'political solution' but in different terms. The *NCNA* correspondent argued that:

> The Palestinian people have carried out a struggle against a 'political solution' which is part of their persistent struggle against aggression and suppression. Particularly since September of last year, the Palestinian people have waged a tit-for-tat struggle against US imperialism and their accomplices over the political scheme of a so-called 'Palestinian state'.
>
> To push ahead with the 'Palestinian state' fraud, the United States and their accomplices have worked behind the scenes *to buy over a handful of Palestinian national scum to hoodwink the people* [emphasis added]. They have also tried openly to sow discord among the Arab nations and the various Palestinian forces. They instigated a number of puppets to join in a chorus of the organisation of a 'free provisional Government of Palestine'. US imperialism also blatantly sent a 'peace mission' to the Middle East to peddle its 'proposal' on a 'Palestinian state'.[51]

The *People's Daily* approached the issue in a different tone:

> US imperialism and social-imperialism collude and at the same time contend with each other in their activities in the Middle East. While intensifying the arming of Israel and engineering military suppression of the Palestinian guerrillas, US imperialism is actively pushing the plot for a so-called 'Palestinian state'. Flaunting the signboard 'for a just and lasting peace in the Middle East', social-imperialism is working in close co-ordination with it in many respects. Such unseemly activities of theirs boil down to one aim, i.e. to make the Palestinian people and the people of the Arab countries give up their struggle against the US-Israeli aggressors, submit to their will and fall victim to their activities of contending for and dividing spheres of influence in the Middle East.[52]

Other activities for Palestine Week included holding a photo exhibition on Palestine, visits by the delegation to factories and a PLA unit, and a meeting with Chi Peng-fei. On 9 May the delegation and Arab journalists met Chou En-lai.[53] Answering Arab journalists' questions, Chou reiterated China's support for the Palestinian cause. During the talks Chou pointed out, according to *al Kifah*, that 'we propose and hope that all Palestinian organisations unite in a practical form and acquire only two institutions to lead the armed struggle, a political one and a military one'.[54]

Before and after Palestine week, *Fatah* magazine paid a great deal of attention to publishing Mao's military writings. According to *NCNA*, *Fatah*

> in its April 23 issue, . . . carried the chapter 'On the purely
> military viewpoint' in Chairman Mao's article 'On correcting
> mistaken ideas in the Party'. The first three sections, 'The laws
> of war are developmental', 'The aim of war is to eliminate war',
> and 'Strategy is the study of the laws of war as a situation as a
> whole', [and] of Chapter One of Chairman Mao's article 'Problems
> of strategy in China's revolutionary war' were carried in two
> instalments on 10 and 13 May.[55]

More significantly, one remarkable outcome of China's invitation to the PLO, almost a year after Black September, was the message transmitted by Chinese leaders of their intention of extending their support to include *all* PLO fronts. Future arms supplies would be given in 'Arafat's personal name as Chairman of the Executive Committee; and 'it will be in his official capacity that he will be responsible for distributing arms among PLO fronts'.[56] The Chinese move aimed to reduce reliance on Fatah as the sole beneficiary of its aid, by widening support to other fronts. Though some argue that China's change of priorities towards the PLO came as a result of Fatah's weakened position after Black September, the indications do not lead solely to this conclusion. Factors indicated earlier should be taken into consideration: the apparent Fatah-Soviet rapprochement, with the former's attempt at enhancing such relations; the emergence of China from the Cultural Revolution, which was to end four years later with the Lin Piao affair; China's imminent admission to the United Nations; and the fact that the Palestinian resistance was characterised by a multiplicity of fronts, to rely on one alone of which, however strong it may be, and which meant China's facing more than one enemy — Israel and certain Arab states — was imprudent. Two other points were made by the

Chinese to the delegation: first, that unity of the PRM was essential for any viable Palestinian movement in the future; second, that future confrontation with Arab regimes, given the experience of Black September, was inevitable. Problems should therefore be anticipated, and the PRM's strategy must be directed not only against Israel but also against the Arab regimes which planned the destruction of the Palestinian movement. Bilal al-Ḥasan of the PDFLP, who was a member of the delegation, summed up China's position on the PRM after Palestine Week, in an interview with *al-Ḥurriyah*:

The Chinese had the following points in mind:

1 Our attitude to the Palestinian cause is a matter of principle and our support is dictated by your international duties and is never subject to other political considerations.
2 We regard your battle against imperialism in the Middle East as of direct concern to People's China and we hope that, through your struggle, you will be able to bring American imperialism and Zionism to the stage of collapse that now confronts it in Indo-China: Vietnam, Cambodia and Laos.
3 Your national unity and your Arab unity are an extremely important element in your ability to reach this aim.
4 You can always be confident of our support for you, and you can be confident that our support for you is unconditional, as it has been in the past and will always be.

Asked what was 'new' in the Chinese talks, al-Ḥasan mentioned three points:

The first was our Chinese comrades' insistence that although imperialism and its instrument Israel are our principal enemies in the area, these forces may employ reactionaries to strike at us from within. Should this occur, reaction will have to be in the forefront of our enemies, and we will have to have plans to confront it. The second point is that it is not enough to talk of national unity in the abstract; this unity must be based on a sound political line. We will have to struggle theoretically and persevere in this struggle until practice demonstrates the truth of the political line. Our Chinese comrades pointed out that if we compare the situation of the Palestinian revolution with that of the Chinese revolution (from the point of view of adopting a sound political line) our situation is more difficult; because in China the differences were within a single party, whereas our differences arise in a front in which there are conflicting intellectual and political trends. The third new important point in these talks was the Chinese attitude which we were informed of officially and which can be summed up as follows: People's China will henceforth provide its aid and support to the Palestine Liberation Organisation, so that this aid may reach every combatant commando detachment; this is the kind of participation by which they are helping to promote Palestinian National Unity. I think that this attitude which expands the sphere of co-operation between People's China and all the commando detachments, will lead to the strengthening of relations. And there can be no doubt that these three points are an expression of People's China's understanding of the development of the situation in the area and of the nature of the internal situation of the Palestinian Resistance, especially at this stage.[57]

China's 'new' policy priorities with the PRM as a whole must not be confused with its consistent and coherent stand on Israel. For it was reported that there seemed to be some sort of improvement in Sino-Israeli relations. Sources for this impression were primarily Soviet Eastern bloc allies and the Israeli press. China's strong denial of such contacts were precise, and included the most minute details. When Israel spread the rumour that direct telecommunications were to be introduced between China and Israel in July, the General Administration of Telecommunications of the People's Republic of China issued a statement, on 28 June, pointing out unequivocally that:

On 22 June 1971 a UPI despatch from Jerusalem said that a representative of the Israeli Ministry of Communications announced on the same day that direct telephone communications between Israel and the People's Republic of China were to be instituted on 1 July. On 23 June, Reuter also sent a similar despatch from Jerusalem. The General Administration of Telecommunications of the People's Republic of China hereby states in all seriousness that the news spread from Jerusalem is groundless and is a wilful fabrication.

The fact is: In April the Shanghai Administration of Telecommunications inquired at the London Post and Telecommunications office about the relay of photo-grams and telephone calls from Shanghai to Nigeria and Colombia. In answering the above inquiry, the London Post and Telecommunications office raised in passing the requests for telephone service with China from Israel and Australia. The Chinese side did not reply to this. Therefore the question of China instituting telephone communications with Israel simply does not exist. As is known to all, the Chinese Government and people have consistently given firm support to the just struggle of the Palestinian and other Arab peoples against US-Israeli aggressors. The Chinese Government and people have no contact whatsoever with the Israeli Zionists. This has been the case in the past and will remain so in the future. This stand of the People's Republic of China is firm and unshakeable.[58]

The Israeli press reported that, when Romanian President Ceaucescu visited China in July, and then Israel, he discussed with Chinese leaders the necessity of establishing relations with Israel for 'exchange of information' and raised the possibility of a visit to China by a member of the Israeli Communist Party. *Ma'riv* claimed, furthermore, that a 'prominent left-wing member of the Israeli government' held talks with Chinese Embassy personnel in Paris at 'the latter's request'. The Chinese Embassy denied this allegation[59] and the Israeli Foreign Ministry denied that Sino-Israeli relations were discussed during Ceaucescu's visit.[60]

During the Palestine Week PLO visit to China, it is very likely that Chinese arms supplies were discussed. A consignment of arms which arrived shortly afterwards led to the first test of wider Sino-Arab relations as a result of Sino-Palestinian relations (as distinct from inter-Palestinian disagreements concerning the recipients of Chinese weapons). A Chinese consignment including tanks, armoured vehicles and light weapons was transported via Algeria to the Syrian port of Latakia. 'Arafat, with the mediation of the Algerian Ambassador in Beirut, sought and pleaded with Ḥafez al-'Assad, President of Syria, to release the consignment on the grounds that it was intended to equip PLA units, which were composed of Jordanian army deserters and some Palestinians stationed on the Syrian border with Jordan since Black September.[61] The importance of this arms delivery is quite clear since its timing coincided with the convening of the 9th session of the PLO-NC in Cairo between 7 and 13 July,[62] and it just preceded the Jordanian army's final attack on the remaining Feda'in presence in the 'Ajlūn Jarash area of Jordan. This final Jordanian attack on Palestinian bases in Jordan was furiously commented upon by the *People's Daily* which stated that 'the Chinese people indignantly condemn the Jordanian reactionaries for this bloody crime and firmly support the Palestinian guerrillas' just action of counter-attack in self-defence. The recent attacks by the Jordanian reactionaries are a continuation of their armed suppression of the Palestinian guerrillas last September'.[63]

In the face of such a momentous task and setback, Fatah's Central Committee met in Syria in early September 1971 and decided to seek aid from a traditional ally, China, and one it hoped to make, the USSR.[64] The delegation sent to China was led by 'Abū Djihad, the most authoritative figure in Sino-Fatah relations, and included prominent members such as Hani al-Hasan and Hamdan 'abd al-Kader. They arrived in Peking on 19 September 1971 and were jubilantly received by Chinese crowds, Chi Peng-fei and Wang Hsin-ting, Deputy Chief of General Staff of the Chinese Staff of the Chinese PLA.[65] The delegation remained in China for two weeks. The day after its arrival, at a banquet sponsored by the official hosts, the Chinese People's Association for Friendship with Foreign Countries (CPAFFC), Wang delivered a speech on the general Chinese stand on the Palestinian question, and included vehement attacks on 'social imperialism', while 'Abū Djihad, recalling the past, presented his requests thus:

> In the dark trying days, the Palestinian revolution and the
> Palestine Liberation Movement (al Fatah) already knew that the
> Chinese people and the Chinese Party are their most sincere
> friends, their most faithful supporters. In the past, the great
> Chinese revolution stood on our side with the ardour of a
> revolution, with the sincerity of a close friend. Today at a
> most difficult time, we have come to you again.[66]

During this extended visit the Chinese press gave little coverage to the delegation's movements, except to mention a meeting held with Chi Peng-fei on 21 September.[67] The delegation attended a dinner in honour of former Jordanian Prime Minister Sulaiman Nabulsi, Secretary-General of the Arab Lawyers' Federation; Shafīk 'Arshidat and Marwān al-Hamūd.[68] Before leaving, on 2 October, the delegation attended China's national day celebrations.

At the time when the UN General Assembly was debating China's admission, and two weeks after 'Abū Djihad's visit, 'Arafat headed a top-level two-week-long visit to the USSR and East Germany, at the invitation of the Afro-Asian Solidarity Committees of the respective countries. The size and composition of the delegation is indicative of the importance attached to its search for political and military aid from the USSR. Besides 'Arafat, there were Khalid al-Fahūm, Chairman of PLO-NC's 9th session (and who with al-Shukairy, was part of the first PLO delegation to China in 1965); Faruk al-Kadūmi, member of Fatah's central and Executive Committee; Samī 'Atarī, General Secretary of the PLO-Executive Committee; Lieutenant-Colonel

Muṣbaḥ al-Budairī and other 'prominent members of al Sa'iqa'. *Hiṣad al 'Asifa*, a PLO publication, stated that the visit was of vital importance for several reasons:

1 The USSR, like PRC, is the most reliable friend of the Arabs. . .
2 The land of Lenin can only be trustworthy for its principles, the foremost being the solidarity with fighters for freedom. . .
3 In spite of *differences in opinion* [emphasis added] on the issue of national rights of the Palestinian people, our people appreciate the USSR's solidarity in this particular period, when a process of annihilation is under preparation.
4 The meeting of the Palestine Revolution and Soviet leaders is given emphasis by the fact that despite all treacherous attacks staged against the revolution, they were not able to demoralise it nor were they able to achieve political annihilation of the revolution which is the only representative of the Palestinian people.
5 The USSR knows very well the capacities and leading force of the Palestine Revolution, and that it is deeply rooted in the people of the area. . . . Thus the USSR appreciates this role and gives it consideration in every *balancing force* [emphasis added] in the area.[69]

Three main points were made before the arrival of the delegation. First, the 'differences of opinion', although apparently strong, were open to negotiations. Second, the generally held view among PRM leaders was that the USSR, in its attitudes to the Arab-Israeli conflict, had always dealt with any state or front according to its ability to influence decisions which concerned the Palestinians. In a way, the Palestinian argument in Soviet-PRM relations had always been based on the Soviet Union's approach to the balance of power in the Arab-Israeli conflict. Lastly, the PLO took into consideration the critical issue of the Sino-Soviet conflict and was aware of the effect it would have on the PRM whenever its 'neutrality' appeared to be in danger; it was thus imperative to consider this factor. During its 10–29 October 1971 visit the delegation held five working sessions with the host Soviet organisation, convening three main meetings: political, military and informational.[70] According to *al-Fatah*, discussions covered three main items: 'the necessity to escalate armed struggle against Israel; the importance of bringing out the Palestinian 'entity' as an anti-imperialist and anti-Zionist body; [and] the importance of achieving unity among the various guerrilla groups'.[71] Before the delegation's departure to East Germany, a joint communiqué was issued which stressed that 'the *Soviet public* [emphasis added] resolutely sides with the Palestinian Resistance movement which is a component part of the national liberation movement of the Arab people' and added that the two sides 'noted the importance of the unity of all the progressive forces of the Arab world and the need for further strengthening their alliance with the countries of the socialist community – the true friends of the Arab peoples'.[72]

The visit to Moscow was most likely requested by the PLO, especially after initial signs of cooling relations with China; but once again, its results were limited compared with those achieved almost a year later. For the delegation not only met no prominent Soviet leaders, but the tone and press coverage of the discussions were at a low level.

China's admission to the United Nations

The recognition of the PRC's government as the sole legitimate representative of China to the United Nations on 25 October 1971 undoubtedly added a strong, new, pro-Arab voice, not only in the General Assembly and the specialised Agencies, but in the Security Council, where the PRC could exercise the veto power of a Permanent Member. Ironically, China was to find itself in a dilemma in debates and votes whenever there was a split in the Arab position on any issue.

Between December 1971 and November 1974, China's voting behaviour reflected this dilemma. In the Council, eight votes were cast positively on issues directly condemning Israel; there was one abstention; and, with Iran, it abstained in six votes.[73] Voting in the General Assembly, though it followed the same pattern, was more complex; each issue and vote will be referred to separately below. On the other hand Arab bloc voting on China's admission was favourable: eleven for, four abstentions (Bahrain, Jordan, Lebanon and Qatar) while only Saudi Arabia voted against.[74]

China's stand on the Palestine question at the UN – i.e. Palestinian right to self-determination and the liberation of Palestine – remained unchanged. This must not be confused with China's wider involvement in the Arab-Israeli conflict in political debates and voting. In his first major speech on behalf of China at the UN, Chiao Kuan-hua referred to the Arab-Israeli conflict in the most direct way, putting China's priorities and stand on the matter:

The essence of the Middle East question is aggression against the
Palestinian and other Arab peoples by Israeli Zionism with the
support and connivance of the superpowers. The Chinese
government and people resolutely support the Palestinian and
other Arab peoples in their just struggle against aggression and
believe that persevering in struggle and upholding unity the heroic
Palestinian and other Arab peoples will surely be able to recover
the lost territories of the Arab countries and restore the
Palestinian people their national rights. The Chinese Government
maintains that all countries and peoples that love peace and
uphold justice have the obligation to support the struggle of the
Palestinian and other Arab peoples, and no one has the right to
engage in political deals behind their backs bartering away their
right to existence and their national interests.[75]

It was further reported that Abba Eban, Israeli Foreign Minister, sent
a message of congratulations to the Chinese Foreign Ministry on the
occasion of China's admission, but the message was seized by the
Chinese Post Office and returned, unopened, to its original destination,
with the explanation that the two states had no postal or telecommunications agreement.[76]

China found itself in a complex situation at the UN at the very
outset, when the French delegation sought the support of the four
other Permanent Members for talks on the Middle East. China refused
on the grounds that it opposed Resolution 242 as a basis for discussions.[77] Thus when the General Assembly discussed the issue and,
once again, favoured this resolution as a basis for 'lasting peace in the
Middle East', China abstained from voting, along with five Arab states
(Algeria, Libya, Morocco, South Yemen and Syria) while the rest of
the Arab bloc voted positively.[78] When the Egyptian Foreign Minister
Mahmud Riyadh met Chiao Kuan-hua and discussed the Arab-Israeli
conflict, the Chinese delegate stated his government's stand on three
basic points:

First, as we stated in our opening speech, priority is given to the
Palestinians' self-determination and their legitimate right to regain
their state through armed struggle. Then we support the Arab
states in their struggle of liberation against Israeli occupation.
Second, we have not changed our position on Resolution 242,
which is an agreement between the two superpowers, or more,
against Arab interests. If any resolution is debated on the basis
of 242 we will reject it. Third, we are concerned with the stand

taken by the progressive Arab regimes and their proposed resolutions at the General Assembly. But if all Arab states take a unanimous stand, we will back them unreservedly.[79]

Yet when on 20 December the General Assembly debated and adopted a resolution (No. 2851) calling strongly upon Israel to 'rescind all measures to annex and/or settle in the occupied territories' China acted as a 'non-participant' while the whole Arab bloc voted for the resolution.[80] None the less both Chiao[81] and other Chinese delegates[82] had continuously and vehemently supported the Palestinian and other Arab causes against Israel at various UN debates throughout December 1971.

The years 1970–1 were marked by continuing support from China for the PRM. China therefore denounced in the strongest terms the Jordanian monarchy and government in their suppression of the Palestinians during and after Black September, and China's military supplies to Fatah reached their highest point during Black September.

After Black September, many lower-level PRM members believed that China began to reconsider its support for Fatah and develop an interest in other PRM organisations. This argument is not supported by the facts: first, Fatah remained the strongest organisation within the PRM, and although it was weakened, other organisations were relatively more weakened as a result of Black September. Second, there is no evidence of China favouring relations with other organisations – this only happened two years later. Third, for China to reduce its relations with Fatah would have been disadvantageous since it would thus have lost its strongest and closest ally within the PRM. Fourth, the only noticeable change in the Chinese attitude after Black September was that its press started to refer to other organisations than Fatah, and to quote their positions. Fifth, China gave no indication of reconsidering its fundamental opposition to the recognition of Israel.

This period also witnessed Nasir's death. This had two implications for the PRM: first it lost one of its staunchest and most valued supporters in the Arab world; second, it was left to deal alone with the difficulties of inter-Arab politics. China's entry into the United Nations constrained its position on Palestine because of Arab disagreements on the policies to be followed. Because China had no unified Arab position to align itself with, it chose its policies according to its own objectives, and therefore its voting on the 'political solution', for example, reflected its own international priorities.

A final point, which is of relevance for the following period, involves the USSR. Prior to Black September Fataḥ had tried to obtain Soviet aid but failed. This made it possible for it to get maximum support from China. As will be seen, the development of relations between the Palestinians and the Soviet Union later had a negative effect on Sino-Palestinian relations.

Chapter 5

Turning point in Sino-Palestinian relations

The Expulsion of the Soviets from Egypt results in the deterioration of Sino-Fataḥ relations

1971 was one of the most crucial years in Sino-Fataḥ relations. Initially China remained consistent in its political support for Fataḥ and, more significantly, continued to provide military training. On the seventh anniversary of Fataḥ's initiation of armed struggle, 1 January, the *NCNA* correspondent in Damascus sent a feature story relating his visits to various Fataḥ commando bases on the Israeli border, condemned attempts by the 'reactionary Jordanian regime' to annihilate the Palestine Resistance Movement, noted the fighting spirit of the commando incursions and the Palestinian aim of liberating their homeland.[1] China's military support continued: 'Abū Khalid of Fataḥ was sent to China at the head of a delegation which stayed three months to 'get acquainted with and to specialise in revolutionary information and guerrilla warfare'.[2] Officially the delegation was invited by CPAFFC and one of its meetings was reported to be with Peng Shao-hui, Deputy Chief of General Staff of the Chinese PLA.[3] The results of the visit were most likely discussed in Baghdad when the Chinese Ambassador fêted 'Arafat at the Embassy on the occasion of the latter's official visit to Iraq.[4]

At this point one major element of China's foreign policy, the Sino-Soviet dispute, probably led to the deterioration of Sino-Fataḥ relations. This coincided with Fataḥ's gradual rapprochement with the Soviet Union as a result of the latter's worsening relations with Egypt. Until July 1972 the Soviet attitude towards the PRM was determined by its support for the 'political solution'. When Sadat visited Moscow during 2–4 February 1972 the joint communiqué reiterated the previous stand on Arab-Israeli conflict that 'the two sides reaffirmed their determination to continue their struggle for a just settlement in the

Middle East on the basis of compliance with all the provisions of the Security Council's Resolution of 22 November 1967, above all for the withdrawal of Israeli troops from all Arab lands occupied in 1967'.[5]

Politically, China's position on the PRM, particularly on the 'political solution' and some Arab states' attempts to bring it about, followed the Palestinian accepted positions. In his attempt to consolidate and strengthen Hashemite rule in the area, and after having successfully curtailed the PRM presence in Jordan, King Hussein sought a new strategy. On 15 March 1972 the King announced a comprehensive plan for the new nation. The plan consisted of twelve points, the most important of which were:

1 The Jordanian Hashemite Kingdom will be called the United Arab Kingdom.
2 The UAK will consist of two provinces: A. Palestine province which consists of the West Bank and any liberated Palestinian territory whose people wish to join to it, B. Jordan province which consists of the East Bank.
3 Amman will be the Central Kingdom's capital as well as that of Jordan [proper].
4 Jerusalem will be the capital of the Palestine province.
5 The Head of State is the King who will be in charge of the Executive branch, aided by a ministerial cabinet.
6 The legislative branch will be attached to the King under the King's personal jurisdiction, and consist of an assembly called the 'National Assembly'. Its members are to be elected through secret balloting, with equal representation of the two provinces . . .
7 The kingdom will have a unified army with the King acting as the Supreme Commander. . . . Any attempt to doubt any part or the whole of this plan will be considered treason to UAK.[6]

The plan, obviously, was not only condemned by the various branches of the Palestine Resistance Movement, but also by almost all Arab states. The Chinese reaction was predictable. The *People's Daily* remarked that:

King Hussein of Jordan has recently dished up a plan to set up a so-called 'United Arab Kingdom'. . . . This is a wicked conspiracy of the Jordanian reactionaries to try to liquidate the revolutionary cause of the Palestinian people, split the unity between the Palestinian and other Arab peoples and undermine the struggle against US-Israeli aggression.[7]

The same day, 18 March, Arab diplomatic envoys in Peking requested a meeting with Chi Peng-fei to brief him on the plan. The Chinese Foreign Minister condemned the Jordanian regime and reiterated China's stand:

> The Chinese Government and people have always supported the Palestinian people and the people of all the Arab countries in their just struggle against US-Israeli aggression. It is our consistent stand that the national rights of the Palestinian people must be restored and Israeli Zionism must withdraw from all Arab territories it has occupied.[8]

Meanwhile a Fataḥ delegation, headed by 'Abū Niḍal and including 'Abū Daoūd, proceeded to China on 30 March,[9] seeking military aid and to discuss the latest political developments in the area. Accorded an enthusiastic reception at Peking airport, and a banquet given by Chi Peng-fei on the day of its arrival (during which the latter reasserted China's position on Hussein's plan),[10] the delegation held separate talks with Chi on 30 March[11] and Chou En-lai on 31 March,[12] then held another round of talks with Chi on 1 April.[13] It visited a PLA unit in Peking the following day[14] and left on 3 April for North Korea;[15] it returned to China on 7 April and once again had discussions with Chou En-lai before leaving on 11 April.[16]

While the delegation was travelling, the PLO-NC held an emergency meeting in Cairo from 6 to 10 April to deal with two main topics. Once again emphasis was put on the necessity for Palestinian unity, though its realisation was as remote as ever. The second matter was condemnation of Hussein's plan in its entirety; and for the first time the movement proclaimed in its resolutions the legitimacy of overthrowing Hussein's regime.[17] On the occasion of the Cairo meeting Chou En-lai sent a message to 'Arafat which, although it made no reference to Hussein's plan, affirmed that 'the Chinese Government and people will unfailingly and resolutely support your just struggle. We will forever stand together with the Palestinian and other Arab peoples'.[18] According to *al-Fataḥ* newspaper the delegation on its return handed 'Arafat a letter from Chou En-lai which stated his 'Government and people's admiration for PRM's emphatic refusal to accept Hussein's plan'.[19] The plan and the PLO-NC's condemnation of it were reported in a commentary in the *People's Daily*:

> The plan for establishing a so-called 'United Arab Kingdom'
> dished up by the Jordanian King Hussein not long ago is exactly
> the latest refurbished version of the political schemes of

imperialism, Zionism and the Arab reactionaries. The 'Hussein plan' was indignantly condemned and firmly rejected at the Cairo meetings [of PLO-NC] . . . . The meetings made decisions to unify the Palestinian revolutionary forces. All this has given a resounding reply to the schemes of imperialism, Israeli Zionism and one or two superpowers to liquidate the cause of the Palestinian and Arab revolution and to divide spheres of influence in the Middle East.[20]

Before the meeting various Arab and foreign organisations were invited by the PLO to send representatives to Cairo to join in condemnation of King Hussein's plan; this solidarity meeting, as well as the open sessions of the PLO's NC meeting was attended by a delegate of the Chinese Communist Party.[21]

One of the main elements in the improvement of Soviet-PLO (Fataḥ) relations was the gradual deterioration of Soviet-Egyptian relations in the second half of 1972. After two decades of intense co-operation the break was apparently, according to Muḥammad Heikal, based on the Soviet withholding arms deliveries and spare parts, and the Soviet's miscalculation over Sadat's leadership and his strategy of winning a limited war 'even ten milimetres' over Israel.[22] These policies led not only to new Egyptian contacts and openness towards the West, and especially the USA, but also frustrated the USSR which, as a result, responded by showing a preference for dealing with other 'radical' Arab regimes and the leading force within the PRM. On 8 July President Sadat met the Soviet ambassador to Egypt, Vladimir Vinogradov and informed him of the following decisions:

1 He thanked the Soviet Union for all the help it had given Egypt through its [military] technicians, but now wished the services of these technicians to be terminated with effect from 17 July.

2 Soviet arms which were in Egypt should either be sold to Egypt and Egyptians be trained to use them, or should be returned [this was a reference to those four reconnaissance aircraft of the latest type].

3 Any remaining Soviet forces should be placed under Egyptian command or be withdrawn.

4 Under the terms of the Soviet-Egyptian Treaty of Friendship [28 May 1971] immediate high-level consultations should be initiated.

5 Any technicians who were in Egypt for training purposes and who came before the main body of experts arrived, should stay.[23]

On 17 July, the day Soviet technicians were to leave Egypt, 'Arafat at the head of a delegation of members of political, military and information committees of the PLO arrived in Moscow at the invitation of the Soviet Committee for Afro-Asian Solidarity. Besides holding talks with the host organisation, and departing from the form of previous visits, 'Arafat conferred 'with officials of the Central Committee of the Soviet Communist Party and members of the Politbureau'.[24] On 27 July 1972, at the end of the visit, during which agreement was reached on future political co-operation and military aid, a joint communiqué was issued, which emphasised three matters: growing Arab need for Soviet assistance, allusions to Egypt's decision to expel the Russians, and a stronger Soviet tone on the role played by the PRM.

China's response was swift. The expulsion of Soviet military personnel from Egypt was welcome news. The first official statement on the affair was made when Muḥammad Maṣmūdī, Tunisian Foreign Minister, visited China in late August. At a banquet given by Chi Peng-fei, the anti-Soviet theme was clearly stated by both foreign ministers. Chi stated, with clear reference to Sadat's decisions, that:

> . . . of late, the Egyptian government has adopted measures to
> safeguard the sovereignty of its country, which are an expression
> of the Egyptian and other Arab peoples' strong determination to
> decide their own destiny and carry their anti-imperialist struggle
> to the end.[25]

In its attempt to minimise the significance of its loss of influence in Egypt, the Soviet Union tried to upgrade the significance of the PRM in the Arab-Israeli conflict. Writing in *Pravda* on 29 August, Pavel Demchenko voiced the strongest Soviet position on the Palestinian cause expressed until then:

> Arab reactionaries and imperialist and Israeli agents have acted
> jointly against the Palestinians, pushing them to extremism in
> order to portray the guerrillas to world public opinion as terrorists
> and thereby to undermine their ties with the Arab masses and
> deprive them of international support. . . . Both Tel Aviv and
> reactionary circles in a number of Arab countries have exerted
> great efforts to prevent the unification of Palestinian organisations.
> They are afraid that, if they were united, the Palestinians would
> be a real force in the Middle East.[26]

Soviet references to the 'just struggle of the Palestinian people' were officially adopted from then on whenever an Arab leader set foot on its soil. Iraqi President Aḥmad Ḥasan al-Bakr visited Moscow during 14–19 September at the time of Soviet attempts to strengthen its influence in other Arab states, and the joint communiqué stated unequivocally that:

> They, Iraq and USSR, regard the Palestine Resistance movement
> as a component part of the Arab national liberation movement
> and declare that they will continue to give material assistance
> and moral and political support to this movement.[27]

After these visits the first known direct arms shipments were reported and they were received through Syria.[28]

Moreover, the Soviet press became more explicit concerning actions taken by the PRM. After the bloody clashes of September 1970 Fataḥ established the Black September organisation, though it never publicly acknowledged responsibility for its actions. Under the direct leadership of 'Abū 'Iyad, the organisation was responsible for terrorist attacks against Israeli interests in the occupied Arab territories, inside Israel and world-wide. On 5 September a group of Black September guerrillas invaded the Israeli quarters at the Munich Olympic Games and held its members hostage, as a bargaining point for imprisoned Palestinians in Israel and in West Germany. The demands were temporarily met and the Palestinians with their hostages were removed to a German military base, where a shoot-out occurred, initiated by the Germans. It resulted in the killing of all nine Israeli hostages, four Palestinians and one German soldier, while three Palestinians were wounded. The Israelis retaliated by heavily bombing, on 8 September, civilian areas on its borders with Lebanon and Syria. The USSR's attitude to the attacks isolated the two incidents:

> The clamour which Israeli propaganda is making over the tragic
> occurrence in Munich is a smoke-screen which will mislead no-one.
> Neither Lebanon nor Syria bears any responsibility for these events.
> The obvious fact that Israel's military operations against the Arab
> peoples were planned beforehand cannot be concealed.[29]

The *People's Daily*, on the other hand, commented only on Israeli attacks on Lebanon and Syria, without mentioning the Munich incident, and condemned the superpowers for the 'no-war no-peace policy' and strongly put forward the Palestinian position:

> The Israeli aggressors claim that their 'security' has been
> threatened. It seems that their bombing of Syria and Lebanon
> has been done out of the needs of 'self-defence' and 'security'.

> This is purely gangsters' logic. . . . The Israeli aggressors also
> assert that once the Arab people cease aiding and supporting the
> Palestinian guerrillas the time would then be 'ripe for peace'.
> This too is a sheer lie with an ulterior motive. The objective of the
> Palestinian people's fight is to recover their lost homeland and
> restore the national rights they have been deprived of. Their
> struggle and that of the Arab countries to recover lost territories
> are an integral whole . . .[30]

China's stand at the UN, by contrast, marked clearly its foreign policy priorities which were emerging and taking a definite course at the time. The two most obvious trends were its rigid anti-Soviet position, regardless of the consequences for third parties, and second, its continued rejection of Resolution 242. This final element obviously fitted in with the PRM's wishes. At the General Assembly's debates on 5 December, on Israel's continued occupation of Arab territories since June 1967, and on attempts to establish settlements in these areas, Huang Hua, Vice-Chairman of the Chinese delegation, argued the whole point with themes which reflected the priorities of China's foreign policy concerning the Arab-Israeli conflict:

> The crux of the matter lies in the two superpowers' deliberate
> creation and strenuous maintenance of a 'no war, no peace'
> situation in which, under the guise of seeking a political settle-
> ment, they may use the territories and sovereignty of the Arab
> countries and the Palestinian people's right to existence as
> stakes for making political deals in order to further control
> the Arab countries, suppress the Palestinian revolution and
> divide spheres of influence. . .
>
> However, while the US Government is supporting the Israeli
> aggressors. . . the other superpower, masquerading as a friend of
> the Arab people, is taking advantage of the temporary difficulties
> of the Arab countries to carry out large-scale infiltration and
> expansion in the Middle East under the signboard of 'help to
> eliminate the consequences of aggression' and 'assist the Arab
> people'. It is more deceptive and more dangerous than old-line
> imperialism . . .
>
> The Chinese delegation would like to take this opportunity
> to reiterate: The Chinese government and people have consistently
> held that Israeli Zionism must completely withdraw from Egypt,
> Syria and all other Arab territories it has occupied; the Palestinians
> must have restored their right to return to their homeland and

their right to national existence. . . The Chinese government and people earnestly hope that the Palestinian and other Arab peoples will further strengthen their unity and support and assist each other in the struggle against their common enemy.[31]

Thus when votes were cast on Resolution 2949, on 8 December, which condemned Israel for continued occupation of Arab territories and called for an end to the state of belligerency and recognition of sovereignty by all states involved, the Arab bloc and the USSR, among others, voted positively, while China and the USA abstained.[32]

To avoid losing its relatively balanced position between the PRC and the USSR, Fataḥ decided that in future 'Abū-Djihad and 'Abū Mahr would be responsible for future Sino-Palestinian contacts, which had shown a certain coolness by early 1973, while 'Arafat, assisted by other members, would be responsible for Soviet-Palestinian contacts, It should be recalled that 'Arafat's last visit to China, as Chairman of the PLO and Fataḥ official spokesman, had been on 21 March 1970. Consequently PRM sources believe that 'Arafat decided to curtail his direct contacts with Chinese leaders as a result of Soviet pressure. On the other hand, should any disagreement occur in Soviet-Fataḥ political relations, a visit by 'Arafat to China would be immediately considered.

'Abū Mahr, leading a ten-member Fataḥ delegation, arrived in Peking on 1 March 1973.[33] Given the composition of the delegation, the primary issues for discussion were military aid[34] and political questions concerning the PRM, particularly China's first hints of disapproval of the closeness of PLO-Soviet relations. On 23 June 1973, the first PDFLP delegation, led by Taiysīr Khalid, arrived in Peking at the invitation of the CPAFFC.[35] This invitation had no military significance, and was purely a political move by China to show its discontent with Fataḥ's growing relations with the USSR. It is worth recalling that in earlier Chinese talks with PRM delegations, for example with al-Shuḳairy, the Chinese encouraged PRM-Soviet talks only to prove the point that the Soviets, unlike them, were not willing to give credence to the PRM's role in the Arab-Israeli conflict. However, when Soviet priorities in the area witnessed a marked change, and this was willingly reciprocated by Fataḥ, China took the matter seriously.

The October War and China's positions

Before the outbreak of the 1973 October War, Sino-Soviet polemics on foreign policy in general, and the Arab-Israeli conflict in particular.

reached new levels of accusations and counter-accusations. The Soviet approach was less coherent and more general;[36] the Chinese argument was concise and often dealt with sensitive problems of Soviet-Arab relations. In a lengthy article by a *NCNA* correspondent, the following major points tracing Soviet-Arab relations since the June 1967 war were put forward:

> The Arab people have not forgotten how the Soviet revisionist leading clique had sworn by heaven that it 'would help the Arab peoples firmly counter' the aggressors during June, 1967. The Soviet revisionist clique sold some arms to Arab countries to show their 'disinterested assistance' and 'reliable friendship' and declared that only with the help of this 'assistance' and 'friendship' could the Arab countries liquidate the consequences of Israeli aggression. But the Arab people are fully aware what kind of stuff is the 'disinterested assistance' of the Soviet revisionists. The arms supplied by the Soviet revisionists are not only costly, but many restrictions are also attached. For example, they did not provide offensive weapons and prohibited their use for recovering lost territories. . . . Soviet revisionist 'assistance' may be useless trash for the Arab people to resist Israeli aggression but it has become a major means of Soviet revisionist penetration and expansion in the Middle East. In past years, large numbers of Soviet military 'advisors' have followed close at the heels of Soviet munition exports. The Soviet revisionists strove to control key departments of some Arab countries and obtain rights to use naval and air bases and ports. They sent a huge fleet to the Mediterranean to play the bully and make a show of force, gravely menacing the security of the Mediterranean countries. Soon afterwards, they stretched their claws of aggression into the Persian Gulf in a bid for grabbing oil resources and strategic points. . . In order to make a deal with US imperialism, the Soviet revisionists have allowed an increasing number of Soviet Jews to emigrate to Israel in recent years. This exploded the myth about their 'reliable friendship'. The number of Jews emigrating to Israel has increased from several hundred in 1970 to 32,000 in 1972. Not long ago, in a bid for 'most favoured nation' treatment from the United States, the Soviet revisionist authorities have formally assured the latter of an end to collecting exit fees from Soviet Jews with a view to facilitating their emigration to Israel. . . . The dirty undertaking of the Soviet revisionists in the Middle East has promoted the awakening of

Arab peoples. The Egyptian government announced in July last year the ending of the mission of Soviet military advisors in Egypt, thus fully expressing the firm will of the Arab people against Soviet revisionist control.[37]

On 6 October 1973 the fourth Arab-Israeli war broke out simultaneously on the Egyptian and Syrian fronts; it lasted 15 days and resulted initially in significant victories for the Arab armies. The Jordanian front remained peaceful, and King Hussein's refusal to join the war hampered Palestinian participation on that front. The PRM forces stationed on the Lebanese border had two tasks: to defend and delay any Israeli advance on this third front, and to act as an attacking force in the event of failure on the Egyptian and Syrian fronts, by using pure guerrilla tactics, i.e. scattered and unsystematic attacks on Israeli forces. But the guerrillas did not play any significant role in the war.[38] Arab strategy aimed at a limited victory, not a 'total war of liberation' or even one to regain the territories occupied in 1967.

China's attitude at the outbreak of the war was one of clear and loud support for Egypt, Syria and the PRM, while its attitude at the UN reflected its foreign priorities on the Arab-Israeli conflict as a whole. However, its support came about *after* there were evident signs that Arab armies on the Egyptian and Syrian fronts were on the advance, which was in contrast to their position in the three earlier wars. It is worth mentioning that Soviet condemnation of Israel took place one day before any official Chinese statement on the war.[39] On 8 October Chi Peng-fei, on behalf of the Chinese government, met the Egyptian, Syrian and PLO envoys in Peking, condemning Israel and stating that 'we will, as always, stand firmly on your side in the struggle of the Egyptian, Syrian, Palestinian and other Arab people against Israeli aggression'.[40] The *People's Daily* added, on the same day, one further note on the reasons for war, which had not been mentioned by Chi:

The Israeli aggressors have been so daring and unbridled as to embark on another war adventure because they have the support and the connivance of the superpowers. US imperialism has been supporting Israeli Zionism and has constantly provided it with a great deal of military aid. Soviet revisionist social-imperialism, while proclaiming its 'consistent support' for the Arab people's struggle, has allowed large numbers of Soviet Jews to emigrate to Israel, thereby supporting the latter with manpower. It is also ready to restore diplomatic relations with Israel. Soviet revisionism has given the Arab countries some weapons, but at the same time shackled them in their struggle to recover their lost land; it is attempting in a thousand and one ways to tie the hands of the Arab countries and people. Soviet revisionism and US imperialism are both contending and colluding with each other in the Middle East, which has caused the Middle East question to remain unsettled for a long time, and they have taken advantage of such a situation to maintain and expand their respective spheres of influence. The frenzied aggression of Israel is just an inevitable result of such a policy pursued by the superpowers.[41]

By the fifth day of fighting, 9 October, the Israeli forces recovered from the initial shock of defeat and took the offensive, especially on the Golan Heights. They counter-attacked heavily on the Syrian flank, the border closest to the Israeli hinterland; this offensive bore fruit on 12 October. On 11 October, Chou En-lai sent a message to Presidents Sadat and al-'Asad reiterating his country's 'unfailing support'[42] and met with the Syrian and Egyptian envoys to Peking.[43] The Egyptian, Syrian, Iraqi, Algerian and Jordanian ambassadors in Moscow met, at their request, Andrei Gromyko on the same day and 'conveyed the sincere gratitude of these states to the Soviet Union for its invaluable all-round assistance and support for the Arab countries which are fighting against Israeli imperialist aggression and upholding their freedom and national independence'.[44]

The most significant development in China's position on the conflict occurred at the UN. It is still a matter of confused debate which of the Arab states, Egypt or Syria, requested the USSR hastily to ask for a cease-fire soon after the outbreak of war, through the UN Security Council.[45] However, from the outset, the USSR and the USA played, as throughout Arab-Israeli history, a leading role at the UN, with other member-states remaining on the periphery and making little meaningful contribution; and in most cases each power represented the interests of one of the antagonists. This picture was altered by China's admission to the UN, as clearly evidenced throughout debates on the October war; China's voting behaviour on the outcome of this war remained consistent: it would not participate in actual decision-making but made strong attacks on 'superpower hegemony'.

Non-participation became a hallmark of Chinese actions after 22 October 1973, when Security Council Resolution 338 came to the vote, 'calling for an immediate cease-fire and the implementation of

Resolution 242 in all its parts'.[46] The reasons for this policy were best expressed by Chiao Kuan-hua and Huang Hua who explained China's stand at the UN.[47] At the centre of the matter lay two factors: the history of rejection of Resolution 242 and total condemnation of 'superpower hegemony', which ensured at the debates and in decision-making that China's role in the world remained *sui generis*. After Resolution 338 was adopted, Israel continued its counter-attacks, and on 23 October Resolution 339 was adopted, calling once again for a cease-fire and requesting the sending of UN forces to supervise the truce agreement. On the same day, during a heated Sino-Soviet argument, Chiao stated China's position in the following way:

Now the Chinese delegation would like to state once again our views on the Middle East situation and on the manipulation of the Security Council by the two superpowers, the United States and the Soviet Union:

1 Since October 6, the broad masses of armymen and people of Egypt, Syria and Palestine have won a series of brilliant victories in their heroic fight against Israeli aggression. . . . The sacred fight against aggression and for the recovery of occupied territories waged by the armymen and people of Egypt, Syria and Palestine has broken the situation of 'no war, no peace' deliberately created by the two superpowers in the Middle East for their respective interests, exploded the myth about the 'invincibility' of Israel and demonstrated the strong fighting will of the Arab and Palestinian people, who have been greatly encouraged.

2 However, we have to point out with indignation here that the two superpowers have played a most inglorious role throughout the incident. It is known to all that the dangerous development of events in the Middle East is caused not by the Arab and Palestinian people but by the Israeli Zionist aggression and provocations with the support and connivance of the two superpowers, the two superpowers having successively supplied arms to the belligerent parties. Here it must be pointed out that in supplying arms to the Arab countries, the purpose of the Soviet Union is by no means to give true support to them in resisting Israeli provocations but to control the development of the Middle East situation so that it will not go beyond the limits it has agreed with the other superpower. . . . In order to further divide up spheres of influence in the Middle East

and reimpose the situation of 'no war, no peace' on the Arab peoples, the two superpowers, after hectic bargaining behind the scenes for their respective interests, produced a draft resolution at the Security Council on the early morning of October 22 in an attempt to use the United Nations and the Security Council as their hired tool to rubber-stamp the deal of the two superpowers. All people with a discerning eye will see clearly that that so-called draft resolution is even more ambiguous than Resolution 242, and is a scrap of paper, a fraud which can solve no problems. Basically speaking, the Chinese delegation was not in favour of this so-called resolution. However, it was only after taking into consideration the desire of certain countries concerned that the Chinese delegation refrained from voting against it and did not participate in the voting.

3 We firmly support Egypt and Syria in their just denunciation of Israel's expanded aggression. No matter what measures the Egyptian, Syrian and Palestinian people may take on their occupied soil for the recovery of their lost territories, they are all just, whereas any slight provocation made by Israel constitutes a criminal act.

4 Following the draft resolution of October 22, the United States and the Soviet Union have today introduced a new draft resolution [Resolution 339] on. . . supervising the cease-fire. This is a fresh insult to the United Nations. Like the previous resolution [338] this draft Resolution is a mere scrap of paper which makes no condemnation of Israel's expanded aggression, puts the aggressor and the victim of aggression on a par and fails to make the slightest mention of the demand for the immediate withdrawal of the Israeli aggressors from all the occupied Arab territories. Fundamentally speaking, the Chinese delegation is opposed to this draft resolution. . . . Nevertheless, out of respect for the countries concerned, we would give consideration to that draft resolution. But we will never allow it to be imposed on us. The superpowers want to force through the draft resolution before it is distributed. What kind of logic on earth is this? If the countries concerned – I repeat, the countries concerned – want such a thing, we have no alternative, but the maximum we can do is to refrain from opposing it.

5 Fundamentally speaking, the days are gone when the two superpowers could manipulate and dominate the affairs of the

world. . . . So long as the national rights of the Palestinian people are not restored and the lost territories of the Arab countries are not recovered, there can be no lasting peace in the Middle East.[48]

On 25 October the war ended leaving a complex military situation to be disentangled by the politicians. On the Egyptian-Israeli front this was clearer, but on the Syrian front, the Israeli army had been able first to contain the Syrian advance and later to strengthen its position, finally occupying more territory than it had in the pre-war period.[49] On 27 October, the first UN forces arrived at Suez City, and plans were set at Kilometre 101 for discussions on the first Egyptian-Israeli disengagement.

Politically, the October war had a serious impact on the Arab balance of power and the international situation, mainly because of the use of oil as a political weapon. Repercussions of the war on inter-Arab relations were evident: for the first time in two decades Arab 'moderates' – Sadat vs Naṣir, 'Asad vs Salaḥ Djadīd (radical leader of the ruling Ba'th party who lost out in the 1967 war) – gained power and momentum. This was further enhanced by conservative Arab oil producers, i.e. Saudi Arabia, with their oil power. Ironically the PLO, though it had historically gained political ground as a result of the weaknesses of the Arab regimes' inability to defeat Israel militarily, became stronger by being recognised as 'the sole legitimate representative of the Palestinian people' at the Arab summit meeting in Algeria at the end of November. It was a move to which King Hussein violently objected, as it was basically aimed at giving the PLO responsibility in future for the Palestinian question; thus the Arab states which were directly militarily involved with Israel were temporarily freed from their historical role as guardians of Palestinian rights. This move, however, gave the PLO political legitimacy and legality in the international scene. The whole episode produced another irony: the USA's gains were greater than those of the USSR, and the former, historically allied with Israel, gained a new ally, Egypt, a crucial state in Middle Eastern developments, as well as remaining close to the conservative Arab oil-producing states whose strength was then emerging.

The aftermath of the October war entailed a new dimension in the PRM's development. The big powers and some Arab states attempted to convene a Geneva conference on the Arab-Israeli conflict, in which the possibility of creating a Palestinian state would be discussed. In preparing for this Geneva conference the USSR tried to influence the

PRM, with two objectives in mind. First, when the conference was to be convened, all major PRM organisations should be unified to have a clear and strong Palestinian bloc, with definite demands for negotiation at the Conference. Second, given the USSR's deteriorating relationship with Egypt, the PRM came to be the major channel for Soviet influence in any final settlement. At the end of November and at the invitation of the Soviet Afro-Asian Solidarity Committee a PLO delegation arrived in Moscow. This was after the end of the Arab Summit Conference in Algeria. The delegation was headed by 'Arafat, and included important leaders like George Ḥaba<u>sh</u> of PFLP, Na'if Ḥawātma of PDFLP, Zuhair Muḥsin of the Syrian-backed al-Sa'iqa, and others. The question of the Palestinian state was at the centre of discussion. Hawatma declared in Moscow that the two sides 'reaffirmed the absolute right of the Palestinian people in the West Bank of Jordan and the Gaza Strip to determine their own future'.[50] 'Arafat went a step further by stating to *Tass* that the October war had 'convincingly confirmed the fruitfulness of the strengthening of relations of solidarity and co-operation between Arab countries and socialist states, with the Soviet Union in the lead, in all spheres — military, economic, political and diplomatic.'[51] Finally, at the end of the visit a joint communiqué was issued in which the Soviet side emphasised its determination to 'continue assistance and support for the struggle which the Arab people of Palestine are waging for their legitimate national rights'.[52]

The Turning Point

The gradual improvement of PLO(Fataḥ)-Soviet co-operation brought a marked coolness to Sino-Fataḥ relations, though it would be an exaggeration to claim that Fataḥ and its leadership were in any sense pro-Soviet. Fataḥ considered that the USSR played a significant role in the Arab-Israeli conflict; its military and political capacities were imperative for the Palestinian cause, whether against Israel and the USA or in inter-Arab politics, and the acquisition of Soviet support added a whole bloc of Eastern European states and Cuba, which previously played only a marginal role. Thus the PLO's success in this field had given it a broad circle of international diplomatic support: the USSR and its bloc, China and its sympathisers (North Korea, Albania and Cambodia), the Third World states in their majority, and the Arab bloc. This support was to become significant at the United Nations. Reacting to Soviet-Fataḥ closeness China sought to extend relations with other PRM

116

organisations: the PFLP, PDFLP, and al-Sa'iqa. However, China's firm stand on Israel had not changed, and all PRM leaders acknowledged China's consistency.

Soviet statements and its position on Palestine underwent a change towards stronger attitudes and active involvement in the following two years. When Isma'il Fahmī, Egyptian Foreign Minister, visited Moscow, 21–24 January 1974, a joint communiqué was issued, stating that:

The Soviet Union and the Arab Republic of Egypt reaffirmed
that the establishment of a lasting and just peace in the Middle
East is impossible without the withdrawal of Israeli forces from
all the Arab territories occupied in 1967 and without the
legitimate rights of the Arab people of Palestine being respected.
It was noted that the Palestinian problem cannot be considered
and resolved without equal participation by these representatives
in the work of the Geneva Peace Conference on the Middle
East as soon as possible.[53]

Soviet-PLO relations were further developed in the hope of convening a Geneva Conference with full PLO participation, and with the hope of a procedural step creating a Palestinian Government-in-Exile. 'Arafat met Andrei Gromyko during the latter's visit to Syria on 7 March 1974 and was officially invited to the USSR.[54] In April, the seven Warsaw Treaty member states met and issued a statement declaring that:

The participants in the conference note the significance of the
Geneva peace conference on the Middle East and the need for
all the states directly concerned and also representatives of the
Arab people of Palestine to take part in it. The participants in
the conference believe that the further continuation of the work
in the Geneva conference should lead, above all, to the solution
of the key problems of the Middle East settlement — the withdrawal
of Israeli troops from all the occupied Arab territories, the ensuring
of the legitimate rights of the Arab people of Palestine in
accordance with their national aspirations, and the guaranteeing
of the security, integrity and sovereignty of all the states of
the area.
  The states participating in the conference are ready to intensify
their activities in order to promote a political settlement of the
conflict and urge all states to contribute towards establishing
a just and lasting peace in the Middle East . . .[55]

'Arafat, nevertheless, continued to consult with the Chinese ambassador to Syria, whom he met on 28 April 1974,[56] on the planned Palestinian state and the Geneva conference, and he sought China's political support for such a development. In mid-May the PDFLP carried out a guerrilla action, infiltrating into Israel from Lebanon's southern border, and held school youths as hostages at Ma'alot; because of Israeli intransigence in meeting the guerrillas' demands, the army attacked, resulting in the killing of the guerrillas and some students. The Israeli air force retaliated by bombing Lebanese villages and Palestinian refugee camps for three days. The *People's Daily* reacted strongly to the Israeli action against Lebanon, but did not mention the Ma'alot incident.[57]

The PLO-NC held its 12th session in Cairo during 1–8 June 1974, apparently after strong disagreements among the participants on the Geneva Conference and the proposed Palestinian state. The ambiguity of the state of affairs manifested itself in the Council's resolutions. Resolution 3 stipulated that the PLO must struggle against any plan for a Palestinian state that demands, in return, the recognition of secure boundaries with Israel and abandoning the Palestinians' right of return to their homeland. Resolution 4 stated that 'any liberatory step accomplished is a continuation of over-all PLO strategy in establishing the democratic Palestinian state formula which was laid down in previous NC resolutions'.[58] In its political declaration, after the meeting, the NC declared that more efforts must be exerted to strengthen relations with socialist states and progressive international forces, and paid tribute to the USSR and China, among the socialist camp, for their aid.[59]

On 31 July a PLO delegation headed by 'Arafat arrived in Moscow for four days of talks, as part of an extended visit to other Warsaw Pact states. This visit was significant for future political and military developments. On the same day 'Arafat had a meeting with Boris Ponomaryev, alternate member of the Politburo and Secretary of the CPSU Central Committee, and Rostislav Ulyanovsky, deputy head of the international department of the CPSU Central Committee; both had a keen interest in the Arab world and played an important role in Arab-Soviet relations.[60] The next day 'Arafat met Vasily Kuznestsov, Deputy Minister of Foreign Affairs.[61] Two significant points appeared in the joint communiqué at the end of the visit:

> The Soviet Union expressed support for the participation of the Palestine Liberation Organisation in the Geneva Peace Conference, exercising equal rights with the other participants. . . . In response

to the request of the Palestine Liberation Organisation Executive Committee, the Soviet side agreed to the opening of a PLO mission in Moscow.[62]

'Arafat's success in finally achieving recognition from the USSR and its bloc was dismissed by other PRM organisations. The crucial issue was what the future Geneva Conference would entail if the parties involved reached agreement. However, there is no doubt that the mere fact of Soviet recognition of the PLO added to Fataḥ's prominence with the PRM. George Ḥabas̲h̲ attacked Soviet policy and Fataḥ when 'Arafat was in Moscow:

> There is an imperialist American scheme for the region but the Soviet line is ineffective in thwarting the scheme because the Russians base their policies on Israel's right to exist. The Soviet Union alone should bear responsibility for its political errors which caused the retreat of socialist movements in the area.[63]

An especially significant element in the PLO's international drive was long-awaited recognition by the United Nations, in which the USSR played an important role. This was undoubtedly discussed during 'Arafat's visit to Moscow. In order to balance matters, a Fataḥ delegation, led by Hanī al-Ḥasan, was sent to China on 29 August 1974. China made its reservations clear about the close PLO(Fataḥ)-Soviet relations, for the invitation was extended by the CPAFFC and, throughout the entire visit the delegation was accompanied by the host organisation's Vice-President, Yang-Chi.[64] It was only on 4 September that a meeting was held with Vice-Premier Li Hsien-nien,[65] but no mention of any other meetings with Chinese government officials or leaders was made.[66] This Fataḥ delegation was the first since 'Abu Mahr's March 1973 visit. In 1974 it was the only Fataḥ visit while China had received both the PFLP and PDFLP delegations after the 1973 October war. On 16 September Hanī al-Ḥasan left Peking alone[67] and the rest of the delegation left on 11 October.[68] Three days after al-Ḥasan's departure, Farūḳ al-Ḳadūmī, member of the PLO Executive Committee and of Fataḥ's Central Committee, met China's ambassador to Lebanon and they discussed the question of the PLO's participation at the forthcoming UN General Assembly meeting.[69]

The plenary meeting of the 29th session of the UN General Assembly, held in the first week of October, saw Palestinian participation in an international body that had always been regarded as a tool of anti-Palestinian aspirations. On 2 October, Chiao Kuan-hua presented

China's views on a wide range of world questions. On the Arab-Israeli conflict Chiao reiterated the Chinese position with apparent dismay at recent developments, giving considerable emphasis to a pro-Palestinian stand and to the 'Arab people':

> The Arab people brought about an excellent situation through fighting the October war . . . . Now a disengagement has been effected between Egypt and Israel and between Syria and Israel, but the Middle East question is still far from being settled.
>
> The essence of the Middle East question lies in Israeli Zionist aggression and the contention between the two superpowers, the United States and the Soviet Union, for hegemony in the Middle East versus the struggle of the Palestinian and other Arab peoples against aggression and hegemonism.
>
> It is well known that the United Nations has held innumerable discussions on the Palestine question and adopted countless resolutions thereon, of which the one referred to most often is Security Council Resolution No. 242 of 1967. All these resolutions have the common feature of twisting the question of restoration of the Palestinian people's national rights into a so-called 'question of refugees'. This is a gross injustice. We have always opposed it and will continue to oppose it.
>
> Now, the Arab countries have proposed to discuss the question of Palestinian national rights at the General Assembly Session, so that all countries may hear directly the voice of the millions of Palestinian people and the 100 million Arab people, and more countries may understand and support their just position. This is entirely necessary.
>
> Restoration of Palestinian national rights and recovery of the lost Arab territories form an integral struggle. There can be no settlement of the Middle East question so long as the lost Arab territories are not recovered and Palestinian national rights are not restored. Whatever manoeuvres they may engage in, the two superpowers will never succeed in their attempt to sacrifice the Palestinian national rights and undermine the militant unity of the Palestinian and other Arab peoples.[70]

China's annoyance with Fataḥ's closer ties with the USSR was made obvious during the PLO's participation in the UN debates, when it was announced that a PFLP delegation arrived in Peking on 19 October 1974, led by Taiysīr Ḳuba'h. This was its first visit to China at the invitation of the CPAFFC, and the delegation was escorted throughout the visit by its president, Chai Tse-min[71] – in contrast with Hanī al-Ḥasan's reception. This delegation met Ho Ying, Vice-Foreign Minister, on 16 October.[72] The next day it was received by Li Hsien-nien.[73] During the discussions Li pointed out China's support in the Arab-Israeli conflict was not confined to the PLO (Fataḥ) but was open to the whole of the PRM. He also pointed out that for any successful Palestinian revolution to achieve its goals, the PRM not only had to carry out a protracted struggle against the enemy, Israel, and that negotiations with the enemy were futile at that stage, but that the superpowers must be opposed, though the USSR carried more blame since it was strengthening Israel by allowing Soviet Jewish migration. To achieve all these aims, the unity of the PRM was imperative.[74]

While the PFLP delegation was in China, the UN General Assembly passed Resolution 3210 on 14 October 1974, inviting the PLO, as 'the representative of the Palestinian people, to participate in the deliberations of the General Assembly on the question of Palestine in plenary meeting',[75] and 'Arafat went to New York for his first historic trip to that international body which had previously been condemned by all PRM forces for unjustly neglecting the Palestinian cause. The Chinese press kept total silence on the significance of the trip and Chou En-lai, when congratulating the convening of the 7th Arab conference in late October, omitted mentioning this development; he merely stated that:

> in the past year the situation in the Middle East has developed in
> a direction more and more favourable to the Arab people and the
> people of the Third World and unfavourable to Zionism and
> big-power hegemonism.[76]

A month after the end of the PFLP visit to China, 'Abū al-'Abid, leading a PDFLP delegation, arrived in Peking on 17 November at the invitation of the CPAFFC. Again, it was escorted by the host organisation's president, Chai Tse-min[77] in an apparent rebuff to Fataḥ. While the delegation was having discussions with Chinese leaders, the UN General Assembly passed Resolution 3236 which reflected the UN's changing attitude to the Palestinian cause:

1 *Reaffirms* the inalienable rights of the Palestinian people in
   Palestine, including:
   a) the right to self-determination without external interference;
   b) the right to national independence and sovereignty;
2 *Reaffirms* also the inalienable right of the Palestinians to return
   to their homes and property from which they have been displaced
   and uprooted, and calls for their return;

3 *Emphasises* that full respect for and the realisation of these
inalienable rights of the Palestinian people are indispensable
for the solution of the question of Palestine;
4 *Recognises* that the Palestinian people is a principal party in
the establishment of a just and durable peace in the Middle East;
5 *Further recognises* the right of the Palestinian people to regain
its rights by all means in accordance with the purposes and
principles of the Charter of the United Nations;
6 *Appeals* to all states and international organisations to extend
their support to the Palestinian people in its struggle to restore
its rights, in accordance with the Charter;
7 *Requests* the Secretary General to establish contacts with the
Palestinian Liberation Organisation on all matters concerning
the question of Palestine.[78]

On the same day the visiting PDFLP delegation in China met Li Hsien-
nien. On 27 October, the *People's Daily*[79] gave the Chinese view on
the UN resolutions:

This [UN Resolution] is a new victory of the Palestinian people . . .
because of the resolute demands of the numerous Third World
countries, the current session of the UN General Assembly invited
for the first time the representatives of the Palestinian people to
take part in the discussion of the Palestinian question. At a plenary
meeting of the UN General Assembly Chairman of the Executive
Committee of the Palestine Liberation Organisation Yasir 'Arafat
made a speech. . . strongly denouncing the monstrous crimes of
Israeli Zionism, refuting eloquently all sorts of fallacies fabricated
by Zionism and superpowers. . . . In the past it [USSR] openly
slandered the Palestinian people's armed struggle as 'adventurous
riots', trying to wipe out at one stroke the Palestinian people's
cause of national liberation; but now it has changed its tone,
pretending to 'support' the 'legitimate national rights' of the
Palestinian people, in a vain attempt to bring their cause of
national liberation within the orbit of its 'political settlement'
of the Middle East question and made this a pawn in its bargaining
with the United States.[80]

After his UN appearance, 'Arafat proceeded, as head of a PLO
delegation, to Moscow from 25–30 November. This delegation was
composed of prominent PRM members including Khalid al-Fahūm,
Chairman of the PLO-NC Farūḳ al-Ḳadūmī, Zuhair Muḥsin of al-Sa'iqa

and Na'īf Ḥawātma of PDFLP. This time it was reported that the delegation had talks with Alexei Kosygin, and had a meeting with Andrei Gromyko on November 29 when they discussed the Palestine problem within the framework of a Middle East settlement and on the basis of ensuring the legitimate rights of the Palestinian Arabs to self-determination and national sovereignty. It was stressed that the rights for which the Palestinian people were fighting under the leadership of the PLO were an essential condition for the establishment of a just and lasting peace in the Middle East.[81]

China's position on the Palestinian question became increasingly determined by the relative degree of cordiality between any PRM front and the USSR: Fataḥ is a prime example. This was clearly noticeable because of the multiplicity of forces within the PRM, and consequently the varying positions which had to be taken into consideration in the Arab-Israeli conflict; and by 1975 the main issues were the Geneva Conference and the coming Lebanese Civil war. Fataḥ and the PDFLP, however, kept their options open in dealing with the USSR and China. In dealing with the PRM, the Soviet Union consistently sought to treat the PLO, and especially Fataḥ's role in it, as the main representative of Palestinian attitudes for any future Geneva conference. Consultations were either conducted directly or through Soviet ambassadors in the Arab world. Fataḥ, however, was keen to keep China involved and informed of developments, particularly lest the Security Council should become involved, in which case it might be desirable for China to exercise its veto power, and as a precaution against any deterioration in Soviet-Fataḥ relations.

On 7 January 1975, 'Abū 'Iyad, member of Fataḥ's Central Committee, met the Soviet Ambassador in Cairo, Vladimir Poliakov, and the East German Ambassador, while on the same day 'Abū 'Iyad and 'Abū al-Lutif met the Chinese and the Cuban ambassadors to Cairo.[82] Andrei Gromyko met 'Arafat during the former's visit to Egypt and Syria on 2 February 1975 in Damascus, where Gromyko 'reaffirmed the Soviet stand regarding the need for representatives of the Palestine Liberation Organisation to take part on an equal footing in the Geneva Peace conference',[83] and it was reported that the talks also covered Soviet arms supplies to the PLO.[84] However, in dealing with PRM forces which were basically and overtly anti-Soviet, and which openly rejected the Geneva Peace Conference, China's approach was cautious. For example, the Chinese Ambassador to Lebanon, Hsu Ming, paid an official visit on 28 February 1975 to a PFLP camp, for the first time, as far as is known. There George Ḥabash and other members received him and talks were conducted on 'mutual and common principles' on the Palestine question.[85] The same day 'Arafat had talks with the Chinese and Soviet Ambassadors to Lebanon.[86] The PLO's careful consultations with the USSR and China stemmed from the PRM's mistrust of Egyptian moves. At that time Kissinger was still attempting to reach agreement between the USA and Egypt about convening the Geneva Peace Conference. Sadat had by then drawn closer to the USA, and was favourable to American positions. However, by the end of March 1975, it became clear that Kissinger's 'shuttle diplomacy' was heading for defeat. On 1 April 1975 the Chinese Ambassador to Lebanon visited both Zuhair Muḥsin, head of al-Sa'iqa and Na'if Hawātma at PDFLP headquarters, and the ambassador pointed out to both of them that the 'step by step' diplomacy was aimed at 'shattering Arab unity'.[87]

The importance of both Soviet and Chinese backing for the PRM became clear on the beginning of the Lebanese Civil War in mid-April. A week before the outbreak of hostilities, a Fataḥ delegation led by Laṭif Sa'īd arrived in Peking on 6 April, at the invitation of CPAFFC.[88] This delegation, as will be shown below, achieved little politically or militarily and, most probably, its demands were not met, particularly in the case of the military equipment Fataḥ badly needed at a crucial moment for its survival.

The Lebanese Civil War proved a dramatic development for the Fataḥ-led PRM. The Lebanese loose super-structure enabled the PRM to struggle for its *last* survival base in the Arab world. For after the September 1970 débâcle in Jordan, no Arab state bordering Israel allowed the political and military presence of the PRM. In all other Arab states the Palestinians are not a dominating force, but play a peripheral role within the existing structure. Lebanon was the last resort for any meaningful political existence, and it was in Lebanon alone that the PRM was, and still is, the dominant force, regardless of the complexities of the socio-economic and political structure of the state. It is in Lebanon, should any Arab-Israeli (or for that matter, Lebanese-Israeli) settlement be achieved, that the PRM's existence and role must seriously be taken into consideration. Of course, the civil war in Lebanon is also a class war: the structure of the state has been shattered. Historically it had been ruled by a dominant class, economically strong and based on traditional families, mostly Christian. However, it is not a religious civil war. The Lebanese state, in its military and political aspects, was based on a haphazard coalition of interests.

124

When war broke out the state, as arbiter between different power groups, became obsolete; it could not even uphold the historical economic structure of the national entity. It seems ironical that two prominent forces, the Phalangist and other Christian groups, and the Israelis who sought to annihilate the last Palestinian stronghold, contributed to the strengthening of the PRM. For any settlement of the Lebanese Civil War cannot fail to take into account the PRM, aided by local Lebanese patriotic forces. The Phalangists, other Christian forces, and Israelis disastrously miscalculated the strength of the PRM in Lebanon.

Officially, the Lebanese Civil War erupted with the Phalangist massacre of Palestinians at 'Aīn al-Rūmmunah on 13 April 1975. Because of this serious threat to its survival, the PRM had to resort to its only outside allies, the USSR and China. 'Arafat visited Moscow from 28 April to 5 May, alone. It was openly announced that the discussions centred, once again, on the Geneva Conference and the fear of a secret Israeli-Egyptian agreement mediated through the USA. The communiqué issued at the end of the visit pointed out that

> both sides expressed themselves firmly of the opinion that unless
> the Palestinian problem was solved in the interests of the Arab
> people of Palestine, there could be no peace and tranquillity
> in the Middle East.
>
> They stressed the importance of a representative of the Arab
> people of Palestine taking part, with equal rights with the other
> interested parties, in the efforts to achieve a Middle East settlement,
> including the Geneva Peace Conference on the Middle East.
>
> They emphasised the special importance in present conditions
> of co-ordinated efforts by Arab states and the Palestinian Liberation
> Organisation in the struggle for a just and lasting peace in the
> Middle East and against any and every kind of bilateral separate
> deal divorced from a comprehensive settlement of the Arab-Israeli
> conflict.[89]

'Arafat's acceptance of the call for Palestinian representation at the proposed Geneva Peace Conference was condemned by the PFLP and al-Sa'iqa, because the earlier PLO official position had been that it would decide whether or not to attend Geneva when it received an official invitation, and not before. The statement also appeared to imply that the USSR would take an active part in ensuring that in the event of an over-all settlement, Israel's sovereignty would be respected. Zuhair Muḥsin, who was not included in this delegation, condemned the Soviet commitment to guarantee Israel's sovereignty and existence within the pre-1967 war boundaries. He declared that 'the Soviets committed a new blunder by offering the firmest guarantees for Israel's independent existence.... They have fallen in the trap which portrays the Middle East Problem as one of lack of security and protection for Israel.... It is the Palestinians in the first place and then the Arab countries who need security guarantees against Israeli aggression'.[90] On 11 May 1975, at the invitation of the CPAFFC, an al-Sa'iqa delegation paid its first visit to Peking;[91] it was a purely military delegation to get acquainted with the Chinese form of guerrilla warfare and it arrived in Peking after 'Arafat ended his Moscow visit. One month later, Hanī al-Ḥasan met the Chinese Ambassador to Beirut and their discussions centred on the possibility of sending a high-level Fataḥ delegation to China to negotiate much-needed Chinese military aid at a critical moment.[92] To balance Fataḥ prominence in the PRM, the CPAFFC invited a PFLP delegation, led by Musṭafa 'Alī 'abd al-Raḥman, member of the Political Bureau; the delegation arrived in Peking on 19 June 1975.[93] This was the PFLP's second and last official visit to China in the period of this study, and it came after Hanī al-Ḥasan's meeting with the Chinese Ambassador and before Fataḥ's proposed high-ranking visit to China in July. The PFLP had condemned both the PLO and the USSR in their joint effort to agree on and further a Geneva Peace Conference. At the time of the PFLP visit to China, 'Arafat was conducting talks on 22 June in Damascus with a Soviet team led by Ponomarev.[94]

The day before the departure of the Fataḥ delegation to Peking, Hanī al-Ḥasan wrote an article in *al-Safīr* which dealt with the significance of the visit, Sino-Fataḥ relations, and sought to play down the apparent coolness in relations. He claimed that this visit had been agreed upon in October 1974, to conduct discussions with the Communist Party of China, and stated unequivocally that 'any future historian will note that the Palestinian people had fought, from 1967 to 1970, with Chinese arms ... and China, Egypt and Syria constituted the backbone of [military and other] aid [to Fataḥ] at the most crucial period, with the Chinese side contributing the bulk of aid'. It should be noted that 'Arafat's last visit to China and his first visit to the USSR both took place in 1970, before Black September. Hanī al-Ḥasan spelled out four elements of Chinese policy:

1 China does not, and has no intention of recognising Israel.
2 China views the Zionist existence as an intruder in the area.

126

Thus it does not recognise such existence, but supports the
Palestinian people in their attempt to eradicate the intruder.

3 When China's strategy corroborates with ours in the necessity
for the eradication of the Zionist entity, its strategy, therefore,
coincides with ours in the belief that armed struggle (this
powerful strategy) is the only way to eradicate Zionism.

4 China refuses the logic of hegemonism and adopts the principle
of self-reliance. Thus Sino-Palestinian relations had never
witnessed an attempt at certain hegemonism and directiveness.
Last year, Li Hsien-nien informed me at the [Chinese] Foreign
Ministry that: 'Any Palestinian decision you adopt, we will
adopt immediately. But any decision which is not *fully
Palestinian* [emphasis added] we will have to evaluate our
position after studying the situation'.[95]

The primary aim of this visit was military, given the erupting civil
war. China's military aid to Fataḥ in particular was necessary for two
reasons: it would help against Soviet pressure, and in the event of a
total show-down in Lebanon, which at the time seemed likely, Fataḥ
would continue to be the dominant force within the PRM and in
relation to the state. Secondly, Li Hsien-nien's statement to Hanī
al-Ḥasan in August 1974 clarified the Chinese view of Sino-Arab
relations, on the one hand, and on Arab-Palestinian approaches to
a solution to the Arab-Israeli conflict, on the other. Li's first note
implied that China still followed the policy it stated earlier; non-
recognition of Israel, unity of the PRM, protracted war, etc. But a
change would occur if parties that were directly non-Palestinian
became involved – e.g. Egypt and Syria – who might seek Chinese
political support at a certain stage, or which could conflict with
Palestinian interests in an inter-Arab question. More significantly,
Chinese decisions would depend on the extent to which Fataḥ chose
to involve the USSR in PRM matters. Increased Soviet-Fataḥ cordiality
ought to be taken seriously, given China's stated opposition to the
USSR. Thirdly, in consequence, was an indication that China's voting
behaviour at the UN, for example, would be dictated by such conditions. Lastly, it seems obvious from the tone of the article that
Sino-Fataḥ relations had reached their lowest ebb since they started
in 1964. Given the composition of the delegation, its timing and broad
publicity, unlike previous occasions, Fataḥ hoped to close the gap in
differences of opinion and to return to its privileged position in China's
dealings with the PRM.

The Fataḥ delegation led by 'Abū Djihad, who had last visited China in September 1971, and which included prominent members like 'Abū Mahr and Hanī al-Ḥasan, arrived in Peking on 17 July. It was received at the airport by Ho Ying, Vice-Foreign Minister and Chai Tse-min, president of the CPAFFC;[96] this reception was low-keyed compared to that of September 1971, as there was no obvious public or press attention. On 18 July the delegation was received by Ho Ying, in the presence of Wang Shang-jung, Deputy Chief of General Staff;[97] and on 21 July it had two separate meetings with T'eng Hsiao-ping and Chiao Kuan-hua, Chinese Foreign Minister.[98] This was the first time T'eng publicly met a Palestinian delegation; there was no mention of Li Hsien-nien, who had long been associated with China's relations with the Arab and Third World. T'eng's prominence could be attributed to his re-emergence from disgrace after the Cultural Revolution subsided, and his being groomed to take over the duties of ailing Premier Chou En-lai. The talks apparently gave no indication that the Chinese were willing to give pre-eminence to Fataḥ in its relations with the Palestinians. On the contrary China showed its intention to keep its options open in dealing with other Palestinian fronts, which in turn would be determined by these fronts' relations with the USSR. In an obvious down-grading of the visit, to which Fataḥ had given wide publicity before the delegation's departure, the *NCNA* reported the delegation's departure for North Korea, on 23 July, with no more than the following comment:

> A Chinese state leader and leading members of the departments
> concerned met and held talks with the delegation in Peking and
> exchanged views on the international and Middle East situation
> and on further developing the militant friendship between the
> people of China and Palestine. The delegation visited a tank unit
> of the Peking units of the Chinese People's Liberation Army.
> Its visit to China was crowned with success.[99]

Clearly alarmed at the outcome of this visit and its possible consequences on arms supplies to enable Fataḥ to sustain the war in Lebanon, the Lebanese Prime Minister, Rashīd Karamī, met Chinese Ambassador Hsu Ming on 26 July, in an apparent attempt to dissuade the Chinese from involving themselves in the Lebanese Civil War. None the less, on the delegation's return the Central Committee of Fataḥ met in Damascus to review the outcome of its discussions with Chinese leaders, and the following points were made:

1 The visit ended the long break which had lasted for two years
   between the highest levels of the two sides. This was the first

delegation since 1973 which included members of the Central Committee [given that Hanī al-Ḥasan's visit in August 1974 had been in the capacity of 'Arafat's personal envoy].

2 The Palestinian delegation succeeded in uncovering, in the most open way, the reasons for the expansion and strengthening of Soviet-Palestinian relations. The Chinese side understood and appreciated these reasons. The Chinese side expressed their understanding, which calmed down anxieties in Palestinian circles and advised that steps should be taken to strengthen Soviet-Palestinian relations, for according to their [Chinese] evaluation the PRM's need for Soviet aid is understandable.

3 The delegation was assured that Peking regards Fatah as the main-stream of PRM, and bases its evaluation on this assumption. Opinions were exchanged on the 'rejectionist front' [PFLP, PFLP-General Command, Arab Liberation Front, who all condemned the Geneva Peace Conference]. From the discussions, Fatah understood that China appreciates its reasoning on this issue and that China supports Fatah's political programme. And China's advice was that Fatah's stand taken on the political programme should not lead to disunity within PRM, and it hopes that Fatah's leadership ought to deal patiently with what Peking called 'the small partners'.

4 Peking expressed its readiness to fulfil all the delegations' demands, and its willingness to exert the necessary support in demanding the expulsion of Israel from the United Nations.[100]

It is obvious, in retrospect, that, contrary to Fatah's claims, there were considerable disagreements on a wide range of issues, and particularly on the increasing Soviet influence over Fatah. On 13 August 'Abū Djihad and 'Abū Mahr met, on their return, the Chinese and North Korean ambassadors 'to discuss and further mutual relations' between the two parties.[101] China's dismay at Fatah was noticeable when it extended an invitation to the PDFLP to visit Peking.

These differences on Geneva and other issues notwithstanding, the evolution and expansion of the Lebanese Civil War faced Fatah with its most serious challenge as leader of the PRM. It must also be remembered that during the turbulent period in Lebanon, Fatah sent a delegation to Peking, led by Aḥmad 'Afani and Ḥusnī Yūnis, on 5 September, on its way from Vietnam. The delegation sought military aid, and the Chinese press reports were brief and uninformative,[102] while the PDFLP delegation arrived on 11 September at the invitation of CPAFFC,[103] and it was reported that Ho Ying[104] met its members, but no mention was made of the presence of the PLO mission's representative at the talks. According to *al-Ḥurriyah*, the delegation had four lengthy meetings with Ho Ying and members of the host organisation. During the talks, China reaffirmed *'its support to Palestinian people, under the leadership of the PLO, and that the Chinese side stressed the importance of strengthening bilateral talks with the PDFLP'.*[105] [Emphasis added.]

Throughout the entire period of conflict in Lebanon, the Chinese press kept almost totally silent on internal developments there, especially on the PRM's struggle to hold on to its last position in Lebanon. Chinese reports were confined to statements on the 'heroic and joint Lebanese army and PRM forces' in either repelling Israeli attacks and/or inflicting casualties on Israeli positions and military intrusions.[106]

In its search for aid, Fataḥ looked to the USSR. However, before 'Arafat's visit to the USSR on 24–28 November, two major developments occurred which influenced the strengthening of Soviet-PLO relations. The first was the successful attempt at the UN General Assembly in November to adopt a resolution equating Zionism with racism, and both the Chinese and Soviet press hailed the occasion.[107] The second was Henry Kissinger's success in reaching a second Egyptian-Israeli Sinai disengagement agreement, which was signed in Geneva on 4 September by the representatives of the respective countries. To symbolise the US-Egyptian rapprochement, Sadat arrived in Washington at the end of November to negotiate such matters as aid for the faltering Egyptian economy, reduction of American support (whether governmental or corporative) for Israel, and 'Egypt's desire for peace'. It was the first time since the 1952 revolution that an Egyptian head of state had visited the USA.

On 9 November the USSR called for the resumption of the Geneva Peace Conference. 'Arafat's Moscow talks were conducted with Andrei Gromyko and Boris Ponomaryev. Yet the USSR, like China, was keeping a watchful eye on developments in Lebanon, and keeping its options open when dealing with various PRM fronts, for there was no certainty that Fataḥ would survive this crisis. In mid-December Na'if Hawātma headed a PDFLP delegation to Moscow at the invitation of the Soviet Committee for Solidarity with Afro-Asia.[108] Although Hawātma and other PDFLP members had visited Moscow previously as part of PLO delegations, this was the first time an official delegation was sent to the USSR.

As Chinese attacks on the USSR became increasingly strident, China also modified its policy towards liberation movements according to their relations with the USSR, and by 1972 this policy had taken firm shape. China sought to give or withhold support on this basis. In the case of Palestine, this tendency was reflected in China's relations with Fataḥ. As Fataḥ's relations with the USSR improved after Egypt's expulsion of Soviet military personnel, China correspondingly reduced its interest in Fataḥ. China tried to downgrade Fataḥ's leadership of the PRM by giving political support to other PRM fronts, by inviting delegations from other organisations to visit China, and by promising to extend military aid to the PLO only, thus implying that this aid would go to any organisation which gained control over the PLO. At a less direct level China's new priorities were to be seen in its voting behaviour at the UN, where positions were taken in opposition to those of the USSR; whenever there was an Arab consensus on any issue and that consensus was in agreement with Soviet positions, China abstained or failed to participate, rather than be seen taking the same position as the Soviets.

Despite this, China could not withhold all support from Fataḥ, which remained the strongest force in the PRM, and Fataḥ continued to claim that relations between itself and China were good. The facts are different: the last high-ranking Fataḥ delegation to China, in July 1975, failed to achieve anything of note, and was also rebuffed by Chinese leaders on several basic issues. It was given a remarkably cool reception from the Chinese press and leadership, which was in noticeable contrast to earlier visits from lower-ranking Fataḥ delegations. This last delegation was even told to 'deal patiently with small partners' within the PRM.

The decline in Chinese interest can be explained only by improved Soviet-Fataḥ relations, and the course of the war in Lebanon weakened Fataḥ's position. China considered that if the Palestinians were defeated it would have backed the wrong ally, and it did not want to take this risk. Further, having established diplomatic relations with Lebanon, China complied with that government's request not to supply military or political aid to the PRM.

The most significant element in changing Chinese attitudes must be repeated: China's anti-Soviet policy. This was undoubtedly damaging to any liberation movement seeking aid from an ally which regarded aid to liberation movements only as an element of its basic foreign policy. These liberation movements, and the PRM in particular, when they started armed struggle, had looked to China, and sought its support politically and materially, because of the model presented by China itself. But China itself had changed and developed; and the applicability

Table 5.1 *Number of Palestine Resistance Movement delegations to China and USSR, 1964–75*

Front (*Organisation*)	*Head*	*China*	*USSR*	*Date*
Fataḥ	'Arafat and 'Abū Djihad	x		March 1964
PLO	'Aḥmad al-Shuḳairy	x		March 1965
Trade Union (PLO)		x		May 1965
PLO Leader	Not specified	x		June 1965
Fataḥ		x		September 1965
Fataḥ (PLO)	'Arafat		x	February 1970
Fataḥ (PLO)	'Arafat	x		March 1970
Fataḥ	Ḥusnī Yūmis	x		August 1970
PFLP	Ḥabash (Transit to N. Korea)	x		September 1970
Fataḥ (PLO)	'Abū 'Amar Sa'ad	x		May 1971
Fataḥ	'Abū Djihad	x		September 1971
Fataḥ (PLO)	'Arafat		x	October 1971
Fataḥ	'Abū Khalid	x		January 1972
Fataḥ (PLO)	'Abū Niḍal and Abū Daoūd	x		March 1972
Fataḥ (PLO)	'Arafat		x	July 1972
PLO	General Federation of Palestinian Workers	x		August 1972
Fataḥ	'Abū Mahr	x		March 1973
PDFLP	Taiysīr Khalid	x		May 1973
Fataḥ (PLO)	'Arafat		x	November 1973
Fataḥ (PLO)	'Arafat		x	July 1974
Fataḥ	Hanī al-Ḥasan	x		August 1974
PFLP	Taiysīr Ḳuba'h	x		October 1974
Fataḥ (PLO)	'Arafat		x	November 1974
PDFLP	'Abū al-'Abid	x		November 1974
Fataḥ	Laṭīf Sa'īd	x		April 1975
Fataḥ (PLO)	'Arafat		x	April 1975
al-Sa'iqa	Hanna Bathiche	x		May 1975
PFLP	Musṭafa 'Alī abd al-Rahman	x		June 1975
Fataḥ	'Abū Djihad and 'Abū Mahr	x		July 1975
Fataḥ	Ḥusnī Yūmis and 'Aḥmad 'Afani	x		September 1975
PDFLP	'Abū al-'Abid	x		September 1975
PLO	Palestine Martyrs' Workers Society	x		September 1975
Fataḥ (PLO)	'Arafat		x	November 1975
PDFLP			x	December 1975

of her own political and military experience had come increasingly under question even in Chinese eyes as the Sino-Soviet rift continued, widened, and assumed ever greater importance in Chinese foreign policy.

Chapter 6

Brief history of the Liberation Movement in Oman

The historical development of the Popular Front for the Liberation of Oman (PFLO) had three distinct political phases. The first was characterised by its 'provincial-local' approach in which the 'Imāmate War can be included; the second saw the dominance of 'revolutionary theory', i.e. the aspiration to extend the revolution from Dhofar to Kuwait, thus including a whole vital area of world oil production. The third phase could be described as 'containment' of the revolution within Oman proper, dictated by the experiences of the previous two phases.

Throughout the 1955–75 period, three main political tendencies shaped the military and political orientation in Oman, in turn influencing the political orientation of the phases above. The first was the outcome of 'Imām Ghalib's dispute with Ṣuḷtan Sa'id bin Taimūr, in which support from both Egypt and Saudi Arabia meant considerable influence by what was fashionably called Naṣirism. The second political tendency resulted from the Arab Nationalist Movement's various branches in the Arabian Gulf and Oman; hence the PFLO's second phase of development went through a 'shift to the left'. The third trend saw a re-evaluation of the movement's internal, regional and international positions, in which it resorted logically, if apparently belatedly, to restricting the struggle according to its own political and military strength.

Before discussing the PFLO itself, it is necessary to outline the events of the 1955–9 'Imāmate War, which played a major role in the creation and development of the Front.

Rise of the Nationalist Movement

The significance of the 'Imāmate War 1955–9

When the 'Imām of Oman, Muḥammad bin 'Abdullah, died in May 1954, Ghalib bin 'Ali, from the Bani tribe, proclaimed himself successor

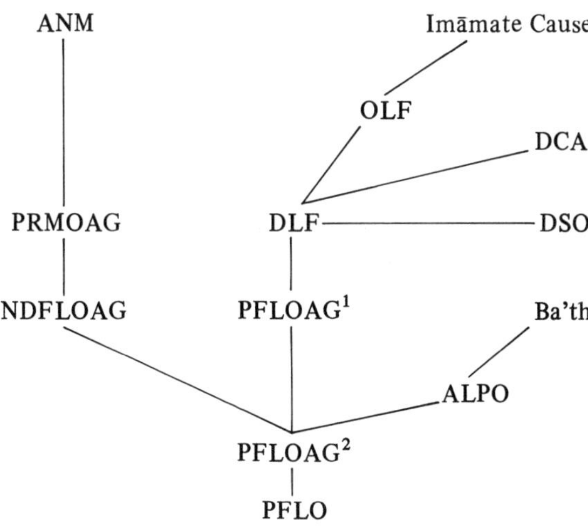

¹ Popular Front for the Liberation of Occupied Arabian Gulf
² Popular Front for the Liberation of Oman and Arabian Gulf

Fig. 6.1 Emergence of Nationalist Movements in Oman 1955–75

to the 'Imāmate of Oman. The rule of the Sultan of Muscat and Oman, Ṣuḷtan Sa'id bin Taimūr, over Oman was based totally on tribal allegiances; until the 1950s he did not exert any power on political conditions in the Omani interior.[1] Ṣuḷtan Sa'id was unable to further the election of any of Ghalib bin 'Ali's rivals, whereas Ghalib's support came mainly from the powerful backing of both Sulaiman bin Ḥimyer and Ṣaliḥ bin 'Isa. Historically, Britain's military assistance to the Ṣuḷtan altered considerably the situation in Oman, as in times of crisis it acted as the Ṣuḷtan's instrument to maintain the status quo. The Ṣuḷtan, unable to thwart Ghalib's nomination, ordered the Muscat and Omani Field Force to occupy 'Ibrī. Ṣuḷtan Sa'id's action was taken for two basic reasons. He aspired, on the one hand, to control the troublesome and unruly tribes of Oman, thus eliminating historically the question of the 'Imāmate in the Sultanate. On the other hand, oil prospecting in the Omani interior seemed likely to be successful, and both the Ṣuḷtan and the British were convinced that 'Imām Ghalib received financial and military aid from Saudi Arabia.[2]

The first encouraging sign of petroleum exploitation in Oman began when Ṣuḷtan Sa'id granted oil concession rights to the British-owned Iraq Petroleum Company (IPC) in 1937. The Ṣuḷtan did not establish any demarcation line for oil exploration between his territory and that of the 'Imāmate in Oman. The unpromising prospects for oil persuaded IPC to abandon its concessionary rights in Dhofar. The Ṣulṭan granted a new concession to Dhofar-Cities Service Petroleum Corporation which held a partnership with the American Cities Service Company and the Richfield Oil Corporation. An agreement was signed on 17 January 1953 between the Ṣulṭan and Philpryor Corporation, half-owned by Wendell Phillips. It is not surprising then that Ṣulṭan Sa'id wished to eliminate all the forces that would constitute a hindrance to oil exploration in Oman. And, as the Ṣulṭan viewed it, the Omani political scene must at all costs be controlled to ensure a status quo beneficial not only for oil exploration, but which would also allow the annihilation of opposing factions within the 'Imāmate. That desire prompted the Ṣulṭan to ask for British military assistance in suppressing any uprisings.

The scramble for oil led oil companies to infringe either Omani or Saudi Arabian territory, for at that time the boundaries were not demarcated. However, in September 1955 the Muscat and Oman Field Force occupied 'Ibrī, a town held by the 'Imām since 1925. In October 'Imām G̲h̲alib took the unprecedented step of applying, through his able brother Ṭalib bin 'Alī, for Oman's full membership of the Arab League.[3] Two 'Imāmate missions were opened, one in Cairo and the other in Dammam, Saudi Arabia. Meanwhile, at the end of October, the Trucial Oman Levies, acting on behalf of the Ṣulṭan and S̲h̲aik̲h̲ S̲h̲ak̲h̲būt of 'Abū Dhabi, occupied the al-Buraimi Oasis and expelled the minute Saudi Police detachment there. By December the Ṣulṭan's forces occupied Nizwa, thereby scattering the 'Imāmate's leaders, and attacked Rostaq, where Ṭalib bin 'Alī resisted in vain before escape to Saudi Arabia. Ṣulṭan Sa'id drove for 600 miles through the desert from Salāla to Nizwā to celebrate his victory; this was the first visit in over a century by a Ṣulṭan to the interior of Oman. Both 'Imām G̲h̲alib and Sulaiman bin Ḥimyer made peace with the Ṣulṭan while Ṭalib bib 'Alī and Ṣaliḥ bin 'Isa al-Ḥarit̲h̲ī established an 'Imāmate of Oman office in Cairo and at the same time raised a 'liberation army' in Saudi Arabia.

It was not until 1957 that active resistance on behalf of the 'Imāmate cause began. By the summer of that year, Ṭalib managed to smuggle arms via Saudi Arabia into Oman and joined forces with 'Imām G̲h̲alib. They first occupied Nizwā and rapidly gained control of all the major towns of Oman, as well as the Green Mountain (Jabal al-Akhdar) which was controlled by Sulaiman bin Ḥimyer, who raised the white flag, symbol of the 'Imāmate. The Ṣulṭan turned to the British government for military aid, and by September 1958 the Ṣulṭan's Armed Forces (SAF) recaptured the area; the most important part was the slopes of the Green Mountain where fierce resistance was apparent. 'Imām Ghalib, his brother Ṭalib, Sulaiman bin Ḥimyer and Ṣaliḥ bin 'Isa fled from Oman in January 1959 and established a government in exile in Dammam. Consequently, by the end of that year, active and organised resistance by the 'Imām and his followers had ceased in Oman, though there were minor mine-laying incidents centring on Dhofar; but these were aimed at keeping the issue alive through international diplomacy.

In short, the 1957–9 attempted uprising in Oman was doomed to failure for several reasons. First, at this stage of political development in Oman the idea of 'People's War' had no significant appeal. Given the fact that the period witnessed Naṣir's political rise and the changes of regime in Iraq in 1958, it is significant that the 'Imām's followers did not attempt to understand the basic causes for the changes taking place in Egypt and Iraq. Second, the revolution's leadership was composed of traditional tribal leaders, thus reducing the revolt and its political strategy to a mere tribal dispute. But, undoubtedly, 'Imām Ghalib had a significant popular following for his cause. Third, the 'Imām was unable, militarily, to face the superior British forces deployed by the Ṣulṭan. Lastly, 'Imām Ghalib's limited military support was external, coming mainly from Saudi Arabia. The Saudis gave their assistance in order to gain control over al-Buraimi; this plan failed.[4] Although 'Imām Ghalib and his followers did not subscribe to the movement of Arab nationalism in its broadest sense they nevertheless were forced to accept its political ideology.[5] There is a striking apparent contradiction between the 'Imām's background and those ideas which he and his followers advocated.[6] Moreover, 'Imām Ghalib opened an official office in Kuwait, as well as those in Cairo and Dammam already mentioned.[7] His government-in-exile was run by a High Council;[8] issuing passports was one of their main occupations. Several other administrative organs were established, such as Military, Financial and Cultural Committees. Through the Arab League, the 'Imām was able to include the 'Question of Oman' from 1960 onwards on United Nations agendas.[9] In 1964, the Moroccan Representative submitted a memorandum in the name of the following Arab states: Algeria, Egypt, Iraq, Jordan, Kuwait, Lebanon, Libya, Morocco, Saudi Arabia, Sudan, Syria, Tunisia and Yemen, requesting that the United Nations support the 'Imām's drive for an independent Oman.[10] This appeal failed as a result of the objections raised by the United Kingdom's representative.

The most significant act of the High Council was the creation, in September 1963, of an Oman Liberation Front (OLF). This front aimed at:

> Firstly, taking practical steps to purify Omani land, from the coast to the interior, from British colonialism. And it must be taken into consideration that Oman is part and parcel of the Great Arab Nation extending from the Gulf to the Ocean.

> Secondly, taking practical steps to fulfil this aim. This must be carried out by organising peoples' struggle in Oman, in a way that conforms with the revolutionary and liberating aims of the will of the people for liberation, independence and equality, promoting and setting up social equality without oppression, racialism or atheism.

> Thirdly, working assiduously to lay the foundations of the new Arab Republic of Oman, which conforms with Islamic Laws and works alongside progressive revolutionary movements which are the hope of free people everywhere.

> The Higher Council, leading the revolution, has entrusted Prince Ṣaliḥ bin 'Isa al-Harithī to represent, temporarily, the National Council of the Omani Revolution and has appointed Mr Ibrahim bin Hamed al-Harithī as Secretary.[11]

Nevertheless, by September 1964, divisions had eroded this short-lived Front. Ṣaliḥ bin 'Isa al-Harithī accused the 'Imām of

> refusing to approve all the sections of the National Declaration which laid down a Constitution. He . . . did not allow the Military Committee to inspect the weapons held by the Front in Dammam; he refused to entrust any army to the fighters; he refused to accept Arab military experts to command military affairs; and he conducted private talks in Kuwait with the British in the hope of returning to Oman.[12]

Although there was little military activity in northern Oman after 1959, between that date and 1964, Omanis were being militarily trained in Iraq and Syria.[13] After 1959, there was no more armed struggle in the 'Imāmate region, but from the early 1960s, isolated armed clashes started in Dhofar, which were later to develop into war under the leadership of the PFLO. Despite the distance between the two regions, there was a clear connection between the movements in so far as soldiers who had been trained to fight for the 'Imāmate were fighting in Dhofar, and the idea of liberation from domination by the al-Bu Sa'id was shared by both movements.

Influence of the Arab Nationalist Movement (ANM)

The second force instrumental in shaping the future of the revolution in Oman was the Arab Nationalist Movement, acting through its Gulf Branch; and to a far lesser extent the Ba'th Party.

As far as the Upper Gulf was concerned, the 1950s witnessed the local impact of the oil boom. This sudden tremendous economic outburst constituted a haven for the disenchanted and wretched Omani population. They sought refuge in places where, by comparison with Ṣuḷtan Sa'id's dark ages, an Omani was free at least to travel and meet his bare economic needs. They came in direct contact with ANM's Gulf Branch. Much of the ANM's early political development has been described earlier; nevertheless, it is worth mentioning that the ANM, in the 'fifties, laid great emphasis on

> national unity rather than class struggle. Its anti-colonialist position
> lacked clarity and was void of theoretical content. Moreover, the
> movement's programme at that time was characterised by a vague
> romantic advocacy of Arab unity that was envisaged to follow
> the German pattern of national unity. Finally, the movement
> took an anti-Communist stance that rejected any attempt at
> alliance with the 'secessionist Communists'. In consequence the
> movement appealed mainly to elements of this prosperous
> bourgeoisie and to those from more or less aristocratic origins.
> As it failed to attract the masses, it remained very small.[14]

Nevertheless, the ANM's Gulf Branch in Kuwait — which at the same time was responsible for Saudi Arabia —

> continued to enjoy an independent political position with minimum
> interference from the centre. Apart from playing an effective role
> as an opposition party inside and outside the Parliament, it formed
> the bulk of Naṣirite movement in Kuwait. Thus the prospect of
> its merger with any other political organisation in accordance with
> the decisions of the National Conference in 1965 did not arise.[15]

But in maintaining their 'ideological' independence, Dr 'Aḥmad al-Khatīb and his colleagues remained aloof from the disputes which were gathering momentum at the centre. The ANM's Kuwaiti branch was unable to contain the leftist trend within its various branches in the Gulf because of its basic inability to comprehend the nature of the struggle and ideological transformation which were taking place in other branches — in particular the Dhofari one. The year 1962 witnessed the first stage of preparing for armed struggle in Dhofar province. In that year, the Dhofari Section of the ANM's Gulf Branch declared its 'independence' and announced the

> creation of the Dhofar Charitable Association which under the
> guise of building mosques and helping the poor, collected money,
> started to make political contacts and recruited members with
> the aim of organising armed struggle against the al-Bu Sa'id rule.[16]

Another clandestine nucleus, called the Dhofar Soldiers' Organisation, was involved in preparations for armed uprising within Ṣulṭan Sa'id's armed forces. This organisation was formed of Omani soldiers serving mostly in Qatar and to a lesser extent in other Gulf Emirates and the Sultanate.[17] During 1959–63 Iraq was instrumental in providing military training for various Omanis.

Creation of Dhofar Liberation Movement

By 1964, the ANM's Gulf Branch, after holding an internal meeting in Beirut, decided to adopt the strategy of launching armed struggle in Dhofar. An effort was made by the Gulf Branch to encourage the two important forces in Oman, the Dhofar Charitable Association[18] (DCA) and the Dhofar Soldiers' Organisation (DSO), to merge into a unified force called the Dhofar Liberation Front (DLF). This merger was finalised at an internal meeting held at Wadī Nahiz in Dhofar which declared officially the launching of armed struggle on 9 June 1965. The DLF aimed primarily at overthrowing Ṣulṭan Sa'id's rule over Oman and it presented no clue to its future political programmes.[19]

Dhofar was chosen as the focal point for armed struggle in Oman for two reasons. First, this area was historically the centre of Omani uprisings and discontent against the rule of a succession of Muṣkatī Ṣulṭans. Consequently the majority of the people forming the DLF came from that area of the Sultanate; this recruitment was reflected initially by its 'provincial' outlook. Second, geographically, Dhofar was ideal for guerrilla warfare, i.e., an unusual area in the Arabian peninsula called 'tropical Arabia'.[20]

At this stage of its development the DLF's strategic aim of concentration on military activity in the Dhofar region seemed logical, with its obvious geographical advantages. However, the Front's subsequent strategy, which will be discussed below, in extending the war to the far end of the Arabian Gulf, would appear to have been impracticable. The small population constitutes a basic hindrance to continuing and developing guerrilla warfare over all of the Sultanate.

The ANM's Gulf Branch's efforts to unite the DCA and the DSO were prompted by several reasons. As to strategic considerations, ANM

> hoped that launching armed struggle in Dhofar would build a
> bridge between the struggle in South Yemen which had started
> in the Radfan mountains under the leadership of the ANM's
> branch there, the National Liberation Front, on 14 October 1963,
> and armed struggle in Oman proper and the Gulf. Secondly, the
> United Arab Republic had set unity between the ANM and the
> Dhofar Charitable Association as a precondition to granting any
> assistance.[21]

Next, the DLF, operating in an area where tribalism constituted the backbone of any mass-orientated movement, had to rely on the various tribes inhabiting the area; prominent among them was the Bayt al-Kathīr tribe. Lastly, the Front adhered to no one political ideology, for its human composition precluded the adoption of any political programme beyond fighting a corrupt Sulṭan and the British presence in the region. This lack of a basic political philosophy resulted in several organisational mistakes with the DLF: the Sulṭan was able to discover — and consequently execute — many members of the cells operating in Muscat and Oman. An eighteen-man Leadership Council was elected to carry out the Front's various tasks.[22] It included representatives of those discontented tribes historically antagonistic to the Sulṭan, Omanis who were either self-exiled in the Gulf and/or intellectuals who had worked in both the Gulf and other Arab countries. The political thinking of the last was tremendously influenced by the idea of Arab nationalism. Up to 1967 the DLF's military activity revolved around creating and organising a mass base for armed struggle; and one of its most spectacular actions was the attempt to assassinate Sulṭan Sa'id in 1966. He was injured, and subsequently resorted to ruthless retaliation against the Dhofari people; he then went into total isolation from the Omani people. At this point the DLF did not establish any military lines and routes to ensure its continuous supplies of armaments. Furthermore Saudi Arabia's support had dwindled at the end of 1966; and Egypt's support ceased after the June 1967 war. Nevertheless the DLF's military activities continued with sabotage, and ambushes of the Ṣulṭan's forces' positions in Dhofar; this it accomplished by dividing Dhofar province into three main military zones: eastern, central and western.

As discussed earlier, the Arab-Israeli war of June 1967 resulted, among other things, in the radicalisation and consequent split of the ANM throughout the Arab world. The radicalisation of the Gulf and Arabian Peninsula elements took place when, at the end of 1967, a Regional Conference was held in Beirut to discuss the future of the 'revolutionary movement in the Gulf'. The Conference was attended by several representatives from Kuwait, Oman-Dhofar, Saudi Arabia, Bahrain, the National Liberation Front of Occupied South Yemen, Qatar, and students and members of the ANM's General Command — the latter representing Na'īf Hawātma's faction within ANM. Hawātma had a tremendous impact on the representatives from the Oman-Dhofar branch.[23] The conference initiated the gradual organisational split into the various branches. However the opening session was devoted to general discussion of the Gulf and Arabian Peninsula, with each representative voicing his point of view. And

> in the course of the discussions, the delegates revealed their increasing dissatisfaction with the autocratic manner in which Kuwait had been conducting the affairs of the Movement. One of the delegates accused Kuwaiti regional Command of imposing its nominees for the leadership upon some regions without the consent of the members concerned. The Omani delegate complained that 'the Command in Kuwait, with its bourgeois social background, was in charge of a potentially revolutionary region'.
>
> Again a divergence of opinion emerged between the Kuwaiti representative in the Conference and the rest of his comrades, when the discussions turned to the strategy of the Movement in the Gulf area. While the former shed some doubt on the feasibility of the proposed strategy of armed struggle, the others insisted that 'our strategy should derive from the consideration that the fight in the Gulf is one fight; that, basically, it is a struggle for national liberation against the military and political presence of British Imperialism in alliance with, and hiding behind, the paper regimes of the shaikhs and all the forces of class exploitation and counter-revolution. A revolutionary armed confrontation to defeat imperialism and its local forces is thus inevitable'.
>
> The majority of the delegates took the view that, while the Movement in the Gulf should take steps to apply the strategy, political circumstances in Oman were most favourable for its

142

immediate implementation especially because in the adjacent territory of Dhofar the revolution had already started.

The resolutions of the Conference on most issues were largely determined by the views of the radical elements, in spite of the reservations of the representative from Kuwait. Apart from adopting the strategy recommended by the majority, the Conference formally denounced the 'patronising' attitude of Kuwait during the previous two years, and condemned the suggestions made for its exemption from the new strategy. To guard against the dominant influence of Kuwait in the future, the Conference decided to entrust the leadership of the Gulf region to an elected Political Bureau consisting of one representative each from Kuwait, Bahrain and Qatar, and three representatives from Oman-Dhofar. Similarly, it was decided that a separate political Bureau should be established in Saudi Arabia, which would periodically meet with that of the Gulf and together with it form the Central Committee for the two regions.[24]

This ideological split, one among many within the ANM, presented a tremendous task to its Gulf Branch. It prompted the 'far left' of the Movement to criticise the Gulf Branch's inability to handle its 'historic tasks', i.e. it was accused of being national bourgeois and failing to achieve revolutionary goals.[25]

The DLF's position in the area was strengthened in November 1967, when the People's Democratic Republic of Yemen (PDRY) achieved independence.[26] A reciprocal strategy was developed in which the PDRY became the DLF's 'secure rear base' while the DLF defended the former's borders with the Sultanate. According to both Omani and South Yemeni sources, had it not been for the DLF's military presence – however limited at the time – the Ṣulṭan, with British and Saudi Arabian assistance, would have been able to occupy a noticeably large portion of the newly-independent state, i.e. the Hadramaut and Mahra regions. It must be noted, in retrospect, that the ANM's Oman-Dhofar Branch discontinued its organisational allegiance with the centre from 1964 onwards, but continued to participate in the ANM's regional discussions.

The shift to the Left

From March 1968 to December 1971 the DLF and the whole Gulf region went through a stage that could be best described as the shift to the left, of which the most significant part, as far as the DLF's

political development is concerned, was the attempt by various movements active in Oman to merge into a unified Front. However, in
January 1968 the ruling Labour Party in Britain announced its intention
to withdraw all British armed forces from the Gulf region by the end
of 1971. Thus the region became the focus of attempts to solve the
problem of the so-called power vacuum; this will be referred to below.

Within this context, the DLF's internal development was acquiring
new characteristics which marked the beginning of a new phase in the
Omani war. In July 1968, before the famous Ḥimrin Conference in
September 1968, the ANM's Gulf Branch held its Second Regional
Command meeting.[27] The Kuwaiti delegate at the meeting strongly
opposed resolutions adopted at the earlier Beirut meeting. He argued
that Marxism could not be accepted wholesale without intensive
study of its applicability to Gulf conditions. He stated that

> 'the movement [ANM] has adopted scientific socialism, but we
> do not yet know exactly what it means', and added that, as far
> as Kuwait was concerned, no man in his right mind 'would think
> of altering the existing regime. There are no toiling groups in
> the country except the bedouins and the Arab workers. Thus
> the question of revolutionary violence in Kuwait does not arise,
> and we do not entertain such thoughts'. The objections of the
> Kuwaiti delegate confirmed the doubts of his colleagues about
> the 'bourgeois' nature of the Regional Command in Kuwait, and
> its unwillingness to go along with the post-June war strategy of the
> Movement. Accordingly, the Conference decided to suspend the
> membership of Kuwait in the movement and asked its delegate to
> withdraw from the meetings of the Conference. At the instigation
> of the Political Bureau for the Gulf, a new Regional Command was
> formed at the end of July. However, al-Khatīb and his associates,
> who continued to enjoy the support of the bulk of the Movement
> in Kuwait, did not recognise the new measures. Thus an open
> split between the Political Bureau and the newly-formed command,
> on the one side, and the leadership of the majority on the other,
> became inevitable.[28]

Nevertheless, after the DLF was renamed the Popular Front for the
Liberation of the Occupied Arabian Gulf (PFLOAG) they argued that
in this regional Conference the left wing faction dominated it and the
following resolutions were adopted

> Reliance on an original line opposing colonialism and reaction
> under the leadership of a revolutionary party, upholding

proletarian ideology which, in turn, will enable it to unite all revolutionary classes in a protracted struggle against colonialism.

Adoption of armed struggle as a form of political struggle.

Condemnation of the 'bourgeois leadership' in the Movement represented by the Kuwaiti section, and the suspension of its organisational role in the Movement.[29]

Consequently the radicalisation of the DLF became inevitable at the Front's subsequent meeting in Dhofar. During September 1–25, the DLF held its second congress since 1964 in Central Dhofar; it became known as the Himrin Congress. The Marxist-Leninist faction, which dominated the discussions, advocated strongly the adoption of new resolutions which culminated in a total change of the DLF's political strategy and programme. Strategically, the congress adopted the following resolutions:

1 To adopt organised revolutionary violence as the sole means for defeating imperialism, reaction, the bourgeoisie and feudalism.
2 To change the Front's name from the Dhofar Liberation Front to the People's Front for the Liberation of the Occupied Arab Gulf, and adopt a comprehensive revolutionary strategy for the whole of the occupied Arab Gulf by linking the struggle in Dhofar to the mass struggle in the Gulf — this being the fine destiny of the revolution in Dhofar.
3 To work towards the unification of the revolutionary tool of the popular masses in the Occupied Arabian Gulf as the healthy and revolutionary prelude to the unity of the area.[30]
4 To establish new committees to solve people's local problems.
5 To nationalise water resources and land; and to make them available to the population.
6 To establish equality between men and women; to assist women to develop their spirit and initiative which has been suppressed by several centuries of slavery.[31]

Given the conditions prevailing in the Gulf at the time, PFLOAG strategy seemed highly idealistic. However, a few points call for some discussion. The word 'occupied' was adopted in the title because leading factions in the Conference considered the whole Gulf region and Oman, with the exception of Kuwait, to be saturated by the British military presence; Kuwait, therefore, was not included in the strategy, which included the 'liberation of the area from Dhofar to

Bahrain only'.[32] PFLOAG's strategy of liberating the whole area seemed impracticable in the light of its military and political weakness and, more significantly for the Gulf, the lack of 'political consciousness among the masses'. PFLOAG had not yet started setting up organisational structures which would enable it to operate effectively at different levels. It was simply, as the title 'Front' implied, a loose grouping of several political and military factions. It was only in 1969, when the first PFLOAG delegation to China returned, and argued the necessity of adopting an organisational structure,[33] that such organisation was established. The adoption of 'scientific socialism', i.e. Marxism-Leninism, per se, was not an *immediate* impediment to the Front's political and military advance in Oman, which, unlike any other country, still lived in the Middle Ages. Sulṭan Sa'id's rule was, to say the least, ruthless and uncompromising, while people living in neighbouring shaikhdoms enjoyed, by comparison, a much higher standard of living and greater individual freedom. Nevertheless the adoption of 'scientific socialism' was a step perhaps too *advanced* for the population even to comprehend; let alone follow. Moreover, it restricted the Front's political room for manoeuvre in the Arab world; this was to be seen in the Gulf and Saudi Arabian rulers' descriptions of the Front as a 'handful of anti-Islamic infidels'. Again, the Front's attempt to nationalise water resources was a practical necessity, given the economic importance of such a vital resource in the area; i.e. the livelihood of nomadic bedouins and herdsmen depended on those rare wells. Launching the idea of women's emancipation was a unique political development in the whole Gulf and Arabian peninsula regions; it proved to be one of the most significant achievements of the Front's early historical development.[34] Finally the Front's resolve to 'work towards the unification of the revolutionary tool of the popular masses in the occupied Arabian Gulf' is a clear indication of the new leadership's awareness of the magnitude of divisions within the nationalist movements in the region. The most important of those arose from the fact that, in October 1968, the 'left wing' of the ANM's Gulf branches held a minority conference at Dubai where a six-man Political Bureau was elected and, after heated discussions, two resolutions were adopted. In the first they declared their organisational independence from the ANM's regional Command in Kuwait and the expulsion of the latter's members, Dr Aḥmad al-Khatīb and his colleagues. The second created the Popular Revolutionary Movement of Oman and the Arab Gulf (PRMOAG), whose main operations were to be in the Omani interior to extend armed struggle and popular uprisings.[35]

146

The Ḥimrin Conference marked a new phase in PFLOAG's history; and after the Congress, the Front launched its most effective military operations and established a highly organised political apparatus in Dhofar. By 1969 the Ṣulṭan's Armed Forces (SAF) had retreated to the Salāla region, giving the Front complete control over the rest of Dhofar. The only SAF units in the province were stationed in the coastal town of Ra<u>kh</u>yūt,

> which was the administrative, i.e. tax collecting, centre of the western sector. On 23 August 1969 there was a particularly heavy monsoon storm, such that no air or sea support could be flown into Ra<u>kh</u>yūt by the SAF. The Front took this opportunity and attacked: Ra<u>kh</u>yūt fell .... Fighting now concentrated on three targets, as the SAF fell back. These targets were the Ṣalāla-Thamrit road — now renamed the 'Red Line' by PFLOAG, the Ṣalāla air base and the eastern province.[36]

Although it would be impossible to calculate accurately military casualties on both sides, it is most likely that the SAF endured most of them; and the war in Dhofar was reaching an unprecedented level. It was in view of this that the Labour Government in Britain promptly decreed special awards for British military and civilian personnel who underwent 'hardships and dangers which have accompanied' their duty in Dhofar.

Another major development took place in June 1970 when the PRMOAG Central Committee met in Muscat and decided to change its name to 'National Democratic Front for the Liberation of Oman and the Arabian Gulf' (NDFLOAG). The term 'occupied' was not included in the name because the Front believed that its main task lay in a protracted struggle against local forces. Although the British presence was given due consideration, changing the socio-political conditions in the Gulf and Oman were seen as first priorities. The newly adopted name was only a *front*; the original organisation continued to operate through it. However their military strategy in the Omani interior, i.e. Nizwā and Izkī, was not as successful as that of PFLOAG in Dhofar.

Less than a month before the Omani palace coup occurred, NDFLOAG attempted, on 12 June 1970, to organise a popular uprising, but it was promptly suppressed by the SAF; the NDFLOAG subsequently went underground and resorted to political rather than military activities. Thus, by 23 July 1970, the date when Kabūs was officially installed as the new Ṣulṭan, there were three main Fronts active in the Sultanate: PFLOAG, NDFLOAG[37] and the Arab Labour Party of Oman (ALPO). The latter was not militarily active in Oman but relied mainly on political organisation. (See Appendix 2 for the background and programme of the party).

Changing Trends in the Gulf

It is important to present briefly three other political factors that had direct effect on the future of the war in Oman. The first is connected with the attempts at the creation of the United Arab Emirates in the Gulf; the second concerns the emergence of Iran as the dominant regional power in the area and the third is the successful coup which installed Ḳabūs on the Omani throne.

The United Arab Emirates

In January 1968 the British Prime Minister announced that Britain would abrogate its long-standing treaties covering defence and foreign affairs with the nine Gulf shaikhdoms, Bahrain, Qatar, 'Abū Dhabi, Dubai, 'Ajman, Fujairah, Sharjah, Umm al Qaiwain and Rās al-Khaymah. The Labour Government's decision to terminate these arrangements by the end of 1971 meant that the shaikhdoms ceased to exist as 'protected states' and consequently had to assume responsibility for their own external and internal affairs. This constituted a grave burden for the shaikhdoms and the

> attainment of independence by the shaikhdoms, while regarded by
> most of the rulers as an inevitable step in the history of the area,
> was neither sought nor universally welcomed. The more traditional
> rulers tended to be content with British protection, which insulated
> them from harsh political realities.[38]

Nevertheless, in February 1968 the rulers of 'Abū Dhabi and Dubai announced their intention of establishing a bi-partite union; soon the other seven requested that they too be allowed to join, and the nine shaikhdoms signed an agreement aimed at creating a Federation. Committees were established to finalise details, but negotiations lingered on for approximately three years. The basic difficulty was the distribution of power between the rulers of the planned Union government. This resulted in the withdrawal of Bahrain and Qatar from the Union (and they announced their independence on 14 August and

1 September respectively). The other seven, with the help of British diplomacy, continued to seek an acceptable formula. The turning point was the coming to power of the Conservative Party in Britain on 20 June 1970. In the same month, Britain's Foreign Secretary,

> Sir Alec Douglas-Home's first move was to begin a series of consultations with Gulf rulers from the Shah of Iran downwards, to see whether a reversal of Labour [party] policy was either practicable or desirable. Many critics in Britain and America believe strongly that it was both, pointing especially to the need to secure the Gulf's vital oil resources (amounting to approximately two-thirds of the non-communist world's proved resources) against Arab intransigence or Soviet-inspired subversion and arguing that the low foreign exchange cost of maintaining the British forces there (estimated at about £17 million a year) was a minimal insurance premium for the £2,000 million or so of annual revenues to western oil companies from their Gulf production. Without the British presence, the critics said, the Gulf might become an area of persistent unrest in which local conflicts between rival Arab states and subversive movements as well as international tension between Arabs and Iranians could erupt and be exploited by the Soviet Union, imperilling western oil interests and supplies.[39]

To further British diplomatic initiatives Sir William Luce was entrusted with finalising a federation formula for the shaikhdoms which would form the basis for retention of a favourable status quo. During his three-week diplomatic consultation tour late in July, Sir William sought the opinion of all parties concerned: Iran, Saudi Arabia and Kuwait were against any continued British military presence in the Gulf.[40] It must be stressed that

> in assisting the rulers during negotiations leading to the federation, British advisers showed a basic concern (shared by most of the rulers) for the protection of British oil interests, including the uninterrupted flow from UAE states – particularly in Abu Dhabi – and also for the continuation of the rulers' practice of banking their oil revenues in London and spending substantial portions of these revenues on British exports. Accordingly, to ensure such continuity, provisions for federal defence were elaborated with great care. A primary objective from the outset was to establish a stable administrative framework that would allow the Trucial Oman Scouts, a British-trained and equipped mercenary force

established in 1952, to become the nucleus of the Union's armed forces. This force, suitably renamed the Union Defence Force (UDF), was actually incorporated into the Union's structure with little difficulty.[41]

Negotiations also continued on the disputed question of power distribution. This resulted in the creation of the UAE's legislative branch, The United National Assembly (majlis al-Waṭanī al'Itihadī), and a 40-member Federal National Council was announced with the following distribution of seats: 'Abū Dhabi and Dubai 8 each; Rās al-Khaymah and Sharjah 6 each; and 'Ajman, al-Fujairah and Umm al-Qaiwain 4 each. Financially 'Abū Dhabi and Dubai agreed to bear most of the costs of the federation, being the wealthiest, while the rest paid nominal contributions. The UAE's upper level decision-making body is called the Federal Supreme Council, with both 'Abū Dhabi and Dubai having veto powers on major issues.

After three years of negotiations between these shaikhdoms and the regional powers concerned, the United Arab Emirates was proclaimed on 2 December 1971. The term 'occupied' Arabian Gulf no longer logically had a place in the PFLOAG's name, since PFLOAG had adopted it on the basis of purely military rather than political or economic criteria. However, the Front's acknowledgement of this change did not take place until its third phase of development, described below. Nevertheless, creation of the UAE left endless boundary demarcation disputes unsolved. It must be pointed out that these Emirates were artificially created; because people's livelihoods, throughout the Emirates, had depended very much on the nomadic economy – i.e. nomadic bedouins settling in different areas while their tribal allegiances rested with a ruler residing outside the defined territories. Incomes were derived basically from herding, fishing and pearl diving (excluding of course oil revenues); consequently tribes travelled according as these pursuits dictated. Although Britain, prior to the establishment of the UAE, did not intervene in these complex matters of undefined areas of tribal influence, she did play the dominant role in finalising the boundaries. Naturally the basic problems over land-acquisition and claims were concerned with oil exploration and revenues. Should more oil be discovered in the future, boundary questions will certainly come alive again.

Another major problem for the UAE was the lingering issue of the al-Buraimi Oasis, to which Saudi Arabia, Oman and 'Abū Dhabi had claims. Jurisdiction over it was solved after Kabūs came to power; in

October 1971, during a state visit to Saudi Arabia, the new Sulṭan managed to cede three major villages adjacent to Oman. Moreover, 'Abū Dhabi and Saudi Arabia agreed, in 1974, to finalise borders between them. Oil exploration and investment in the area were left to 'Abū Dhabi to arrange; however, oil revenues were to be shared by the three parties concerned.[42]

The emergence of Iran as a regional power

The second factor that had a direct effect on the war in Oman and the whole Gulf was the emergence of Iran as the most important regional power, though the other two relatively powerful states of the region, Iraq and Saudi Arabia, must not be neglected. For two decades Iran had concentrated on building itself into a military power capable of playing a significant role in the Gulf area. Iran's development of her air, ground and naval forces surpassed that of all other states of the Gulf and Arabian Peninsula. Iran became qualitatively superior to Iraq and Saudi Arabia in air power as a result of its purchase of highly sophisticated combat aircraft. Similarly, Iran's build-up of its ground forces led it to expand its helicopter fleet, thereby exceeding the power of both Iraq and Saudi Arabia. The importance of helicopters lies in their ability to provide ground combat support. This became an invaluable element in Iran's involvement in the Omani war. The effectiveness of Iran's naval forces was far greater, and its offensive possibilities more advanced, than those of Iraq and Saudi Arabia combined.[43]

These factors, added to a considerable defence industry, made Iran the logical inheritor of Britain's protective role in the Gulf, filling the 'power vacuum' when Britain was due to leave. Moreover, the Gulf is Iran's only vital maritime outlet to the rest of the world – i.e. Iran's coastline extends for 1300 kilometres from the Shatt al 'Arab to the Gulf of Oman and Iran's richest oil fields of the south-west are only a few miles from the Gulf shores; its flow of oil, then, must be secured.

It was with this in mind that Iran occupied the islands of 'Abū Mūsa, Greater and Lesser Tumbs at the tip of the Gulf. However, before this occupation and on the eve of the UAE's announcement of Federation

> Iran and Sharjah came to an agreement on Abu Musa Island, under which Iran would provide 3.75 million dollars a year aid to that sheikdom until revenue realised from oil in the island or its offshore waters reached 7.5 million dollars. Thereafter oil revenues were to be split equally. In the ambiguous agreement

neither side acknowledged the other's sovereignty although the Sheikh of Sharjah agreed to allow Iranian troops to occupy half the island. The Sheikh of Ras al Khaymah refused a similar settlement. On November 30, the last day of formal British protection, Iranian troops occupied Abu Musa island by agreement and the still disputed Tumbs by force, with the resultant loss of perhaps seven lives on the Greater Tumb.[44]

All Gulf shaikhdoms, Saudi Arabia, and Iraq had prior knowledge of Iran's intention to take military action. In the final analysis, Iran's military prominence in the region led it to play a significant role in the Omani war; and its gradual involvement in the war signalled a major change in the area.

The overthrow of Sa'id bin Taimūr

The third, and most significant, development was the successful palace coup that placed Kabūs on the throne. There can be little doubt about the British role in the coup. Given that both PFLOAG and NDFLOAG had made substantial advances, and the two other factors mentioned above, the only obstacle to change in Oman was the policy of Ṣulṭan Sa'id bin Taimūr. After the Conservative Party won the elections on 18 June 1970, both the British

> Foreign Office and the Ministry of Defence were worried that an unstable situation in Oman could well prejudice the smooth withdrawal from the Gulf in the following year. Accordingly, the British Government let it be known that its officers should not stand in the way of a change of government. . . . Some of the seconded and contract officers in Oman went a stage further than this, and actively helped Kabūs organise the stroke against his father.[45]

And on Thursday 23 July 1970, Shaikh Turaik al-Ghafarī, son of the Governor of Dhofar and close friend of Kabūs, stormed the palace with a few followers and demanded the abdication of the Ṣulṭan. It must be remembered that Ṣulṭan Sa'id trusted the British to organise his palace security; none of them was present that day. In the shooting that ensued the Ṣulṭan was injured and subsequently abdicated in favour of his son Kabūs. He was then flown to Britain, and three days after the palace coup the new Ṣulṭan announced to the Omani people the new situation.

R. Fiennes, who served at the time with the SAF, recalls that

> People liked Tom Greening; he was quiet and unassuming. He had
> done well as Intelligence Officer in northern Oman, discovering
> arms caches and more besides. So no one thought twice about
> his many visits to Ḳabūs, the carefully tethered heir to the
> Ṣulṭan Sa'id bin Taimūr. Few remembered that the two men
> had been at Sandhurst together. Tom took over Intelligence in
> Dhofar in July 1969 and almost at once a harvest of pertinent
> information reached the army from sources that Tom seemed
> to acquire overnight. His success was phenomenonal.
>
> He spoke D̲jebali, the language of the Kara, and was everywhere
> at once. No one had reason to think that the handsome young
> Intelligence Officer had the time, let alone the intention, to plot
> against the Sultan . . . . He had come from the house where Ḳabūs
> lived and passed by to the court of Bareik, son of the Walī of
> Ṣalalah. It was no secret that Bareik disliked the Sultan and his
> feudal dicta. But few people knew what passed between Bareik
> and the Intelligence Captain. To act too soon or too late would
> be disastrous and they all held important positions, in the
> banking community of Oman, in the oil company, in the army,
> and in the Foreign Office in Whitehall.[46]

Thus the end came for the 'last' corrupt and ruthless sovereign in
Omani contemporary history, and the new Ṣulṭan undertook to make
major changes that would transform the country's medieval form of
oppression. The choice of Ḳabūs to oust his father had nothing to do
with his experience in governing or his intellectual calibre, but was
mainly because he had undergone military training at Sandhurst. When
he returned from his training, he was put under virtual house arrest.
His uncle, Ṭariḳ bin Taimūr, on the other hand, had long experience
in serving the country both before the coup and after when he was
appointed Prime Minister temporarily (1970–1); but he was considered
by the British to have 'nationalist attitudes' and was therefore not
favoured.

These three political developments, especially the change of authority in Oman, had a tremendous impact on the war. The most serious
threat to PFLOAG was an internal uprising on 12 September 1970.
This calls for discussion despite the difficulty of establishing in detail
exactly what occurred.

Development of the Nationalist struggle in the 1970s

The 12 September uprising

In the eastern region of Dhofar controlled by PFLOAG, a number of factions considered, after the July coup, that the change of authority in the Ṣulṭanate and Oman's which resulted in opening to the outside world were positive steps which called for an attempt to reach some sort of rapprochement with Ṣulṭan Ḳabūs. In their view this could be done either by negotiations or by infiltrating the Ṣulṭan's armed forces and governmental apparatus *after* a formal agreement to end hostilities had been reached.[47] The idea of rapprochement with the Ṣulṭan was not new. Some six months before Ḳabūs's coup, Ṭariḳ bin Taimūr had sent a personal letter to the Front, through PFLOAG's office in Cairo, asking if negotiations could begin between himself and PFLOAG on 'joining forces' to end the rule of Ṣulṭan Sa'id bin Taimūr. The Front not only rejected this important offer, but thought it a bluff, and considered it against their principles to rally support for a member of the al-Bu Sa'id family.[48] The crux of the matter was that the Front was unable to grasp the significance of a power change in Oman and consequently to exploit this opportunity. After Ḳabūs came to power, the Omani population felt the change, however slow, in their daily lives, as jobs became more abundant and attempts at modernisation were made.

The Front, faced with this unprecedented move within its ranks, resorted to public executions without conducting trials. Several leading members of the Command of the Eastern sector — particularly the Military Commander — rejected this uncompromising approach by the leadership and advocated some sort of agreement with the Ṣulṭan. The leadership was adamant and accused this faction of being spies and counter-revolutionaries; it demanded that they should be tried, which would have meant their execution. This faction, sensing the grave situation, gathered strong support throughout the militia and other Front forces in the Eastern sector and blockaded the whole region, making it physically inaccessible to the forces of the leadership. In return for obedience and adherence to the leadership, this faction requested that the latter send representatives to negotiate some sort of agreement on the outstanding issues. The leadership refused to do this. By this time, the Omani intelligence services — guided by the British — were aware of these developments and infiltrated the militia, inciting them to extend the crisis.[49] However the Centre, in this dead-lock situation, moved large segments of the PLA to the East, and the

154

dissident faction, feeling that their execution was now inevitable, either escaped to the Suḷtan's side or left the region altogether. Few gave themselves up pending their 'public trials'.

It would be highly misleading to attribute what occurred solely to the whims of 'counter-revolutionary forces' in instigating such an uprising, and even worse to regard the British-Ḳabūs intelligence services as the prime movers of this affair.[50] For one thing, those who were involved had a long history of allegiance to the cause of the Front in Oman. For another, the PFLOAG had, as described above, important military and political forces stationed in the Eastern sector; should a counter-revolutionary uprising occur, it would seem highly unlikely for the majority of those cadres to be docile and unconcerned about it. The time lapse, from Ḳabūs's July coup to the uprising in September, was too short for the joint Ḳabūs-British intelligence services to set up an incident as important, well-organised and -executed as this. Until this period, PFLOAG had exerted firm control over the area that it dominated, even though the Eastern sector is geographically separate from the central and western sectors. In short, Suḷtan Ḳabūs's palace coup created an opportune moment for PFLOAG to reconsider its priorities; but unfortunately its leadership was unable to comprehend the magnitude of the change that was about to come over the area. It was a grave error for the leadership not to analyse accurately the *reasons* for the uprising, and to react with military action rather than sympathy and understanding. As a result this incident acted as a catalyst for 'defections' from PFLOAG's ranks.

The merger of the Fronts

Although both PFLOAG and NDFLOAG had issued a joint statement on 2 December 1970 calling for unity of action and the creation of the 'broadest national front',[51] the total merger did not come about until a year later. PFLOAG held its Third Congress on 9 June 1971 at Raḵhyūt in western Dhofar. The Congress's resolutions primarily dealt with internal conditions and problems faced by the Front during the period between the Second Congress and Ḳabūs's accession to power. Briefly, the resolutions dealt with the creation of 'people's councils' in the liberated areas, nationalisation of all land in the countryside, the abolition of slavery, and support for women's liberation.[52]

Nevertheless, from the Third Congress to December 1971, during which time the three significant developments discussed above occurred, the two Fronts reached agreement on the future course of the war in

Oman. Subsequently they held a Unification Congress, on the Ho Chi Minh Line at Ihlish, in Dhofar, on 22 December 1971. They also established contacts with the scattered cells of the Arab Labour Party in Oman, to develop a joint political platform; and the latter agreed to limited co-operation. The Ihlish Congress adopted, for the first time, three main resolutions

1　To amalgamate the People's Front for the Liberation of the Occupied Arab Gulf and the National Democratic Front for the Liberation of Oman and the Arab Gulf into one front under the name, People's Front for the Liberation of Oman and the Arab Gulf.
2　To discuss and approve the national democratic working plan and the internal organisational statutes forwarded by the preparatory committee.
3　To elect a single leadership for the People's Front for the Liberation of Oman and the Arab Gulf.[53]

For the first time PFLOAG agreed to delete the label 'occupied' from the Front's new name. By this date, the problem facing Oman and the Gulf, from the Front's point of view, was the continuing power of the existing rulers. This does not mean that the Front neglected the presence of foreign forces; on the contrary, the Iranian presence in Oman was to reach an unprecedented level in 1974–5. For Ḳabūs had secured Iranian military backing during his state visit to Iran in October 1971. At the same time he was able to harmonise Oman's relations with Saudi Arabia. The Ṣulṭan paid an important state visit to Saudi Arabia on 11 December 1971.[54] Saudi Arabia agreed to withdraw its support from 'Imām Ghalib and to grant Oman generous economic assistance. Saudi Arabia's opposition to all 'subversive activities and communist oriented movements' led it to even closer relations with Ṣulṭan Ḳabūs's troubled country. During this period Oman was admitted to both the Arab League (on 29 September 1971, despite the opposition of 'Imām Ghalib, PFLOAG, and the PDRY), and to the United Nations (on 7 October 1971, by 117 votes to 1 with two absentions). The one negative vote came from South Yemen (PDRY), and Oman became the UN's 131st member. Thus, the end of 1971 saw the war in Dhofar on the verge of new developments.

The establishment of government control

The third phase in the history of the war in Oman extends from January 1972 to July 1974 when the PFLOAG was forced into unprecedented retreat. During this phase Oman's oil revenue increased; this in turn enabled the government to allocate some of its revenue for the building of schools, hospitals and other public facilities; but defence expenditure reached 60 per cent of the total.[55]

Militarily, the SAF's major offensive began in late 1971, using air and ground forces, and especially helicopters, hoping to cut off PFLOAG's supply lines to the Eastern sector; but it resulted in high casualty rates for the SAF. Despite Ṣulṭan Ḳabūs's claim at the time, that the 'rebellion' in Dhofar had been 'contained and reduced by defection', the winter offensive proved otherwise. The British government remained equivocal about the scale of its involvement in the war, being in a delicate diplomatic position. *The Guardian* reported from Oman that

> officials are secretive concerning the presence of the SAS in the
> Civil War. The Sultan . . . is reluctant to admit that he is
> dependent on outside forces to lead his troops and the Oman
> government is trying to play down the size of the rebel problem.
> But it was learned yesterday that British soldiers have figured
> prominently in all major actions against the rebels. And they
> are also responsible for most of the intelligence and military
> planning of the war.[56]

By June 1972 PFLOAG still had the upper hand over the SAF in the Eastern sector, and the Front had 'succeeded in cutting off Jebel from the plain. Trade has virtually stopped and just by their presence they are draining the economy.'[57]

On 19 July PFLOAG launched its strongest attack on the eastern coastal town of Mirbat; this was the last major offensive that the Front's PLA units carried out in the Eastern sector. At this offensive

> an estimated 250 guerrillas were involved in the dawn attack
> on a position that contained a platoon of soldiers, some members
> of the British army training team and 30 *Firgats* — irregulars
> drawn from the hill tribes owing allegiance to the Government
> and paid by it. They left 29 dead and another 12 were captured.
> The retreating force was seen dragging many corpses and the
> SAF's 'conservative' estimate was that 60 were killed. The
> consequences for the guerrilla leadership may have been grave:
> intelligence reports said 25 were killed in subsequent internecine
> conflict, and the results achieved would have taken 'a whole
> series of battalion operations'. Establishment of the 'White
> City' and Jibjat posts are said to have given the people in that

area 'a tremendous boost in confidence'. Important in this context
are the *Firqats*, who, having either withdrawn their allegiance
from PFLOAG or fled from them to the plain, have returned
armed and in the pay of the Sulṭan.[58]

According to a PLFOAG General Command source the attack on Mirbat
was aimed at the Omani military leader who was stationed with the SAF
at Mirbat at the time of the attack, because he had been the Military
Commander in PFLOAG's Eastern sector who led the 12 September
1970 uprising. This leader fled the Front's area after the uprising
failed, and the leadership sentenced him to death. He subsequently
joined the SAF's ranks and the latter appointed him at Mirbat.[59]
PFLOAG forces withdrew from the town of Ṭaqa after this disastrous
operation, and gradually the Ṣulṭan's military power in the Eastern
sector began to grow. Meanwhile the Front was facing grave internal
troubles, some of them structural. (See Appendix 3).

The Ṣulṭan's attempt to gather Arab and foreign support for the
war bore fruit in April 1972, when a Jordanian delegation visited
Oman.[60] At the same time a Saudi Arabian military delegation made
a field study of the Dhofar province, and in this way the whole Arabian
peninsula became involved in ensuring the stability of the area. David
Housegs, reporting from Kuwait, disclosed in the *Financial Times* of
25 June 1973 that Saudi Arabia and the Gulf States had set up a joint
intelligence organisation to exchange information about and concert
action against subversion in the region.

However, the most significant development of the war was Iran's
support for Ṣulṭan Ḳabūs, which became large-scale in December
1973. Despite the presence of Iranian and Jordanian forces in Oman,
and to a much lesser extent Saudi Arabian assistance up to that date,
the British presence continued in key military positions within the
governmental structure. Iran's significant military contribution was
paratroopers and helicopters. Initially, Iranian military involvement
was denied by all parties concerned as too diplomatically embarrassing
to admit at the time. On the one hand two years had gone by since
Iran had occupied the islands at the tip of the Gulf; on the other, had
Iran's intervention been confirmed by the Ṣulṭan it would have aroused
strong nationalist feeling. The Iranian forces aimed to cut PFLOAG's
supply link — the Red Line — thereby denying the whole of the Eastern
sector to the Front. And in March 1973

Iranian paratroopers reportedly opened up the land link between
Salālah, the coastal capital of Dhofar and the rest of Oman. In

December, in 'Operation Thimble', launched by an Iranian
contingent nine hundred strong, helped the twelve thousand
British-led troops of the Suḷtan to consolidate his gains.[61]

It was beyond PFLOAG's logistic capacity either to deter or resist
these military operations. Its forces had to retreat to the PDRY's
borders with Oman, and after the end of 1973 the Front's military
infiltration in Dhofar was carried out at high cost, human and material.

By March 1974, the over-all military and political situation was in
favour of, and under the tangible control of, the Suḷtan. During that
month Suḷtan Ḳabūs paid a state visit to Iran after which a joint Iranian-
Omani communiqué declared inter alia that

> the two heads of State noted with satisfaction the ever expanding
> and mutual relations between the two countries and reaffirmed
> the readiness of their governments for close cooperation in the
> political, economic and cultural fields and the establishment of
> security within the region. . . expressed their firm belief in full
> cooperation between Iran and Oman in all fields aimed at the
> maintenance of stability in the region and the free passage of
> ships and freedom of movement through the Hormuz straits and
> adjoining seas, which is of vital importance to both countries.[62]

These changes around PFLOAG prompted it to take another step
which should have been taken, at the latest, by the end of 1971. The
Front convened a general congress on 1 July 1974, at which three
significant resolutions were adopted:

1 Organisational independence for the PFLOAG sections in the
   different political entities of the area, and the right to form
   specific policies and programmes as required by regional
   political conditions.
2 Organisation of the PFLOAG branches in the regions of Oman
   within the framework of an independent national organisation,
   under the name *Popular Front for the Liberation of Oman*.
3 Election of a Central Command for the Popular Front for the
   Liberation of Oman.[63]

These resolutions reflected the Front's decision to contain revolutionary activities within Oman proper, after nine years of adherence
to the idea of 'liberating' the area from Dhofar to Kuwait. The Front's
National Programme adopted the strategy of 'protracted war' and
acknowledged, for the first time, the 'enemy's military superiority'.[64]
The new Programme called for recognition of the fact that the Gulf's

internal political developments, in the states ruled by different ruling families, were to be based on progressive factions in each state, but that the newly-formed front was not responsible for taking an active stand against all these regimes. The programme advocated the unity of all 'progressives' in the area, without commitment to specific action, as advocated earlier. Though the programme touched every economic, social and political aspect of Omani society it made clear without reservations that current tasks must concentrate on Oman only.

Despite this necessary, though belated, move, the Front was unable to regain the initiative militarily or politically. After further offensives by Iranian and other forces, their military situation was extremely weak. The Ṣuḷtan's mounting military superiority by 1975 would have made it suicidal for the PFLO to continue military operations in Dhofar; and as Sa'id Mas'ūd, a Front leader, put it, 'we were faced with the decision whether to hold to the land and be annihilated or retreat to save the revolution'.[65] There was no question as to what the choice and outcome would be. PFLO retreated to Hauf, beyond the PDRY border, where it stationed all PLA units and conducted its foreign relations from its office in Aden. Ṣuḷtan Ḳabūs tried to define the problem of discontent in Oman, spearheaded by PFLO, as a diplomatic issue between the Sultanate and the PDRY. For the Front's basic activities and infiltrations could now come only from the PDRY's territory. By then PFLO, after its military retreat from Dhofar, was unable to rally viable regional, Arab and international support around its cause. Only the PDRY and Libya were continuing their support, and offices were opened in Algeria and Iraq, but the latter's support fluctuated according to circumstances. It came as no surprise that Ṣuḷtan Ḳabūs announced on Oman's fifth national day, in November 1975, that the 'question of war in Dhofar has ended'.[66] The PFLO nevertheless rejected this claim, on the basis that the 'war in Oman' is by nature a 'protracted' one.[67] That argument, however, could be justified *only* if the PFLO had some military ground to manoeuvre in; this significant element of guerrilla warfare was completely neglected by them, especially during the second phase discussed.

PFLO's international relations

Of the communist world, during the period covered by this study, the USSR and East European bloc gave help to the PFLO, which was not self-sufficient. China withdrew its support at the most crucial period in circumstances discussed in the following chapter. It should be noted that the PFLO's relations with the USSR and Eastern Europe began only *after* the Chinese change of attitude at the end of 1972.

The PFLO, throughout its history, had constantly acknowledged the aid received from China; internationally, it never criticised the USSR directly, but indirectly alluded to lack of USSR aid on occasions. In a speech delivered in Pyongyang, where PFLOAG representatives had been invited to the Anti-Imperialist Journalists' Congress, between 18 and 26 September 1969, they spoke strongly against the Ṣulṭan, the neighbouring 'artificial' shaikhdoms, western domination, etc., and stated unequivocally that 'after four years of armed struggle and people's war, we are sorry that in the free progressive world only the PDRY and China understand and support our struggle'.[68] However, it is most likely that the PFLOAG relations with the USSR and the Eastern bloc, unlike those with China, started through the Aden Office of the Front. It is not precisely clear, however, why PFLOAG-USSR relations did not develop until after China withdrew its support in 1972; but all indications suggest that China had great influence in keeping PFLOAG on its side of the Sino-Soviet dispute. The USSR criticised, in vituperative terms, the regime of Ṣulṭan Sa'id bin Taimūr in Oman in the press throughout the Oman war.[69] USSR comments on the palace coup were, naturally, unchanged:

> The old Sultan, said one writer, had been removed only because
> he had refused to spend his money on modernizing his army in
> order to ensure the safety of oil production. Any reforms by the
> new Sultan would serve only the imperialists; they would not
> affect the country's social structure.[70]

The USSR and East European bloc's support for the PFLOAG came about at a critical moment in the development of the Front,[71] but was limited because of the Front's inability to counter the Ṣulṭan's military advance in Dhofar. In April 1973 the PFLOAG despatched, for the first time, a high-ranking delegation to tour the USSR, Eastern Europe and China, soliciting aid. In *Saūt al-Thawra*[72] this tour was given prominence, but the countries which the delegation was to visit were not mentioned; the editorial merely stated that the mission was directed to the 'socialist bloc' by contrast with earlier delegations to China when editorials had given prominence to China's role in 'spearheading revolution in the world'. The PFLOAG's shift to the USSR bloc came too late, and the Front was unable to respond to the bloc's willingness to extend aid because of its weakness on the ground by 1975. Secret correspondence which fell into the hands of the Omani security forces revealed this inability to cope with Soviet aid:

> The Soviet Union is asking for a course consisting of 30 (thirty) people. We sent a message to ADEN to the effect that we could not spare that number, but we could spare 5 in addition to the previous course so that they could be trained on anti-aircraft rockets.[73]

Of the 'socialist bloc' only Yugoslavia and Rumania had recognised and exchanged envoys with the Ṣulṭan of Oman in April 1973. The USSR, unlike China, could choose to support or withhold aid from the PFLOAG. Up to the time of writing, it has *never* withheld support from the Front; but the USSR has leeway to withdraw such support and substitute for it that of one or more of its bloc members.

It has often been claimed that the PDRY exerts a 'great influence' on PFLOAG decision-making on strategy and tactics. This claim must be viewed with reservations. First, throughout the development of the PFLOAG, the PDRY *never* played any significant role in shaping its political orientation, let alone decision-making. Second, unlike the PFLOAG or any other front that operates in the Arabian peninsula, the PDRY, as a state, is bound by international legislation, and, for example, the stationing of PFLOAG military forces within the PDRY's borders creates a situation which is bound to become critical. Third, the PDRY is mainly concerned with its own national security, and its economic and political development. Consequently, measures are taken to ensure that its national interest is not put in jeopardy. This does not mean that the PDRY must 'terminate' or curtail the PFLOAG's military and political existence; it simply implies that the latter *must* depend on its own abilities to advance whatever programme it adheres to. And should this programme fail or erode, as argued above, the PDRY can hardly be blamed. Fourth, put into historical perspective, the two respective parties shared one significant element in their existence: each acted as the 'defender' of the other's territory, according to their respective spokesmen. Had it not been for the PFLOAG military presence beyond the PDRY's borders, either Saudi Arabia or Oman, or both, could have easily sliced the PDRY into various territories, i.e. the Sixth and Fifth Governorates of the PDRY could have been attacked at a time when the nation was about to complete 5 years of independence. Finally, the PFLOAG, throughout its period of military and political activity in the region, had solid backing from a hard core within the PDRY's ruling National Liberation Front. It is often alleged that *one* man – Abdul Fataḥ Isma'īl, the NLF's Secretary-General –

162

exerted a 'tremendous influence in containing and curtailing the activities of the PFLOAG'.[74] Though it is beyond the scope of this study to discuss power distribution in the NLF, it would seem hardly likely that *a single leader* could dominate the whole course of the PFLOAG's activity. Simply argued, the NLF's power base is not determined by one man's political whims; it is a combination of several contending views. Nevertheless Ṣuḷtan Ḳabūs has been able, diplomatically, especially within the Arab sphere, to project the 'problem' as one between Oman and the PDRY.

It is through this diplomatic effort that the Ṣuḷtan hopes to exert the maximum 'influence' on the PDRY's policy towards the PFLO; for as the Ṣuḷtan argues, if it were not for PDRY support for the 'rebels in Dhofar' and its acting as 'exporter of revolution' the whole issue would have been solved much earlier. In addition, Iran's military involvement had limited Ṣuḷtan Ḳabūs's diplomatic freedom. Although the Gulf States and Saudi Arabia recognised the necessity of stability and maintenance of the status quo in the area, the presence of Iranian troops in Oman, and its occupation of the islands and military dominance in the Gulf, aroused doubts about Iran's intentions.

Chapter 7

China's attitudes to, involvement in, and withdrawal from, the Omani War, 1955–75

China's relations with the Omani Nationalist Movement during the period under study, 1955–75, can be divided into three periods. The first period began with 'Imām Ghalib's Movement and ended in 1968. It was characterised by political support of the 'Imām's Movement. The 'Imām's representatives refused offers of military aid from China. The second period coincided with the radicalisation of the Nationalist Movement in Oman from 1968 to early 1972. During this period China was the *only* foreign nation that gave military support to the PFLOAG which depended heavily on China's assistance. During this period so-called 'Maoist' ideology exerted a tremendous influence on the political and organisational orientation of PFLOAG. The third period, from 1972 to 1975, saw the withdrawal of Chinese support. Three basic factors underlay China's change in policy. The first was the development of China's global foreign policy when the Great Proletarian Cultural Revolution subsided. The second was Iran's influencing China's withdrawal of support for the PFLOAG. The third was China's concern to establish relations with existing Arab regimes, while the PFLOAG's political and military programme called for their overthrow.

Phase One: 1955–68

China's relations with the Omani nationalist movement was its first political involvement in the Arabian Peninsula. Relations began as a result primarily of earlier Sino-Egyptian political contacts during the period of anti-British sentiment in the Arab world.

This period is characterised by China's political support for the 'Imāmate cause against the Ṣulṭan and the British; it was later transformed into China's willingness to give military aid to the 'Imām. China's political statements on the nationalist movement in Oman were made before 1959. For example, after the Ṣulṭan occupied the Buraimi oasis with British military aid, a *People's Daily* commentator argued that

> The occupation of the oasis on October 26 by the forces of the
> Sultanate of Oman, under the command of British officers, was
> motivated by the rich petroleum resources of this oasis which had
> been coveted by certain western countries. . . . This is why Britain
> is grabbing it, in the capacity of 'protector' and 'ally' of Oman. . . .
> [And] for many years British forces repeatedly intruded into the
> oasis and clashed with Saudi Arabian authorities, trying to compel
> Saudi Arabia to agree to special colonial privilege for Britain over the
> oasis. Finding threats useless, Britain is now occupying it by force.

He went on to state that it was basically a Saudi-British problem; and that is why Faiṣal, Premier and Foreign Minister of Saudi Arabia at the time, regarded the incident as an act which 'violates international law and principles'.[1]

It is worth noting here that from 1955 until Ḳabūs's palace coup in 1970, China always associated the former Ṣulṭan Sa'id's rule with British 'imperialism and the oppression of the Omani people'. China has never denounced any other Arab head of state over such a long period and with such intensity.

Reporting on 'Imām Ghalib's rebellion in 1955–7, China initially confined itself to quoting foreign sources. But when 'Imām Ghalib opened an office in Cairo in 1957 China sought to make its first contacts with the 'Imāmate forces. According to the *Observer*, 'Shaikh al-Harithī, official envoy of the 'Imām of Oman in Egypt, said in Cairo . . . that the Imam has declined an offer of aid from Communist China in the present dispute in the territory'.[2] Chinese aid to the 'Imām was not forthcoming mainly because of the latter's reservations about dealing directly with a Communist state. The scheme against Oman, in the Chinese view was an extension of 'imperialist alliances between Britain and the USA' directed at 'slicing' Oman for their own interests.

The *People's Daily* commentator stated that

> Though the 'dirty deal' on Oman between Dulles and the British
> authorities was not disclosed, there were indications that the two
> countries might have reached some compromise for the time
> being. . . . That would be freedom of action in the Buraimi oasis
> for the United States and in Oman for Britain, as the Cairo

representative of the Imam has pointed out. . . . To maintain its colonial interests along the Persian Gulf, Britain had to protect itself against being dislodged by the United States and to subdue the national independence movement of the Arabs. But the Oman situation in the past weeks made it imperative for Britain to concede some interests to the United States in return for support.[3]

It seems that China's stand on Omani internal developments and their relationship to Saudi Arabia was clouded with uncertainty over the nature of the political attitudes of the various parties involved in the dispute. Although China had originally clearly sided with Saudi Arabia during the Buraimi dispute, two years later China's analysis of the dispute shifted, seeing it as a dispute between two external powers: Britain and the USA, implying that the latter had a free hand in manoeuvring Saudi Arabia over the Buraimi issue. To China the whole affair was reminiscent of Anglo-French-Israeli action against Egypt during the Suez Crisis of 1956.[4]

China also threw its political support behind the 'Imāmate cause through its embassy in Cairo. From there it was announced that:

> The Chinese people sympathise with the Omani people in their struggle against imperialism, Chinese Ambassador Chen Chia-kang told the Director of the Oman office, Mohamed el-Harsy [al-Hari<u>th</u>ī] when the latter called on the Ambassador today.
>
> The Omani representative told the Ambassador about British aggression in Oman and asked whether he had received the memorandum of the Arab League soliciting support for the Omani people from the Bandung Conference countries.
>
> The Ambassador said he had received the memorandum and would forward it to his government as soon as possible.[5]

From the Chinese perspective the only method of countering British-American involvement in Omani internal affairs was for the Arab people to rely on 'the world forces of peace led by the Soviet Union [which] firmly supported every action of the Arab people against colonialism'.[6]

When the question of Oman was referred to the United Nations Security Council by all the members of the Arab League, but was not discussed by the Security Council mainly because of Britain's stand, the *Kwangmin Daily* commentator wrote in support of a *Tass* statement of 20 August 1957, that it was the duty of the UN to 'halt British aggression.' He added:

this statement demonstrates the just stand of the Soviet Union in supporting the colonial peoples' liberation movement and shows that it is the true friend of the people of the Middle East.[7]

The USA abstained on the issue of discussing the Omani question at the Security Council. The *People's Daily* argued that by its abstention the USA

> was actually backing the British aggressors against the Arab
> people's fight for independence. . . . Realising its awkward
> position in the Middle East. . . the United States was relying on
> clandestine dealings with Britain in exchange for British support
> of United States subversive activities against Syria.[8]

On the same day, 23 August, the Chinese Ambassador in Cairo declared that 'the Chinese people resolutely oppose the British government's armed intervention against the people of the 'Imāmate of Oman and its indiscriminate bombing in Oman'. This statement was made in a Chinese Government note sent by the Chinese embassy here to the Arab League in reply to the League's memorandum soliciting support for Oman from the Bandung countries.[9]

By 1958 China viewed the 'Imāmate cause as one of several 'national independence movements' in the Arab world. Chou En-lai, in a speech delivered to the Fifth Session of the First National People's Congress on 10 February 1958 declared that:

> In the past six months, the peoples of countries in the Near and
> Middle East and in Africa, especially those of the Yemen, Algeria,
> Ifini of Morocco and Oman have waged unremitting and heroic
> struggles against colonialism, in which they have won the sympathy
> and support of all peace-loving peoples.[10]

From this date onwards, China kept in close contact with the 'Imāmate office through its embassy in Cairo; at the same time it reported on Omani internal and external developments.

The next step towards closer relations was announced when Ṣaliḥ bin 'Isa al-Ḥarit̲h̲ī, Deputy 'Imām of Oman, granted an interview to a *NCNA* reporter in Cairo. The Deputy declared that:

> all Asian-African countries were united in opposition to
> imperialism and Oman would soon send delegations to all Asian
> and African countries, including China, to explain the Omani
> cause and ask for help. As regards China, he affirmed the Omani
> people's full support to the just struggle of China to restore
> Taiwan; he also asked that the best wishes of the Omani people

be conveyed to the Chinese government and people, thanking them for their support of the Omani struggle. He emphasised that he was in complete agreement with Chairman Mao Tse-tung's statement that 'imperialists and all reactionaries are paper tigers'.[11]

It is most likely that a Chinese invitation to the Deputy was made after that date. For on 14 January 1959, Ṣaliḥ bin 'Isa led a three-man delegation to tour India, Burma and Indonesia soliciting support for the 'Imāmate cause among Bandung Conference member states. No prior announcement was made concerning the delegation's intention to pay an official visit to China. The Deputy's visit to China lasted twenty-four days, 29 January–20 February 1959.

On 29 January the Deputy 'Imām of Oman, at the head of the delegation, arrived in Peking in response to an invitation from the Chinese Islamic Association (CIA). The invitation did not come from the Chinese Government or the CCP, or from the Chinese Afro-Asian Solidarity Committee. It was extended by an agency that corresponded to the political outlook of the 'Imāmate leadership at that time. Moreover, the Chinese reception party was overwhelmingly dominated by non-governmental and non-party officials.

The following day, Burhan Shahidī, Chairman of CIA, gave a banquet in honour of the visiting delegation. Ṣaliḥ bin 'Isa thanked 'the Chinese people for their resolute support' of the 'Imāmate cause and pointed out that this visit would enhance further co-operation between the 'Imāmate of Oman and China. Burhan Shahidī replied by stating, although without mentioning Ṣulṭan Sa'id bin Taimūr by name, that:

> The struggle of the Omani people, led by the 'Imām of Oman,
> against the British imperialists, is an internal [integral] part of the
> Arab people's movement for national independence and against
> colonialism. . . . We are convinced that the Omani people in
> their struggle against colonialism, firmly supported by the Arab
> countries, the Afro-Asian countries, and all peace-loving countries
> and peoples of the world, will win final victory if they persist in
> their struggle to the end and maintain sufficient vigilance towards
> all the intrigues and plots of the United States and British
> imperialism.[12]

Thus the crux of 'Imāmate/Sultanate rivalry was not yet expressed in a way that would indicate, implicitly or explicitly, China's stand. On 5 February the Chinese Committee for Afro-Asian Solidarity, the Chinese People's Committee for Cultural Relations with Foreign

Countries (CPCCRFC) and the Chinese Islamic Association sponsored a 'mass rally' in Peking welcoming the delegation. Burhan Shahidī declared in his welcoming speech that 'the Chinese people. . . demand the immediate cessation of imperialist aggression in Oman and the withdrawal of all foreign forces from the Gulf of Arabia [viz. Arabian Gulf]'.[13] It was the first time that a Chinese spokesman had referred to the whole Gulf as being occupied by 'foreign forces'; moreover, the Gulf was referred to as Arab rather than Persian. But the speech did not mention the role of Ṣulṭan Sa'id.

Three days later the Deputy and his entourage had an audience with Mao Tse-tung,[14] although no specific issues concerning Sino-'Imāmate relations were discussed. The next evening, the National Committee of the Chinese People's Political Consultative Conference gave a banquet welcoming the Omani delegation. At the ceremony Chen Shu-ting stated that 'Prince Harthy's visit would undoubtedly promote the mutual understanding and the development of friendly relations between the peoples of China and Oman'.[15] Such promotion of understanding occurred the following day when the Deputy met Chou En-lai.[16] According to unconfirmed sources Chou offered military aid to the 'Imām but Ṣaliḥ bin 'Isa declined it and asked in return only for financial support. The Chinese were non-committal about this request.[17] Finally, at the end of his tour, in Kunming, the Deputy cabled Mao Tse-tung expressing his gratitude 'for the tremendous support given to the Omani people in their struggle by the Government and people of China'.[18] The Chinese replied by inviting the Deputy through the Central People's Broadcasting Station to make a speech to the 'Chinese people'.[19]

This early phase of Sino-Omani contacts was characterised by Chinese moral and propaganda support to the 'Imāmate movement. China was not able to provide military assistance for the simple reason that the 'Imām had neither a regular nor an irregular army. Nor was it possible to send any Omanis to be trained in China. The 'Imām had accepted minor Saudi Arabian military aid, most of which came ultimately from the USA. Moreover, as was pointed out in the preceding chapter, almost all Omani nationalists were trained in Iraq and/or Syria.

By the time Ṣaliḥ bin 'Isa and his party arrived in Peking the 'Imāmate movement was facing increasing military set-backs. Sino-Omani relations began basically as a result of Sino-Egyptian relations, especially because of the role Naṣir played in Arab politics. At the time of the Deputy's official visit to China, Sino-UAR (Egypt and Syria) relations had cooled. It would have been unlikely for the Deputy to accept China's offer of military aid without prior consultation with Naṣir, who exerted considerable influence on the 'Imāmate movement. This deterioration in Sino-UAR relations was prompted by the former's disenchantment with Naṣir's persecution of communists and his anti-Iraqi sentiments. Chou En-lai, in his Report on Government Work delivered to the First Session of the Second National People's Congress, 18 April 1959, and during the Deputy's visit to Peking, did not mention the 'Imāmate movement as being one of the 'national independence movements' in the Arab world, in contrast to his speech a year earlier to the National People's Congress. This time, Chou stated China's support for Arab causes in the following way:

> The Chinese people have always expressed their sympathy for all struggles against imperialism, colonialism, aggression and intervention, because our country itself was not long ago a semi-colonial country suffering greatly from imperialist aggression, and even now imperialist forces are still occupying our territory of Taiwan. We are ready to give support and assistance to the full extent of our capabilities to all national independence movements in Asia, Africa and Latin America. In the Arab nation's anti-imperialist struggles over the past years we have always stood on the side of the Arab peoples. A complicated situation has arisen recently in the Arab national independence movements. Some people in power in the United Arab Republic have launched an attack on the Republic of Iraq, and then also attacked the Soviet Union, the great friend of the Arab peoples. Obviously, such actions are injurious to the cause of independence of the Arab nation and therefore cannot enlist the sympathy of the Arab people. . . . We hope that a way may be found to overcome this difficulty now facing the Arab cause of national independence so that the imperialists will not succeed in their sinister scheme to harm the Arab nations.[20]

This was a clear reflection of deteriorating Sino-UAR relations, and of China's association of the 'Imāmate movement with Naṣir. It did not mean that China believed the 'Imāmate movement against the Ṣulṭan had ended or been defeated. China's press releases supported the 'Imāmate movement *after* Sino-UAR relations were harmonised.

Less than two months after the Deputy concluded his visit to China, Yu Chao-li (pseudonym) wrote an article in *Hung-ch'i* discussing at length the thesis that 'imperialism is the sworn enemy of Arab national liberation'. Commencing with an unequivocal attack on

Naṣir's policies towards Iraq and local communists, he proceeded to discuss the Arabian Gulf and Peninsula and Oman:

> petroleum, the life-blood of the Arab peoples, is now still basically controlled by imperialism. 99.9 per cent of the oil deposits in the Middle East (including Iran) and 99.7 per cent of the oil output are still in the hands of monopoly capital in the imperialist countries . . . . Not only in the Arab states, but in all countries fighting for or safeguarding national independence, every political force must make this choice: either to break away from imperialism, rely on and call forth the strength of the masses of the people and unite with the socialist countries and all the anti-imperialist forces of the world, and, by doing so, make it possible to achieve complete success in the struggle against imperialism; or to compromise with imperialism, to be afraid of and even suppress the forces of the masses of the people and be hostile to the socialist countries and all anti-imperialist forces and, by doing so, inevitably betray the national interests. Farūk [Egypt], Faiṣal the Second [Iraq], Sa'id [Oman], and Shishaklī [Syria] represented such national traitors in the Arab states.

After this first official visit by the Deputy 'Imām of Oman, until the end of 1959, China's support for the 'Imāmate movement marginally intensified. For example, the Chinese Afro-Asian Solidarity Committee issued a statement on Oman Day — a resolution had been passed among Bandung Conference members designating 19 July a day for Oman — in a show of solidarity. The *People's Daily* expressed the 'wholehearted support of the Chinese people for the anti-imperialist struggle waged by the people of Oman and Southern Yemen'.[21]

There are certain fixed points in China's attitude to the 'Imāmate movement during this period. First, it supported the 'Imāmate line on the historical separation between Muscat and Oman, and the former's annexation of Oman with British aid. Second, Oman and the Arabian Gulf were linked as being under total British domination, with oil as the reason. Third, consonant with the perpetuation of political domination, the British had to rely on the support of local 'puppet' rulers such as Ṣulṭan Sa'id. Fourth, the USA's role in Oman was a subordinate one. No allusion was made to US military support, via Saudi Arabia, to the 'Imāmate movement in its initial phase. Finally, no allusion was made to the tribal outlook of the 'Imāmate movement; Chinese commentators simply referred to 'Omani nationalists'.

China's relations with the 'Imāmate movement in the first half of

171

the 1960s were influenced by two major factors: the endorsement by Afro-Asian nations of the 'Imāmate movement, and Sino-Egyptian relations.

The Chinese Afro-Asian Solidarity Committee was the main channel for Sino-'Imāmate contacts. The second Afro-Asian People's Solidarity Conference (AAPSO) was held in April 1960 in Conakry, Guinea. The communist-oriented delegates' main task was to transfer the Secretariat headquarters from Cairo to Conakry as a further step in reorganising AAPSO; such moves were aimed at reducing Naṣir's influence within the organisation. The Chinese delegation to the Conference was the largest and most impressive present. Although by this date the Sino-Soviet dispute was surfacing, the dispute itself was not an issue at the Conference. Two of the basic issues from the Chinese point of view were attainment of 'social revolution' – i.e. the triumph of communism in the under-developed countries – and opposition by the under-developed states to all forms of colonialism and imperialism. Chu Tzu-chi stated at the Conference that

> it is imperative for the Asian and African peoples first of all to oppose and end colonial rule, liquidate the control and bondage of the imperialist forces of aggression, and completely wipe out its influence in all fields before they can obtain a solution to the social problems facing them and achieve a social programme.[22]

It was within this context that China saw the 'Imāmate movement in Oman and 'Imāmate-Naṣir relations. China's support for the Omani case at Conakry was without reservation,[23] although it was regarded by the Chinese as part of the 'nationalist movement' in the under-developed world. The 'Imāmate delegation succeeded in getting the Conference to reiterate its support for observance of 18 July as 'Oman Day'. On 18 July 1960, one month after the Conakry Conference, and as part of Oman Day celebrations, Ibrahim al-Harithī, 'Imāmate representative in Damascus, granted the *NCNA* reporter there an exclusive interview:

> in which he quoted Chairman Mao Tse-tung's famous thesis, i.e. people's war, and summed up the present situation in Oman . . . . Referring to the friendly relations between Oman and China, he enthusiastically praised China for its lofty stand of giving support to all Arabs' just struggles and all oppressed peoples' struggles including the Omani people's struggle for independence and freedom. . . . He stressed that Chairman Mao's speeches and articles on military thinking had greatly inspired the Omani leaders and fighters.[24]

It was the first time that an 'Imāmate official not only paid tribute to Mao's thought on liberation, but also stated that it actually exerted some 'influence' on policy makers. The second assertion must be treated with some scepticism. It would seem, given the nature and composition of the 'Imāmate leadership at that time, that it was too *early* a date for such an 'inspiration' to have had any practical effect on the Omani leaders. What is most probable is that such assertions were made during a period when the 'Imāmate movement had reached its lowest ebb in Oman itself, but not internationally. China was an exception as a non-Arab state lending political and propaganda support. Furthermore, on the day of the interview, the Chinese Committee for Afro-Asian Solidarity in Peking sent a message to Ṣaliḥ bin 'Isa, Deputy 'Imām, on the occasion of 'Oman Day', declaring that:

> the Chinese people sternly condemn the imperialists' aggression
> against Oman and their slaughtering of the Omani people and
> resolutely support the Omani people in their just struggle against
> imperialism and for independence and freedom.[25]

The second element in Sino-'Imāmate relations related to Sino-Egyptian relations. It is significant that Chinese press releases, while relaying erroneous claims about the 'heroic struggle of the Omani people in the battlefront', had totally neglected the creation – in name only – of the Oman Liberation Front which, as stated earlier, resulted in a split within the 'Imāmate leadership.[26] *NCNA* articles are clear illustrations of this. For example, in a long article on the 'anti-imperialist armed struggle' being waged in Oman, the reporter argued that:

> The Omani people's armed forces have grown in strength from ten
> thousand men to fifteen thousand this year [1963]. . . they have
> ambushed British patrols, laid mines in lines of communication,
> raided major British ports, demolished its ordnance depots and
> inflicted heavy losses on the enemy.
>
> Situated in the south-east of the Arabian Peninsula and having
> a total area of two hundred and ten thousand square kilometres,
> Oman freed itself from British colonial rule after the great
> uprising of 1913 and became independent under the 'Imām. In
> 1920 Britain was compelled to recognise its independence.
> Refusing to become reconciled to this set-back and shaken by
> the rising anti-colonialist movement in the Middle East, Britain
> incited its protégé, the Sultan of Muscat, to invade Oman at the
> end of 1955. In July 1957 a greater uprising broke out in the
> country and the Omani people soon routed the troops of the

Sultan of Muscat commanded by the British officers. Then
British troops went into action and the Omani people's forces
withdrew from Nizwā to the mountains and carried on guerrilla
warfare against the British invaders.[27]

Sino-Egyptian rapprochement by the end of 1964 gave the 'Imāmate
cause a tremendous political boost. The basic cause of unfriendly
relations between Egypt and China was the former's strong support
for India when the Sino-Indian border clashes took place in 1962.
Chou En-lai headed an impressive fifty-member delegation on an
extended visit to fourteen African, European and Asian countries.
The delegation arrived in Cairo on 14 December 1963. It was the
first high-ranking official visit by the Chinese to Egypt since the two
countries established diplomatic relations in 1956. The most significant result of the Sino-Egyptian talks was expressed in a joint communiqué. It clearly 'illustrated the extent to which Peking was prepared
to go in supporting Arab causes and particularly Cairo's leadership in
order to impose its image and restore its limited influence in the Arab
world'.[28] Although the joint communiqué indicated some sort of
compromise between the two powers – e.g. China's support for almost
all Arab nationalist movements in return for the UAR's unconditional
and strong support on the Taiwan question – the Chinese side seemed
to be 'required' to follow a line of total support for Arab causes. This
seemed clear enough from China's attempt to lay emphasis on 'general'
Arab issues rather than specific ones. The communiqué, published in
the *Peking Review* in its entirety, was supplemented by the Chinese
version of points of emphasis; the Arabic version contained no such
gloss.[29] The Chinese version declared that:

> Premier Chou En-lai solemnly indicated that China has consistently
> stood for and faithfully abided by the Five Principles of Peaceful
> Co-existence and the Ten Principles of the Bandung Conference.
> In accordance with these principles *the Chinese Government has
> unswervingly taken the following stand in handling its relations
> with the Arab countries:*
>
> 1 *It supports the Arab peoples in their struggle to fight
>   imperialism and to win and safeguard national
>   independence.*
> 2 *It supports the governments of Arab countries in pursuing a
>   policy of peace, neutrality and non-alignment.*
> 3 *It supports the Arab people in their desire to bring about
>   solidarity and unity in the form of their own choice.*

4 *It supports the Arab countries in their efforts to settle
   their disputes through peaceful consultation.*

5 *It holds that the sovereignty of Arab countries should be
   respected by all other countries and that encroachment and
   interference from any quarters should be opposed.* This is the
   same stand the Chinese Government has consistently taken in
   handling its relations with all other African countries. President
   Naṣer expressed full agreement with and appreciation of the
   above stand of the Chinese Government enunciated by Premier
   Chou En-lai.
   The Chinese side declared its full support to the people of
   Palestine in restoring their legitimate rights and in returning
   to their homeland. For this the Arab side expressed deep
   gratitude. The Chinese side reaffirmed its support to the people
   of Yemen in their struggle to safeguard national independence
   and the people of Oman in the fight to win their independence.[30]

This carefully drawn-up communiqué indicated Chinese priorities:
Oman ranked below the others. None the less, 'Imām G̲h̲alib and the
'Imāmate Office in Cairo declared their gratitude for Chou's and the
Chinese government's support 'as a source of great *moral strength*
[emphasis added] for our fighters and is also a real expression of the
policy of the Chinese people in support of the nationalist movements
and a symbol of the Bandung Spirit'.[31] The inclusion of the 'Imāmate
cause in the communiqué had undoubtedly furthered amicable relations
between China and the 'Imāmate leadership, and the Chinese press
made no mention of the creation of the Oman Liberation Front. Such
divisions were reported *only* through second-hand sources. China's
silence for over two years on the divisions clearly indicates its non-
committal approach to both sides. It referred to the so-called Omani
struggle against imperialism and the Ṣulṭan only through the label of
Omani 'nationalists' which, at the time, was void of any political
significance.

China's involvement in, and withdrawal from, Omani Wars, 1967–75

In tracing China's involvement in the Omani war it should be noted
that there are certain events — such as the precise dates of the Sino-
PFLO exchanges of visits — that cannot be accurately determined. This
section is only concerned with Sino-PFLO relations; other related issues,

such as Sino-Iranian relations during this same period, are discussed separately. The case of Iran is singled out, in contrast with those of the PDRY and Iraq, because of its significance in China's withdrawal of aid to the PFLO.

The first mention of the Dhofar Liberation Front (DLF) came through *NCNA* reports from the Cairo office of the Front.[32] The Cairo office of the DLF had played a major role in contacting the Chinese embassy there and arranging the first DLF delegation to Peking. There are conflicting reports on the nature of the talks held in Cairo between the Chinese and DLF representatives. According to one source the Chinese asked and were 'highly concerned' with whether the DLF had sought political and military support from the USSR.[33] The DLF response was negative and the Chinese offered them aid. Current PFLO spokesmen deny this.[34] None the less, such reports seem likely to be true in view of the anti-Soviet propaganda the Chinese were carrying out at the time. It is not clear in retrospect why the DLF sought Chinese aid rather than aid from the USSR, since the latter's potential was far greater. According to Khalid 'Amīn, a PFLO spokesman, the Front was 'eclectic' in its approach. China at the time was championing 'world revolution through armed struggle'; the contacts with the Chinese embassy in Cairo began *after* the June war during which Arab official feeling was one of disappointment at the lack of Soviet aid. Further, when contacts were established the DLF leadership had no clear notion about the 'background and basis for the Sino-Soviet conflict'.[35]

The first DLF delegation, invited by the Chinese People's Institute for Foreign Affairs (CPIFA), arrived in Peking on 23 June 1967, exactly two years after the establishment of the DLF, two weeks after the Arab-Israeli June War, and at a time when China was in the middle of the Cultural Revolution and its resulting radicalisation of foreign policy. The delegation was headed by Muḥamed 'Aḥmad al-Ghasanī, member of the DLF Council. It included 'Salim 'Alī Musalam, member of the Political Committee and Aḥmad Suhayl Faraḥ, member of the Military Committee.'[36] The delegation met members of the host organisation and conferred with the Chinese Defence Ministry. The Chinese promised to supply the DLF with nominal aid: light armaments – e.g. machine-guns, grenades, etc. – and $35,000 which would cover the freight expenses; also included in the shipment were Mao's writings and the Red Book and other Marxist literature. The first Chinese aid shipment was sent to Tanzania and transported thence to the Front. At the time, Tanzania assisted the Front with minor commodities, such as tea and sugar. Chinese aid had a tremendous impact, for it was the first significant aid the Front received. The only other outside aid had been from the Front's cells and organisations in Kuwait and, to a lesser extent, in the rest of the Gulf.[37] This aid, although minor, meant a turn in the *intellectual* transformation of DLF members: because of this Marxist literature the DLF began to pay more attention to Marxism, and particularly its Chinese form. Moreover, the aid arrived at a time when the DLF was on the verge of transforming its whole political structure and outlook to adopt Marxism as a guide. From this point onward the future leaders of the PFLOAG began to support the Chinese side in the Sino-Soviet conflict, although this was not overtly obvious from available literature.

From the inception of Chinese aid to the DLF to the latter's transformation into PFLOAG, China was completely silent on internal developments within Oman and the role the DLF was playing in the region. When the Ḥamrīn Conference was convened in September 1968, during which the Front took radical positions, two Chinese visited and attended the conference in Dhofar. They were invited by the PFLOAG to observe the working and progress of the revolution. One was an *NCNA* reporter and the other an official of the Chinese Communist Party.[38] They stayed for one month observing the various changes and the political situation in the area. They returned to China with favourable impressions of the new political line advocated by the newly-formed front. The Chinese supported the political programme endorsed at the Conference: e.g. total revolution in the Gulf, adoption of scientific socialism, women's rights and equality, etc. Immediately after the conclusion of the Conference the PFLOAG despatched a delegation for political and military training in China. When they returned they became *political commissars* in the various units of PFLOAG; they were selected from Dhofaris living in the Gulf.[39] The first group of PFLOAG members sent to China had a tremendous impact on the future organisation and orientation of cells and political education among the cadres. Their task in China was not solely to be trained militarily, but also politically. Despite these increased contacts, Chinese press articles on the various liberation fronts and local upheavals throughout the world up to 1969 totally neglected the Omani war. *Peking Review*, 18 October 1968, for example, contained a sketch map showing that in the Arab world there were two 'excellent world situations' where popular armed struggle had either triumphed or was in the process of doing so: the PDRY and Palestine (see Chapter 1, Map 1.1).

Following the return of the first group of Dhofaris from China, a high-ranking delegation from PFLOAG's Central Committee paid an official visit to China. In Peking they met both Chou En-lai and members from the Defence Ministry during which they were promised an increased amount of military aid. This aid consisted of anti-aircraft missiles, explosives and light machine-guns — substantial aid in relation to PFLOAG's limited capabilities. From this point on the Chinese welcomed several PFLOAG military, political and technical delegations. One such delegation was sent to train in technical matters and at the end of the period of training the Chinese offered PFLOAG a broadcasting station. PFLOAG throughout this period was almost completely dependent on Chinese aid — this stemmed from PFLOAG fulfilling its earlier promises. At the same time, the Front's image, both locally and internationally, began to be portrayed as 'Maoist'; it was unable to either confirm or deny this charge. If it had confirmed it, it would have implied that the Front was following a one-sided political line; if it had been denied it would have harmed its relations with China.[40]

It was through the two Chinese who attended the Ḥamrīn Conference in September 1968 that the first extensive descriptions of life in Dhofar began to appear in the Chinese press. These reports were the basis for allegations that PFLOAG had acquired a pro-Chinese attitude. It also confirmed fears that the Front was totally dependent on one non-Arab source for vital aid. Furthermore, political education and literature within PFLOAG's ranks were undoubtedly influenced by the Chinese political line. After their tour of Dhofar the Chinese related the many-faceted influence of China's aid on the PFLOAG. One article, describing a fighter's adherence to the thought of Mao Tse-tung, stated that:

> On his way to the garrison quarter of a unit of the army's Western Command on the morning of August 27 [1969] this correspondent met four PLA [People's Liberation Army] fighters who were cocking their sub-machine-guns and escorting more than ten war prisoners from Raⱨẖyūt to another place. A young fighter, patting the sub-machine-gun in his hand, said to this correspondent: 'Chairman Mao had said: "everything reactionary is the same; if you don't hit it, it won't fall". We must resolutely wipe out the enemy who refuses to surrender'.[41]

The correspondent's keen observation of the difficulties the Front were encountering was reflected in another article describing the high level of illiteracy:

As a result of the protracted colonial rule, the Dhofar people still have no written language of their own. Many fighters from remote villages or mountains do not understand Arabic. Political instructors in the armed units explain Chairman Mao's works to these fighters in the local language. Many fighters have managed to learn by heart a large number of quotations from Chairman Mao.[42]

On women's rights in Dhofar, the correspondent wrote:

In Dhofar, the women who are the most oppressed under colonialism and feudalism for generations have also been mobilised. Many of them have come out of their homes to study politics and to learn how to read and write. Many young women have encouraged their husbands to join the People's Liberation Army. Braving hails of enemy bullets, some woman carried water and food to the fighters who were fighting against the enemy, and took care of the wounded.[43]

The PFLOAG for its part paid tribute to China's internal political development, giving particular support to the radical elements who were waging the Cultural Revolution. On celebrating the 20th anniversary of the founding of the PRC, *NCNA*'s correspondent in Aden was told to convey the Front's

warmest congratulations to the Chinese people who uphold Marxism-Leninism-Mao Tse-tung Thought. . . . We resolutely support all the resolutions adopted at the Ninth National Congress of the Communist Party of China. We firmly support China's Great Proletarian Cultural Revolution.[44]

Such endorsements not only supported the radical elements in China's internal power struggle, but were also intrinsically anti-Soviet. For the Ninth National Congress of the Chinese Communist Party, held during 1-14 April 1969, was convened after three years of national upheaval. The Congress aimed at accomplishing three main tasks: summing up the experience of the Cultural Revolution, the election of a new Party Leadership, and the adoption of a new Party Constitution. Lin Piao was at the centre of all these changes. He was officially designated as Mao's successor. Lin Piao, in his opening speech to the Congress, devoted an important section to China's new course in international relations. Stress was laid on the Sino-Soviet dispute and the Soviet Union's 'revisionist' path. Although he omitted any reference to the PFLOAG's role in the Omani war when discussing China's support for wars of national liberation, extracts from his speech were later repeatedly quoted by PFLOAG spokesmen.

The PFLOAG's adherence to the Chinese line is most evident in its analysis of the over-all world political situation. Although there was no direct attack on, or mention of, the USSR and other socialist countries, PFLOAG literature followed the Chinese line on the role of the socialist countries in supporting wars of national liberation in Asia, Africa and Latin America. *Saūt al-Thawra*, marking 1 May 1969, pointed out in a lengthy article that for the strengthening of 'the dictatorship of the proletariat' in the socialist countries, the parties holding power must enrich such power by 'holding high more than one banner of proletarian culturalism' and their role must consist of aiding the 'proletarian class in the advanced industrial states onto a correct Leninist line' and launching an international education programme to 'expose and repudiate opportunistic and chauvinistic theories and all that may defame Marxist-Leninist proletarian revolutionary thought'.[45]

Such a call for militancy stemmed from the leaders' adherence to a basic political line that was transmitted among the population of Dhofar under the control of the Front through educational classes and cadres' directives. In February 1970 two noted commentators, Fawaz Ṭrabulsī and Fred Halliday, accompanied by PDRY officials, visited areas in Dhofar under the PFLOAG's control. Ṭrabulsī noted that:

> political education is divided into the following: firstly, the Front's own writings; secondly, the official agenda which the General Command drew up after the Second Conference of the Front. This includes the *Communist Manifesto*, Lenin's *Selected Works*, Mao's Red Book, Stalin's *Dialectical Materialism*, books available in Arabic of Ho Chi Minh, Guevara, Kim Il-sung, NLF [South Vietnam], Popular Democratic Front for the Liberation of Palestine, and *al-Huriya* magazine. Thirdly, because the above two presuppose a certain level of literacy which few fighters had reached the Front has laid down a unified political education programme that is carried out by political commissars in the form of lectures. This programme constitutes, besides the Red Book, basic political education in Dhofar. It is divided into twenty-five lessons encompassing four main topics: 1) characters of a struggling revolutionary; 2) organisational disciplines (democratic centralism); 3) principles of Marxism-Leninism; 4) internationalism, national liberation and class struggle.[46]

Both commentators pointed out the importance of 'Mao's Thought' for PFLOAG cadres. Their explanation of the reasons for the spread and influence of 'Mao's Thought' in an area like Dhofar is rhetorical. This was due, they said, to its content and form. Ṭrabulsī argues that these two elements are significant because

> the thought of Mao Tse-tung is a Marxist ideology and that is most progressive and encompassing for national and social issues in a colonised and semi-colonised world. This is the basic reason why this thought exerts a wide influence in Dhofar (and other places). However, the argument that this influence is due to China's aid to the revolution, which some foreign reporters who visited Dhofar advocated, is simplistic and must be rejected. Egyptian peasants do not read Lenin, despite tremendous aid from the Soviets. As far as the form is concerned, Mao's thought is the 'people's thought'; that is, it aims at poor and middle peasants, sons of tribesmen, and workers of colonised cities. The people of Dhofar do not differ from these.[47]

Such an argument is analytically deficient. It is one thing to concentrate on aid, whether military aid or in the form of political rhetoric, during a movement's infancy, and another thing when the movement reaches a certain stage of maturity. It should be borne in mind, and this is acknowledged by current leaders of the Front, that the PFLOAG had no extensive knowledge or understanding of either the Sino-Soviet conflict or the historical background to the triumph of the Chinese Communist Party. The Front sought Chinese aid at a time when the latter was advocating a certain international militancy that aimed at, among other things, discrediting the Soviet Union. To consider Mao's writings, although they are undeniably one form of Marxism, as applicable to Dhofari conditions, is simplistic. It is so because Mao's writings are directed precisely at the Chinese peasantry whose historical, sociological, political, and more importantly, economic conditions differed from their Dhofari counterparts. The argument that the existence of poverty, oppression and backwardness in a traditional society leads to revolution needs to be viewed with considerable reservations. Such conditions do not necessitate the triumph of an indigenous revolutionary movement. Dhofar is only one example of this. This is one of the basic reasons why the Chinese themselves tell scores of representatives of liberation movements on pilgrimage to Peking, the PFLOAG included, that they must act according to conditions prevailing in their own surroundings; almost all these delegations regard such Chinese attitudes as 'pure modesty'. Finally, while both writers claim that the Vietnamese experience had some impact on the PFLOAG's education it seems that the PFLOAG drew few lessons from it. Vietnamese conditions were remarkably suited to Mao's thought; yet the Vietnamese did not merely copy the Chinese model.

Responding to an invitation extended by the Chinese People's Association for Friendship with Foreign Countries, the PFLOAG despatched a delegation headed by Ṭalal Sa'ad Muḥamad, member of the Executive Committee-General Command,[48] to China from 28 February to 4 April 1970. After touring southern China and visiting conventional tourist spots, the delegation conferred on 2 April with Chou En-lai, Huang Yung-sheng, Chief of the General Staff of the Chinese People's Liberation Army, and Chi Peng-fei, Vice-Foreign Minister.[49] At this meeting the Chinese affirmed their 'support to the PFLOAG'; and pointing out the front's political role in the area promised to send heavy and light armaments — e.g. anti-aircraft missiles, explosives, sub-machine-guns, grenades, etc.[50] On his return to Aden Ṭalal Sa'id gave an interview to the *NCNA* correspondent there in which he stated, inter alia that:

> all cadres and fighters of the People's Front for the Liberation
> of the Occupied Arabian Gulf are determined to study Marxism-
> Leninism-Mao Tse-tung Thought in the course of armed revolution-
> ary struggle and carry the struggle in the Dhofari region and the
> Arabian Gulf through to the end.[51]

China's involvement after this visit intensified both militarily and politically. The PFLOAG's acknowledgement of aid was expressed on various occasions. Celebrating the fifth anniversary of the 'June 9 Revolution', the Front held a mass rally in Aden at which Li Chiang-fen, the Chinese Chargé d'Affaires was present on 'invitation'.[52] At the rally, Ḥasan Ghassanī from the PFLOAG's office in Aden delivered a ceremonial speech in which he expressed the Front's 'heartfelt thanks to socialist countries, particularly the People's Republic of China, for their moral and material support and aid to our revolution'.[53]

The *People's Daily*, in its comments on such occasions, although it restricted itself to the Front's activities in Dhofar, presented brief historical accounts of foreign involvement. It described British and American collaboration with the 'country's own reactionary party' in suppressing the local population and concluded that after 'five years, the armed struggle in the Dhofar region has developed fast and the situation is very promising'.[54] China's widened interest included the welcoming, albeit cautiously, of armed struggle in the Omani interior, launched on 12 June 1970 by the NDFLOAG. China took the view that the leadership of PFLOAG was more advanced than that of NDFLOAG. A Chinese editorial argued, adding a clear Chinese note to the war and giving secondary place to the role played by the NDFLOAG, that:

the heroic Dhofar people, led by the Popular Front for the Liberation of the Occupied Arabian Gulf, had with their guns liberated more than 90 per cent of the villages and some cities of Dhofar. They had fought out a brand new situation of surrounding the cities with villages. Not long ago, several guerrilla organisations united to form a democratic fighting line to liberate the peoples of Oman and the Arabian Peninsula. The guerrillas led by this organisation vigorously attacked the British colonial army and mercenary troops and had won brilliant victories.[55]

China's view of the role played by the NDFLOAG in Oman was apparent through its low-level commentary and rather unorthodox way of marking the Front's founding. The worker commentators group of Peking's Machine Tool Plant No. 2, for example, entitled their essay 'New Storm on the Arabian Peninsula', in which they wrote that:

The new storm of the armed struggle of the Oman people is a continuation and development of the armed struggle of the people in the Dhofar area under the leadership of the People's Front for the Liberation of the Occupied Arabian Gulf. This fact has once again eloquently testified to Chairman Mao's brilliant and absolutely correct thesis that 'revolution is the main trend in the world today'.[56]

China remained officially cautious in confirming its political and military assistance to the PFLOAG cause. Its state-to-state relations with the PDRY, whose support for the Front constituted one of its basic foreign policy objectives, is a striking example. From 1–13 August 1970, Salim Roba'ya 'Alī headed a delegation to China to discuss the mutual interests of the two countries. In honouring the Yemeni Chairman, Vice-Chairman Tung Pi-wu said at a banquet in Peking, making an explicit distinction, that

in international affairs, the Government and people of Southern Yemen support the Palestinian and other Arab peoples in their struggle against US-Israeli aggression, support the people of the Arabian Gulf in their revolutionary armed struggle against imperialism.[57]

To which, Chairman Salim Roba'ya in reply affirmed explicitly his country's support for the PFLOAG and all other 'revolutionary forces' in the Arabian Peninsula. China expressed its implicit support for the PDRY against Saudi Arabia and to a lesser extent the other ruling regimes in the rest of the Peninsula. At the end of the official visit, the two sides issued a joint statement declaring that:

> The two sides express firm support to the people's armed struggle in the Arabian Gulf under the leadership of the People's Front for the Liberation of the Occupied Arabian Gulf. The Chinese side express *admiration* [emphasis added] for the firm stand taken by the government and people of Southern Yemen in support of the anti-imperialist struggle of the people of the Arabian Gulf and for their aid to it in various forms.[58]

Direct Chinese denunciation of Gulf and Arabian Peninsula rulers in Saudi Arabia and Oman is absent in its press coverage of the whole area at the end of 1970 and on into the decade. The overthrow of Sulṭan Sa'id by Ḳabūs was almost totally neglected. More significantly, the new Sulṭan was never described, as his father was, as a 'reactionary lackey'; equally, there was no condemnation of the attempted creation of the United Arab Emirates as a by-product of 'British imperialism' in the region. The Chinese press continued to report the PFLOAG's military activities, relying on its communiqués as evidence of the continuation of the war. But there were no political commentaries explaining the various political changes concerning the Front. When the PFLOAG and NDFLOAG, for example, announced their merger on 2 December 1970, *NCNA*'s correspondent in Aden referred to the content of the communiqué in general terms,[59] neglecting the most crucial reasons for the merger that the communiqué itself had emphasised (see previous chapter).

By 1971 China's reserved reporting and coverage of events became more evident and the emphasis shifted to secondary sources dealing with the Gulf and Oman in general. A *NCNA* correspondent in Aden, reporting on the opening of a 'week of solidarity with the revolution', which the Chinese ambassador to the PDRY attended, quoted the Yemeni official 'Aziz al-Ḍali as having 'condemned the reactionary policies pursued by the Sheikhs and Sultans in the Arabian Gulf and their collaboration with colonialism to prolong the life of foreign petroleum firms which are monopolising the oil wealth of the Arabian Gulf'.[60]

The first Chinese reference to the overthrow of Sulṭan Sa'id by his

184

son Ḳabūs and the formation of the United Arab Emirates appeared almost one year later, quoting a second-hand source.

Chinese support for the PFLOAG had diminished by 1972, and was finally terminated when China sought and acquired diplomatic recognition from Iran and Kuwait and was seeking recognition from Saudi Arabia and the rest of the Gulf. Before turning to Sino-Kuwaiti and Sino-Iranian relations in detail, and the reasons for China's withdrawal of political and military aid to the PFLOAG, the following descriptive methodology of China's changing priorities in the area is offered.

The first official Chinese reservations over its involvement in the Omani war occurred in 1972 when a high-ranking delegation of the PFLOAG was despatched to Peking and Pyongyang. On his departure, the leader of the delegation, Aḥmad 'abd al-Ṣamad, declared that the purpose of the visit was to 'confirm the ties of revolution and struggle binding the people of Oman and the Gulf to those of China and North Korea'.[61] Although Chinese sources are totally silent on the visit by the PFLOAG, the latter's sources give the date as the last two weeks of July 1972.[62] The most obvious reason for this sudden despatch of a PFLOAG delegation was the failure of a high-ranking PDRY delegation to persuade the Chinese leadership to continue their support to the Front.

The PDRY delegation, headed by Abdul al-Fataḥ Isma'īl, member of the Presidential Council, made an official visit to China during 8–17 July 1972. The PDRY delegation sought further strengthening of bilateral economic ties and technical assistance, but the question of support for the PFLOAG was a central concern of the PDRY. On 9 July, in the Great Hall of the People in Peking, Abdul al-Fataḥ Isma'īl delivered a speech in which he warned his hosts that 'we comrades, as you know, are facing conspiracies from American and British imperialists and Arab reaction headed by Saudi Arabia and the puppet regime of Muscat and Oman, who are backed by British imperialism'; these conspiracies were aimed first and foremost at the PDRY by crushing the 'struggle of the people of Oman' led by the PFLOAG. He went on to reaffirm the PDRY's full support to the PFLOAG's armed struggle in the Gulf and its aim of unifying the whole area.[63] Replying to the Yemeni leader, Chou En-lai neglected to mention the PFLOAG and the whole of the Gulf, but stated in equivocal terms that 'your Government and people strongly support the Palestinian people and the rest of the Arab peoples in their just struggle to regain national rights and lost territories.'[64] Chou's formulations were reiterated in the joint communiqué at the end of the visit, in which nothing was said of Chinese 'admiration' as stated in an earlier communiqué, of the PDRY's support for PFLOAG.[65]

This lack of enthusiasm on the Chinese side prompted the Front hastily to despatch a delegation. While the PFLOAG delegation was in Peking discussions were held in a manner that the delegates thought 'unrevolutionary'. At the discussions,

> the Chinese, for the first time, put forward their point of view on the course that the revolution must take. They concentrated on the negative aspects of the revolution; in particular the feasibility of its totality in the Gulf, which they doubted. And they argued that the logical course the revolution must take is, firstly, liberating Oman, then proceeding to the rest of the Gulf. Moreover, the Chinese argued that the basic hindrance to tne revolution is the existing regimes in the area which the revolution [PFLOAG] is incapable of countering, let alone overthrowing. After these discussions we clearly acknowledged that China could not be relied upon in its aid. We therefore began to reassess our previously held notion about the Soviets being 'revisionists'; thus we contacted the Soviets in Aden for future collaboration.[66]

Officially, both sides played down their disagreements; this resulted in several sources continuing to believe that the Chinese were aiding the PFLOAG. This belief was reinforced by the Sultan's forces capturing large caches of arms from the Front. The misconception was reinforced by official spokesmen of the Front; e.g. Muḥamad 'Abdullah, member of the Central Committee, declared in an interview that 'China had influenced the movement's ideology, but it remained only a supplier of arms, seeking neither to organise the campaign nor to send troops'.[67] The Front remained, officially, cordial and friendly towards China. *Saūt al-Thawra*, for example, continued publishing congratulatory messages to Chinese leaders on all possible occasions.[68] On the 24th anniversary of the founding of the PRC, the Central Committee of the PFLOAG sent a congratulatory message to Mao Tse-tung noting the 'unbreakable relations between the two revolutions'.[69]

Nevertheless, Ṣulṭan Ḳabūs' sources were quick to realise the existence of this friction. Attributing the date to the Chinese Foreign Minister's visit to Iran (see following chapter) and the latter's stated conditions for recognition of China, the official Sultanate newspaper, *Oman*, declared that 'China had reduced, if not withheld, its support for the rebel movement in Dhofar'.[70] From this date forward the PFLOAG concentrated on actively seeking Soviet aid, primarily through

PDRY diplomatic channels. Moreover *Saūt al-Thawra* argued, in several major articles, for the need to establish firmer ties with 'all' in the socialist camp.[71] The Front celebrated its eighth anniversary in Aden with the marked absence of the Chinese Ambassador or any other representative from China.

The change in China's foreign policy in favour of establishing ties with the existing regimes in the Gulf prompted China to drop all support – propagandist or military – for the Front. When Salim Roba'ya 'Alī of the PDRY visited China in April-May 1975, he declared at a banquet in the Great Hall of the People that his country supported 'the people of Oman' under the leadership of the PFLO in their 'struggle to achieve their aspirations' and strikingly added that 'we thank our Chinese friends for their support to our Arab people's struggle, especially the Palestinian and Omani'.[72] Replying to the speech, T'eng Hsiao-p'ing was silent on China's support to the PFLO and, remarkably, any previous references to the Gulf and the Arabian Peninsula as being solely under 'Western imperialism'. He confined his remarks to an assault on 'superpower hegemony' and declared China's support only for the Palestinian cause in the Arab world.[73]

On the formation of the PFLO in 1974, with its new strategy of confining the 'revolution to Oman only', which the Chinese had strongly favoured since 1972, China remained adamant in withholding aid to the Front. The PFLO's Executive Central Committee sent a last 'appeal' to their Chinese comrades, who were celebrating the 26th anniversary of the founding of the PRC, in an unprecedented form:

> Our people in Oman have taken up arms and have been fighting for 10 years under the leadership of the PFLO, but they are today facing imperialist and reactionary conspiracies and a tyrannical invasion by Iranian militarism, contrary to all modern and contemporary conventions and aimed at subjugating our people and silencing the guns of their revolutionaries. For this reason, our people appeal to you and all the freedom and peace-loving peoples of the world for more support and backing for their struggle, to enable them to rout the invaders and colonialists.[74]

China by then saw internal conflicts in the Gulf as less important than relations between the two superpowers. The Chinese formula of unity for all Gulf and adjacent states to oppose 'superpower hegemony' was applied without regard to disputes between Gulf states, to whom the Chinese view seemed unrealistic. These states were united on one matter: the need to suppress, by whatever means necessary, all existing internal opposition within each respective country. Yet the *Peking Review* argued in a feature article entitled 'United struggle against hegemonism' that the regimes of the Gulf had achieved their ultimate goal of unity in facing the impending superpower hegemony in the area, especially that of the USSR, by diplomatic channels. The author argued that because of the 'great strategic importance' of the Gulf, with one of the richest oil deposits in the world, its OPEC members had 'heightened their vigilance. . . and stiffened their resistance' against the superpowers in various ways: Iran and Iraq reached an accord on their border disputes; Iran and Saudi Arabia had 'decided to fight together to defend common interests of all countries in the area'; Saudi Arabia and Iraq reached a final agreement on demarcation of boundaries; Saudi Arabia and Kuwait concluded a lasting agreement on the demarcation of the neutral zone; and finally, Kuwait sought economic unity among the Gulf states. The above lead the commentator to the conclusion that such unity 'shows the fiercer the rivalry between the two superpowers, the more dispute there is in the world and the greater is the threat to third world countries. And this in turn makes their unity in the struggle against hegemonism all the more urgent and compelling'.[75] Such themes in China's foreign policy, however unrealistic in the eyes of indigenous rulers in the Gulf, have been continuously espoused by its diplomats in the area.

Chapter 8

China and Kuwait

Introduction

Kuwait is the largest Emirate on the western coast of the Arabian Gulf and has historically been a merchant state. On 23 January 1899 Shaikh Mubarak al-Ṣabah signed an agreement with the British government pledging himself and his successors not to cede, sell, lease, mortgage or allow the occupation of Kuwaiti land for any purpose by any other foreign power, or to receive any foreign representative without the prior consent of the British government. In return Kuwait would obtain the protection of the British Crown. Kuwait had historically concerned itself primarily with establishing balanced relations with neighbouring states, such as Iraq, Saudi Arabia and Iran. The al-Ṣabah family has ruled with absolute power and stability over the tiny shaikhdom for almost two centuries, save for the 1938 events.[1] Since the beginning of the twentieth century all major decisions in Kuwait have been taken by the ruler with the advice of the British Political Resident. The Emirate's foreign relations and contacts required British consent.

This situation was altered formally in June 1961 under the rule of Shaikh 'Abdullah al-Salim al-Ṣabah, commonly regarded as the father of modern Kuwait.

During the period of British domination over Kuwait, oil was discovered, thus giving Britain control over one of the most prosperous oil-producing states in the world. As oil had already been discovered in Iran, the protectorate agreement of 1899 bound Shaikh Mubarak 'not to give a concession in this regard [oil exploration rights] to anyone other than a person nominated and recommended by the British Government'.[2] The first oil concession was signed on 31 December 1934 between the Kuwait Oil Company (KOC), a newly-formed British company, and Shaikh 'Aḥmad al-Djabir al-Ṣabah, granting the KOC full rights to exploration and marketing of Kuwaiti oil. Later, in July 1948, the American Independent Oil Company (Aminoil) was granted a concession on the Kuwaiti part of the Saudi-Arabian-Kuwaiti Neutral Zone. Commercial oil production did not, however, start until 1950. Oil exploration in Kuwait was seriously affected by the nationalisation of Iran's oil in 1951 by Prime Minister Mossadegh. This brought retaliation from the international oil monopolies which boycotted Iranian oil and thus relied more heavily on Kuwaiti production. The Mossadegh government was subsequently overthrown in 1953 by the joint efforts of the British and US Governments and the 'competing' oil companies. Three years later Japan entered the Arabian Gulf oil exploration, bringing with them a competitive approach. Initially they concluded a deal with Gulf Oil Corporation for the purchase of Kuwaiti oil, and this crude oil was supplied by the Kuwait Oil Company which was jointly owned by British Petroleum and Gulf Oil. The contract was to last 15 years.[3] In July 1958[4] the Japanese-owned Arabian Oil Company (AOC) concluded an agreement with Sha<u>kh</u> 'Abdullah al-Salim al-Ṣabah for the exploitation of oil in the neutral zone and off-shore. This agreement was more favourable to Kuwait than any of its earlier agreements, in terms of profits and joint decision-making; but because of the 1899 Treaty, British consent was needed. The British Government refused to consent until the former Japanese Foreign Minister, who was then consultant to the AOC, gave assurances in London that his company wanted 'to work hand in hand with the world's existing firms'.[5]

There appear to be a number of reasons for Japan's entry into this previously British preserve, which also marked the reduced importance of the 1899 Treaty. First <u>Shaikh</u> 'Abdullah al-Salim had determined a course for Kuwait's gradual independence from foreign domination, and he achieved this by using his skills as a statesman; second, Kuwait wished to be associated with the general rise of Arab nationalism, which manifested itself mainly through Naṣir's prestige. Third, the British Government feared the recurrence of a Mossadegh-type development and wanted to ensure Kuwait's internal stability; had the al-Ṣabah family been overthrown, the problems of finding new rulers for Kuwait would have been serious, calling for more than a mere coup. Fourth, the Japanese concession was off-shore and at that time off-shore oil exploration seemed unlikely to become profitable.

Sino-Iraqi relations

An understanding of Iraq is essential to the discussion of relations between China and Kuwait, since Iraq long claimed Kuwait and the politics of Gulf States are closely interrelated. On 14 July 1958 the Iraqi monarchy was overthrown by 'Abdul Karīm Ḳasim and 'Abdul Salam 'Arif. At first there were fears that the West would intervene to restore the monarchy, and President Naṣir flew to Moscow, where he sought assurances for Iraq's protection against such intervention. Unlike Egypt and Syria, the Communist Party in Iraq had substantial power and influence in the new regime. China seized this opportunity, on 16 July 1958, to extend recognition to the new government. On 17 July the Iraqi government restored diplomatic relations with the UAR, the Soviet Union and China. One week later the first shipment of Chinese goods arrived in Baghdad and on 6 August two *NCNA* correspondents were posted to the Iraqi capital.[6] Chou En-lai went so far as to assure Ḳasim of China's support by sending him a message on 29 July stating that:

> We have great admiration for Your Excellency and the Iraqi
> people under your leadership . . . . I would like to assure Your
> Excellency that the Chinese Government and people will give
> every support to your government and people in your struggle
> to safeguard national independence and oppose imperialist
> aggression.[7]

Sino-Iraqi relations then saw a rapid development: between December 1958 and September 1959 eight Iraqi government, public and Communist Party delegations visited China and between December 1958 and July 1959 three Chinese delegations went to Iraq.[8]

Kuwait, as always, was concerned with the uncertainty of political development in neighbouring countries, particularly in Iraq, where Communist influence was growing. In what appeared to be an agreement with Jordan, Kuwait expelled a number of so-called communists, including Syrians and Iraqis, and handed them over to the Jordanian authorities. The *NCNA* was quick to react, and from Baghdad wrote:

> Informed sources here disclosed today, 29 May 1959, that the
> Government of Kuwait had handed over to the 'Amman authorities
> more than two hundred Jordanian refugees. Some of them fled
> their country following the US-inspired overthrow of the nationalist
> Sulaiman al-Nabulsī cabinet of Jordan in April nineteen fifty seven.
> Others received heavy sentences of imprisonment in absentia by
> the Jordanian court for their struggle against the reactionary regime.
>
> Before the handing-over, the Jordanian refugees were in the
> service of the Government and private firms in Kuwait.[9]

This development took place shortly after Naṣir started to repress communists in his country in December 1958. Sino-Egyptian relations were at a low ebb, the Chinese press taking a strong position against Egypt and Naṣir personally over the persecution of Egyptian and Syrian communists, following the Soviet line in this.

Kuwait's independence and conflict with Iraq

Despite this condemnation the Chinese press continued to keep a close eye on developments in Kuwait, and particularly on the positions taken by <u>Shaikh</u> 'Abdullah al-Salim concerning any Arab states that were labelled as 'reactionary'. When the ruler of Kuwait visited Jordan, among other Arab states, on 17–18 February 1960, the *NCNA* reported the visit without giving any indication either of support or of condemnation.[10]

<u>Shaikh</u> 'Abdullah al-Salim set the course for Kuwait's national independence, and its restructuring on modern lines by setting up a Parliament. China's attitude to this is significant.

On 19 June 1961 agreement was reached between <u>Shaikh</u> 'Abdullah al-Salim and the British Political Resident giving Kuwait its independence in foreign relations and ending the 1899 Agreement.[11] Two days later Kuwait applied for membership of the Arab League and was welcomed by all Arab states except Iraq. Caught by surprise because of the secrecy and speed of developments, Iraq sent a message to <u>Shaikh</u> 'Abdullah al-Salim which welcomed the abrogation of 'the false and unlawful 1899 Treaty which was signed between Kuwaiti political agent <u>Shaikh</u> Mubarak without the knowledge of Iraqi authorities, which was legally established'.[12]

Ḳasim was adamant in his demand for the incorporation of Kuwait, although no substantive historical evidence in support of Iraqi claims was adduced. Because of the expected threat from Iraq, and Kuwait's inability to defend itself, the letters exchanged between Britain and Kuwait on 19 June 1961 provided that: 'Nothing in these conclusions shall affect the readiness of Her Majesty's Government to assist the Government of Kuwait if the latter request such assistance'.[13] As the Iraqi threat developed <u>Shaikh</u> 'Abdullah al-Salim asked for British military assistance on 30 June 1961, and informed Arab Governments of his action. The next day British troops landed in Kuwait.

China's actions throughout this period show the uncertainty of its policies. After hesitating, China recognised Kuwait on 28 June,[14] thus miscalculating forthcoming events. China was caught in a dilemma: Iraq,

China's closest Arab ally, was threatening military action against Kuwait, the first independent Arab Gulf State and the richest in oil production for the 'western imperialist camp'. Recognition would irritate Ḳasim, who was then planning its takeover. The USSR's attitude to the abrogation of the 1899 Treaty was one of disbelief, and it supported Ḳasim.

China's unsureness was evident in a message sent by Chou En-lai to Shaiḵẖ 'Abdullah al-Salim to mark independence day, 19 June. The message was sent on 30 June:

> On the occasion of the proclamation of independence of Kuwait,
> I have the honour, on behalf of the Government of the People's
> Republic of China, to extend hearty congratulations to the
> Government and people of Kuwait. May the people of Kuwait
> achieve further successes in the cause of opposing imperialism
> and colonialism, safeguarding national independence and building
> their country. May your country attain prosperity and its people
> enjoy happiness.[15]

China was the first communist country to recognise Kuwait.

China's uncertainty was reflected in its political commentaries, in which severe condemnation of British 'military occupation of Kuwait' was combined with cautious reports on Iraq's claims and arguments. China's knowledge of Kuwait's external and internal developments was quite remarkable, although its press reporting was variable. Two months before the proclamation of independence, Kuwait assumed full power over its judicial system. *NCNA* reported from Cairo that:

> Kuwait has assumed full judiciary powers on its territory as from
> April first [1961], according to a MEN [Middle East News] report
> from Kuwait.
>
> In the past there were two kinds of courts in Kuwait: 'Shari'a'
> courts which ruled according to the Koran and before which all
> natives appeared and the 'British Mandatory House' which was a
> special court set up by Britain for the trial of British subjects in
> Kuwait. A few months ago Kuwait reorganised its entire judicial
> system and there are now in Kuwait ordinary courts besides the
> Shari'a courts.[16]

The Chinese press reported on Kuwait's independence on 22 June 1961.[17] It was forceful in its condemnation of Kuwait's request for British military aid: on 2 July 1961 *NCNA* commented from Peking on the event with obvious reservations:

British ground, sea and air forces landed in Kuwait on Saturday morning in the name of 'assistance' to Kuwait and *once again effected military occupation* [emphasis added] over Kuwait which Britain recognised as an independent and sovereign country on June nineteenth. Iraqi Premier Ḳasim said at a press conference on June twenty-fifth that Kuwait 'is an inseparable part of Iraq'. During the time of the Turkish Empire Kuwait was part of Iraq's Basrah Province, he said. The Iraqi Government would promulgate a Republican decree appointing present Shaikh of Kuwait as Governor of Kuwait County of Basrah Province.[18]

The Chinese press kept a close watch on the Iraq-Kuwait dispute after attempting to expose the negative Kuwaiti side of the affair. However, throughout the crisis China never directly condemned Shaikh 'Abdullah al-Salim or the ruling of al-Ṣabah family, but Kuwaiti actions were seen in terms of British 'military occupation' of Kuwait. The first week of July 1961 provides a good example: when the Arab League began to mediate in this conflict, the Chinese press presented only the Iraqi version.[19]

The British military response to Kuwait's request received severe condemnation: condemnation of the British government's declaration that it would reinforce its military forces in Kuwait,[20] condemnation of the use of Cyprus as a base of transit for the troops,[21] Lebanese 'public opinion' criticising Britain was mentioned,[22] and an exaggerated allegation was made that the number of British troops in Kuwait had reached 'ten thousand men'.[23]

As a result of a request from Iraq and the UK on behalf of Kuwait, the United Nations Security Council met on 2 August 1961 to discuss the dispute. Though no substantial conclusions emerged from the debates they helped clearly to indicate the positions of the various Security Council members on the dispute. Chinese press coverage gave tacit support to the Iraqi cause by extensively quoting anti-Kuwaiti arguments:

> The United Nations Security Council yesterday [5 July 1961] resumed its discussion of the situation in Kuwait, according to a *Tass* New York report.
>
> Soviet Delegate V. Zorin demanded that the Security Council take vigorous measures to make it binding upon the British government to withdraw its troops from the territory of Kuwait at once. Zorin objected to the Representative of Kuwait — a country entirely occupied by the British troops — taking part

in the work of the Security Council because, he said, with the British authorities controlling the Kuwait Administration, he could not represent a sovereign state, and his participation would not be conducive to an objective consideration of the question before the Council.

Iraqi representative Pachachi said that British troops had now entirely occupied Kuwait and were trying to suppress the national liberation movement in the country. The Iraqi representative spoke at length on the history of the Kuwait people's struggle against the British colonialists. It had been historically proved that Kuwait belonged to Iraq, and its government intended to restore its rights to Kuwait by peaceful means.

The representatives of Britain and Kuwait tried to justify the military occupation of Kuwait by the claims that this act of aggression allegedly thwarted Iraq's 'aggressive designs' on that principality.[24]

The Kuwaiti case at the Security Council was supported by the Representative of the Republic of China (Taiwan), whose arguments obviously reflected the position of the bloc led by the UK, the USA and France. On 14 July 1961 the Iraqi embassy in Peking gave a reception celebrating the third anniversary of the Republic of Iraq's National Day. Leading Chinese personalities representing Party and Government were present. The Iraqi ambassador 'Abd al-Hak Fadil spoke first and, according to *NCNA*:

He strongly condemned the British troops for having occupied Kuwait. . . . 'Kuwait is a part of the Republic of Iraq just as Taiwan is a part of China and Goa is a part of India.'[25]

A significant development in the Kuwaiti-Iraqi dispute took place when, on 20 July 1961, the Arab League agreed to a Moroccan resolution, despite the Iraqi representatives' strong protest. The resolution stipulated that:

1 (a) The Kuwait government undertakes to request the withdrawal of British forces from Kuwait territory as soon as possible.

(b) The Iraq government undertakes not to resort to force to annex Kuwait to Iraq.

(c) [The League] supports any wish expressed by Kuwait for unity or [federal] union with other state members of the Arab League's pact.

> 2 (a) [The League] welcomes the State of Kuwait as a member of the League of Arab states.
>
> (b) [The Arab States] support the application of the State of Kuwait for membership of the United Nations.
>
> 3 The Arab States undertake to offer effective assistance to safeguard the independence of Kuwait on the basis of her request — and the Council empowers the Secretary-General to undertake the necessary measures to carry out this Resolution at the earliest possible moment.[26]

This resolution was only opposed by Iraq, and boosted Kuwait's image as an independent state. Incidentally this was the first opportunity for the Arab League to exercise military power in an inter-Arab dispute. China found itself in a difficult situation, and kept total silence on the decisions. This was because accusations of 'military occupation of Kuwait' were no longer credible, while China's closest ally in the dispute was confronted with a unanimous Arab decision. The Chinese press refrained from mentioning the episode until September 1961, except when on 25 July *NCNA* jubilantly noted from Baghdad that 'three British soldiers of the British occupation forces in Kuwait were captured by the Iraqi army together with a British reconnaissance armoured car in which they were riding.'[27] The *NCNA* followed their trial closely.[28]

As far as Kuwait was concerned, one outcome of this episode was the creation of the Kuwait fund for Arab Economic Development. Given its small size, Kuwait found that its position in the Arab world would be enhanced if it provided economic aid to Arab states in the form of loans and other assistance, such as the building of schools and hospitals. Although at first sight economic, this approach really reflected Kuwait's political positions and, through its oil revenues, gave it an influence in inter-Arab relations which it could obviously not have achieved on the basis of its military capacity.

On 10 September 1961 the first units of the Arab League Peace Keeping Force arrived in Kuwait, and British troops began their gradual withdrawal to Bahrain and surrounding area. This development was noted by the Chinese press. On 14 September Shaikh 'Abdullah al-Salim, after receiving assurances that the rest of the Arab League forces would be stationed at the borders by 20 September, announced his request for the further withdrawal of British forces from Kuwait in a move to assure Kasim that an Arab army was readily available to defend Kuwait's independence. The Chinese understanding of this request was different:

The Ruler of Kuwait, Shaikh Abdullah al-Salim al-Ṣabah yesterday [September 14] officially demanded that Britain withdraw its aggressor troops who have occupied Kuwait since 1 July, according to a report from Kuwait.

This was announced by the Kuwaiti Government in an official communiqué which said that the Shaikh made the request because of the arrival of an Arab force.

In defiance of the protests lodged by the peoples of the Middle East and the world, Britain has continued its military occupation of Kuwait under various pretexts in the past two months and more.

In the middle of August the leader of the Arab League and the ruler of Kuwait asked Britain to withdraw its troops. Iraq, a member state of the Arab League, voiced its opposition to the sending of an Arab force to Kuwait.

The Arab Security Force formed by the United Arab Republic, Saudi Arabia, Morocco, Jordan and Sudan has arrived in Kuwait in the past few days.[29]

Withdrawal of British troops from Kuwait left China with two issues to condemn: the movement of British troops from Kuwait to other parts of the Arabian peninsula and the Gulf, and the 'negative' aspects of Kuwaiti oil policies.

China expressed certain reservations on the movement of British troops which had been stationed in Kuwait:

The last group of British aggressor troops in Kuwait left the country yesterday, 9 October 1961, according to a Middle East News report from Kuwait today.

It was reported earlier that most of the British troops would be transferred to nearby Bahrain, a rear base of the British interventionist troops, and Aden, another British military base on the Arabian Peninsula.

Britain effected its military occupation of the oil-rich Kuwait at the beginning of July, in the name of 'protecting' that country. This aggression has stirred up strong opposition among the Arabs and people in the rest of the world.[30]

The same theme was followed throughout the Gulf, whenever there was a sign of British troop movements. *NCNA*, for example, reported from Baghdad that:

A demonstration was held in the Shaikhdom of Qatar, a British Protectorate in the Arab Gulf, on Saturday, and the demonstrators shouted slogans against imperialism, according to a report from Dubai (Trucial Oman).

The report was carried by *al-Shark* Iraqi newspaper today, 27 February 1962. The people of the Arab Gulf demanded the withdrawal of the British imperialist bases from Kuwait for they regarded the maintenance of the British imperialist forces in Kuwait as the maintenance of colonialism in the entire Arab Gulf, the report said.[31]

Kuwait's relations with China before recognition

On oil policy, Shaikh 'Abdullah al-Salim had considerable achievements to his credit. In 1962 he concluded an agreement with KOC whereby the company relinquished over nine thousand square kilometres – i.e. half its original concessionary area – and turned the area over to the Kuwait National Petroleum Company (KNPC). The KNPC was established in October 1960 as a joint-stock company with the government holding 60 per cent of the shares, while the remaining 40 per cent were owned by the Kuwaiti public; the basic aim of the company was to handle local marketing. Added to this Shaikh Abdullah al-Salim re-introduced democratic forms, which had been suppressed after the 1938 movement, by instituting free elections for the Parliament. The Parliament was invested with legislative powers and played an important role in ratifying, amending or rejecting the Government negotiations with the oil companies.

Kuwait, as a major world oil producer, was at the mercy of the international oil companies, and particularly of the seven which had a virtual international monopoly on world energy resources. The need of the oil producing states for machinery for formal negotiation arose in 1959 when, in February of that year, the oil companies decided

without prior consultation with the governments concerned to cut the price of Middle Eastern oil by 18 cents per barrel; and in spite of the uproar that the companies' action provoked in oil exporting countries, and of the clear signs of a gathering storm in the Middle East, and notwithstanding the Arab warning in the shape of a resolution adopted by the Arab Petroleum Congress [April 1959 under the auspices of the Arab League] calling on oil companies to consult the producing governments before making any price alterations, the companies decided to cut prices again in August 1960 by an average of about 9 cents per barrel.[32]

These unilateral decisions by oil companies prompted Iran, Iraq, Kuwait, Saudi Arabia and Venezuela to meet in Baghdad in September 1960 to lay the foundation of the Organisation of Petroleum Exporting Countries (OPEC) in order to deal with the threat to their depleting commodity. The first decade of OPEC's history was a period of minor achievements by comparison with those of the oil companies; but OPEC became a major international economic force by its very existence.

China's attitude to the oil question remained stereotyped. When <u>Shaikh</u> <u>D</u>jabir al-'Aḥmad, then Minister of Finance and National Economy, granted an interview to a Middle East News correspondent in Kuwait in which he discussed oil production for 1962, *NCNA* quoted the interview with minor adjustments:

> About 80,000,000 tons were produced by the 'Kuwait Oil Company' which is jointly and equally owned by US and British capital (the Kuwait Oil Company was formed by the Gulf Oil Corporation and the Anglo-Iranian Oil Company which were granted a joint concession in December 1934 by the <u>Shaikh</u> of Kuwait).
>
> The US 'Independent Oil Company', since 1948, in its concession in the part of the Neutral Zone belonging to Kuwait, produced about 9,000,000 tons. (The Neutral Zone, a desert land between Saudi Arabia and Kuwait, was separately administered by both Saudi Arabia and Kuwait).
>
> The Japanese Arab Oil Company, which was granted a concession in 1958 and whose contract was based on the exploration of the off-shore oil resources of Kuwait, produced about 1,000,000 tons. The Shell Company which obtained its concession in 1961 was still prospecting, al-Ṣabah said. Kuwait oil deposits are estimated at 898,200,000,000 tons, exceeding known deposits in the capitalist world. Its present rate of production is the highest in the Middle East. The whole Kuwait territory is covered by the four concessions mentioned above and all its oil industry is monopolised by US, British and other foreign capital. 20 per cent of the population in Kuwait are oil workers. The US and British monopolists have made enormous profits by taking advantage of the favourable natural conditions and by exploitation of the workers.[33]

Since independence, Kuwait had sought diplomatic recognition from various nations in order to strengthen its international position in countering Ḳasim's claims and, by June 1962, seventy-one states had extended recognition to Kuwait.[34] In a rash response, Ḳasim severed diplomatic relations with any state which recognised Kuwait. However on 9 February 1963, Ḳasim's regime was overthrown, and he was subsequently executed by the Ba'thists in a military coup. Kuwait consequently reapplied for UN membership and was accepted on 14 May 1963 as an independent state. It is noteworthy that when Kuwait applied for the second time, in November 1961, to be admitted to the UN, the USSR, under Iraqi pressure, used its veto to block Kuwait's membership. China's support for Iraqi claims, and accusations about the British occupation of Kuwait, ceased completely with Ḳasim's death, and commentaries on Kuwait-Iraq relations took a new tone. Kuwait used the opportunity of the coup in Iraq to try to obtain diplomatic recognition from Iraq. Delegations were exchanged, including, notably, an Iraqi delegation on 10 May 1963 which comprised Defence Minister Ṣaliḥ Mahdi 'Amash, Foreign Minister Ṭalib Husain al-Shabik, and Air Force Commander Hardan al-Takriti.[35]

On the second anniversary of Kuwait's independence, Chairman Liu Shao-chi sent <u>Shaikh</u> 'Abdullah al-Salim a message of congratulation which, in contrast with Chou En-lai's of 1961, failed to include a phrase on the 'safeguarding of national independence', but merely stated that:

> On the occasion of the second anniversary of the independence of Kuwait, I have the honour to express congratulations to Your Highness and the people of Kuwait. I wish prosperity to your country and well-being to its people.[36]

Iraq's recognition of Kuwait was finally secured when the Kuwaiti Heir Apparent and Prime Minister, <u>Shaikh</u> Ṣabah al-Salim, visited Iraq on 2 October 1963 and reached an agreement with Prime Minister 'Aḥmad Hasan al-Bakr, whereby Iraq recognised Kuwait's independence within its current boundaries.[37]

Kuwait's foreign policy was low-keyed until 1967. Historically, it is centralised around the al-Ṣabah ruling family, although other forces — neighbouring states, parliament, etc. — had some influence on decision-making. But a pattern has appeared which can be likened to four concentric circles. The inmost, covering matters of the highest priority, concerns the main bordering states of Iraq, Saudi Arabia and Iran. In this area can also be included the interest of sustaining the conservative status quo of the region. The second area of Kuwaiti foreign policy is the Palestinian problem and the complex situation it has created in inter-Arab politics as a result of the Arab-Israeli conflict. This has led Kuwait to be open to ideas of Arab unity, and its oil revenues have to some extent been used politically and economically to this end. The third area is merely auxiliary, and concerns other states' positions on the Palestinian question. Last is the attempt to retain, as far as possible, a balanced neutrality.

Kuwait has used its oil policy to derive the maximum possible international advantage. From 1967 to 1973 its foreign policy objectives were to achieve a more central position in the Arab world. After October 1973 the emergence of Saudi Arabia's power in the Gulf and the Arabian peninsula became noticeable. The upsurge of Saudi conservatism in the area was accompanied by Iran's increased role in the Gulf. Kuwait's foreign policy, after 1974, was heavily influenced by Saudi Arabia, and the repercussions of this influence were seen clearly both in Kuwaiti internal developments and in its regional, Arab and international alliances.

After the Kuwait-Iraq border dispute subsided, and Iraq recognised Kuwaiti sovereignty and independence, the Chinese press turned its reporting to the 'positive' side of the Kuwaiti government's decisions on various issues, and its condemnation of 'capitalist' oil companies' exploitation of Kuwaiti oil was noticeably milder.[38] A remarkable development in this period was the visit to Peking in February 1965 of Shaikh Djabir al-'Ahmad al-Sabah, Minister of Finance, Industry and Commerce. This arose out of Kuwait's attempt to adopt a more neutral foreign policy and its attempt to use trade to this end. For example, in 1964 Western Europe and the USA accounted for 63.3 per cent of Kuwait's total imports.

The Western bloc's positions on the Arab-Israeli conflict hardly favoured the Arab side. To change this, the Kuwaiti government tried to diversify its pattern of trade, and at the end of 1964 decided to encourage trade with the communist bloc. Shaikh Djabir al-Ahmad was entrusted with this responsibility. He visited the USSR in November 1964 and then other states in this bloc. When an invitation was extended by Fang Yi, Chairman of the Commission for Economic Relations with Foreign Countries, he set off for Peking.

Certain questions concerning this visit remain unanswered, particularly since it showed little sign of success. As stated above, China had recognised Kuwait in June 1961; but Kuwait did not reciprocate, most probably because of western influence. Kuwait itself, given its readiness to accept recognition from anywhere in the world, had no objections of its own to extending reciprocal recognition, and it did so with the USSR and the Eastern bloc. Another reason may be that, of all states in the Gulf, and the Arabian Peninsula, only Iraq and Yemen had recognised China, whereas both Saudi Arabia and Iran, the strongest states in the area, were conservative in their attitude towards diplomatic relations with communist bloc states. Finally, recognition of China by Kuwait meant withdrawal of recognition from the Republic of China, since this was a condition made by the PRC. The problem remained unresolved until 1971, and is dealt with later. It was new to Kuwait, which had not faced this dilemma earlier when it had recognised both East and West Germany, as well as North and South Korea, unconditionally. As far as recognition was concerned, Shaikh Djabir's visit was fruitless, from the Chinese viewpoint.

Trade relations, Shaikh Djabir's main concern, were improved, and trade between the two countries doubled.

The delegation arrived in Peking on 11 February 1965 and was met by an impressive group of Chinese representatives. Beside Fang Yi and members of his department, who had extended the invitation, there were Ting Hsi-lin, Vice Chairman of the Commission for Cultural Relations with Foreign Countries; Ḥadj Yūsuf Sha Meng-pi, Vice-President of the Islamic Association of China; the Vice-Ministers of Light Industry and Commerce; and Lin Chao-nan, Deputy Director of the Department of West Asian and North African Affairs of the Foreign Ministry.[39] The day after its arrival the delegation was received by Premier Chou En-lai and Vice Premier Chen Yi,[40] and on 13 February the delegation had a meeting with Chairman Liu Shao-chi.[41] It is certain that no agreement on recognition was reached, but it was agreed that trade relations could be developed. On the day before the delegation returned to Kuwait, 17 February 1965, a joint communiqué stated that:

> On February 12 and 13, the Kuwait delegation held talks with
> the Chinese party headed by Fang Yi, Chairman of the Commission
> for Economic Relations with Foreign Countries of the People's
> Republic of China. The two parties conducted discussions on all
> aspects relating to economic co-operation and development of trade
> relations between the two countries on the basis of equality and
> mutual benefit. In order to realise this co-operation, the head of
> the Kuwait delegation invited China to send a delegation to visit
> Kuwait. The invitation was welcomed by the Chinese side.
>
> The talks between the two parties were held in an atmosphere
> of friendship, full understanding, sincerity and co-operation. The
> implementation of the points discussed during the talks will bring
> enormous benefits to the two friendly governments.[42]

China was keen to develop trade with Kuwait as a basis for the establishment of diplomatic relations, and took up the invitation with speed. On 5 June 1965 its delegation arrived in Kuwait and was received by Shaikh Djabir al-'Ahmad. The delegation was led by Nan Han-chen, member of the Standing Committee of the National People's Congress, Chairman of the China Council for the Promotion of International Trade and Chairman of the Board of Directors of the Bank of China.[43] Besides holding talks with Shaikh Djabir al-'Ahmad on trade relations, the delegation met, on 6 June, the 'Amir of Kuwait, Shaikh 'Abdullah al-Salim, and handed him a letter from Chairman Liu Shao-chi,[44] and on 8 June, Shaikh Sabah al-Salim, Crown Prince and Prime Minister, received the delegation which handed him a letter from Chou En-lai.[45] The Chinese delegation, however, was unable to reach an accord on recognition, or to negotiate any agreement on oil, for Kuwait at this time had no control over the marketing of its oil. The only Kuwaiti oil company was the KNPC and its function was merely to deal with local marketing. Shaikh Djabir al-'Ahmad claimed it was impossible to negotiate an oil deal with the Chinese delegation and confined their mission to exploring 'possibilities of expanding mutual industrial potential'.[46]

China, for its part, sensing that the deadlock on recognition would not be broken, had intentionally sent Nan Han-chen, in his capacity as Member of the Standing Committee of the Chinese National People's Congress, to hold a meeting with his Kuwaiti counterpart. The Kuwaiti parliament could exert pressure on the government given sufficient support among its members. The Chinese delegation was unable to accomplish its aim, primarily because of the Government's unwillingness to withdraw recognition from Nationalist China, which would have entailed the expulsion of its representative in Kuwait. If the Government had been willing to extend recognition to China through the Kuwaiti Parliament, a majority in this body, mostly pro-Government members, would have voted positively on the issue. However, on 10 June when the delegation ended its visit, the joint communiqué listed no meaningful achievements:

> The Chinese delegation and the Kuwaiti delegation. . . held talks.
> The two parties discussed questions on the development of
> relations of friendship and co-operation between the two countries
> in accordance with the interests and desires of the two peoples
> and on the basis of the Five Principles of mutual respect for
> territorial integrity and sovereignty, mutual non-aggression,
> non-interference in each other's internal affairs, equality and
> mutual benefit, and peaceful co-existence.

The two parties also exchanged views on the development of
economic and trade relations between the two countries with a
view to expanding the exchange of commodities between the two
countries. The Chinese delegation expressed the willingness to
purchase chemical fertilisers and other products from Kuwait.
Both parties agreed that a Chinese economic exhibition will be
held in Kuwait. The time for holding the exhibition will be fixed
later on by both parties.[47]

The sale of fertilisers to China was not agreed until 1969, mainly as
a result of pressure on the Kuwaiti government by the oil companies
and their respective states. Thus there was a cooling of relations until
late 1969 and early 1970. The 1965–8 period witnessed no significant
breakthough in Sino-Kuwaiti relations, the main contact taking the
form of exchanges of letters of greetings on government changes in
Kuwait. On 26 November 1965, Shaikh Ṣabah al-Salim succeeded the
previous 'Amir after his death: Chairman Liu Shao-chi greeted the new
'Amir and hinted that hopes of 'friendship between the peoples of
Kuwait and China grow with each passing day'.[48] Chou En-lai's message
of congratulations to Shaikh Djabir al-'Aḥmad on his assumption of
the post of Prime Minister, in December 1965, said:

> May your Excellency and the Government of the State of Kuwait
> achieve continuous successes in the cause of safeguarding national
> independence and carrying out national construction. May the
> relations of friendship between the peoples of China and Kuwait
> develop with each passing day.[49]

Between these two messages, a Kuwaiti delegation, led by Hamid
Yūsuf al-'Issa, Under-Secretary at the Ministry of Finance and Industry,
visited China during 3–10 October 1965.[50] China, for its part, was
extremely careful in selecting the members of delegations to Kuwait.
On 11 June 1966, for example, a Chinese Muslim delegation, headed
by Ḥadj Muḥamad 'Alī Shang Chi, who was also a member of the
National People's Congress, paid a visit to Kuwait.[51] This was obviously
to show sensitivity to Islamic feelings and the role played by the
Kuwaiti Parliament in influencing the government. There were however
no indications that the delegation met any prominent members of the
Kuwaiti Parliament.

As a result of the 11 June 1965 Joint Communiqué, a Chinese trade
exhibition was opened on 17 January 1967, almost two years after the
visit. The hopes for some success in establishing diplomatic relations

were not realised through this exhibition despite the fact that the trade delegation was led by the Chinese Ambassador to Iraq, Chao Chih, who came specially from Iraq,[52] and had an audience with Shaikh Djabir al-'Ahmad, Prime Minister and Crown Prince, before his departure. According to the Ambassador this meeting

> pointed to the long-standing friendship between the two countries
> and expressed his conviction that it would be further developed
> in the common struggle against imperialism, colonialism and
> Zionism. The Kuwait Premier . . . said that Kuwait and China
> shared a common aim in their common struggle against imperialism
> and colonialism and should unite to face their common enemies.[53]

At the opening ceremony on 18 January 1967, which was attended by Shaikh 'Abdullah al-Djabir, Chao Chih gave a eulogy of Mao's Thought, which was a common occurrence at the height of the Cultural Revolution:

> The products of heavy and light industry, agriculture, handicrafts
> and the photos on display at the exhibition gave a general picture
> of the brilliant achievements scored by China in socialist revolution
> and construction under the leadership of Chairman Mao and the
> Chinese Communist Party during the last seventeen years. All
> these achievements are the victories of Mao Tse-tung's Thought.[54]

If nothing significant was achieved in diplomatic relations, this was due partly on China's side to the radicalisation of its foreign policy, which resulted in its giving wider attention to the area, and particularly to developments in Oman and to Fatah. At the same time, Nationalist China tried to strengthen trade relations with Kuwait during the Cultural Revolution, and thereby to disrupt Sino-Kuwaiti trade contacts. From 21-27 February 1968 a group of Nationalist Chinese businessmen held a trade exhibition;[55] at the end of the month, the first Nationalist China oil tanker arrived at al-'Ahmadi port, and the Chinese ambassador gave it considerable publicity.[56] A second trade exhibition was held in Kuwait 20 October–3 November 1968.[57]

Kuwait's desire to improve relations with the communist bloc and thus strengthen its position as a neutral state, as well as to rid itself as much as possible of western political influence, manifested itself in the establishment of diplomatic relations with Albania on 30 June 1968. This may have caused concern to Nationalist China, which conducted a trade drive at the end of the year.

The breakthrough in Sino-Kuwaiti trade relations came the following year when the first shipment of Kuwaiti fertiliser was sent to China after arduous negotiations and despite the opposition of foreign oil companies. The following account of the background of Sino-Kuwaiti contacts was kindly provided to the author by the Kuwait Chemical and Fertiliser Company (KCFC). Although the figures presented in these tables go beyond 1969, they are presented here up to 1973 for the sake of coherence. The following are the official minutes of a number of interviews with responsible members of the KCFC who were directly involved in negotiating these deals.

KCFC was registered during 1964 as a Kuwaiti shares company between PIC [Petrochemicals Industrial Company] 60%, Gulf Oil Company 20% and BP/Bermuda 20%. This company started a Fertiliser Complex in Shauiba comprising an ammonia plant of 400 t/d capacity, a Urea plant of 500 t/d, an Amsul plant of 500 t/d and Sulphuric Acid plant of 375 t/d.

The complex production was as follows:

(1,000 M.T. Year)

	1966	1967	1968	1969	1970
Urea	—	44.5	65.6	135.1	162.2
Amsul	30.9	66.2	73.5	35.2	71.1

During 1968, PIC decided to erect two Ammonia plants of 880 t/d and two Urea plants of 800 t/d. Production was expected to start during 1971.

KCFC, who was charged with marketing the total production of PIC in addition to its own production, had to develop many more markets for its products, expecting a huge production increase. During the period 1970/71 the fertiliser market for Urea and Ammonium Sulphate was very bad. The world's largest buyers were: China, India, Pakistan, Egypt and Indonesia. Almost all the largest buyers of fertiliser, except China, were receiving most of their fertiliser requirements from the large traditional producers in Japan and West Europe, either on soft loans or under various development schemes.

The USA AID [Agency for International Development] was providing several hundred thousand tons of fertiliser products to India, Pakistan, Indonesia and Vietnam almost free of charge. Kuwait was finding it very hard to start business with these large buyers under the prevailing conditions. This was made even more difficult because Kuwait had no AID schemes to most of the fertiliser importing countries. Furthermore, while a very large country like the People's Republic of China was buying freely millions of tons of fertiliser without asking for credit or help, KCFC was not entertaining any business relations with this customer. Unfortunately, at that time Nationalist China had an Embassy in Kuwait, while Communist China was officially not represented in this country. However, Communist China was having a very large trade with Kuwait involving export of all kinds of foodstuff, manufactured goods and building raw materials.

The Kuwaiti authorities had no objection to importing or exporting to mainland China from Kuwait. The only political difficulty was that Communist China refrained from opening an embassy in Kuwait on the grounds that National China (Formosa) was part of mainland China and should not be recognised as an independent state nor be authorised to open an Embassy. Nevertheless, in spite of this political difficulty Kuwait has never stopped having normal relations with Communist China.

KCFC decided to start the first approach with Peking for the sale of fertiliser on the ground that China is already having a normal commercial relationship with Kuwait. First contact was made directly with SINOCHEM/Peking. The difficulties then started with the board of KCFC where the representative of Gulf Oil Company protested against this action and expressed his worries that his Company may not like to see one of the joint ventures in which Gulf has 20 per cent interest trading directly with China. This also might not be acceptable to the Government of USA. BP representative declared that his company would not like to see KCFC trading with China unless it is absolutely vital. PIC representative objected that:

A — KCFC is a Kuwaiti Company.
B — There is nothing in Kuwait to prevent a Kuwaiti company doing business with Communist China.
C — That West European and Japanese fertiliser producers, whose countries have not recognised Communist China, are selling millions of tons of fertilisers to this customer without any restrictions.
D — That KCFC and PIC cannot afford to neglect this market particularly after the start up of the new plants.

The Board of KCFC has finally ruled that KCFC may sell to China up to 60 per cent of its production which represents the shares of

PIC in KCFC. This decision opened the door officially to KCFC to start trading fertiliser with communist China. The following deals were since then concluded with this country:

Year	Place of negotiations	Tonnage concluded M/T	Total Production of KCFC/PIC for this year (round figures)	Percentage of the Chinese deal to total sales
UREA				
1969	Peking	50,000	135,000	37.0
1970	"	75,000	162,000	46.2
1971	"	150,000	182,000	82.4
1972	Kuwait	231,750	514,000	45.1
1973	"	203,000	580,000	35.0
AMMONIUM SULPHATE				
1973	Kuwait	24,000	119,000	20.0

(Interviews were conducted and tables compiled during 1975–6 in Kuwait. The KCFC members prefer their names not to be mentioned, and insisted on the official minutes being published as above).

Several points arise from these negotiations. First, all negotiations and subsequent agreements on trade were reached in Peking *before* Kuwait's recognition of China. Second, the noticeable increase in China's purchases occurred *after* Kuwait extended recognition to China, and the latter's gradual emergence from the upheavals of the Cultural Revolution and its admission to the UN. Third, the decision to sell fertilisers to China encountered opposition from the foreign shareholding companies in the KCFC, reflecting their respective states' desire to 'contain' China; the same foreign companies simultaneously sought to monopolise the Chinese market, which gave them good prices. This gave substance to Chinese allegations that Kuwait's national resources were under the domination of foreign oil companies of the 'capitalist world'. Fourth, there seems to have been a keen desire on the part of the Kuwaiti Government to break into the Chinese market,[58] thus laying the foundation for the eventual establishment of diplomatic relations. This is suggested by the fact that 82.4 per cent of total sales to China occurred only a few months prior to Kuwait's recognition of China. This proportion was reduced by half in the following year, 1972, indicating that China, too, sought Kuwaiti recognition and used trade to obtain it. After recognition, China's purchases from the KCFC were based on its international trade balance rather than on political considerations. Lastly, the value and quantity of Sino-Kuwaiti trade gave it the third place in Kuwait's exports, after Saudi Arabia and India (see Table 8.1). The doubling of Chinese imports yearly between 1971 and 1973 is a further indication of China's use of trade as a political tool, and the same observation can be made of Kuwaiti imports from China over the same period.

1971–5: Kuwait and China establish full diplomatic relations

Before Kuwait's recognition of China, Chinese press commentaries and reports looked at the 'positive' aspects of matters of vital importance to Kuwait. Ranking high in the Chinese order of priority for press treatment was condemnation of oil companies backed by their governments. The *People's Daily*, for example, argued:

> To safeguard their state sovereignty and protect their resources, the ten member-states of the Organisation of Petroleum Exporting Countries (OPEC) which includes Iran, Iraq, Algeria, Libya, Kuwait and Venezuela, have been waging a resolute struggle recently against the oil consortiums of imperialism headed by the United States. These oil-producing countries, which have been the victims of wanton plunder by imperialism for a long time now have united together and taken concerted action to cope jointly with the rapacious and ruthless international exploiters. . . . The demand of OPEC member-states for higher oil posted prices and tax rates reflects the strong desire of the broad masses of people of these countries to get rid of the imperialist plunder and exploitation and is fully justified.[59]

The early months of 1971 witnessed active diplomatic contacts between China, Kuwait and Iran simultaneously. Recognition by these two states had vital implications in the area. Kuwait was willing to extend recognition to China for several reasons. By the end of 1970 it had become evident that China's admission to the UN was imminent, and this meant that China would have an important role to perform in Arab affairs, particularly the Arab-Israeli conflict. In order to normalise relations with Iran, China had to satisfy Iran that it would no longer give military and political aid to the PFLO. It was beyond Kuwait's diplomatic capacity to reach an agreement with China on this, so the issue was left to Iran, and the Shah in particular. For China, recognition by Kuwait meant opening the doors of other Gulf states, in particular Saudi Arabia; this, again, was beyond the diplomatic

Table 8.1 Kuwait imports for 1964–73   جدول رقم ٨/١ واردات دولة الكويت للفترة من عام ١٩٦٤ إلى عام ١٩٧٣

الواردات عن طريق الدول (بالأسعار الجـارية)

IMPORTS BY COUNTRIES (AT CURRENT PRICES)

1973	1972	1971	1970	1969	1968	1967	1966	1965	1964		Selected Countries	اسـم الدولة :
in %	In thousand K.D.								Per-centage	in thousand K.D.		
					Arab Countries الدول العربيـة							
1.6	4,828	4,295	2,904	3,148	2,616	2,765	3,793	1,337	1,451	1.1	1,318	Iraq	العراق
0.7	2,056	2,238	1,978	1,808	2,274	2,528	1,899	1,167	1,156	0.9	1,021	Jordan	الاردن
4.3	13,340	13,545	10,654	9,743	8,173	8,037	6,702	4,121	3,381	2.6	3,048	Lebanon	لبنـان
0.5	1,649	1,631	1,408	1,866	2,921	3,148	1,945	1,459	1,319	1.1	1,236	Syria	سـوريا
0.4	1,205	962	561	706	348	33	203	272	57	—	5	Saudi Arabia	المملكة العربية السعودية
0.1	242	291	204	317	235	192	243	183	164	0.1	143	Arabian Gulf Countries	دول الخليج العربي
0.3	1,028	847	775	982	1,562	2,841	1,280	511	515	0.6	694	Egypt	جمهورية مصر العربية
—	70	117	143	166	77	112	123	77	24	0.1	62	North Africa	دول شمال افريقيا
0.1	372	85	97	107	125	102	49	55	37	0.1	72	Other Arab	دول عربية أخرى
8.0	24,790	24,011	18,724	18,843	18,331	19,758	16,237	9,182	8,104	6.6	7,599	Total	الاجمالـي

				African Countries	الدول الأفريقية								
1.1	3,434	2,909	2,631	1,796	1,796	1,132	1,130	1,005	1,297	0.7	823	Total	الاجمالي
				Asian Countries	الدول الآسيوية								
0.5	1,561	1,215	800	1,815	2,017	1,014	1,020	1,436	855	0.6	709	Ceylon	سيلان
2.6	7,963	7,595	7,384	8,337	11,044	8,811	6,713	4,456	3,960	3.3	3,822	India	الهند
1.5	4,504	3,754	4,047	3,795	2,843	3,600	3,919	4,349	4,320	3.6	4,063	Iran	ايران
17.9	55,542	41,967	32,789	33,946	33,782	27,894	26,488	17,907	12,773	9.9	11,362	Japan	اليابان
1.4	4,448	4,024	3,181	3,482	2,500	3,546	1,970	3,085	2,092	1.6	1,879	Pakistan	باكستان
3.5	10,778	8,456	7,629	7,269	8,920	8,323	6,608	5,439	4,358	1.8	2,095	People's Rep. of China	جمهورية الصين الشعبية
1.6	4,923	4,335	3,872	4,729	3,903	3,801	3,119	2,490	1,708	1.5	1,679	Hong Kong	هونج كونج
6.0	18,666	10,980	7,460	5,451	4,025	3,890	2,434	1,566	2,138	1.0	1,164	Other Asian Countries	دول آسيوية أخرى
35.0	108,385	82,326	67,162	68,824	69,034	60,879	52,271	40,728	32,204	23.3	26,773	Total	الاجمالي
				European Countries	الدول الأوروبية								
30.0	93,175	84,988	80,655	78,086	82,635	74,663	72,391	60,945	51,613	41.1	47,331	European Common Market	دول السوق الاوروبية المشتركة
4.1	12,538	12,401	10,512	8,702	8,692	8,718	8,056	6,730	5,067	4.2	4,772	Other Western Europe Countries	دول أخرى بغرب أوروبا
4.1	12,972	9,636	11,219	10,419	10,120	9,467	9,952	7,920	5,823	3.7	4,265	E. European Countries	الدول الأوروبية الشرقية
38.2	118,685	107,025	102,386	97,279	101,447	92,848	90,399	75,595	62,503	49.0	56,368	Total	الاجمالي

Table 8.1 continued   تابع جدول ٨/١

1973 % in %	1972	1971	1970	1969	1968	1967	1966	1965	1964 Percentage	1964 In thousand K.D.	Selected Countries اسم الدولة
			بالألف دينار كويتي in thousand K.D.						النسبه المئوية Per-centage	بالألف دينار كويتي In thousand K.D.	
				American Countries	الدول الأمريكية						
14.1	43,783	34,328	33,622	29,595	34,277	37,334	45,897	34,713	27,518	18.0	20,769	United States of America الولايات المتحدة الأمريكية
0.8	2,604	3,869	1,087	1,402	1,458	1,674	703	797	268	0.3	314	Other American دول امريكية أخرى
14.9	46,387	38,197	34,709	30,997	35,735	39,008	46,600	35,510	27,786	18.3	21,083	Total الاجمالي
				Oceanic Countries	الدول المحيطيّة						
2.7	8,613	7,466	6,590	5,353	4,234	4,449	5,091	3,242	2,805	2.1	2,434	Total الاجمالي
0.1	288	243	105	175	291	251	165	20	—	—	—	Other أخرى
100.0	310,582	262,177	232,307	223,267	230,778	218,325	211,893	165,282	134,699	100.0	115,080	Grand Total الاجمالي الكلّي

المصدر : مكتب الاحصاء المركزي ــ جهاز التخطيط ــ الكتاب السنوي للاحصاء بدولة الكويت ، الكويت عام ١٩٧٤ ، ص ــ ١٩٩

Source: Central Statistical Office, Planning Board, *Statistical Yearbook of Kuwait*, Kuwait, 1974, p.199.

capacity of Kuwait. The Gulf area was a potential market for Chinese products, and development of trade was one of the justifications that the Kuwaiti government gave for establishing relations. This was not very convincing, for Sino-Kuwaiti trade declined *after* recognition, as evidenced by the downturn in China's fertiliser imports. By 1970, Kuwait was clearly following a more neutral foreign policy: Saudi Arabia's influence was not noticeable before 1973, while both Kuwait and Iran shared a common interest in the recognition of China. The period coincided with China's emergence from the Cultural Revolution, when Chinese foreign policy was once again to achieve recognition from as many states as possible. It is also the case that Chinese propaganda attacks against a state are terminated when relations are normalised with it; the propaganda thereafter concentrates on the 'positive' achievements of the regime in power, regardless of the implications for local anti-government forces.

The Kuwaiti government had taken certain steps to justify publicly the establishment of diplomatic relations with China. Prior to the announcement of recognition, the Kuwaiti Government invited the Chinese Ambassador to Iraq, who arrived on 8 March and stayed until 22 March 1971, after recognition was secured.[60] His lengthy stay suggests that Kuwait still hoped to obtain an agreement with China whereby both the People's Republic of China and the Republic of China would maintain diplomatic relations with Kuwait. But the PRC stuck to its stated condition of recognition of its government as the 'sole legal Government of China', and the Kuwaiti Government had no option but to yield. Ambassador Kung Ta-fei's negotiations were carried on with Kuwait's Foreign Minister, <u>Shaikh</u> Ṣabaḥ al-'Aḥmad, and the Under-Secretary Rashīd al-Rashīd, who then arranged a meeting on 15 March for the Ambassador with the Crown Prince and the Prime Minister[61] to reach final agreement. The official move to recognise China began on 2 March 1971, when Rashīd al-Rashīd informed a Press conference at the Foreign Ministry of the likelihood of the establishment of diplomatic relations with China.[62] The Kuwaiti press, at Government instigation, began to point out the advantages of such a move. The pro-Government, conservative newspaper *al Ra'i al-'Ām*, in an editorial of 14 March 1971, argued the case thus:

Why doesn't Kuwait recognise People's China? Is it the fear of communism? Then we should not have recognised the USSR or other communist states! Or are we following the USA? If this is the case, which we think unlikely, then the USA does not deserve special treatment. . . . But it needs our enmity only. It is the contrary: China supports our causes, while the USA is against us, for it supports our enemy Israel and supplies it with arms, finance and men. We recognise the USSR which supports the 'political solution' while China supports totally our right in Palestine and has continuously supplied the Palestinian guerrillas with arms, expertise and moral and political support . . . . For those who do not know, we state that the only foreign state that supplied arms to the guerrillas during Black September was China, in addition to Algeria . . . . Regardless of all this, Kuwait cannot ignore a state which constitutes one third of the world's population just because this state is a communist one, or because an island called Formosa has taken this title.

To ignore the existence of China is a short-sighted diplomatic approach.[63]

On 22 March a joint communiqué was issued in Kuwait, stating that:

The Government of the People's Republic of China and the Government of the State of Kuwait, in accordance with the principle of developing the common interests of the two countries and the desire to promote relations between the two countries in all fields,

in view of the noble stand of the People's Republic of China in supporting the Arab struggle against imperialism and Zionism,

in view of the stand of the Government of the State of Kuwait in recognising the Government of the People's Republic of China as the sole legal government of China,

have decided to establish diplomatic relations at the ambassadorial level and exchange ambassadors within the shortest possible period.[64]

Three days later, 'Abd al-'Aziz Ḥusain, Kuwaiti Minister of State, declared that

official recognition of the PRC and the exchange of ambassadors is only an added element to the 'reality' of the existing relationship between the two states. For our trade relations are immense, and we have always voted for the PRC's rightful place at the UN. Moreover, His Highness the Crown Prince had visited China many years ago at the invitation of the Chinese government.[65]

The day agreement on recognition was reached, 22 March 1971, the *People's Daily* gave a glowing account of the 'struggle of OPEC' member-states against western oil companies[66] and gave a brief, similar, account of Qatar and Abu Dhabi.[67] On the establishment of diplomatic relations with Kuwait, the *People's Daily* paid tribute in an editorial to two aspects of Kuwaiti political development: it clearly differentiated between the Kuwaiti people and the Government and emphasised the 'positive' aspects of the Kuwaiti Government's decisions:

> The establishment of diplomatic relations between China and Kuwait fully conforms to the fundamental interests and common aspirations of the people of the two countries who were oppressed, trampled underfoot and looted by imperialism in the past and face the same task of opposing imperialism today. Similar experience and common struggle have linked our two people together. The Kuwaiti people are courageous and industrious people. In order to oppose the imperialist and colonialist rule, the Kuwaiti people had carried out a protracted struggle. . .
> To safeguard their state sovereignty and national resources, the Kuwaiti government and people, together with other petroleum exporting countries, carried out recently a powerful struggle against the imperialist oil monopolist groups headed by the United States. . .[68]

Steps were taken to open embassies in Kuwait and Peking, and the first Chinese ambassador to Kuwait, Sun Sheng-fei, presented his credentials on 24 August 1971.[69] Kuwait took an active part in supporting China's admission to the UN, and it opposed the American resolution for representation of 'two Chinas' in the international body.[70] When China was admitted to the UN, <u>Shaikh</u> <u>D</u>jabir al-'Aḥmad, Heir Apparent and Prime Minister, sent Chou En-lai a message welcoming the event on 28 October 1971.

Thus China was the last communist state to be recognised by Kuwait. The new relationship brought little by way of initial diplomatic gain in the rest of the Gulf or Saudi Arabia. On 3 December 1971, for example, the President of the newly-independent United Arab Emirates, <u>Shaikh</u> Zayid bin Ṣulṭan, sent the customary diplomatic note to Chou En-lai on the founding of the UAE, as Kuwait had done in 1961 to both the PRC and the Republic of China. China's recognition of the UAE came on 8 December 1971[71] in a letter from Chou En-lai to <u>Shaikh</u> Zayid. But, as Kuwait in 1961, the UAE did not reciprocate; the reason was Saudi Arabian pressure, for the UAE, unlike Kuwait in 1961, had every justification to recognise China. (Saudi Arabia was the only Arab state which voted against admitting the PRC to the UN). The delay in reciprocal recognition by the UAE was seen with dismay in the Chinese press. The *People's Daily* commentary came a week later, and showed implicit disappointment at the absence of developments:

> In 1820 Britain occupied the area which is known today as the United Arab Emirates and made the Emirates British 'protectorates'. *The colonialists' oppression and exploitation of the Emirs stimulated the people of these countries to resist* [emphasis added]. On 2 December 1971, the Emirates — 'Abū Dhabi, Dubai, Sharjah, 'Ajman Um al-Qaiwain and Fujairah — declared the founding of the United Arab Emirates after the exclusive treaties which they signed with Britain had expired.
>
> On December 3, the President of the United Arab Emirates, Zayid bin Ṣulṭan, telegrammed Premier Chou En-lai on the founding of the United Arab Emirates; on December 8 we telegrammed Zayid bin Ṣulṭan to declare China's recognition of the United Arab Emirates and expressed our congratulations. The Arab League and the United Nations had already decided to accept the United Arab Emirates as their member state.[72]

China and Iran

Before considering further Sino-Kuwaiti relations, it is necessary to examine Sino-Iranian relations, which are essential to an understanding of China's relations in the Arabian Gulf as a whole, and particularly in Oman. Sino-Iranian relations can be divided into three phases. The first extends from the 1950s to the early stages of the Cultural Revolution: during this period China gave consistent support to the Tudeh Communist Party and other nationalist forces in Iran. During the second phase China supported only opposition splinter-groups which were purely anti-Soviet and supported Chinese international policies. In both these phases China strongly opposed the Shah's regime. The third phase is notable for the total reversal of China's priorities and its support of the Shah and his regime.

The anti-Shah period

For almost two decades Sino-Iranian relations revolved around China's support for opposition Iranian organisations, the Tudeh party in particular, condemnation of the Iranian government's oppressive measures inside and outside Iran, and vehement attacks on Iran's regional and international alliances, mainly its alliance with the USA. Throughout this period Iran was a strong supporter of the Republic of China and had trade relations with it.

Up to the mid-'60s China's support concentrated on the Tudeh Communist Party, which itself was closely aligned with the USSR. When the PRC was proclaimed in October 1949, the Tudeh party was banned, because of an attempt to assassinate the Shah, and all communist movements in Iran went underground. But unofficially the Tudeh continued to operate through Front organisations and in other ways. Tudeh's support for China came about during the brief rule of Premier Mossadegh, when Iran went through a liberal phase. While critical political developments were going on, the Tudeh underground party, in mid-August 1953, persuaded Prime Minister Mossadegh to pursue more radical policies and

> the party's Central Committee, in a series of communications to the Prime Minister, appealed for the creation of an anti-imperialist front and demanded legalisation of the Tudeh party, a release of all political prisoners, an end of martial law in the southern oil fields, the expulsion of the US military mission to Iran, the rejection of foreign military aid and cancellation of the 1947 Iran-US agreement, nationalisation of the American-owned Bahrain oil fields, and recognition of the People's Republic of China.[73]

On Iran's regional and international relations, the Chinese press concentrated its heaviest attacks on the Central Treaty Organisation (CENTO) which had been created under US influence in August 1959 and included Turkey, Iran, Pakistan and Britain, following the disintegration of the Baghdad Pact. Iran's neighbour, the USSR, feared that the USA might use Iranian territory to station nuclear weapons, thanks to Iran's membership of CENTO. China, for its part, considered this move with its military implications as a serious threat to the leading socialist state.

On 9 June 1960, Peking hosted the 11th session of the General Council of the World Federation of Trade Unions (WFTU) during which a declaration was adopted on 'the executions and arrests of Iranian workers and patriots':

> Since 1959 there has been a reign of terror in Iran.
>
> The large-scale strike of 30,000 brickworkers in Teheran last summer and powerful student demonstrations in the Iranian

capital last January were bloodily put down by the military armed forces and American imperialism.

On 4 May 1960, the Iranian government ordered the execution in Tabriz, provincial capital of Azerbaijan, of five Iranian patriots. . . sentences ranging from ten years' imprisonment to forced labour for life were passed on seventeen patriots and workers including one woman. They were condemned by a military tribunal which met behind closed doors in a hasty session which completely disregarded the principles of judicial procedure.

Frightened by the popular demonstrations in Turkey, the Iranian government ordered a further wave of arrests of Iranian patriots of whom four. . . have just been condemned to death.

The General Council of the World Federation of Trade Unions expresses its deep solidarity with the workers and the Iranian people, and protests vigorously against the repressive measures of the government of that country; it demands that the executions of the condemned be not carried out, that an end be put to the reign of terror and the imprisoned patriots set free.

At the same time it calls upon all the trade union organisations and upon workers of every opinion and affiliation to strengthen their support of the workers and people of Iran in their legitimate struggle.[74]

Until the Cultural Revolution, the Chinese press constantly and strongly attacked Iran's international and regional alliances, and noted the 'negative' side of the Shah's internal political, economic and repressive military measures. On 17 May 1961, for example, *NCNA* reported that:

the Shah of Iran, Mohammed Reza Pahlevi, left Teheran today in his personal aircraft on a seven-day state visit to Norway, according to a Teheran report. The route the Shah took to the airport today was heavily guarded by troops and police to prevent any demonstration against him . . . . On the eve of the Shah's departure, many arrests were made in Teheran by the Iranian authorities in the name of 'anti-corruption'.[75]

The Chinese press continuously reported, until 1966, on Iran's 'deteriorating economic predicament'[76] and throughout these years supported the Tudeh Party's political activities.[77]

Pro-Chinese splinter groups in the Opposition

By 1967 China was deeply involved in the Cultural Revolution and its

218

foreign policy was in the process of radicalisation, with consequent intensification of anti-Soviet policy. Iran's young intellectuals and political activists within and outside Iran, many of whom were associated with the National Front coalition of ten years earlier, sought to study other political experiences, such as those of Algeria, Cuba, Vietnam and China. The pro-China tendency became evident when splinter groups emerged, even within the ranks of the Tudeh party, and Sino-Soviet polemics started among Iranians. The pro-Chinese elements held in the words of two commentators:

> the view that Iranian society is in essence no different from that
> of China when Mao Tse-tung was engaged in revolutionary war,
> and thus conclude that Mao's views must be exactly applied to
> Iran: 1) people's war in the countryside, 2) alliance with national
> bourgeoisie, 3) establishment of a national democratic government
> under the leadership of the proletariat. [78]

Tudeh, on the other hand, advocated a strong pro-Soviet line and strongly condemned all Iranian splinter groups that took a pro-Chinese position. The General Secretary of the Tudeh party, Radha Radmaiyshi, addressing the international communist parties meeting in Moscow in June 1969 strongly condemned China's, and in particular Mao Tse-tung's, 'adventurist' and 'chauvinist' internal and external policies. He condemned the policies of the CCP led by Mao and denounced the Iranian pro-China splinter groups. [79] By contrast, the Chinese press paid considerable attention to the Iranian splinter groups: on the 21st anniversary of the foundation of the PRC in 1970, for example, the *NCNA* reported a message from 'Iranian revolutionaries' without stating which group it came from. [80]

The Pro-Shah period and the establishment of diplomatic relations

China's relations with Iran are an excellent illustration of the dramatic changes of priorities in Chinese foreign policy since the 1960s. As we have seen, the Chinese changed their support from one opposition group to another in Iran according to both China's and these groups' positions on the Soviet Union. After the Cultural Revolution, the Chinese took their position to its logical conclusion and chose to support the Shah's regime because of its anti-Soviet stand. This decision resulted in the total abandonment of one of the previously most revered principles in Chinese foreign policy, namely, support for 'people's war'. Concretely this meant the withdrawal of military and political aid from the PFLO and all other forces which opposed ruling regimes in the Arabian Gulf. This dramatic change was clearly to be seen in the Chinese press, which ceased publishing any critical reports on internal developments in these states. We will here deal with the period when diplomatic relations were established and the two following years, which are relevant to our study, 1971–3.

Iran's interest in establishing diplomatic relations with China emerged in December 1970, when it was reported by *Dawn* that the

> Iranian government has set in motion a detailed study of long-term
> advantages which Iran might expect from recognising Peking, a
> reliable source disclosed today. . . . The report was ordered 'at
> the highest level', the source said, but there was for the moment
> no intention to break with Nationalist China. . . . Observers
> recalled that Iran abstained in the recent United Nations vote
> on the China admission question, rather than vote against us as
> in past years. Iran's imports from Taiwan are at present six and
> a half times bigger than its inports from China, but exports to
> China exceed exports to Taiwan.[81]

Before Iran's formal recognition of China, it was clear that the two sides wanted to achieve this goal, but failed to reach a decision until August 1971, most probably because of Iran's demand for China to reduce, and ultimately terminate, all aid to PFLO. The interests they shared were evident. First, China shares a long border with the USSR, and in the eventuality of a military conflict with the USSR, it could, under suitable circumstances, use Iran's neutrality, if not its aid. Though there is no known military pact binding the two states against a common enemy, such as the USSR, both are watchful and fearful of its military strength. Second, by 1971 Iran had asserted itself as indisputably the dominant military power in the Gulf, and was already beginning to expand its naval power in the Indian Ocean, where the USSR was an obvious major contender for control. Iran was very concerned with 'stability' in the Gulf, particularly since the UAE at that time had not yet proved itself as a stabilising factor, and the guerrillas in Oman appeared to be successful, thus presenting a threat in Iran's view. China's support to the PFLO was vital to its continuing success. It was therefore part of Iran's strategy to neutralise this support, and if possible put an end to it. China's tacit agreement to Iranian domination of the area was most obvious when Iranian troops occupied the 'Abū Musa and two Tumbs islands, on 30 November 1971, the last day of formal British protection in the Gulf. The Chinese press remained totally silent, despite the fact that this action was a blatant conquest

220

of foreign territory. Similarly, later on, China remained silent when Iranian troops became involved in Sulṭan Ḳabūs's efforts to defeat the PFLO in Dhofar, where the Chinese press had previously continuously advocated the 'people's war' waged against the ruler. Third, the Gulf region is the main oil supplier to the western world. The oil-producing states in the Gulf, and their revenues, as the Chinese press noted so often, had historically been looted, exploited, and the inhabitants of the region oppressed, by western monopoly oil companies which in turn represented the interests of their respective governments. Fourth, it is imperative to note that the Shah's regime was most certainly allied and to a large extent heavily influenced by the USA. For at the time of Sino-Soviet 'ping-pong' diplomacy and eventual agreement between the two, Iran was given American consent to court China. For all these states shared many common and mutual interests, e.g. anti-USSR, strategic importance of 'securing' oil through the Gulf etc.

The identity of Sino-Iranian interests, which culminated in the establishment of diplomatic relations in August 1971, was shown by two major visits within a short period of time. Both these visits took place before recognition, and Pakistan played a mediating role between the two states. On 14 April 1971, Her Royal Highness Princess Ashraf Pahlavi arrived in Peking 'at the invitation of the Chinese government'. She was met by Li Hsien-nien, Kuo Mo-jo and a group of prominent Chinese personalities.[82] That same day the delegation met Chou En-lai[83] and that evening a banquet was held in its honour. There the reasons that diplomatic relations did not exist between the two states were given a discreet interpretation by Chou:

> Her Royal Highness Princess Ashraf Pahlavi is a friend whom we
> know well. We met each other in April 1965 during the celebrations
> of the tenth anniversary of the Bandung Conference in Indonesia
> . . . . In modern times, particularly since the Second World War,
> there have been fewer contacts between our two countries as a
> result of imperialist obstructions and sabotage. However, the
> Chinese people have always followed with interest and attention
> the Iranian people's efforts in their struggle against foreign
> aggression and for national construction. In order to safeguard
> state sovereignty and protect their national resources, Iran,
> together with other members of the Organisation of Petroleum
> Exporting Countries, have recently waged effective struggles
> against the western imperialist oil monopoly consortiums and
> won victory. We express support to your just struggle and
> sincere congratulations on your victory.[84]

Her Royal Highness's speech was cautiously written and, despite her disclaimer, her statement had political implications affecting recognition and China's curtailment of her activities in the Gulf region:

> I come to China, Mr Prime Minister, not at the head of an official
> delegation, but on a voyage of personal discovery. My remarks
> are therefore brief and should be regarded as non-political.
>
> But for the benefit of those who invariably attribute political
> innuendoes to my moves, let me say this: my brother and sovereign,
> the Shahanshah of Iran, has always maintained that in this world
> of boundless diversity, co-existence and co-operation based on
> principles of mutual respect and reciprocal goodwill, between
> countries with differing socio-political systems is perfectly
> possible. I believe my presence here amongst you bears testimony
> to the validity of this dictum.[85]

The delegation left on 19 April 1971.[86] It is unlikely that negotiations on recognition were concluded then, but the basic principles were probably set out. For ten days later, on 30 April 1971, Princess Fatamah Pahlavi arrived in Peking at the head of a delegation which included the wife of the Iranian Prime Minister and Madame Rahim Khan, wife of the Commander-in-Chief of the Pakistan Air Force.[87] The delegation was received with as much ceremony as the previous one. The inclusion of Madame Khan was an indication of the role played by Pakistan, which had amicable relations with both states. The most significant achievement of this delegation, before its departure on 13 May 1971,[88] was that China and Iran finally agreed on the issue of recognition. The first step was taken when Iran and Albania established diplomatic relations on 25 May 1971.[89] And finally, on 17 August 1971, the Chinese and Iranian ambassadors in Pakistan signed the agreement on the establishment of diplomatic relations. The communiqué issued in Islamabad stated that:

> The Government of the People's Republic of China firmly supports
> the Imperial Government of Iran in its just struggle to safeguard
> national independence and state sovereignty and protect its national
> resources.
>
> The Imperial Government of Iran recognises the Government
> of the People's Republic of China as the sole legal government of
> China.[90]

On two consecutive days the *People's Daily* carried editorials marking the occasion. The first, on 18 August, dealt in a flattering and distorted way with historical developments in Iran. For example, an account of the role of Islam (which was in fact introduced after military conquest) made no mention of the Arabs; the article glorified Nadir Shah, who is well known for having expelled the Afghans from Persia and recovered provinces which had been taken from Persia by the Ottomans and the Russians in 1736. In brief, the account given by the Chinese press was sheer propaganda, masquerading as history, to justify contemporary political ends.

The second article focused on two themes: the first praised the regime's accomplishments and linked the 'two peoples' aspirations'; the second, unlike previous Chinese statements on such occasions, took a hard line on the question of Taiwan and the 'two Chinas' issue. The latter was probably defended by the Iranians during the period of negotiations and the Chinese still felt the need to press their viewpoint.

From the time of recognition onwards, China's support for the PFLO showed that China had yielded to Iranian demands: it gradually diminished and was soon terminated. As noted earlier, the Chinese first asked the PFLO leaders to confine their strategy of liberation to Oman alone, and when the response was not encouraging, the Chinese put an end to their relationship with the PFLO. Thus the PFLO lost the only strong non-Arab supporter for its cause.

The following two years saw the growth of Sino-Iranian relations at governmental level: the Empress of Iran paid a visit to China in September 1972,[91] when she was received with great jubilation, and her reception matched that given to Kim il Sing of North Korea, China's closest ally. Trade delegations[92] were exchanged with greater frequency than with any other state in the area. In June 1973 a fertiliser contract was discussed when a Chinese chemical engineering delegation paid a visit to Teheran.[93] This visit was reciprocated on 28 September[94] by the Iranian Chairman of the Board and General Managing Director of the National Iranian Oil Company. A high point in Sino-Iranian relations came when the Chinese Foreign Minister, Chi Peng-fei, paid a visit to Iran on 14 June 1973. At the airport, Chi issued a written statement declaring that:

> Our common lot and common tasks have bound us closely
> together. I am confident that, through my present visit to your
> country, the mutual understanding and friendship between the
> Chinese and Iranian peoples will be enhanced and the friendly
> relations and co-operation between our two countries further
> developed.[95]

Chi went further to state precisely the aims of his visit in the course of a banquet tendered him by his Iranian counterpart:

Iran is an important country in the Persian Gulf and you have every reason to feel uneasy at this situation. We have consistently held that the affairs of a given country must be managed by the country itself, and the affairs of a given region must be managed by the countries and peoples of that region, and world affairs must be jointly managed by all countries. Iran and some other Persian Gulf countries hold that the affairs of this region should be jointly managed by the Persian Gulf countries and brook no outside interference. This is a just position, and we express our firm support for it.[96]

What is particularly significant in this speech is that China gave every possible justification and support for Iran's military role in what the Chinese press referred to as the Persian Gulf (when the Chinese press commentaries are aimed at Arab states in the Gulf it utilises the term 'Arabian Gulf'). On the day of his departure, 17 June 1973, Chi gave unequivocal support to Iran's military actions in the Arabian Gulf when he stated that the Shah 'has the right to reinforce Iranian military potential to fight subversive activities in the oil-producing countries of the Gulf'.[97]

China tries to use Kuwait as a stepping stone in its relations with the Gulf

Once diplomatic relations were established with Kuwait, China hoped to improve its position in the area by opening a trade exhibition in Kuwait. Through this means, and others more direct, Chinese products would flow to Saudi Arabia and the rest of the Gulf.[98] China sought, unsuccessfully, to secure Kuwaiti mediation in its effort to obtain diplomatic recognition from Saudi Arabia and the other Gulf states. It was clear to China that Saudi Arabia was the key to recognition from the other states in the region because of its dominant position. Kuwait was unable to persuade the Saudis; but China continued pressing the Kuwaitis to use their good offices to bring about Saudi recognition.

One of the largest Parliamentary delegations to visit China arrived in Peking from Kuwait on 14 July 1972 at the invitation of the Standing Committee of the National People's Congress.[99] The delegation was led by Yūsuf Khalid al-Mukhalid, Vice-Speaker of the National Assembly, and included five other members: Rashīd 'Awad al-Djuisri, Salim Khalid al-Marzuk, Samī 'Ahmad al-Munayis, 'Abd al-Karim Hilal al-Djahadlī, and 'Abd al-Muṭalib al-Kazmī. China's cordiality towards

224

the Parliamentary section of the Kuwaiti regime was certainly aimed at gaining further support in its drive to persuade Kuwait to assist its diplomatic manoeuvres in the area. The delegation was granted a very friendly reception by the Chinese authorities, who arranged a significant meeting with Chou En-lai on 15 July 1972.[100] In the course of the discussions Chou made a number of points concerning Kuwait and Arab conditions.[101] He first pointed out that China had achieved self-sufficiency in oil production and used this production 'frugally', therefore China had no need to import foreign oil. Second, he re-iterated China's support for the Palestinian Resistance Movement and the delegation responded with its gratitude and admiration for China's position. Chou then went on to attack the great powers' hegemonistic approach in the Middle East and singled out the USSR's recognition of Israel for criticism, reminding his audience that China had always refused to recognise that state. Some of the members of the delegation expressed support for China's anti-Soviet line. Fourth, he was cautious in discussing the clashes which were then taking place in Lebanon: instead of stating China's position on the crisis, he asked the delegation's opinion on the situation, and all its members took a pro-Palestinian stand. Lastly he raised the question of the large numbers of Palestinians in Kuwait, and pointed out that it constituted a burden on the state; although he was not specific concerning the implications of this, he talked about the need for Kuwait to establish an industrialisation programme to combat unemployment. The delegation returned home from Shanghai on 18 July 1972 and made two points in its report to the National Assembly. First, it pointed out that 'the discussions with Chinese authorities, especially Chou En-lai, were highly fruitful, and the delegation noted the complete Chinese support to Arab causes, and in particular the Palestinian one'. Second, the members hoped that relations 'between the two parliamentary bodies would develop and hoped that a Chinese parliamentary delegation visits Kuwait'.[102]

At that time relations between the Kuwaiti executive and China were not deeply rooted and saw no noticeable progress. On 2 December 1972, Kuwait's Commerce and Industry Minister, Khalid al'-Adasānī, arrived in Peking[103] for discussions on furthering trade relations. On 5 December his delegation had an audience with Chou En-lai.[104] The three-day interval between the delegation's arrival and this meeting indicates a certain Chinese hesitancy about joint Sino-Kuwaiti economic co-operation. This was mostly due to the terms offered by the Kuwaiti minister, which were contrary to China's principles for aid to the developing countries. China was further disappointed at Kuwait's inability to further its diplomatic thrust in the Gulf and with Saudi

Arabia. Chou made the following main points (see Appendix 4 for the full minutes): first he mentioned Saudi Arabia's policy of non-recognition of China and his hope that this would be resolved in due course. Second, he explicitly singled out the year 1955 as that when Sino-Kuwaiti trade was established, although there is no evidence to prove this.[105] Third, he said that al-'Adasāni's formula for Sino-Kuwaiti industrial co-operation reflected Kuwait's unawareness of Chinese principles of foreign aid. Fourth, Chou emphasised China's adherence to 'self-reliance' in building its industry; it was therefore unwilling to rely on Kuwait alone for its imports of chemical fertilisers. Finally, al-'Adasāni's complaint about the uneven balance of trade between the two states was not reciprocated by any promises to attempt to close the gap. When the Kuwaiti trade delegation returned home on 9 December 1972[106] Sino-Kuwaiti trade relations, basically political in nature, had made no noticeable progress.

The October 1973 War and China's attitude towards Arab oil policy

The October War and the oil embargo which accompanied it gave a further opportunity to the Chinese to manifest their support for the Arab position. Although there had been much talk of using the 'oil weapon' in the struggle with Israel, it was only in 1973 that the oil producers were finally in a position to employ it without heavy risks to their income; the war also conveniently broke out at a time when OPEC was taking a firm stand with the oil companies and, at last, asserting control over prices and extraction of their valuable resource.

Although China supported the Arabs in the embargo, this had little practical effect. China's position on the international oil market is difficult to establish since it was not then a major oil exporter and only supplied oil to other countries for political purposes or in exchange for technology. The latter exchanges took place mainly with Japan. Evaluation of China's potential as an oil exporter is hampered by the relative lack of figures on production and internal consumption. Oil exports for political reasons were most likely to be to bordering states, in South-east Asia and Japan. Finally, if China were to become a significant oil exporter, it would need to consider membership of OPEC, which would give an added dimension to its anti-superpower policies, since all OPEC members belong to the Third World, by Chinese definition.

Throughout the 1973 crisis the Chinese press expressed jubilation at Arab actions. Three weeks before the Arab boycott of oil to the USA and Holland and the use of the 'oil weapon' for political ends, Chiu Pei-chiang argued that the 'scramble for energy and resources' had several dimensions, but he did not foresee that Arab oil producers might take united action against the USA; thus his main emphasis was on a different aspect:

There is growing discussion about the danger of the United States finding its oil resources depleted. To ease the shortage, the US Government decided to import oil, chiefly from the Middle East. In 1972 US oil imports accounted for 27 per cent of its consumption, and the figure will go up to 33 per cent in 1973.

The energy problem which faces Japan and West European countries, however, is different from the one the United States has to tackle. Oil-poor, these countries have been depending on imported oil and natural gas from the very beginning . . . . It must be added that a considerable amount of these imports are procured through the distributing network of US oil firms. This is especially so in the case of Japan.[107]

When war broke out on 6 October 1973, the Chinese press was sceptical that the Arab oil producers would implement an oil boycott,[108] and when the boycott was decided on 17 October it hailed the occasion, and gave considerable attention to Saudi Arabia's role[109] — unlike its attitude in previous comments.

The most thorough discussion on the whole crisis was put forward by a certain Tschen Shen-chen two years later.[110] His article discussed the whole oil crisis at great length and more lucidly than is usual in China. Though the arguments are cogently presented, they are sometimes self-contradictory. Asking rhetorically how the oil crisis of October 1973 came about, Tschen gave the following analysis, tracing oil history from before the First World War and indicating Britain's major role:

The Middle East is the treasure holder of world oil. Nearly all countries in this area have been proved to own oil. Ranging about 1,200 miles in length and 500 miles in width, this oil reserve region has a total reserve of over 61 billion tons of oil which accounts for two thirds of total certified deposits within the capitalist world . . . . The Mid-East oil is not only the prime source of profiteer undertakings of the imperialist, it also forms the main source of

> motivation for warring machines . . . . It cannot be forgotten,
> further, that the Mid-East area joins the continents of Europe,
> Asia and Africa, its position has vital military strategic meaning.[111]

Throughout his historical analysis of the oil concessions, the writer totally neglected one significant factor, namely, the consent given by local rulers to the western oil companies to exploit and market their oil; he even avoided mentioning the role of Mossadegh in the nationalisation attempt of the 1950s. The author further (intentionally?) ignored the fact that oil had not been used as a means to a political end during the June 1967 war, for at that time major Arab oil producers refused to take such an approach.

His second point centred on a more fashionable argument in Chinese propaganda, though this time he used elaborate means to condemn the USSR's role in the crisis:

> The focal point of the US-Soviet Union power struggle centres
> upon Europe, but over 80 per cent of the petroleum consumed in
> Europe comes from the mid-East. The Soviet revisionists can
> control the oil transit leading to Europe if they can assume
> control of the oil transport lines in the oil producing regions of
> the Mid-East and Persian Gulf.
>
> The Soviets' eagerness to control and exploit the Mid-East oil
> arises of course from its long-term military strategic needs. Although
> the Soviet revisionists have their own oil reserves, but around
> 87 per cent of these reserves are scattered in Siberia, the Far East
> and Central Asian region. The tapping and putting to use of these
> reserves requires considerable finance.
>
> The revisionist Soviet New Tsar. . . inherited the old Tsar's
> southern expansion strategy in infiltrating on an enormous scale,
> with a view to replacing the American imperialists and to assume
> sole dominance in the Middle East.[112]

He gave the examples of Iran, Iraq, the PDRY and Syria as countries which fit the above description. Third, Tschen pointed out the weaknesses of these oil-exporting economies:

> The imperialist exploitation of Middle East oil has resulted in
> abnormal development of the Middle East national economy, vast
> land has been turned into the leased land for oil, the country farm
> has gone bankrupt, agriculture is destroyed and their people's
> food and daily necessities are primarily imported.
>
> More shocking is the fact how the oil work-force are being

exploited. The American oil monopoly companies would squeeze
in the 1960s from each individual worker something like US $4,700
annually, and about 40 thousand US dollars from the Kuwaiti oil
worker annually. The average earnings of the Kuwaiti worker is
less than 1/6 of his American counterpart.[113]

Surprisingly, the deduction from these facts about the relations of oil
producers with the western oil companies was a eulogy of the achievements of OPEC governments, though they never effected any substantial mitigation of the lot of Kuwaiti oil workers. Finally the author
went on to link the crisis of 1973, and its implications for the oil
producing governments' decisions on international economic and
political issues, with the theory of the Three Worlds, and China's
position within it:

> China is a developing country. It also belongs to the Third
> World. A common purpose and the need for struggling have
> firmly united the people of developing countries in Asia, Africa
> and Latin America.[114]

There are numerous flaws to this analysis. First, the author totally
ignored the effect of the oil crisis on the internal economic development of the oil exporting countries. Second, his argument was selective:
as pointed out earlier, the failure to discuss the 1967 war and the fact
that the oil weapon was not used then, is in marked contrast with
Chinese press statements in June 1967. Thirdly, all favourable developments after the oil crisis were attributed to the oil producers' regimes,
their errors in the use of oil revenues ignored. Lastly the claim that
China belonged to the Third World, which also included all OPEC
members, was of no relevance, for the primary reason that China gave
no *practical* assistance in the oil crisis; in fact it benefited from the
rise in oil prices.

Sino-Kuwait relations in 1974–5: sports diplomacy

Throughout this period Chinese relations with Kuwait were characterised by 'sports diplomacy', ties with the Kuwaiti parliament, and
concentration on the 'success' of Gulf and Peninsula states at achieving
some sort of regional co-operation. The last element is interesting
because all the surrounding states – with the exception of Iraq and
the PDRY – are conservative, basically anti-Communist and particularly
anti-Soviet. For China, although a communist state, showed clear

anti-Sovietism, agreed to withhold military and political aid from local opposition in these states (as it did with the PFLO), and welcomed the conservative positions taken by these states against the superpowers.

Once diplomatic relations were established with Kuwait and Iran, and China withdrew support from opposition movements in the Gulf which threatened the status quo, attention shifted to areas where these two states could assist China's thrust in the international arena. Sport was one of these areas. Before the Asian Olympic Games in Teheran in November 1974, Chinese diplomats were active in both Teheran and Kuwait in preparation for the games and the subsequent expulsion of Taiwan from the International Olympic organisation.[115] Initially the Chinese proposal was advanced during the visit of a high-ranking delegation of the Olympic Committee of Kuwait (OCK) when it was in China on 17 February 1974[116] and had a meeting with Wang Meng, Minister of the Chinese Physical Culture and Sports Commission.[117] The Kuwaiti side agreed to the Chinese proposal to consider the All-China Sports Federation as 'the sole national sports organisation governing all sports activities in the People's Republic of China', which implied that Taiwan must be replaced in the organisation. The delegation's concurrence with Chinese demands was 'dictated by the fact that OCK's decisions are an extension of the Kuwaiti Government's recognition of the PRC and voting for it at the UN. Moreover, OCK is, legally, an organ of Kuwaiti Government. This decision by OCK was taken in view of China's acceptance and support for an Arab forthcoming request to terminate Israel's participation in all Olympic games'.[118] When the delegation returned home

> members of the Chinese Embassy in Kuwait paid a visit to OCK's
> headquarters with their written proposal. This was followed by
> visits by members of the Iranian embassy. The two sides agreed
> to co-ordinate their efforts for the forthcoming Asian Olympic
> Games at Teheran in November 1974.[119]

Before China's final admission to the Asian Olympic Games, the Speaker of the Kuwait National Assembly, Khalid al-Ghanim, arrived in Peking on 9 March 1974, at the invitation of the Standing Committee of the National People's Congress of China.[120] As there are no indications that the visit had any official significance, it appears that the Speaker was fulfilling a personal ambition to visit China, and he travelled with his wife and office secretary.[121] He did however meet some people, particularly on 10 March when he met Chu Teh, Chairman of the National People's Congress, and attended a grand Banquet at the

Great Hall of the People, where speeches were exchanged. After the banquet, a meeting with Chou En-lai lasting one and a half hours was held. Discussion centred on general issues which had already been discussed with Kuwait's Minister of Commerce and Industry Khalid al-'Adasānī in 1972 as well as the Kuwait National Assembly delegation in the same year. However, according to the Kuwait Embassy's report to the Foreign Ministry,[122] Chou expressed his admiration for Kuwaiti diplomacy, and remarked that President Boumedienne of Algeria had informed him of the 'effective role Kuwait played in reconciling Bhutto and Mujib al Rahman'. It appears that the Speaker's visit to Peking was also used to further Chinese aims: 'the Chinese had insinuated to Arab ambassadors, including that from the Yemen Arab Republic, China's desire for Kuwait to lay the basis for negotiating with Saudi Arabia on establishing diplomatic relations'.[123] The Speaker left for Kuwait on 14 March 1974 from Kwangchow,[124] having achieved nothing specific except for sight-seeing.

Finally, the importance of Saudi Arabia in Chinese eyes can be clearly seen in Chinese press reports of Saudi Arabia's every attempt to increase its influence in the Gulf region. When the Saudi Crown Prince, Fahad ibn 'Abd al-'Aziz, paid a visit to Kuwait and Iraq in June 1975, in an apparent attempt to reassert Saudi Arabian influence on the former and reach some accommodation with the latter, the *NCNA* reported the visits approvingly.

The following month Prince Fahad was in Iran to further the idea of 'Gulf security'. *NCNA* once again gave the visit prominence, and stated after Fahad's discussions with the Shah and the Iranian Prime Minister:

> They discussed questions of the region and ways and means of preserving peace and security there and keeping the region free from Big Powers' intervention and contention . . . . The Crown Prince's visit to Iran was regarded by Iranian public opinion as another big step, after the visit to Saudi Arabia last April [1975] by the Shah of Iran, in the strengthening of the relations between the two countries and in the promotion of defence co-operation in the region.[125]

Despite these evidences of China's desire to establish relations with the emerging power and the Gulf, and its acceptance of Saudi policies, Saudi Arabia remained adamant in its refusal to recognise China.

Table 8.2 *Kuwaiti trade agents for Chinese products as at December 1975*

Name of Agent	Items
Sū'ūd 'Audjan and Bros.	Canned Mutton, 'Great Wall' Brand; Canned beef
Ra'ad Stores	Frozen Broilers; Frozen Mutton
Sulaiman al-'Abd al-Karim & Bros.	Canned goods, 'Malin' Brand
Husain Maki al-Djum'h	Woollen mixed-piece goods
Bahman Trading Corporation	Sanitary wares, 'Victory' brand; Glazed wall tiles, 'Three Ring' brand; Acid resisting glazed ware pipes and fittings; bed sheets; machine-embroidered bed sheets (Shanghai); pillowcases; nails; singlets and sweaters, 'Double Mull' brand
'Ahmad Bahman and Bros.	Leather shoes; rubber shoes; plastic sandals; enamelware
'Isā and 'Abd 'Ali Bahman Co.	Machine-embroidered bed sheets
'Abd al-Rahim 'Ali 'Akbar	Embroidered blouses, 'Pony' brand
al-Radan stores	Staple fibre blankets
al-'Ahli Trading Exhibition	Garments (100% cotton)
'Ali 'Abd al-Wahab Sons & Co.	Carpets (Tientsin Branch); 'Camel' steel safes; Chairs (Peking Branch)
'Ahmad Muhamad al-Rashid	Vacuum flasks; footballs; kerosene cooking stoves; cotton-piece goods No. 90700
Fahad Sultan	Fountain pens, 'Youth' brand
Mansūr Maki al-Djum'h	Sewing machines, 'Butterfly' brand
Muhamad 'Ahmad al-Basam	Picture frames
al-'Amir Trading & Contracting Est.	Cell batteries
Salam Trading Co. Ltd.	Toys
Faisal Bozie al-Yasin	Lubricating grease
Yūsuf Khalid al'Adasāni	Medicines
Muhamad al-Djasim	Sanitary towels; bandages
Sa'adi 'Abū Darir	Malleable iron; pipe fittings
Faūd Mustafa	Cigarettes, 'Pony' brand
'Abas 'Ali al-Hazim	Carpets (Shantung branch)
Nūr Trading Co., W.L.L.	Transformers
Muhamad 'Abd al-Rahman al-Bahr	Shipping
United Shipping Trading and Contracting Services, W.L.L.	Shipping
'Abd al-Khadar Behbehani	Dactylo-mycin tablets, 'Great Wall' brand

Source: Privately drawn list for the author by Kuwait Ministry of Commerce, December 1975.

232

Conclusion

The three case studies above illustrate the changes which took place in Chinese foreign policy during 1955-75. There were three main phases of Chinese policy towards the Arab World: 1955-66, 1967-70, and 1970-75. China's re-evaluation of its foreign policy priorities can be seen from its changing attitudes towards the Arab World in these three phases, particularly the third. These changes were dictated by China's perception of the world as a whole, and not specifically by the conditions prevailing in these three cases: in the cases of the two liberation movements, the PRM and the PFLO, the Arab side had a consistent and unshakeable belief in China's 'revolutionary' foreign policy. The changes occurred as a result of China's desire to fill a gap and achieve leadership status in the Third World. In the process China's priorities in the region altered.

From its creation in 1949, the Chinese state was faced with a hostile policy of 'containment' by the USA, which not only forbade any American trade with China but also put pressure on other states to withhold recognition from China, to support the US strategic materials ban, and generally to reduce economic relations with it to a minimum. This policy was effective for many years and China was, for historical and ideological reasons, closely associated with the Socialist camp under the leadership of the USSR in its early years. The Bandung Conference in 1955 gave China an opportunity to break this American blockade and open and develop relations between itself and the Third World. Its success was limited, but the Conference gave China an opportunity of dealing directly with Arab states, at the time of Naṣir's leadership. Diplomatic relations with Egypt were established during the crucial period of the Suez Crisis, and Arab states' relations with China were much influenced by Egypt's position on China: once Egypt had recognised and established diplomatic relations with China, other Arab states followed suit.

China's support for Arab nationalist movements was closely linked with Naṣir's leadership of the Arab world: for example, its support for the 'Imāmate cause and the Algerian revolution in the late 1950s and the early 1960s was in tandem with Naṣir's. This is apparent from the fact that China's support for the 'Imāmate cause came long before its support for Palestine, although the Palestinian issue already existed. Furthermore, up to 1967, the Palestinian cause was judged by China on the basis of the extent to which it was accepted by the Arab states, led by Naṣir.

Throughout this period China *did* follow the USSR's policies in the Arab world, whether support for nationalism and/or for local communist parties. But for a decade China made no diplomatic breakthrough in the Arab world.

Publicising the Sino-Soviet dispute, which continued at a low level from 1960 to 1966 because of internal Chinese developments involving pressing questions, theoretical and practical, on how to build socialism, further hampered China's diplomatic thrust. China was now faced with an additional hostile power, the USSR, whose strength lay mostly in the Socialist bloc (except Albania and North Korea, who were not internationally significant) and with a number of important Third World countries, including Egypt and the Arab World. Moreover local communist parties, especially Arab ones, were firmly committed to the USSR. China thus had to face hostility from two directions and to depend on its own strength, which came mainly from its historical experience.

The Third World, the Chinese claim, is under-developed, poor, and faces immense economic, political and cultural obstacles, as did China. Power in China was gained through armed struggle, as the history of the Chinese Communist Party attests. China was not in a position to meet these countries' economic needs and to assist their transformation to a developed stage to the extent to which the USSR, for example, could. Where, then, does China's strength in the Third World come from? The two cases we have studied, that of the PRM and the PFLO, show that even in 1967, China provided military aid which was substantial in relation to the size of these movements. Both sought military aid during the Cultural Revolution period. The extent of Chinese willingness amazed them, as did the amount of material assistance they received. Of course the degree of support was different in each case, but clearly the PRM was in greater need and operated on a larger scale. The 'people's war' element in Chinese foreign policy was a matter of diplomatic tactics, though, undoubtedly, several Chinese leaders did recognise the potential of 'people's war' in the Third World. It is note-worthy that armed struggle and 'people's war' in the Third World *did not* wither away when the Cultural Revolution ended. On the contrary, the national liberation movements who are pursuing armed struggle and 'people's war' are more than ever desperate for aid, to resist the mounting pressures from advances in weapons technology and the economic strength of the 'imperialist forces'. Oman is only one example.

China now often advocates the principle of 'self-reliance' as a corner-stone for development in the Third World. This is applied by the Chinese both in reference to liberation fronts and to states. How relevant and applicable is this concept to our case studies? Politically both the PRM and the PFLO operate within closely limited geographical areas. The former is, for example, effectively stateless: no military bases can be established within Palestine and this prevents the movement from reaching a high stage of development. Its inherent weaknesses were clearly illustrated by Black September. PFLO, on the other hand, though it did not lack base areas, was desperately short of man-power, for which its adherence to Chinese ideology did not compensate. Self-reliance in this case was hardly sufficient: what was most needed was military aid, training and equipment. China's own experience of 'people's war' was totally different. The famous Yunnan years in the history of the CCP, and the endurance of the party in an isolated part of China, afforded the CCP an opportunity to reach a remarkable stage both of political and military development. Moreover, although China did not advocate as imperative the establishment of a commu-nist party in Third World countries as the basis for a successful move-ment, it naturally approved any such development. The Chinese press on numerous occasions noted with enthusiasm the PFLO's acceptance and implementation of Marxism-Leninism, and particularly of 'Mao Tse-tung Thought'. The PFLO's unique and short history clearly demonstrates that adherence to such a political ideology could result in serious setbacks; for the conditions it operated in were those of a traditional system and its uncritical application of theory was hardly an asset in its struggle. The historical conditions under which the CCP was able to live, like a parasite, on its opponent's weakness, and thus surmount many socio-economic and cultural problems, in the 1930s, were totally different from the conditions prevailing for the PRM or the PFLO.

Kuwait is obviously a different case. The Kuwaiti authorities do not even consider the idea of 'self-reliance'. As we have noted before, Kuwait is a 'monoculture' economy and Chou En-lai has stated more than once that Kuwait, given the high rate and availability of Arab and other foreign labour, should industrialise, since oil is a depleting commodity. But industrialisation is hardly considered by the ruling élite, for to embark on such a programme, though logical and feasible in the medium term — say, three decades — implies the emergence of a labour force of significant size. The rulers of Kuwait consider the emergence of a 'proletarian class' would present dangers to their own existence. The current élite is closely associated with western forms of a free enterprise economy; this, given world market conditions, brings them to the conclusion that local industrialisation would be comparatively less profitable than other economic activity. Because of the lack of industry, trade is important to Kuwait. The state does not want to rely on restricted sources for its trade and, as we have seen, Kuwait's trade with China has considerable political undercurrents.

The aftermath of the Cultural Revolution has produced some valuable insights in China's foreign policy objectives in the Third World. The question is, why did China choose to include itself in the Third World, in its division of the world into three? In this loose bloc of states China takes the first rank in that it can, and does, give aid to other Third World countries. Scholars who tend to accept the similarities of 'historical development and poverty', claimed by China, tend to exaggerate the extent of such similarities. Taking foreign aid as the indicator, China's position within the bloc is the highest, and at several stages its aid exceeded that of the USSR, as in 1972. Undoubtedly Chinese aid to these countries is more principled, and sometimes more favourable to the receiving states. The question remains as to why, given its status as a poor Third World country, China stretches itself to such an extent. Many answers have been given, but practically it seems that the ultimate goal of this aid is to *compete* with the 'superpowers' by setting an example, to gain influence for its political programme of Third World unity against 'superpower hegemonism' and to put forward the idea of China's ability to replace other foreign aid. The Chinese, of all people, learned from their own history that aid is a potent element in foreign policy. Chinese precepts for Third World countries to unite in solidarity against 'superpower hegemonism' is irrelevant in many of these countries. Many states in this bloc are aligned and prefer *both* 'superpowers' to China; this has less to do with these countries being under the influence and 'domination' of either superpower than the fact that the ruling élites of almost all of them owe their power and very existence to such an alliance. The remedies they put forward to solve their internal problems are linked to political and other aid they receive from the superpowers rather than, say, China's experience.

Since China's emergence from the Cultural Revolution, support for liberation movements and 'people's war' has been low on China's list of priorities. On the one hand it has willingly withdrawn aid from a given Front in order to establish diplomatic relations and develop solidarity, however vaguely, with the very state which a few years earlier it was seeking to overthrow through its aid to the Front. It is one thing to establish diplomatic relations with regimes of different political and economic systems from China's. It is another thing completely to withdraw aid from local forces and Fronts which adhered to Chinese precepts, followed the Chinese example and relied on Chinese aid at crucial moments of their existence. The PFLO did precisely this and was rewarded disastrously by China. It is often argued that China stops aiding Fronts which have 'no future', and that these Fronts must 'go it alone'. In the case of the PFLO the turning point came in 1972 when there was sufficient room for continuation aid. It can further be said that China's withdrawal of support directly contributed to weakening the PFLO. It cannot be ignored that the PFLO's leadership consistently adhered to the Chinese political line internationally; it even went as far as to reject aid from the USSR at one stage. The outstanding fact about Sino-PFLO relations is not the latter's failure on the ground, but China's policy of gaining a foothold in the Gulf through existing regimes: it thus abandoned the PFLO to establish diplomatic relations with one of the world's most repressive regimes, Iran.

In this later period China has also shown reservations on the policies of Fataḥ, the main body of the PRM. Their relations have cooled. Undoubtedly, China's aid to Fataḥ is a highlight of foreign aid to the Palestinian cause, but a gap in relations has developed over Fataḥ's closer ties with the USSR, which is considered the main enemy by the Chinese. However, given the multiplicity of Palestinian organisations, China, as well as the USSR, is in a position to play one Front against the other in various ways, through, for example official invitations, political support, and the extension of military training to more than one Front. The issues in Sino-Palestinian relations are basically two: first, Palestine remains the main focus point as an *Arab* cause, though different Fronts and Arab states have different attitudes and solutions to it, and therefore China cannot ignore it as it did the PFLO. Second, Fataḥ remains the main organisation in the PRM and for China to antagonise it openly would not be favourable.

Conclusion

Although it is often claimed that China does not seek leadership and hegemony, particularly in the Third World, only time will demonstrate the validity or otherwise of this claim. The answer lies in the 'dialectical' approach to power. While these Third World countries' situation is deteriorating, and their ability to sustain themselves in the contemporary world growing more doubtful, China is developing, and its thrust in the Third World is gradually exceeding that of both superpowers.

Appendix 1

Fatah military study on China

Introductory note

This Fataḥ study of the Chinese experience in guerrilla warfare against Japan was published immediately after the June 1967 war. Two points emerge. The first is Fataḥ's keen desire to learn from other experiences, regardless of ideology. Fataḥ's non-adherence to any defined ideology was one of the greatest assets to its growth. Its interest in the Chinese experience was purely military. Thus the pamphlet is devoted to the organisation, objectives and applicability of such guerrilla warfare to Palestinian conditions. It draws heavily on Mao Tse-tung's *Selected Works, Volumes 1 and 2*, in the discussion of the Chinese experience of resistance against Japan. The second point is that this period in Chinese Communist Party history was chosen because, as Fataḥ saw it, both the Palestinian and the Chinese experiences had a common factor: foreign invasion. It is because of this historical similarity that Fataḥ chose the Chinese resistance to Japan's invasion, and from it tried to draw the conclusion of a certain 'military similarity' between the two experiences. Needless to say, Fataḥ did not ignore other experiences: the period after June 1967 saw a flourishing of studies on the Algerian and Cuban experiences, among others.

The influence exerted by the Chinese experience over the Palestinian resistance movement was considerable. It was not a matter of 'copying' Chinese experience in Palestinian conditions, but rather following China's 'world outlook' and its implication for the Palestinian Resistance Movement – seeing several camps of 'friends, enemies and neutrals', which any liberation front must assess if it is to progress towards its goals. Despite the contention of Fataḥ's top leaders that the Sino-Soviet dispute should not be allowed to divert the Front from its basic principles, there are signs that this was a difficult decision for the leadership to make in the historical development of the Palestinian

Resistance Movement. The problems are complicated in the Palestinian case. First, the Palestinian Resistance Movement, as its name implies, consists of a number of Fronts. This, in the final analysis, is a source of weakness rather than strength; decisions must be taken, for example, whenever the Palestinian presence in an Arab state is at stake, which must not only obtain the agreement of all parties, but must be executed unanimously. Any forceful bloc can accordingly pose a serious threat. Second, the Palestinian question has historically always been an Arab dilemma. The Palestinian Diaspora, unlike that of the Jews, was not scattered throughout the world, and Israel was created directly at Arab expense, regardless of whether or not a unified Arab nation existed at the time. Consequently, any attempt to 'eradicate such alien existence' meant decisions on Arab states, particularly those sharing borders with Israel. At any point, any of these Arab states could choose not to involve itself in a war with Israel. Because of the creation of Israel, the Palestinians were forced to establish their forces in Arab states and consequently, at certain points, their intention to achieve specific goals was bound to conflict with the interests of the 'host' state. Third, given the economic, political and military backwardness of the Arab states, the need for some powerful non-Arab state to make good these deficiencies is immense. In a sense, it has developed to a point where international politics must be taken into consideration, with two major powers playing important roles: the USA and the USSR.

In their long search for a solution to such complex problems, the forces of the Palestinian Liberation Movement had to look to China to draw conclusions on the applicability of the theory of 'people's war' to their conditions. The three chief forces were Fatah, the PFLP and the PDFLP. The peaks of intellectual activity in these Fronts, and their attempt to study and be influenced by the Chinese experience, occurred twice: after June 1967 and September 1970.

One point requires emphasis: *all* thinkers of the Palestinian Resistance Movement had reservations about adopting the Chinese form of Marxism-Leninism, or Maoist policies, in the Palestinian war of liberation. What interested the Palestinian Resistance Movement in the Chinese experience was the *eclectic* study of several liberation movements, so as to select the best and most appropriate approach to its own problems. There was however a clear dividing line between Fatah on the one hand, and the PFLP and the PDFLP on the other, concerning ideological similarities with the Chinese experience. Throughout China's dealings, contacts and discussions with members of the Palestinian Resistance Movement, the Chinese showed a marked preference for

Fataḥ's 'ideological' stand on – i.e., its nationalist approach to – the process of liberation.

Both the PFLP and the PDFLP constantly argued the necessity to establish a Marxist-Leninist party to lead the Palestinian and then the Arab revolutions in the process of liberating Palestine. The PFLP advocates that 'we must lay a demarcation line between the forces of revolution on the Palestinian scene based on class structure' and 'the Palestinian workers and peasants are the base and the leading force of the revolutionary class . . . . The Palestinian bourgeoisie does not live in refugee camps. The camps are inhabited by workers, peasants and the petty bourgeoisie whose livelihood is not drastically different from that of peasants and workers'.[1] Asking rhetorically how weak people oppose imperialist technological superiority, the PFLP stressed, referring mainly to Mao's writings, the imperative need to establish a people's movement and a people's war, based on a Marxist-Leninist party.[2] Once this is provided to create the basis for a Marxist-Leninist leadership, the front must co-operate with and organise a wider Arab revolutionary front. Although this is not one of the tasks of the Palestinian revolution, the necessity arises to extend this revolution to Arab states, given the fact that its military existence is dialectically connected with the surrounding Arab states. It is imperative to establish 'an Arab Hanoi as a revolutionary base'.[3] Once the Arab side is established, internationally, the allies of the Palestinian revolution are 'all the oppressed peoples who suffer from colonialist and imperialist exploitation', China, which has gone through this stage of colonial domination and is still suffering from imperialist containment, the USSR and the rest of the socialist camp. Moreover 'to complete this chain to contain Israel, Zionism and imperialism' the interests of these forces must be attacked and resisted on a world scale.[4]

The PDFLP, in its political and military formulae for the Liberation of Palestine, does not differ markedly from the PFLP – both Fronts originally sprang from the mother organisation, the Arab Nationalist Movement. The reasons and general trends of the split between them were considered to be between the 'left' and 'right' factions of the mother organisation. Its analysis of the path which the liberation process should follow laid more stress than the PFLP on the 'intellectual revolutionary' nature of the Palestinian Movement. This should not be confused with the Marxist-Leninist precept of establishing 'a revolutionary movement based on a worker-peasant alliance as a leading force behind the Palestinian Resistance Movement'. The PDFLP's literature reflected a modified 'theory' of the role revolution should play in the 'developing and less developed' countries. In this it laid emphasis on Chinese notions in order to suit its own objectives.[5]

Fataḥ's doctrine on achieving the strategic goal of liberation, formulated in simple and straightforward terms, has been its greatest asset. No doctrine of comparable effectiveness has been propounded by the other Palestinian Resistance Movement Fronts and organisations. It claims that the primary contradiction in this war is with Israel, against which all efforts must be directed.

The Arab states which compose the front line safeguard the continuity of the revolution. They have always been something of a problem to the revolution. The front-line states – Egypt, Syria, Jordan and Lebanon – have all at one point or another dealt harsh blows to the existence of the Palestinian Resistance Movement. But, Fatah argues, when one of these states attempts the military liquidation of the Palestinian Resistance Movement, then the primary contradiction will have to shift *temporarily*. The rest of the Arab world, given its complex political alliances with the East and the West, obviously affects the political role the Palestinian Resistance Movement plays in the Arab-Israeli conflict. But the Palestinian Resistance Movement should in no way get entangled in internal Arab politics. To do so would not only be a waste of effort: it would effectively exceed its capacities. It would be irrational, for example, for Fataḥ to attempt to bring down 'reactionary' Arab states by all means available, at the expense of its primary conflict with Israel. Third, in the international arena, contradictions must be clearly defined. The primary task here is to oppose states that perpetuate the existence of Israel – e.g. the USA – and neutralise in various ways the states which have traditionally been pro-Israeli in the conflict, while maintaining strong ties with the socialist camp and all other forces in the world which are sympathetic to the cause of the Palestinian Resistance Movement.

It is in this third field that differences have developed among Fataḥ members over the Sino-Soviet conflict, and the implications of Russian and Chinese policies towards the Arab-Israeli conflict. The Sino-Soviet dispute is dealt with even-handedly among the Fataḥ Central Committee members. In his attempt to outline the reasons to certain unnamed Fataḥ lower level cadres, drawn mostly from the Fataḥ intelligentsia, all of whom had made a respectable contribution to the Palestinian cause, Ňazih 'abū Niḍal[6] argues as follows regarding Fataḥ's relations with China and the USSR. He states that when armed struggle began in 1965, Fataḥ sought to study several experiences in the world which could prove helpful. Mao's writings had a tremendous influence in shaping the political outlook of certain cadres in Fataḥ. China's prestige among Palestinian guerrillas was enhanced by the availability of Chinese arms. But the 'feeling of cordiality' with China was modified in 1972 when Fataḥ cadres began to question China's international diplomacy: for example 'why does China, the cradle of revolution, receive Nixon, the champion of American imperialism? Why does China support the Shah of Iran's regime and receive his sister as a noted leader . . . while there is in Iran a mass revolutionary movement which needs support? . . . . Then these questions became objections and rejections, especially after China supported al Numīrī's massacre of Sudanese communists.'[7]

By contrast Arab and Palestinian attitudes towards the USSR were initially hostile because of the latter's recognition of Israel and its role in the partition of Palestine. When the Cold War erupted the Arab mass media, representing Arab states, clearly took the American position and attacked Soviet policies in the Arab world. Ñazih 'abū Niḍal argues that this attitude began to change when, in 1955, the USSR lent Egypt the aid it needed. As far as the Palestinian revolution was concerned there was a wide divergence of opinion between it and the USSR on the general goals of the revolution, and the USSR had constantly relied on Arab communist parties as spokesmen and leading forces in the Arab world. But the October 1973 war changed this relationship. There emerged a certain closeness of aims of both parties in the area. The PLO began to depend more heavily on the USSR, realising the potential of the latter's support. At this juncture, the pro-Chinese faction in Fataḥ, says 'Abū Niḍal, began asking anti-Soviet questions about the USSR's stand on international and Arab issues. This took a form which followed China's concept of the 'three world division', accusing the Soviet Union of being 'social imperialist', etc. The trend towards taking sides and following either the USSR or China's line in foreign policy became more acute among Fataḥ's intelligentsia. Nadjī 'Alūsh wrote an extended criticism of one of the supposedly pro-Chinese members of Fataḥ, Munīr Shafīḳ, severely accusing the latter of 'blindly' following Chinese positions which are, to say the least, harmful for the Palestinian Resistance Movement.[8] There is no evidence whatsoever in Munīr Shafīḳ's writings to corroborate 'Alūsh's accusations, and Shafīḳ rejects these allegations on the ground that none of his views ever advocated the Chinese line, nor did his actions ever lead to the conclusions that 'Alūsh tried to draw.[9]

This document, according to PRM sources, was written by Chinese military authorities for Fataḥ. Fataḥ added its own introduction to it. Its significant element is its lack of any Marxist-Leninist rhetoric.

Studies of revolutionary experiences: The Chinese experience [*Text*]

Introduction

Guerrilla war should be dynamic and in a continual state of movement. Quiet intervals constitute the main factor impeding the success of guerrilla war since they give the enemy a chance to achieve better control over the country and provide rest for its soldiers. Such intervals also help to weaken the masses' zeal in joining or supporting the guerrilla fighters. Strategically, guerrilla warfare differs from regular warfare in that it avoids classical battles, and tactically it avoids clashes which would normally cause losses. Guerrilla war also breaks one of the rules of regular warfare, namely that of 'concentration' in relation to the two fighting parties, as dispersal is one of the basic principles which ensures the safety of the guerrilla fighter and the success of his operations, thus concentration is substituted by dispersal. Moreover an important factor in guerrilla warfare is the relationship between the location and the number of fighters. This proportion has been clarified by T. E. Lawrence in his book 'The Arab Revolution' where he states that, against the Turks, it is essential that a protection fort should exist in each 4 square mile area provided 20 men are available for such a fort; thus the Turks needed 600,000 men to control the area while they only had 100,000 men. Although this ratio is an important factor, it is subject to others such as the geographical nature of the country, the quick movement and morale of the two parties. Guerrilla operations which gave priority to safety would soon fade out and vanish. Guerrilla war is basically carried out by a minority which depends on the support of the majority. An essential part of guerrilla warfare is training, how to mobilise the masses, and in this respect a guerrilla fighter must be politically educated before he learns how to use a gun. The main element in this type of war is the human being, which causes the guerrilla leaders to spend more time in the organisation and guidance of people, setting up riots and circulating propaganda, rather than fighting, since their basic task is to win popular support.

Guerrilla warfare

Guerrilla warfare has its own characteristics and objectives. It is the weapon used by a weak nation against another hostile one which has huge military force. It is appropriate first to define clearly our political aims and to evaluate our responsibility in the realisation of these aims.

The target of our policy is to create a unified nation against the Japanese Front, which is the policy we follow to achieve the liberation of the Chinese nation from Japanese invasion. There are a number of basic measures which must be taken for the realisation of this aim, namely:

1 Mobilisation and organisation of the masses.
2 Achievement of internal national political unity.
3 The establishment of bases.
4 Preparation of the fighting forces.
5 The people's recovery of confidence and strength.
6 Destruction of the enemy's forces.
7 Recovery of the occupied territory.

Guerrilla warfare without political objectives will definitely have no success, and if its political objectives do not conform with the aspirations of the people, it will not obtain the people's sympathy, support or assistance. The true nature of guerrilla warfare is a revolution. It derives its strength from the masses and their support for it, and this type of warfare cannot exist or flourish without their support and co-operation.

Organisation of the troops

How is guerrilla warfare organised?

Although the troops formed from the people at the beginning suffer weakness in their organisation, their characteristic is the ability to be properly organised given time. It is essential that a political and military leadership is assigned to each guerrilla unit, and this applies to all units without exception regardless of their size or origin. The leaders of guerrilla units should be strict in the execution of their policies, determined, loyal, faithful and brave. They should also have a revolutionary education, be confident, endowed with self-control, and capable of resisting enemy propaganda. In brief, such leaders should be able to overcome any negligence or disorder that may initially prevail among their forces, eventually establishing order among their forces and increasing their strength and ability to fight.

A chaotic guerrilla warfare cannot get close to victory. On the other hand, those who attack the guerrilla movement and accuse it of being a mixture of vagabonds and anarchists are not aware of the activities of guerrilla warfare. We do not deny that there exist corrupt groups who carry out scandalous acts under the guise of being guerrilla troops. We do not deny that at the beginning, guerrilla movements suffer from lack of organisation and qualified people, which might lead to tragic results. It is imperative to educate the fighters and improve their conditions in the light of our previous experience. But corruption is not latent in guerrilla war itself; rather it exists in irresponsible chaotic acts or in chaos itself.

What is the fundamental strategy of guerrilla war?

The strategy of guerrilla war basically depends on awareness, ability to move quickly, and attack. This strategy must be correlated to the enemy's position, the geographical paths and lines of communications, the relative capabilities of the fighters, climatic conditions and the backing of the masses. In guerrilla war one should select a tactic to attack from the west when the enemy expects to be attacked from the east. One should avoid the strong enemy and attack the weak one, attack and withdraw at lightning speed and take firm and rapid decisions. Should the troops clash with the enemy, they must withdraw if it advances, terrify the enemy if it stops, strike if it is tired of marching, and follow it if it withdraws. The vital positions in the strategy of guerrilla war are the rear of the enemy, its wings and its weak position; in all such positions it is necessary to terrify, attack, tear up, exhaust or destroy the enemy.

It is appropriate to distinguish between two types of guerrilla war. The fact that guerrilla war depends on the masses of the people does not, as such, mean that the organisation of guerrilla units is impossible in a war which lacks revolutionary character. The guerrilla war of liberation is the result of historic developments and it is governed by the concepts of such development. A guerrilla war which violates the concepts of historical development is for example the one used by hostile forces against the people, such as the Italian war against Ethiopia. Such fighters are easy to destroy because they lack a wide popular base. The most distinctive feature of guerrilla war in a civil war is being a fortified internal civil war. It is easy for a certain class of people to unite and fight fiercely and determinedly, but in the case of a revolutionary war, guerrilla fighters have to face the problem of unifying various classes of people, and this requires propaganda.

The guerrilla war carried out by the Moroccans against the French and the Spanish differs from the Chinese war, and these differences are due to the characteristics of the different nations in various areas. While there is a similarity in the nature of such struggles, there is a difference in their form. In this respect it would be necessary to go back into history to find the prevailing circumstances with respect to environment, economic development, political ideas, national character and traditions, and level of civilisation. It would be appropriate to study carefully the actual circumstances which lead to fighting since circumstances vary according to political and economic positions and the realisation of popular targets. Such progressive changes in circumstances create new types of fighting.

Relations between guerrilla war and regular war

The general features of regular warfare, i.e. positions and mobility, basically differ from those of guerrilla war. Similarly guerrilla war differs from regular warfare in the system of organisation, armament, equipment, supply, tactics and leadership as well as the concept of front and rear. The basic feature of guerrilla warfare is that it is dependent on the masses for the organisation of its units. As a result organisation in guerrilla warfare depends on regional circumstances. The level of supply of equipment and materials is of minor importance, but it has to rely on civilians for the troops' subsistence. The strategy of guerrilla warfare differs from that of ordinary warfare since the basic tactics of guerrilla warfare depend on continuous activity and movement. The phrase 'decisive battle' or 'defensive positions' does not exist in guerrilla warfare. The transformation of mobile positions to defensive positions of vital sites does not develop in guerrilla warfare. And the general features of exploratory operation, comprehensive or partial dispersal of the fighting forces, and development of attack, which occur in regular warfare, do not occur in guerrilla warfare.

In addition there is a difference in guidance and leadership. In guerrilla warfare independent small guerrilla units play a major role, and interference in their operations should be avoided. On the other hand, leadership in regular warfare is centralised in order to co-ordinate the organisation of military efforts of various fighting sectors; this is undesirable and even impossible in guerrilla warfare. Groups which are close to each other may co-ordinate their efforts to a certain extent. The guerrilla fighters' duty is to destroy small enemy units, terrify and weaken its larger forces and compel it to disperse its forces. It is possible to develop guerrilla units gradually, composed of ordinary people, into regular army units.

Guerrilla war in history

Historical experience has shown that the success of guerrilla war depends to a great extent on strong political leaders who are devoted to the cause of national unity. Such leaders concentrate their efforts on the masses. Experience has shown that prior attention must be given to attacking the enemy politically and militarily. It is likewise essential that fighting should develop vigorously since guerrilla warfare on its own is unable to achieve final victory.

Organisation of guerrilla warfare

The following points must be considered:

1 How the guerrilla troops are formed.
2 How the guerrilla troops are organised.
3 How to arm the guerrilla troops.

What are the elements which form a single guerrilla unit?

A guerrilla unit may be formed of:

1 Ordinary citizens.
2 Units of the army which have temporarily withdrawn from the army for this purpose.
3 Army units which have permanently withdrawn from the army.
4 A combination of regular soldiers and individuals of the public.
5 The national guard.
6 Retired army members.
7 Vagabond bands.

In the first case, troops are formed from the public and this is essential for the protection of the people against the enemy. Whenever the enemy comes to attack, the leaders of the masses call the troops to resist with old weapons or any available ones, and as a consequence of this a unit is formed. In this type of unit young students, teachers, local officials or technical workers assume the leadership. One may come across someone who claims that he is a student or peasant and does not know about military techniques. This attitude is unacceptable as there is no basic difference between a peasant and a soldier. The basic requirement is to be brave, then it will be easy for him to abandon his farm and become a soldier. By carrying weapons one becomes a soldier and, when organised, one becomes a member of a military unit. Guerrilla warfare is the university of war. Hence after fighting bravely and vigorously several times, he may become a leader of his group. We may therefore discern that the origin of guerrilla warfare (can) be found in the masses who organise this type of war by themselves.

The second type of formation of a guerrilla unit is tantamount to a group from the regular army which, whenever necessary, distributes its members in the form of units to carry out guerrilla activities. This type of guerrilla formation is necessary for two reasons: 1. In the case of a war of mobile positions, the organisation of troops to cope with ordinary operations is essential. 2. Until the development of guerrilla war on a larger scale there will be no-one who can perform the tasks of guerrilla warfare other than the regular forces. History has proved that regular forces are unable to endure the difficulties of guerrilla warfare for a long time.

The third type represents groups of the regular army who are permanently detached to carry out guerrilla operations in the enemy's rear lines, thus constituting the backbone of the guerrilla organisation.

The fourth type is formed when certain guerrilla troops are sent to work under the command of a local leader. Should such troops be politically and militarily trained, they develop to become the guerrilla nucleus in that area.

The fifth type is composed of the national guard, the police and the popular militia. Such troops should be available in all areas, since the revolutionary government believes that the people should be available in areas of military operations. Such troops are bound to comply with government instructions.

The sixth type consists of those who have left military service with the regular army in the Japanese treacherous units. It is essential to stimulate propaganda among those units to encourage them to leave military service with the Japanese. Such units should be organised and educated to become successful and loyal guerrillas. Political activity in their ranks is of major importance.

The seventh type consists of vagabonds whose political beliefs should first be rectified.

Despite apparent differences in the basic forms of units we have discussed, it is rather easy to unify them to become a comprehensive collection of troops. (The ancient people say this mountain is great because it does not disdain a handful of dust and these rivers and seas are deep because they absorb the waters of little streams.)

How to organise troops

Let us for example take a geographical division of a certain area and divide it according to contours. A military leader and political delegates should be appointed for this area, as well as military and political officers who work under the control of those leaders. The army head-quarters consist of the general staff, their assistants, supply officers and medical staff; all of them work under the command of the chief of staff who operates according to the instructions of the leader.

The political headquarters has an office for the organisation of propaganda, motivation of the masses, and other affairs; this office is headed by the political executive. The same area should be divided into a number of sectors according to its topography and the enemy's position, as well as the stage reached by the guerrilla war. Duties are assigned to soldiers according to the number of guerrilla units available in that area. In order to ensure that the leadership has a good command over the troops and organises the political and military efforts in the area properly, a committee composed of seven people selected from among the officers and political cadres is set up in each region. Such a committee considers military and political matters. The people in each region should arm and organise themselves in two groups, a fighting group and a defensive group.

The fighting units are formed as follows

1 The squad, which is the smallest unit of guerrilla groups. It consists of 9 to 11 men including their leader and his assistant. Its weapons consist of two to five locally-made rifles, shotguns, spears or swords. Every two or three squads form one platoon.
2 The platoon, which consists of two or three squads. The platoon has a leader and an assistant leader. If the platoon operates alone, it should have a political instructor to carry out political propaganda. The platoon's weapons consist of ten guns and some other shotguns or swords.
3 The company, which is composed of two to four platoons. The company has a leader, assistant leader and political delegate. All the units mentioned are under the command and direct control of the military leader of the region concerned.
4 The regiment should be properly organised and better equipped than the above-mentioned units. The number of soldiers and size of the machinery in the regiment excel those of the other units. Should the regiment be formed from among the units operating in the area, men and weapons should be withdrawn from the guerrilla units operating there, to form the regiment. Armed groups such as the militia or the police should be available in a small area to maintain security. The guerrilla fighters should not be attached to such armed units.

5 The brigade should be better controlled and organised than the regiment. In each of the brigade's squads there are ten people, and every three squads form one detachment. Similarly three detachments form a regiment and every three regiments form one brigade.
6 The division. Two brigades form one division. All the units of the regiment, brigade or division have a leader, deputy leader and political officer. All the guerrilla units, including smaller and larger ones, are fighting groups which receive their supplies from the central government.

The defensive units are formed as follows

All people of both sexes aged 16–45 should be organised in defensive units provided that such organisation be done on a voluntary basis. The first step for volunteering is that the volunteer bring a weapon and thereafter he takes the necessary military training. The duties assigned to these people are to guard local places, obtain information from the enemy, seize traitors and prevent the distribution of enemy propaganda. In the event of enemy attack on the region, such local guerrilla units must try with the weapons they have to mislead the enemy, hinder its progress, and spread terror in its ranks. This is the type of assistance which the defensive unit gives to the fighting guerrilla units. They also assist in bringing stretchers for the wounded and food for the fighters. The formation of such defensive troops assists in the elimination of traitors, vagabonds and rioters. Such defensive forces will gradually develop to become the reserve for the official armed forces; such defensive groups should be based on choice rather than obligation. Operating teams should also not be separated from the locality they live in. Everybody in the defensive units should at least have a weapon, whether it is a knife, a spear or a pistol. In all the areas where the enemy operate, the defensive units should form small guerrilla teams of 3 to 10 people armed with pistols. Such groups should not leave the place they live in. To sum up, the masses must be induced to co-operate with the guerrilla groups of their own choice. We should not force them to do so, otherwise the impact will be minimal and therefore this fact should be carefully taken into consideration.

Military equipment of the troops

We must remember that guerrilla troops are armed groups who launch light attacks, a matter which requires light equipment. The type of equipment depends on the nature of the tasks entrusted to the troops. For example, a group which is responsible for the destruction of a railroad should be better equipped than one which is responsible for a less difficult task. The weapons and equipment available do not necessarily match what the fighters require or need; they should rely on what is available for their use. It is not easy to supply troops with weapons immediately, and usually some time is needed to meet such requirements; this must always be taken into consideration. The question of equipment covers all weapons, ammunition, blankets, wireless equipment, means of transport, and facilities to spread propaganda, whether they are to be distributed or replaced. The most difficult part is the supply of weapons and ammunition at the time of the formation of a guerrilla unit, but this problem can soon be solved after a period of resistance when it becomes possible to increase available equipment by taking it from the enemy. The enemy is the main source of weapons.

The minimum required articles of clothing, etc. are

One summer uniform, one winter suit, one blanket and a bag to carry food. On this point, we cannot depend on the enemy's clothes as we do not allow any soldier to take the clothes of his captives. For other fighting forces there would be no need to wear a uniform, and even telephones and radio sets could be dispensed with. It is however essential to supply brigades and divisions with telephones and radio sets. It is essential to have good medical supplies and equipment in the guerrilla army in general and in the guerrilla bases in particular. Medicines and doctors must also be available. Although the troops can, to a certain extent, depend on the enemy for their medical supplies they should, in general, depend on contributions. In the event of nonavailability of medical drugs, basic medical prescriptions should be prepared locally.

Transport is needed in the North. Every leader, staff officer and higher rank officer should be allocated a riding animal, or at least have one animal to be shared by two. Officers responsible for emergencies do not need riding animals.

Propaganda materials are absolutely essential. Every large unit should be supplied with a printing machine and a typewriter to prepare publicity leaflets. They should also be supplied with chalk and erasers. The printing of training brochures is of major importance. In addition to the above-mentioned equipment, it is essential to have field-glasses, compasses and military maps. The leaders should provide the troops with the necessary weapons, but in the meantime the troops should depend on acquiring such weapons themselves.

If the troops become too dependent on senior officers, the psychological effect could be to weaken the feeling of resistance among them.

Structure of the guerrilla fighters

The fighters are composed of soldiers and officers. The officers should have endurance and despite all difficulties they should set an example for their men and be able to mix easily with the people. The officer and his soldiers should have a good morale to strengthen resistance against the enemy. If the officer wants to achieve victories, he should study war tactics. Officers are people who have good moral qualities which can improve as the fighting develops. The most important of these qualities is a firm belief in the liberation of the people. If this belief is there, other characteristics can be developed. Thus, to select an officer from a group, he must have proved himself to be endowed with these qualities. Officers should be selected from among the inhabitants of the area where they operate, which facilitates relations between them and civilians, considering that they are fully acquainted with prevailing conditions in that area. Should such officers be difficult to find in a certain area, then groups of local inhabitants must be trained and educated to reach the standard necessary to become officers. Given that the enemy exploits weak-willed people and induces them to join the guerrilla troops to be spies, it is important that the officers continuously educate the people and stimulate nationalist feeling in them. It is necessary to discover traitors among the guerrillas' ranks and dismiss them from service. In such cases, officers should invite the soldiers to a meeting to explain to them the facts of the case, in order to arouse in them hatred and malice for the traitors. Such procedures act as a warning to the rest of the soldiers. In the event of an officer being discovered to be a traitor he should be discretely punished. The elimination of traitors in the army, however, starts with the elimination of traitors among the public. The success of guerrilla warfare is dependent on the goodwill and purity of its members.

Political problems of guerrilla warfare

Initially we should point out that political activity depends on the education of the political and military leaders and their appreciation of anti-Japanese concepts. The leaders' thoughts will then be transmitted to the soldiers. The soldier's hostile feelings towards the Japanese should not be established simply on account of his being a member of a guerrilla group. Hostility to the Japanese should exist wherever he is, and should this fact be ignored, we shall be an easy prey to the enemy's seduction, or get captured through cowardice. Those who do not fully understand the concept of the liberation of the people are likely to be hesitant in their belief in revolutionary doctrine. It is essential to clarify and define political aims to the people in the guerrilla areas to awaken their national feeling. In this respect, it is appropriate to explain the current political system not only to the guerrilla fighters but to all who are trying to achieve our political aims.

The search for national organisation implies the need for basic unity between the soldiers and the people. It is very important for the guerrilla officers to study and know the political aims of the war against the enemy. There are some officers who claim to be concerned only with military aspects and to have nothing to do with politics. Such officers must understand the relationship between military and political affairs. Military operations are the means used in the achievement of a political aim and it is difficult to separate one of these factors from the other. There are three political issues which should be taken into consideration:

1 Political activity among the soliders.
2 Political activity among the people.
3 Political activity among the enemy.

There are also three basic problems:

1 The spiritual unity between the army and the people.
2 The spiritual unity and coalition between officers and soldiers in the army.
3 Destruction of army unity.

The revolutionary army enjoys a system based on limited democracy. In all armies all over the world, obedience to a senior is compulsory and this applies to the guerrilla fighters as well, but on the basis that the matter is left to the individual's conscience.

It is true that the military system of guerrilla troops is not as strict as that of the regular army; however, circumstances make it necessary to establish a system which must be automatically followed when the soldier realises why he is fighting and why it is his duty to obey one who is senior to him. This system represents consolidation among the ranks of the guerrilla fighters and it is the sole system which can create a co-ordinated relationship between the soldiers and the officers. A different system would mark the relationship between officers and soldiers with distance. Another secondary characteristic of the guerrilla military system is the freedom allowed to officers and soldiers. In the revolutionary army, all enjoy political freedom and may discuss the question of the liberation of the people, rather than take it for granted. Propaganda must also be encouraged by all. The life of the officers and soldiers in the revolutionary army must not differ much, and the officers must live under the same conditions as the soldiers. This is the only way officers will win the respect and confidence of their soldiers which is vital in the war. While it would be incorrect to apply the principle of equality in all aspects, it is necessary to practise equality in facing the difficulties and risks of war. In this way, we would be able to create unity between the officers and soldiers, a horizontal unity between the guerrillas and a unity of depth between the junior and senior ranks.

Concerning the spiritual unity between the troops and the people, the following three rules and eight remarks have been laid down:

1 All operations are subject to an order from the leader.
2 Do not steal from the people.
3 Do not be selfish or oppressive.

Remarks:

1 Return the door when you leave the house (during the summer soldiers used to break off the doors and use them as beds).
2 Fold up the mattress you slept on.
3 Be polite.
4 Be honest in your dealings with others.
5 Return what you have borrowed.
6 Don't bathe in the presence of a woman.
7 Repair what you have broken.
8 Do not search anyone you have arrested without prior permission.

The guerrilla fighters can be described as fish and the people as the sea, so if the fish come out of the sea, they die. In order to destroy the enemy, we have to circulate propaganda among its soldiers, treat enemy captives and wounded well; failing to do this we will indirectly strengthen solidarity with the enemy.

The guerrilla strategy in fighting the Japanese

Taking the Japanese-Chinese war into consideration, the guerrilla fighters should perform the following tasks:

1 Carry out war on the external borders.
2 Set up bases.
3 Expand the fighting areas.

The participation of the guerrillas in fighting does not imply that only guerrilla tactics are used; on the contrary there are a number of strategic considerations which must be taken into account before we start tackling the practical aspects of the guerrilla war. It would be appropriate to note the basic undisputed facts on which all types of military operations depend. These facts comprise the preservation of our forces and the destruction of the enemy's forces; concerning this, we must ask if the sacrifices necessitated by war are in conflict with the concept of self-preservation. The answer is no, since the sacrifices required are necessary to destroy the enemy and preserve ourselves. Sacrificing the lives of some people is necessary to safeguard the whole, and all military considerations follow this principle. We should also remember that the guerrilla units start with very few individuals and then start growing. The basic methods we must choose to guarantee the safety and development of our forces and the destruction of the enemy can be summarised as follows:

1 To always take the initiative, be alert and carry out premeditated tactical attacks in strategic defence.
2 To organise activities with the regular army.
3 To set up bases.
4 To be familiar with the relationship between attack and defence tactics.
5 To develop attack to a mobile operation.
6 To ensure competent leadership.

Although surprise attacks exist in regular warfare, they are more common in guerrilla warfare. Speed is essential in guerrilla warfare: the movement of guerrillas should also be of the utmost secrecy so that the army be taken by surprise. There should be no room for procrastination in the execution of plans which have been drawn up, and passive or positive defence should not be allowed. The principle of extensive distribution of troops in most local battles should be ignored. The basic method to be adopted is to attack violently and deceptively. The defensive tactic has no place in guerrilla warfare. Should there be a need to impede the enemy's progress, the most suitable places to choose are mountain passes, river crossing points and villages where it is possible to foil the enemy's plans and destroy it. The enemy is much stronger than we are and we can impede its progress, keep it busy, disperse its forces and destroy it in one go with the distribution of our forces. Although guerrilla warfare is the war of fighting units scattered over various places, it is sometimes recommended to concentrate forces against a relatively weak enemy and destroy it.

Initiative

In all battles and wars the struggle between the two fighting parties is based on taking the initiative since the initiator has freedom of manoeuvre. Should the army lose the initiative it loses its freedom, and then its role becomes negative and it is liable to defeat and destruction. It is more difficult to take the initiative when fighting within boundaries than when attacking them. We should then recognise the enemy's superiority over us and the need for unity and experience among the ranks of our soldiers. The guerrilla fighters may however take the initiative if they take into account the enemy's points of weakness. It would be possible to maintain initiative only through our correct evaluation of the position and by taking suitable military and political measures. An evaluation which is excessively pessimistic or optimistic will result in losing the initiative. Initiative is not a natural talent, it is only the leader who can take the initiative through a study and proper estimation of the position. There is no specific way to describe the method of taking the initiative since this depends on the position of the two parties at the time.

Caution

Leaders of the guerrilla war should recognise that the application of caution and vigilance is necessary to take the initiative and vital in relation to its effect on the position of the enemy, circumstances, road conditions, topography of the area, and prevailing local conditions. The leader is like the fisherman who throws and pulls in his fishing net according to his knowledge of the depth of the water, the strength of the currents, and other factors. The fisherman is able to control his net through its main ropes and in the same way a guerrilla leader maintains contact and control of his units. The fisherman changes his position according to need and the guerrilla leader should do the same. Through dispersal of forces, concentration and continuous change of position, the guerrillas should use their strength. In general guerrillas disperse for work under the following conditions:

1 When the enemy is in a strong defensive position and the guerrillas do not have enough forces to concentrate against it,

then the guerrillas should scatter to frighten the enemy and weaken its morale.

2 When the enemy attacks the guerrillas and withdrawal becomes easy.

3 When the nature of the terrain does not assist the performance of operations.

4 When available supplies are insufficient.

5 When it is necessary to expand activities to a larger scale.

Regardless of circumstances prevailing at the time of dispersal, it would be necessary to take the following precautions:

1 To keep a large section of the soldiers as a central force and not to use or distribute the remaining forces in groups of equal number but rather in groups of unequal number so that the leader will be able to act according to existing circumstances.

2 To define and fix the responsibility of each unit. Orders should specify the place where the unit should go, the time it should leave, and the place, time and method of meeting with other units.

Guerrilla fighters resort to concentration when the enemy is advancing towards them, where there would be a good opportunity to attack and destroy it. Concentration is advantageous and recommended if the enemy is in a defensive position and the guerrillas are planning to isolate part of its forces in order to dominate and destroy them. By concentration we do not mean the bringing together of all forces of the guerrillas, we only mean to concentrate the forces necessary for a particular assignment; the remaining guerrillas are responsible for impeding and hindering the enemy and destroying its isolated forces or circulating propaganda among the people.

In addition to dispersal and concentration of the guerrilla forces, the leader must be familiar with the phrase 'cautious movement', when the enemy feels the danger of the guerrillas' progress and sends regiments to attack them; in this case the guerrillas should evaluate the situation and determine the time and place of combat. Should the guerrillas feel unable to fight, they should change position; for example if the guerrillas destroyed a part of the enemy's forces in a certain place, they may move to another place to attack and destroy another section of enemy forces. Should circumstances present a danger, the guerrillas should rapidly leave the place; their tactic must be deceptive and confusing to the enemy. They must let the enemy expect an attack from the east or north while they actually attack from the west or south. They must strike the enemy and disperse quickly and their movements must take place at night when changing position. The initiative of the guerrillas is evident in their dispersal, concentration and the cautious movement of forces. Stubbornness and stupidity will lead the guerrillas to passive attitudes which may be their end. Skill lies in the application of these tactics.

Planning

Premeditated planning is essential if we wish to achieve victory in guerrilla warfare. To arrange a plan is essential whatever the size of the unit is. It is essential to study the situation carefully, then determine the relative duties. The plan should include political and military instruction, such as the flow of supplies and equipment, and the question of co-operation with the local civilians. Victory may not be achieved without wise planning, co-ordination with the civilians and cautious surveillance. Even in a situation of defence we should direct all our efforts towards the return of an offensive position, which is the only way to weaken the enemy and preserve our forces. Being in a state of defence or withdrawal does not help or destroy the enemy, yet it is a temporary advantage in the preservation of our forces.

Relationship between guerrilla war and regular war

There are three types of co-operation between guerrilla fighters and regular forces:

1 Strategic co-operation
2 Tactical co-operation.
3 Co-operation in battle.

Guerrillas which frighten and hinder the enemy and paralyse its supply lines weaken the enemy and strengthen the morale of the people and their power of resistance. Such operations are described as strategic co-operation. The destruction of railroads, paved roads, and operations complementary to those of the regular army are treated as tactical co-operation. To complete guerrilla operations satisfactorily guerrilla fighters must be able to communicate by wireless or radio. The duty of guerrillas on the battlefield is to co-operate closely with regular forces by hindering the enemy, collecting information on the enemy's plans and doing night watch in front positions. Such tasks can be performed without prior orders from the leaders of the regular army.

The setting up of bases

We must give considerable attention to the problem of the establishment of bases since war is long and cruel. We may not be able to recover areas we have lost except through strategic counter attacks; and it is possible that this can only be achieved when the enemy has advanced further and further in China; thus we expect the enemy to occupy a small part of China or even most of it, and if this happens our newly-acquired land would be at the rear of enemy positions. Our duty is to carry out a strong and violent guerrilla war within vast areas and to transform the enemy's rear into another battle front, thus forcing the enemy to fight continuously. To subdue occupied areas the enemy will increase its violence and oppression.

The base of the guerrilla fighters can be defined as an area located in a strategic position which enables the guerrilla fighters to train and protect their men and organise their operations. The ability to wage war without the existence of a rear is a basic feature of guerrilla war, but this doesn't mean that guerrilla fighters can exist and operate for a long time without any bases. We can understand the concept of guerrilla bases better if we take the following points into consideration.

1 The existence of various types of bases.
2 The guerrilla areas and the location of the bases.
3 The setting up of bases.
4 The development of bases.

Bases can be divided according to their respective locations: first mountain bases, second plain bases and third, river, lake and gulf bases. The importance of mountain bases is evident but in general the plain does not benefit the guerrilla; however, this does not mean that guerrilla warfare cannot take place in such regions or that the setting up of bases is impossible. It can be possible to set up seasonal bases in plains in the winter when the rivers freeze and in summer when the crops grow. It is also possible to set up temporary bases when the enemy is busy with other things. So when the enemy advances, the guerrillas present in the plains counter-attack, and should the guerrillas withdraw to mountain areas they leave behind groups of soldiers distributed along the plain. Guerrilla groups move from one base to another according to the theory which states that the guerrillas are here today and somewhere else tomorrow. There are many examples of the lake, river and gulf bases, and there is a difference between the base area and the guerrilla base; the base area is the area surrounded by lands occupied by the enemy. There are some areas where garrisons are available, such as cities and areas adjacent to railroads. The guerrillas cannot expel the enemy from these areas and accordingly they remain guerrilla areas. At any time the base area can be changed to a guerrilla area either as a result of our mistakes or due to the escalation of enemy operations.

It is evident that any contested area will eventually either come under our control, be lost to the enemy, or divided between us and the enemy. So leaders should do their best to retain those areas in our possession or at least to keep them divided between us and the enemy. There is another basic factor in the establishment of bases and this is co-operation between the guerrilla unit and the people. We should spare no effort in spreading the principle of 'anti-Japanese Armed Resistance', supplying the people with weapons, organising national defence units and training guerrilla units. We should arouse the political feeling of the people and promote their military zeal. It is essential to organise workers, peasants, liberty explorers, youth and children to realise their strength against the enemy. The united strength of the people is the factor which puts an end to traitors, regains our lost political strength and retains and improves what is left for us.

The economic policy we should follow can be summarised as the protection of trade and business insofar as possible. Contributions should be proportional to the people's wealth, the peasants should contribute a portion of their crops. Confiscation of property is prohibited and can only be applied to traitors. It is essential to re-emphasise the development and expansion of bases as well as the organisation of the people and their military training.

Every guerrilla base has its own attack and defence problems, and in general the enemy will try to destroy the guerrilla's bases by directing numerous forces against it from various directions. While expecting this, we should break up the siege by counter-attack. Since the enemy troops are not supported by reserves in such cases, it is necessary for our main forces to draw up a plan to take one of the enemy's forces by surprise and then concentrate our secondary efforts in deceiving and terrifying the enemy. At the same time the rest of the guerrilla forces try to isolate the enemy's protective forces by attacking its lines of supply and communication, and engaging his regiment one by one. When we defeat the enemy in a certain area we must make use of the time it needs to reorganise and intensify our attacks accordingly. We should not attack a target when we cannot win and it is more appropriate to concentrate operations on relatively smaller areas to smash the enemy and eliminate traitors there. We should expand our operations to include cities and lines of communication where no strict vigilance exists and we may be able to occupy such places for a short time if not permanently. This is our task in strategic defence, the purpose of which is to lengthen the period when the enemy takes a defensive position. We should also expand our military operations and organisation among the masses, attack and destroy with the same determination as the enemy. Thereafter we should allow the guerrillas a period of rest and instruction, preferably when the enemy is in a defensive position.

Development of a mobile war

The development of the guerrilla war to a mobile war is not an easy operation and it constitutes a vital objective. In order to achieve such a development, it would be necessary to introduce some improvements to the guerrilla war in quantitative and qualitative respects. Basically we should increase the number of army recruits and improve our type of equipment and standard of training. We should concentrate on political training and the improvement of organisational methods, the use of weapons and tactics. We should give the soldier a political education and guerrillas should be developed into regular forces. It is also imperative that there should exist administrative offices and political and military staff as well as a military system comparable to other existing systems. Considering that the guerrilla formations function independently and that such formations represent the primary view of the armed formation, centralisation of leadership would be of little importance, lest guerrilla activities become restricted. We should however co-ordinate guerrilla activities among the respective troops on the one hand with those of the regular forces on the other, and the responsibility for this must be taken by the leaders and war staff. In the guerrilla bases, leadership centralisation is· essential for strategic reasons and should be divided for tactical reasons. Strategic centralisation of leadership takes into account the administration of guerrilla units and the organisation of their efforts in fighting and also the control of the general policy of the bases of guerrilla areas. Apart from what has been mentioned centralisation of leadership implies interference in guerrilla activities. In brief the proper policy of the guerrilla war is to create a unified strategy and independent activities.

ORGANISATION OF AN INDEPENDENT GUERRILLA FORCE

Company Commander

Executive Officer

Political Delegate
(mobile propaganda unit)

Company Command:

Despatch section
Administrative section
First Aid & Hospital section
Intelligence section

First Platoon
section

Second Platoon
section

Third Platoon
section

ORGANISATION OF THE COMPANY

Ranks	*Individuals*	*Type of Weapon*
Troop Captain	1	Pistol
Political Officer	1	Pistol
Executive Officer	1	Pistol
Company Command		
Head of Despatch section	1	
Signal section	1	

Ranks	*Individuals*	*Type of Weapon*
Head of Adm. section	1	
Liaison officers	3	Guns
Commissioned staff	2	,,
Barber	1	
Cook	10	
Medical officer	1	
Asst. Medical officer	1	
First Aid & nursing staff	4	
Head of Intell. section	1	Guns
Intelligence staff	9	,,
Platoon commanders	3	,,
Squad commanders	3	,,
9 Squads – 8 persons each	72	,,

ORGANISATION OF THE GUERRILLA DIVISION

DIVISION COMMANDER

Executive officer   Political Delegate

The Company Command and 3 Companies

The Administrative section   4th Company
  " Machinegun   "
  " Medical   "   3rd Company
  " Signal   "   2nd Company
  " Intelligence   "   1st Company

Remarks

1. Each squad consists of 9 to 11 men and in the event of the non-availability of a sufficient number of men or equipment, the third platoon can be dispersed and one of the squads can be made a company command office.
2. Members of the mobile propaganda unit are exempt from their main duties in order to circulate propaganda when not fighting.
3. If the staff number is not sufficient for a certain section, the medical section may be attached to the administrative section instead of being an independent section.
4. If there is no barber available the troops should do without him, and if the number of cooks is not available some members of the company may be selected to do the job.
5. Each warrior must have a rifle.
6. The maximum number of company members should be 180 divided into 12 squads each consisting of 11 men and the minimum number should be 82 divided into 6 squads each consisting of 9 men.

Appendix 2

Arab Labour Party of Oman's study on the historical development of Oman

Introductory notes[1]

As one of the consequences of the June 1967 Arab-Israeli war, several 'disenchanted' Omani members of the Ba'th Party, who inhabited mostly the present-day United Arab Emirates, regrouped and organised what became known as the Arab Labour Party of Oman. The founders were previously attached to Ba'th Party cells in both Iraq and Syria, and very few independent political activists from the Gulf area agreed to join them. All of them originated from the intelligentsia of the society; none had suffered from the political hardships prevailing under the rule of Ṣuḷtan Sa'id bin Tai'mūr, i.e. jailing, assassination etc. When ALPO was organised on party lines, the founders withdrew their allegiance from the Iraqi and Syrian branches of the Ba'th Party through their relationship with the Syrian branch, especially its intelligence apparatus, was kept marginally alive on a personal basis.

It must be pointed out here, at the outset, that ALPO must not be confused with Dr George Ḥabash's Arab Socialist Labour Party (ASLP). It has constantly been taken for granted that the latter originated from the Arab Nationalist Movement.[2]

In order to change the status quo in Oman, ALPO was basically planning to infiltrate the Ṣuḷtan's Armed Forces and the main government agencies which were in existence at the time, and, consequently, to bring about dramatic changes 'from the top'. This approach, as subsequent events demonstrated, proved to be futile.

ALPO's organisational cells were to be found in the following areas:

a) basic cells in Dubai, Sharjah, Rās al-Khaymah and 'Abu Dhābi,
b) minor cells in the other Emirates, Sūr, Muscat and Matrah, and
c) scattered and largely inactive cells in the rest of the Gulf.
    None was active in the Dhofar area.

Throughout its existence, ALPO's military operations, i.e. armed struggle, in Oman and the Gulf, were of minor importance. Its activities centred first around the areas inhabited by the Shiḥuḥ, Rās al-Khaymah, in an attempt to 'mobilise' tribal discontent; but the regime's intelligence was able to curtail swiftly its magnitude in 1972. Next, it collaborated with both the PFLOAG and NDFLOAG to 'put an end' to Sir William Ince's diplomatic initiative in the Gulf to create, among other things, the UAE. The three organisations agreed to kidnap Sir William Ince and, if this was not feasible, to assassinate him. According to PFLO sources, the plan's success was 'imminent', but there was an ALPO leakage of information, and the authorities were alerted. Subsequently the plan was abandoned. Finally a plan was drawn up by ALPO and NDFLOAG to launch armed struggle jointly in the interior of Oman. According to NDFLOAG sources, the former however broke the agreement and carried out the scheme single-handedly on 12 June 1970. Consequently, future collaboration between the two fronts was terminated.

Two final matters in the development of ALPO should be mentioned: its short-lived relations with the other two fronts, and its political analysis of Oman in contrast to the others. When ALPO came into existence the Dhofar Liberation Front was on the verge of changing its whole ideology and structure, and NDFLOAG was totally out of the military scene. After the DLF was transformed into PFLOAG, ALPO's political and strategic programme on Oman was almost identical. However, the question of unity between the two remained unsolved for three basic reasons.

First, the background from which the two originally sprang differed significantly, which entailed, second, the necessity for organisational independence within each front. Third, in contrast to PFLOAG, ALPO was an organisation based on party lines rather than a front. This was one of the weakest points in PFLOAG's earlier development. ALPO, however, wasted no time in creating a front organisation, which it named Omani Peoples' Forces Organisation (OPFO). OPFO was to act as a front to gather support from all sections of the population, and throughout its brief existence its spokesmen continued to deny publicly any allegiance to ALPO.[3] When OPFO was announced, NDFLOAG had already declared its political programme and the former launched its first public and indirect attack on NDFLOAG's political viewpoints.[4]

However, relations between ALPO and PFLOAG existed in general tacit agreement, and it was agreed that the two fronts must operate independently of each other. None the less, by the end of 1972, when Oman and the whole Gulf witnessed significant political changes, the two organisations deemed it necessary to call for unity in the face of mounting pressures. As a result, the two issued a joint communiqué containing the following significant agreement:

> *Differences in opinion* [my emphasis] concerning the scope of the revolution cannot stand in the way of reaching agreement and establishing closer relations, starting from the necessity of reaching an organisational framework to translate these new relations into action against the common enemy.
>
> Agreement has been reached as follows:
>
> 1 To form a joint regional leadership.
> 2 To struggle within the framework of PFLOAG.
> 3 To form a joint central committee.[5]

It should be noted that ALPO did not attempt to seek such rapprochement with NDFLOAG, whereas the latter had sought a coalition with PFLOAG. By the end of 1972, ALPO was obviously unable to maintain a stronghold in Oman, and so was forced to adhere to article 2 of the above agreement. This agreement marked the initial phase of ALPO's fading away from the Omani scene, and by gradual recruitment of its cells' members into PFLOAG's ranks, ALPO's organisational erosion was speeded up and, by the end of 1974, the Party had virtually ceased to exist as a viable force.

Throughout its existence, ALPO's political analysis differed from those of PFLOAG and NDFLOAG on priorities for action in Oman. The document which follows is an obvious example. It is apparent that, judging from its historical analysis of Omani society, this document was written before Ḳabūs's accession to power in 1970. Written at an earlier stage, this political analysis of Oman's politico-economic structure is far more extensive and elaborate than the later minor contributions presented by the other two fronts. However, the best document this can be compared with is PFLOAG's *Oman: a class analysis*; NDFLOAG's intellectual contribution in this field was almost negligible.

In short, the document's[6] contribution to the intellectual history of one of the movements involved in the Omani war is vital background material to our understanding of the methodology of the Fronts' approach.

Outline of the national democratic revolution in Oman: historical background of the Omani society [*Text*]

The criminal policies of British colonialism managed to isolate Oman entirely from the advance of civilisation and progress, and also from current Arab and international events. British colonialism managed at the same time to paralyse the creative culture initiated by the Omani People in their continued struggle for development and progress; it also managed to smear the features of all authentic revolutionary traditions adopted in the course of that brave struggle.

The Omani struggle has always been part of the Arab struggle, because Oman is an integral part of the Arab Nation as it has one language, one history and the same traditions in common with the rest of the Arab Nation. In pointing out the geographical location of Oman, we do not mean to divide a part from the whole; we aim only at indicating the geographical location of this country on the map of the Arab world.

SITE: Oman is located in the south-east of the Arabian Peninsula. To the south, it is bounded by The People's Democratic Republic of Yemen and the Arabian Sea; to the east by the Gulf of Oman; to the north by the Arabian Gulf; to the west by the Kingdom of Saudi Arabia. Oman has played an important role in human civilization because of its strategic location, particularly in maritime communications, acting as a vital bridge for the transportation of goods from India and South-east Asia, from East Africa to the Arab countries and Europe, in addition to transporting local produce to the above-mentioned countries. Thus, we can perceive the seriousness and positiveness of the Omani People and their ardent endurability to hardships and difficulties.

The Omani People had to be on the alert throughout their struggle, to be always ready to defend their homeland against the colonialist conquerors, who tried again and again to dominate Oman because of its important position, along communication routes they needed to maintain their persecution and exploitation of the people of Asia and Africa. They knew that Oman was the main naval power in the Indian Ocean, therefore, unless that power was smashed, it would be impossible for the colonialists to continue plundering and persecuting the peoples of Asia and Africa. It must also be recalled that despite the importance of naval activity to the Omani economy, it never played the main role in the economy, for agriculture has been of the greatest importance to most of the Omani people. Efforts were made to extend agriculture in order to make it a basic source of economy; hence hundreds of irrigation canals were dug in a marvellous geometric system which revealed the high level of civilisation achieved by Omani society in the Middle Ages. Progress in the field of agriculture was reflected in such local industries as the textile industry, sugar industry, ship-building industry, pottery and mining, together with the basic refining of minerals and in particular an iron industry in the Nizwā-Hata areas.

As far as culture is concerned, Oman has played a prominent role in the history of the Arab Nations, especially in the intellectual, cultural, political, literary and astronomic fields. Among famous Omani poets and men of letters were Aḥmad bin Sa'id al-Sastalī, Khalil bin Aḥmad al-Farāhīdī, who was a philologist and the one who introduced the alphabet, points and vowel-points into the Arabic language; al-Muhlab bin'Abi-Ṣufia, Naṣir bin Murshed al-Ya'rbī, and Aḥmad bin Sa'id Āl-bū-Sa'īd, were among the famous political leaders; as for sciences, Aḥmad bin Madj was an astronomer and geographer. There were also many others.

During the reign of the Ummayed and Abbasids, Oman was a center of intellectual and political leadership; it was also the center of revolt against absolute authoritarian central rule, which indicates the intellectual and political level reached by Omani society at that time.

While most parts of the Arab homeland were suffering from Turkish colonialist domination, and the Turkish dissemination of theological thought, Oman used to be in possession of a huge naval force, and had a policy independent from that of the Caliphate or Sublime Porte; Oman also used to keep out the colonialists and get rid of their filth all over the area in order to save the people from colonialist domination, chasing the colonialists across the Indian Ocean to East Africa, and conveying ideas of fraternity and peace to the Asian and African peoples. Unfortunately, these ideas were not concretised because the feudal outlook was unable to put them into practice — regardless of its statements and its being reformative — due to its inability to give up its authoritarian outlook on one hand, and the absence of a vanguard consciousness of the causes of struggle on the other hand. For all these reasons the Omanis were unable to step out of the framework of the thinking which was dominant at that time. Therefore, they established the States of Zanzibar and Mombasa which used to pay tribute to Muscat, which was ruled by Ṣuḷtan Sa'id, an absolute ruler; he was himself the law-giver and the executive authority at home and abroad, against the free will of the people of that area. Baluchistan area (Makran), with its capital (Gwadar) was different from Zanzibar because it had to cope with the same exploitation and persecution which the Omani people and the peoples of East African countries were suffering under the rule of the al-Bu Sa'id Dynasty. Baluchistan area was suffering from national chauvinistic persecution carried out against it by the feudal authority in Oman. In view of these facts, the feudal authority wanted to further its expansionist ambitions and managed to establish its influence in these areas. It is noteworthy that Turkish colonialist domination played a role in transporting the feudal expansionist conceptions based on theological thought. This is a brief outline of Omani civilisation which has started to develop, then gradually gave way to regression. This regression started with the 1798 Convention which was the first agreement concluded in the Arab Nation with western colonialism, and was a starting-point for colonialism to attack Arab civilisation and culture, and fight the aspirations of the people for a better future and new society. As a counterpart, the colonialists managed to disseminate illiteracy, charlatanism and theological thoughts based on superstitions. This is why Oman has, since the late eighteenth century and up to the present time, been living in dreadful intellectual and social backwardness. Dependency, pessimism and defeatism have replaced the revolutionary values acquired through the sacrifices of our people. All this pessimism and defeatism was an outcome of the then prevailing superstitious atmosphere. For resentment against deteriorating situations and the desire to eradicate exploitation and persecution are already there. Therefore, it is imperative that our Party and all the revolutionary forces make great efforts to defeat the reactionary colonialist cultural institutions, combat illusions, disseminate revolutionary ideology, and activate positiveness in our people so as to be able to eradicate exploitation and persecution, push forward the Arab and World liberation movement, and establish peace and stability in the whole world.

The feudal situation in Oman

The feudal situation in Oman dates back several thousand years (the period cannot be precisely determined owing to the absence of historical sources). We can, however, determine that the history of feudalism goes back thousands of years because Oman had commercial relations with the world at the time the Phoenicians were in Oman; the Phoenicians were famous for their wide commercial contacts in East Africa, the Mediterranean countries and India. (This is a proof of the existence of the feudal system in Oman thousands of years ago.) Despite the coincidence of the introduction of western capital with colonial infiltration, the feudal situation still prevails in our society to the present moment. The politico-economic system of feudalism was characterized by the following:

1 The natural economy in Oman is based on self-sufficiency in agriculture, fishing, herding and pearl-diving. Farmers used to

produce the agricultural products that they needed, in addition
to various handicraft products. Nevertheless they have, throughout the feudal period and until the early fifties of the twentieth
century, been terribly exploited and heavily indebted to their
feudal usurers. Farmers only obtained a very small percentage
of their own production, which could hardly meet their needs.
Hence they were always at the mercy of the feudalists and
subject to torture and torment. This, in many cases, placed them
in the same category as serfs.

2 Commercial exchange played an important role in the politico-
economic position in Oman throughout the feudal period,
primarily because of the geographical position of Oman; this
gave rise to a class of workers or seamen suffering from inhuman
persecution and exploitation. They were also quasi-serfs as a
result of their accumulated debts year after year due to feudal
usury; they were thus compelled to toil — against their will — in
the feudalist's ships, by the latter's representatives in power as
a token of their greed and arrogance.

3 The feudal system in Oman is not only based on the slavery of
peasants, but there was a more miserable class — the serfs themselves, who were deprived of the simplest human rights. The serfs
had to toil night and day for nothing more than bare subsistence,
just enough to enable them to go on serving their masters. They
were also beaten, bullied, imprisoned, killed, sold and purchased
every day. Feudalism depended on that class besides the peasant
class, for the accumulation of more wealth to satisfy the feudalists'
whims and expand its influence.

4 Pearl-diving labourers were a mixture of slaves, farmers and
fishermen, harshly exploited by feudal ship-owners. They were
often subjected to starvation, thirst, beating and killing, being
dragged along behind their ship; they were quasi-serfs, deprived
of their own production which was usurped by the feudalists;
they had to pay unwarranted debts alleged by the feudalists,
which the labourers dared not deny. Therefore, the seaman could
not work according to his own will, because he was compelled
to work with this feudal master or that, according to the law
laid down by feudalism (you may forget but the debts notebook
does not).

The feudal system which dates back thousands of years
remained throughout that period, practising economic exploitation and political persecution; peasants and seamen lived

under the sway of feudalism like starving and miserable slaves; beside feudal power, was the power of the State, which was in reality the supreme form of the feudal power, responsible for the suppression of the farmers and working masses, and forcing them to work under brutal feudal conditions, in addition to corvée forced by the State on labourers digging up canals, transportation of cereals and levying heavy taxes etc.

5 Feudalism in Oman found the right background to practise persecution and exploitation at times when Oman was subjected to foreign invasion. For example, during the Portuguese occupation of Oman in the sixteenth century, there existed in Oman scores of insignificant feudalists under the rule of authoritarian princes. The same thing occurred when the Persian invaders managed to occupy the Batinah coast in the eighteenth century where existed many independent and authoritarian feudal lords who inflicted misery and slavery on the people. This characteristic became more visible and clearer under British occupation; the Emirates and the Ṣuḷtanate of Muscat were ruled by feudalists who practised economic exploitation and political persecution, depriving the masses, especially labourers and farmers, of the most elementary human rights.

During that feudal period, the feudal state in Oman had not developed central government, but used often to undermine the central authority and divide Oman into feudal units ruled by feudalists who used their political influence to achieve economic exploitation. In the sixteenth century when the central feudal authority was in the hands of the Banī Nabhān, Oman was invaded by the Portuguese, and was consequently divided into several feudal units, each of which was ruled by an authoritarian prince. In the meanwhile the peasants and all labourers were persecuted, exploited, killed and tortured. Therefore it was necessary for the peasants and all the working masses to overthrow the authoritarian feudalists because it was the main problem in the aftermath of the Portuguese invasion. In the first half of the seventeenth century, a great popular uprising broke out under the leadership of Nasir bin Murshed aiming at getting rid of all feudal units administered by local authoritarian feudalists who supported the division of the country, and subjected the peasants and people to the worst kinds of persecution and exploitation. That great uprising was able — after long fierce battles — to finish off local feudal rule, and unite Oman under

one central rule; it also managed to free the peasants and the
masses — though only for a little while — from the feudal yoke.
That uprising was not only aimed at fighting feudalism or the
enemy at home, and unifying Oman, but it managed to expel
the Portuguese colonialists from Oman, to East Africa and India;
it also liberated the Indian Ocean from the Portuguese colonialists.
We conclude that the main objective of that uprising was to fight
feudalism and expel the colonialist intruders. Therefore the
uprising was a comprehensive revolution against feudalism carried
out by the masses. But because that popular revolution was not
led by an enlightened vanguard who had a healthy conception
and definite channels of activity, it was only normal that the
new power should use the same inherited feudal ways and not
abandon them except in partial reform. This was why the new
central feudal regime did not survive, and Oman fell back into
the hands of local feudalists. The feudal local and central rule
was absolutely authoritarian, which can be seen by an example
indicating the continuity and ugliness of the feudal system in
Oman. On 8 July 1958 Sa'id bin Taimur, the feudal ruler of
Muscat, sold the region called Gwadar, its land and inhabitants,
to the Pakistani Government for 20 million rupees. This is not
the only example of the ferocity of feudalism in Oman, but there
are many other similar crimes. In addition, the feudal regime
nominated — on its own behalf — Governors of the provinces,
levied heavy taxes, and administered courts of law assisted by the
local forces (soldiers). Oman turned from an independent state
into a quasi-colonized state since the agreement on the organization of trade concluded in 1798 between Ṣulṭan bin Aḥmad
the feudal governor of the then Ṣulṭanate of Muscat and Oman,
and the British colonialists (it was the first agreement concluded
in the Arab world with western colonialists). That agreement was
not in fact a pure trade agreement but had definite inherent
political objectives meant to transform Oman into one of their
colonies. When colonialists and feudalists decided together to
plunder the wealth of the Omani people, they began to plan
and conspire against our struggling people. In 1809, colonialists
and feudalists launched a fierce attack against Rās al-Khaymah,
but were repelled. Another attack was launched, and was also
foiled. Again in 1819, colonialists and feudalists launched a third
aggression in which they killed and burned the masses in Rās
al-Khaymah who resisted courageously; feudalists in that area

concluded an agreement in which they gave full concessions to the colonialists and allowed them to act against the people's will on land, sea and air. Thus Oman changed from a semi-colonised into a colonised country. That agreement was extended in 1863, although that extension was only formal, since the survival of colonialists does not depend on agreements but on the feudal class itself and the guns aimed at the people. Therefore the British colonialists made every effort to support the feudal system and its superstructure in particular, for the sake of their colonial interests. The question is: did the colonialists keep the feudal economic structure? Of course, why not? Colonialists came to the East in search of raw materials and consumer markets for their industrial products; this is why the natural feudal economy based on natural self-sufficiency is a stumbling block in the way of world capitalism and its appetite for the exploitation of nations. Therefore British capitalism did not, in general, keep that feudal economic structure. The consumer economy dealt a blow to the natural economy since foreign capitalism considered Oman as a consumer market for its products and bound Oman's economy to the imperial economy; consequently agriculture did not constitute the backbone of our economy, and the local handicrafts disappeared, whereupon our economy became largely dependent on foreign products. As regards maritime transport Omani trading liners were replaced by the ships of the monopoly companies, and Omani ships no longer held the front position in maritime transport as in the past.

The economic structure in Oman collapsed because of world imperialist policies and their impact all over the world; only the feudal superstructure remained to help the British imperialists stay in Oman; for this reason they were careful to enable that structure to survive, whereupon the imperialists were able to extend their exploitation and intensify their persecution of the people.

Oman does not differ from the under-developed countries in general, and the Arab countries in particular, because of policies aimed at binding the economies of under-developed countries with imperialist economy. This is why that change in the economic structure did not lead to the creation of a local industrial economy for the sake of promoting the Omani economy and making it somewhat self-sufficient. For in reality, the simplest commodities are imported from abroad, to the benefit of both imperialists and feudalists whose existence runs counter to any new productive forces (national bourgeoisie and labourers). The new class which has emerged now are the 'Compradors' (monopolizing importers) who act as intermediaries, who flourish and grow in the absence of local production, because their existence is essentially bound to the imperialist/feudalist status quo at present. Thus, our society has changed from a feudal and semi-colonized society into a semi-feudal and colonized society.

The power of the present feudal class, represented mainly by the princes and sultans, does not depend fundamentally on the land, after the changes which have taken place in the economic structure; it is due to their almost complete dependence on the profits they earn from foreign monopoly companies as a result of betraying their country and people by giving concessions to the companies for oil prospecting, investment and the domination of the entire economy of the country. Thus they became closely connected with the colonial presence and the basic economy became principally based on commercial exchange, therefore agriculture and fishing accordingly took a subsidiary position. The present economy is, however, based on petroleum.

The feudal superstructure, with the support and collusion of the colonialists, did not allow the productive forces to grow, i.e. it did not allow national capital to create national industries; this was achieved through the troubles fomented by colonialists and feudalists against national capital in the industrial field, channelling it into serving their foreign monopolizing countries through importing and creating a comprador class which was the second base, as well as through several other factors which hampered the development of national capital. The most important of these factors are:

1 Fear of colluding with colonial interests lest it should compromise its own interests.
2 Seeking quick profit through imports yielding guaranteed profit.
3 Since the larger part who own huge capital are foreigners, they refrain from investing their money in national industries owing to existing political factors.
4 The novelty and lack of expertise on the part of the comprador.
5 The division of the country of Oman has been one of the factors hampering – in the past and at present – the establishment of national industries.

These factors are added to the main factor, i.e. the troubles inflicted by the colonialists and feudalists upon national capital for fear of creating a revolutionary class committed to a progressive economy which would pull down these theological structures, instigate the masses to overthrow these enemies and march past them towards real new horizons.

The collapse of agriculture as we have mentioned before, and the continuation of the feudal superstructure which does not allow the establishment of national industries and subjects the farmers and simple producers to more misery and hunger, which renders them unable to live in Oman; this is also due to the existence of monopoly companies in some areas of the Gulf where it is possible to take a job and make a living. Consequently, Oman witnessed a large-scale emigration of farmers, simple producers, craftsmen to these areas to work under the difficult circumstances imposed by the monopoly companies which resorted to the vilest kinds of exploitation and persecution. However, after oil was extracted in Oman, it was possible for large numbers of Omani labourers to make a living, and constitute a new class leading the struggle against colonialists and their feudal and comprador agents. Nevertheless, the public enemy assisted by his two class allies, pursued a criminal policy which prevented labourers from being stationed in the companies, while this enemy employed foreign semi-mercenary labourers biased against the Arabs of Oman, thus imposing an odd and grave twist on the march of the Omani revolution.

Colonialist domination over Oman

The history of colonialism in Oman dates back to the sixteenth century when the Portuguese discovered the Cape of Good Hope. This discovery was a green light for the Portuguese to realise their ambitions to reach the Orient 'the Arabian Gulf, India and South-east Asia'. At that time they wanted to prevent the Mameluks from forestalling other colonialist states in occupying those areas, and building strongholds which would give them complete domination in those areas. Consequently, the Portuguese launched a savage attack on the Omani area in 1506 A.D., when they sent a naval force under the leadership of Admiral Albuquerque, who assaulted the Arab warships and burnt them in Omani territorial waters. Afterwards he occupied the town of 'Kalhat', then marched on to 'Ḳariyat' then to 'Ṣaḥar' and 'K͟hurfakān', where he was met by popular resistance.

However, the Portuguese were able to overcome this resistance and occupy the town. It is worth mentioning here that the Portuguese based their strategy on a careful assessment of their own strength and that of the people whom they were invading. This strategy demanded the use of terrorist methods, the waging of swift and sudden attacks and the torturing and mutilating of the inhabitants of that region. They monopolized trade. They continued these policies of intimidation and terror throughout their period of occupation. But the saying that 'Injustice breeds resistance' must always be present in our minds. Our people were not daunted by these barbaric and repressive measures. They carried out their struggle to the end. It is perhaps apt to note here that for the Portuguese, the task of occupying our land was facilitated by what was happening in Oman at the time. The country was then divided and under tyrannical feudalist rule. But even that did not stop our people putting up a gallant resistance.

The presence of the Portuguese in our country was an unacceptable anomaly. The honest and sincere people amongst us were aware of this. Thus, and as a response to the desire of the people, they started their movement to unite the land in the face of the invaders; yet the feudalists whose interests were tied to those of the invaders opposed this movement. But despite all this, the people rallied round Nasir bin Murshed and their resistance developed into a war of national liberation which destroyed all the fortresses and strongholds that the enemy had established on the Omani coast, and expelled them from Omani ports and regional waters. Furthermore, the resistance movement pursued the fight into the Indian Ocean and continued its victorious process by liberating regions in India and East Africa which had been under Portuguese domination, and replaced it with a strong and prosperous administration.

Colonialist rivalries

In the last decades of the sixteenth century, and towards the end of the period of Portuguese hegemony, three other imperial powers appeared on the scene. These were Britain, France and Holland. The main rivalry was between Britain and France. The rivalries between these powers passed through two stages. The first was the stage of commercial competition which started when the British established the East India Trading Company, an act which exposed it to competition from the Portuguese, French and Dutch. The second stage was distinguished by rivalries between Britain and other colonial powers. The rivalries at this stage were not of a purely commercial nature. After the end of the Seven Years' War (1756–63) British colonial policy changed dramatically, as a result of the Paris Treaty which ended the war, and according to which France ceded to Britain most of her possessions in the Indian Ocean. In fact, France was left with only the 'Island of

France' in that area. Thus it gave Britain a freer rein in the region (see *Kitab al-Dawla Al-bu Sa'īdiya*). However, France's surrender of her possessions was in fact a tactical move aimed at easing the struggle between the British and French colonialists at the expense of the peoples of the region. The French did try to establish relations and conclude agreements with Oman, where the ruler at the time was Aḥmad bin Sa'īd. The French succeeded in this and were able to establish good relations with him: then followed an exchange of messages and trade between him and the rulers of France. But the British grew wary of this threat to their interest in the region. So, at a time when national feelings in Oman were aroused, immediately after Napoleon's Egyptian Campaign, the British took this opportunity and concluded the famous 1798 treaty, which was the first agreement between Britain and the rulers of Muscat. It was also the first treaty of its kind with an Arab country. This treaty was followed by the McCullam Mission, the result of which was a further treaty with the Ṣulṭan, confirming the one reached in 1798. This new treaty made provision for the appointment of a permanent British Resident in Muscat. He was to be the agent through whom all dealings and communications between the two countries would be conducted. The local regulations governing dealings with foreigners were no longer applied in the case of the British.

The beginning of the British presence

There is no doubt that the 1798 treaty and its confirmation by the 1800 treaty were a shattering blow to Omani sovereignty. They also marked the start of the systematic plundering of our wealth, as well as the beginning of a policy of terrorising and intimidating our people. In addition they inaugurated a criminal colonialist policy which aimed at crushing the forces of liberation, enforcing domination over the Arabian Gulf and the Indian Ocean, and giving imperialism a foothold in our land. Thus the imperialists found their chance to tighten their grip over our lands through the treacherous al-Bu Sa'id rulers of Muscat, who did not control all Omani territory. The northern region of Oman was in fact fully independent of their rule. It represented an obstacle in the face of imperialist ambitions and dealt successive blows against the colonialists. At the same time it constituted a real threat to the treacherous rulers of Muscat. So the British and the rulers of Muscat started working hand in hand to bring the northern region under the authority. They launched three sea and land campaigns to encircle that part of the land and Rās al-Khaymah in particular. The first of these campaigns was undertaken in 1809. The plan of the campaign was for the rulers of Muscat to despatch a land force while the British were to attack from the sea and to destroy the fleet at Rās al-Khaymah and lay siege to the town. This campaign failed because of the brave resistance that the people put up. Another campaign was sent in 1812 and met with the same fate as the previous one. But the British imperialists with their aggressive nature and because they represented the interests of their bourgeois classes, would not accept the realities of the situation. And as long as they were there, they would continue their aggression against the people. So in 1819 they launched their third and most ferocious and ruthless campaign, supported by the treacherous al-Bu Sa'id who supplied a huge army to back up the British warships. However, our people made a gallant stand in the face of the invaders and made tremendous sacrifices before the British were able to subjugate the northern region and Rās al-Khaymah in particular. However, our people would not have stopped fighting even after the fall of Rās al-Khaymah had it not been for the surrender of the feudalist leadership. Thus, through criminal plotting against the Omani people, the treacherous al-Bu Sa'id and the British imperialists were able to control the land of Oman.

Our people did not remain idle in the face of these plots and intrigues which were designed to smother their aspirations, rob them of their resources and isolate them from the outside world. The uprising of 1914 was clear proof of our people's unrelenting resistance, their complete rejection of the colonialists and oppressors and of the extent of their heroism and perseverance concerning the national question and the question of their destiny. Faced with this situation, the British resorted to more intrigues; they made it appear that the Ṣulṭan was the main culprit while they, the imperialists, had no connection with what was happening.

The Ṣulṭan, faced with the wrath of the people, identified himself even more with his masters. The Ṣulṭan concluded more treaties which would secure his position on the throne and abort the people's rebellions against the colonialists. Thus came the Sib Agreement, as a compromise between the Ṣulṭan and the revolutionaries. The imperialists took advantage of the new situation by working out their strategy, which aimed at encircling the interior of Oman on the one hand, and dividing up the country on the other. They also exploited tribal divisions in Oman and planned further fragmentation of the country. They separated the northern part of Oman from the rest of the country, and furthermore divided it into seven so-called states: 'Abū Dhabi, Dubai, Sharjah,

'Ajman, Umm al-Qaiwain, al-Fujaira and Rās al-Khaymah which were all, through various agreements under treaties, under their authority. All these treaties purported to legalise British presence in the area and to declare all these states British protectorates.

A very clear example of the absurd attitude of the rulers of these Emirates is the so-called 'Abū Dhabi Treaty of 1892, in which the following is stated:

> I . . . do hereby solemnly bind myself and agree, on behalf of myself, my heirs and successors, to the following conditions:
>
> That I will on no account enter into any agreement or correspondence with any power other than the British Government.
>
> That without the assent of the British Government I will not consent to the residence, within my territory, of the agent of any other government.
>
> That I will on no account cede, sell, mortgage or otherwise give for occupation any part of my territory, save to the British Government.

The methods resorted to by the British in order to establish their authority in our country

1 *Playing on tribal differences*: It is a well-known fact that British policy depended upon stirring up troubles and divisions amongst the people. So they worked at deepening tribal difference and inflaming devastating tribal feuds, exploiting the conflict between the Hana'is and the Ghafiris. This was a political dispute, ensuing from a difference of opinion over the question of the 'Imām appointed in the early part of the eighteenth century. The 'Imām in question was a minor and so had no right to the office. Muḥammad bin Naṣir al-Ghafiri led the party which opposed the appointment of the 'Imām, while Khalaf bin Mubarak al-Hana'i led those who supported it. Hence those who rallied behind Khalaf were called the *Hana'iyya*, while those who supported Muhammad bin Naṣir were called *Ghafiriyya*. As a result of this serious dispute, the Omanis were divided into two factions: Hana'i and Ghafiri. This resulted in devastating wars which paved the way for the division of the country and its control by British colonialism, and for the creation of numerous weak feudal estates.

The ferocious wars fought between these two factions were quite different from the tribal clashes that took place in Oman from time to time. The colonialists took advantage of these tribal feuds to strengthen their position, implement their plans for exploiting and dominating the country and to consolidate the positions of those rulers who accepted their policies. They also used these differences to deepen even further the division of the country, to deprive the people of education and to distract their attention by those problems in order to make them forget their real enemy which was British imperialism. The colonialists succeeded to a great extent in carrying out their plans, as a consequence of which the Omanis are still suffering from ignorance, disease, homelessness, deprivation of basic human rights and the undermining of their national unity throughout the country.

2 *The creation of disputable spheres of influence*: British imperialism used every means within its power to serve its interests in our country and to divert the attention of our people away from their fundamental problems. One of the methods that the imperialists had recourse to, was the creation of disputable spheres of influence which were to be a bone of contention between the so-called states that they themselves had created. For the success of this policy, they secured the sincere co-operation of their stooges, the Ṣulṭans and princes, who in order to please their masters carried out their plans to the letter. Evidence of the fact that the fragmentation of the land and the creation of these spheres of influence were the work of the imperialists abounds. The village of Masafī, for example, was divided into two parts, one belonging to the State of Rās al-Khaymah and the other to al-Fujaira. The discord between the two parts often led to open hostilities with each shaikh supporting the part of the village under his jurisdiction. We also find that the Khiṣb area, which is in the northern coastal region of Oman, was part of the domains of the Ṣulṭan of Muscat, while the Kilba region in the Gulf of Oman was under the rule of Sharjah. There is also the Masfut region which lies beyond the frontiers of Rās al-Khaymah, bordering on the Sultanate of Oman — we find that this region constitutes part of the 'Ajman Emirate. There is also the Dabā region which best illustrates the disputes over these spheres of influence. This policy was continuously diverting the attention of our people from their basic problem, which was the struggle against the imperialists and their lackeys, the rulers, emirs and sultans. Through such policies the imperialists aimed at consolidating their position in our land. To achieve this aim they tried various methods. One of these methods was the creation of the Council of the Trucial States which, at this time, is doing all it can to weaken the national struggle against imperialists. This they hope to achieve by building a few clinics, some roads, and digging artesian

wells in the rural areas. All these tricks and futile attempts will ultimately fail to water down the resentment and hatred that the masses have for imperialism.

3 *Foreign immigration*: A method which the imperialists adopted in order to add to existing conflicts and problems of our country, and to facilitate the process of plundering our national wealth, was to open its gates to foreign immigrants. This also served as a means of alleviating the pressure on the imperialists, by creating frictions between the natives and these immigrants, who were brought in to exploit our people, despoil our land, create a centre for spying and intelligence services and provide the means through which our national wealth would end up in the banks of London, Washington, Tel Aviv, Bonn and all the other capitals of the imperialist world. Through this policy of immigration the imperialists were aiming at creating on the coast of Oman communities which could be used against the rising tide of revolution and at the same time provide cheap labour and prevent the native Omanis from making a living in their own country, thus forcing them to leave their native land and seek employment abroad. This policy also aimed at dealing a blow to the national economy and agriculture and preventing the emergence of an Arab working class and a national capital which would threaten its monopoly. And as if the social, cultural, political and economic damage of this policy were not enough, the imperialists recruited mercenaries to strengthen their armies and establishments. The Defence Forces of the coast of Oman, and the army of that imperialist lackey, the Ṣuḷtan of Muscat, and the security and police forces throughout the country, were full of these mercenaries. This is all aimed at suppressing the spirit of revolution among the vanguards of this struggling nation. The imperialists thought that by such stupid measures they could achieve their aims. However whatever they do they cannot stop the movement for national liberation or arrest the will of the Arab people. Nor can they tie down the hands which will deal imperialists and their criminal designs a shattering blow to destroy all those who stand in their way and exploit their country and all those who serve the interests of the imperialists.

4 *Evacuation and the call for union*: Of late, the imperialists have realised that all their old methods and designs have been uncovered and that they no longer serve their strategy in a satisfactory manner. So they formulated their new devilish plan which aims at reducing their forces of direct occupation and resorting to a less direct form of

colonialism through their stooges, the emirs and sultans. At the same time, the imperialists are aiming, by playing this new tune, at easing the resentment of the masses, on the one hand, and containing the national liberation movement on the other. So they declared that they are going to withdraw their forces by the end of 1971 and that at the same time they would bring in special mobile military forces to protect their spheres of interest – a policy which would no doubt reduce the costs of maintaining their presence and at the same time dampen the revolutionary spirit of the Omani people. Simultaneously with this declaration of their intention to withdraw, the imperialists prepared the ground for the creation of the so-called union of the Emirates. It is worth mentioning here that the imperialists have been imposing their direct authority upon our people for the last two centuries. Their presence has been represented by their military bases scattered throughout our territory. The most important of these bases are at Masirah, Sharjah, Bait al-Falaj, al-Manāmah and Salālah. The presence of these bases has been a direct provocation to our national sentiments. When the imperialists realised that their old strategy was in need of a change they substituted for it the 'East of Suez' strategy – a criminal design aimed at extending the presence of imperialism on our soil. So the imperialists made a big show of the idea of the so-called Union of the Emirates. This idea was presented as a progressive step, while in reality it is nothing of the sort. This is not a union of the people of the same country but a union of imperialist monopolies. The orders for its creation were issued from the capitals of the imperialist powers, led by America. The British imperialists played a double role of planner and propagandist of this union. Then the ignorant Emirs of the region began to execute the policies of their masters which aimed at suppressing the staunch opposition to imperialist presence and at substituting direct colonialism with another sort – one which is more vigorous and keener on exploiting and monopolizing the economy of the region and more intent on shattering national unity.

The counter-revolutionary forces: Knowing one's enemies and one's friends is of the utmost importance in revolutionary struggle. Without resolving this problem in the proper manner, it is impossible for us to continue with our revolution on the right path, so as to destroy our enemies completely and end their domination. This appears clearly in the repeated failures of the Arab revolution and its miserable inability to finally bring to an end imperialist domination. The imperialists are still in control of our national wealth and of our policies. This is due to the fact that the elements and groups who shouldered the responsibility of leading the revolution were not able to determine who their true friends were, and unite them against the real enemies. The reason is that their class outlook and positions did not give them proper insight to do so. Therefore, in order to accomplish our revolutionary objectives, it is our duty to realise clearly who our enemies are and who our friends are. This will not be achieved except by the study of the nature and realities of our society which in its turn determines the economic status of all classes and the attitude of each class towards the revolution.

Who are the counter-revolutionaries in Oman? From the above analysis we realise that Omani society is a colonised and feudal society. There is no doubt that the principal enemies of the Omani people are imperialism, feudalism, and the comprador bourgeoisie, whose interests are closely tied to those of British colonialism and international imperialism. In addition there are the political 'front' men, such as managerial staff, senior officials and some of the intelligentsia who in one way or another are connected with imperialist establishments. Their number is increasing day by day due to expansion in these establishments. These establishments are a means by which the imperialists dominate and continue in authority. This group of officials plays a dirty role in opposition to the aspirations of the masses. They mislead them by spreading reactionary ideas. They constitute, on account of their bourgeois education, a real danger for the cause of the revolutionary masses, which aims at destroying imperialism, feudalism and the comprador bourgeoisie. They play their misleading role by presenting what is happening as something that is progressive and nationalistic. This group of people enjoy numerous privileges and are getting rich at the expense of the masses. This comes as a result of the facilities they are accorded by the imperialists and the ruling classes. These forces together block the way to Omani progress and collaborate in oppressing and exploiting the Omanis.

It is obvious that international imperialism is the most formidable of these enemies. In the case of Oman, imperialism with its political and military power is a more serious enemy than all the others combined. It has consolidated its presence by establishing scores of military bases – air bases, naval bases and army bases. Through its military forces, imperialism has committed all kinds of atrocities against the Omani people. These forces have killed people, starved them out and banished them. The Omani people have been subjected to the worst kinds of oppression since the signing of the first treaty between imperialism and the traitor Ṣulṭan bin Aḥmad al-Bu Sa'id, the ill-reputed imperialist lackey who committed crimes against the people. British imperialism, supported by the forces of this stooge, made attacks on northern Oman and in particular the region of Rās al-Khaymah in 1809, 1814 and 1819. During these raids they committed massacres, killing women, children, innocent and old people. They devastated, burned and pillaged villages. British imperialism in Oman is an example of imperialism at its worst, on account of the barbaric and inhuman methods that it has been employing.

In 1821 a number of military campaigns were made to crush the Omanis in the region of Dja'lan, which was mercilessly shelled and some of its peace-loving inhabitants killed; some were taken captive and sent to India and Britain, where they were put into slavery, and since then nobody has heard anything of their fate. This happened because they rose up to rid themselves of the imperialists and their stooges the al-Bu Sa'id.

Again in 1914 the people rose in revolt against foreign occupation. This revolt started at Nizwā and Samayil. This was also ruthlessly suppressed by the imperialists and the al-Bu Sa'id traitors, the despotic feudalist stooges of imperialism. Khaṣab was also bombarded by the British navy in 1937, when her people rose against the al-Bu Sa'id, the natural allies of the British imperialists and their right arm in carrying out their criminal policies against the Omani people. These blood-thirsty criminals were not satisfied with the crimes that they had so far committed against the Omani people. So they continued plotting and carrying out their campaign of brutal suppression and destruction by dropping hundreds of tons of explosives and bombs on our people at Nizwa and al-Jabal al-Akhḍar in 1957. In all this the imperialists were always aided by their friends and natural allies the feudalist rulers of Muscat.

Knowing the nature of Omani society, which is a semi-feudalist colonial society, it becomes clear to us that the two foremost enemies are imperialism and feudalism which between them control all the resources of the country. Their domination is represented by the British army of occupation, the Ṣulṭan's army, the Omani Coast Defence Force, the 'Abū Dhabi Defence Force and the new force which has been designated 'The Scouts of the Omani Coast', which has been approved by the Supreme Council of the so-called Union of Emirates. In addition to these there are the local police forces in each Emirate. These local forces are being rapidly increased and are receiving more and more attention, to make them a more efficient instrument in suppressing the people. Moreover, the bourgeoisie, that is the compradors, are in alliance with imperialism and feudalism. They emerged as a class with the advent of imperialism. The bourgeoisie or 'comprador' class lends support to the present situation because of the privileges they are getting from the international imperialist companies and the facilities accorded them by feudalism, the rulers and the British colonialists. This class is satisfied with the present situation and are convinced that any attempt to change it would be an invitation to disorder and chaos.

From the above it becomes clear that the main enemies of the Omani revolution, at the national democratic stage, are imperialism, feudalism, the princes-rulers and the comprador bourgeoisie. The Omani revolutionaries must prepare themselves for a long struggle to crush these vicious enemies and in particular, British imperialism and the feudalist rulers and sultans, who have suppressed and are still suppressing with utter ruthlessness all the national movements in Oman. As the ruling system in Oman is autocratic, tyrannical and unjust and does not allow even peaceful struggle towards change for a better society, there is only one option: armed struggle. This is the only means that all revolutionary forces have open to them. The experiences of all other revolutionary forces in the world, in the Arab world and even in Oman itself, have shown that the enemy will never budge in response to speeches or peaceful action and that violence is the only language that they understand. Without armed struggle talking about revolution is only rhetoric. Armed struggle is the highest form of revolutionary struggle. It is the only form of struggle that truly reflects the hopes of the masses who aspire to getting rid of the tyranny and servitude to which they have been subjected in the past and up to the present day. When we give armed struggle priority in our revolutionary activities we do not neglect the effectiveness of other means of action which augment armed struggle. Faced with these obstinate and vicious enemies, the Omani revolution is going to be a protracted and intensive war at the same time. This is the inevitable result of the frenzied greed of the imperialists in robbing the wealth of our land. We could not achieve the national democratic revolution if we viewed the Omani revolution as sporadic resistance actions which would lead to the fall of imperialism and feudalism. Such a view would be contrary to the nature of the growth and solidarity of the revolutionary forces, which will not be well-equipped for their role except through the long-term struggle which will strengthen them and give them the necessary experience to overthrow both the national and the class enemies.

The motive forces of the revolution: Our study of Omani society reveals the nature of the political oppression and economic exploitation to which the masses are subjected by the feudalist class represented by the Suḷtan, the rulers, the tribal chiefs, and their hostility to anything progressive. There is also the collaboration of the monopoly comprador class, whose destiny is tied to that of imperialism and feudalism and who would defend the present situation with whatever means they have. Of late, there has also appeared on the scene a group of political 'front' men for imperialism and feudalism. This is represented by the managerial staff, senior government officials and some of the intellectuals who are in one way or another connected with the imperialist establishments. This group is on the side of the counter-revolutionary forces. Now that we have described these anti-revolutionary forces, it remains for us to distinguish the motive forces of the revolution in order to unite them and crush the opposing forces.

So what are the motive forces of the revolution? The motive forces of the revolution comprise the petty bourgeoisie, the peasants, the working class, the revolutionary intellectuals and all labourers. They are brought together by the oppression and exploitation they are subjected to. To fulfill the requirements of the national democratic revolution all these forces must be united in a broad front led by the working class as represented by their revolutionary party, in order to crush the domestic enemy and the class enemy. It is important to study the economic position of these forces.

The petty bourgeoisie: To embark upon an analytical study of the petty bourgeoisie class in backward societies — Omani society is no exception — is a very intricate proposition. This is because of the involved nature of the interests of the sections that constitute this class. Its right and left wings constitute a major contradiction within its framework. The right wing desires to climb up into the upper classes while the left wing is more attached to the lower classes. The association of the right wing with the upper classes, however, does not alter the nature of their oppression and exploitation by these classes. This is enough proof that the petty bourgeoisie is a class oppressed and exploited by the imperialists, the feudalists and the big comprador classes. Here we must ask the question: what are the sections that constitute the petty bourgeoisie in our country? The answer to this question is included in a preliminary analysis of the Omani social classes prepared by our Party and guided by scientific theory. According to this study the petty bourgeoisie consists of the following sections:

1 *Small tradesmen*: they run small shops and employ few or no assistants. Some of them can work their way upwards into the upper classes while others go bankrupt and are relegated to the lower strata of society. They are exploited and oppressed by the upper classes. They would support the revolution but at the same time they are doubtful of its ability to succeed.

2 *Small contractors*: they usually use a few employees. Their position is one of speculation. Quite a number of them move into a higher economic bracket and a few of them suffer bankruptcy. They are exploited by the imperialists and their middle-men, the compradors, who control the building materials. They constitute a minor section of the petty bourgeoisie and their attitude towards the revolution is similar to that of the previous section.

3 *Ship owners*: by these we mean the owners of small transport and fishing vessels. They employ between 3 and 15 people on their ships. Their economic position is a precarious and deteriorating one, because of the competition they face from the monopoly companies who run the large transport and passenger ships. This section is exposed to great perils and lives under the threat of bankruptcy. They have a high spirit of adventure and live with the aspirations of the class to which they belong. They are extremely backward intellectually. They would support the revolution but they are not certain of its ultimate success.

4 *Engineers, doctors and teachers*: these enjoy certain privileges in our society. They are enlightened. They share the same attitude towards the revolution as do the other sections of the petty bourgeoisie because they are oppressed by the feudalist class which obstructs their aspirations. They constitute a tiny section of our society.

5 *Junior officials*: they work in government departments and in the establishments of the public and private sectors. Their economic situation is precarious on account of competition from foreign communities who are satisfied with lower wages and who are preferred by the employers. But they earn enough to satisfy their basic needs. They are oppressed and exploited by the imperialists and related establishments. They are enlightened and they are aware of the realities of a

colonised society. They react actively to what is happening and at the same time are desirous of revolution.

6 *Craftsmen*: this section includes carpenters, blacksmiths, weavers, goldsmiths and other craftsmen. They hire no workers, or at most between one and three. They are badly exploited and oppressed by the comprador class. They belong to the slave category. They support the revolution with great enthusiasm in spite of their intellectual backwardness.

7 *Students*: the students do not constitute a separate class or stratum. They are placed in the petty bourgeoisie category because of their political stance, their family origins and their living conditions. Students play the role of agitators against imperialism, feudalism and the compradors. They have a keen political sense and they are naturally opposed to the trilogy of oppression which often denies them the right to continue their studies. A good example of this is what is happening in the interior of Oman where the authorities often prevent them from leaving the area because they are afraid they might continue their studies elsewhere. There are only two schools in this region at a distance of 320 km from each other. The students are always under the threat of unemployment because of the deliberate imperialist policy of preferring aliens. The students have played an eminent role in opposing imperialism in and outside Oman. A striking proof of this is the demonstrations of 1956 in protest against the trilateral attack against Egypt and the massive student demonstrations which took place in Dubai in 1963 during the negotiations for the tripartite unity in which all the toiling masses participated. During these demonstrations one demonstrator was killed and a number were wounded as a result of the brutality of the imperialist and feudalist security forces. These demonstrations reflect the close connection between the Omani revolutionary movement and the Arab revolutionary movement. The connection represented by the students is a sincere expression of the aspiration of the Arab people in Oman. However, students often tend to be subjective, individualistic and impractical in their thinking. However, it would not be an exaggeration to say that students are of a more revolutionary disposition than other sections of the petty bourgeoisie.

From this brief analysis of the different sections of the petty bourgeoisie, it becomes evident that this class is exposed in our colonial and semi-feudal society to oppression and exploitation from the ruling classes who are backed up by imperialist policies and in particular those of the Anglo-American imperialists who planned and are still planning to tie our economy to its own. This has exposed the petty bourgeoisie and the other exploited classes to poverty, wretchedness and deprivation of even basic human rights.

By reviewing all the social classes of which the petty bourgeoisie (which is undergoing all sorts of oppression and exploitation) is one, it is clear that this class has an interest in the revolution. The role it plays in the revolution is dictated by its economic realities. From these realities emerges the role of the petty bourgeoisie as a motive force of the revolution and as a reliable ally. This class, however, cannot achieve their liberation except under the leadership of the proletariat, nor can they successfully carry out revolutionary work without it. Owing to their large numbers and the fact that they are educated and well-informed they can play an effective part in the progress of the national democratic revolution. But all this should not conceal from us the real nature of the petty bourgeois as a wavering and irresolute class which tends to put forward empty and unrealistic slogans. They are easily influenced and tempted by the enemy. They also tend to exaggerate their revolutionary role and can go to extremes in their revolutionary radicalism. Their vacillation becomes more obvious when they are in positions of leadership. Here, they cannot go beyond their concept of private ownership, which reflects their desire to hold on to these positions. Once in these positions the petty bourgeois are under two opposing pressures, each reflecting the interests of a certain class. So once they are in positions of leadership their vacillation becomes more apparent as a result of these opposing pressures because they try to reconcile them in order to safeguard their interests and at the same time keep their positions of leadership. Here lies the danger of this class for the revolution when they are in leading positions, because they would work for reform and not for radical change. But in its historical development within the progress of the revolution the petty bourgeoisie leans generally more to the left than to the right. What we have gained from our own experiences in particular, and from the experiences of other people in general, confirms the validity of what we are saying. Out of our own local experiences we can say that the organisations of this class – the petty bourgeoisie – have failed to fully understand the realities of the present situation, to rally the masses and to work out appropriate plans for the liberation of our people from servitude and exploitation. Its policies have always been unrealistic and doomed to failure. Examples of this are the Arab Nationalist Movement and the Ba'th Party, whose minor conflicts are given precedence over the major conflict against imperialism. In the final analysis these policies have been of great service, though indirectly, to imperialism and its allies. On the other hand, we find that these petty bourgeois organisations have paved the way for the emergence of the true vanguard which fully understood the problems of our society and brought to prominence the major conflict against the oppressive trilogy of imperialism, feudalism and the compradors, while at the same time trying to lessen the minor conflict amongst the exploited and oppressed classes. The Arabs' experience testifies strongly to the fact that the petty bourgeoisie plays a fundamental role in the cause of national liberation. At the same time it cannot fulfill the demands of the national democratic revolution in the absence of the proletariat and its party in the Arab arena. The defeat of 5 June 1967 is yet another example of the vacillation and irresolution of the petty bourgeoisie and its capitulation in the face of imperialist pressures as reflected in the Security Council resolution. On the other hand, they are known·for putting forward hollow slogans, and for their fear of and inability to mobilise the masses and the neglect of their real interests. All this would indicate that the petty bourgeoisie, wherever it is, would participate within certain limits and conditions in the different stages of the struggle for liberation. But whatever role it plays would be subjected to its own realities within the motive forces of the revolution. When it is in a position of leadership it can hinder the fulfilment of the objectives of the revolution. But when it is under the leadership of the proletariat it can play an effective role in fulfilling these objectives.

The peasantry

The situation in the rural areas: Before discussing the present social situation in the countryside and the conditions in which the Omani peasant lives, we will briefly mention some factors which have played a major role in making the position what it is.

1 *Tribal feuds*: Tribal feuds and wars have played a major role in weakening and fragmenting the rural economic structure. This results from the methods adopted in waging these wars, e.g. destruction of crops and water resources, forcible seizure of cattle and murder. This has caused a great deal of misery and made the life of the peasant most unsettled. These feuds and wars have at the same time provided the feudalists with another source of wealth and given them the chance to tighten their autocratic grip.

2 *Lack of a central authority*: The lack of a unified central authority has made it easier for the feudalists to fragment the Omani economy and exploit and oppress the peasants as they please.

3 *Imperialist intervention*: The feudal lords of Oman divided up the country amongst themselves. This resulted in the creation of weak and scattered rival feudal estates. This made the task of occupying Oman by the imperialists easier. Once the imperialists had a foothold in the country they threw their weight behind the feudal lords, thus consolidating their own presence in the country. Furthermore, they followed a policy of deepening the conflicts between the tribes and encouraged tribal feuds and wars. These factors played an important part in weakening the economy and have led to further fragmentation.

4 *Feudal terror*: As a result of feudal terror, Omani society has been in a state of fragmentation and economic shambles. The feudalists have used coercive and destructive means to subdue the people. Internment in fortified places, killing and torture were the methods they resorted to in order to consolidate their authority. They used the peasants as corvée labour. They also employed highwaymen to pillage the peasants' property and kidnap them to sell as slaves, and offer as gifts. This led to the emigration to East Africa of some of the wealthier peasants. The futility of tilling the land under these adverse circumstances compelled peasants to abandon agriculture and emigrate or seek employment as manual labourers and as hands on merchant and fishing boats. Such jobs provided a relatively better life away from direct feudal terror.

This situation has disastrous effects on agriculture, which has been relegated to a secondary position in our economy. As a result of this we have become dependent to a great extent on foreign agricultural imports. In addition to this we find that in certain areas some landlords who are now interested in growing fruit trees, e.g. citrus trees, are employing cheap foreign labour. Such labour has been coming into Oman in large numbers. This would undoubtedly be yet another obstacle in the way of local peasants coming back to their land. These foreign labourers are subjected to the same oppression and exploitation by the landlords but they perhaps find conditions here slightly better than in their own countries.

This brief exposition of the situation in rural Oman is by no means a comprehensive study of the problem. The question of the Omani peasants demands a more detailed and deeper study and day to day experience of the lives of these peasants. However, it is hoped that what has been said will give an idea of what they are enduring.

Let us now turn to the social and economic status of the different sections of the peasantry.

The rich peasants: They form not more than 4 per cent of the rural population. They either use farm labourers or engage in labour themselves. They let a part of their land, partake in commerce and own merchant or fishing boats. They practise usury and ruthlessly exploit poor peasants. In their turn they are subject to exploitation and oppression by the imperialist-backed feudalists. As a result of unjust taxation and restrictions on the marketing of their produce imposed by these feudalists, rich peasants are pessimistic about the future and bear a grudge against the present regime which denies them any political rights. They have the desire to change this system but they would not welcome a radical change. They do not have enough courage to stand against authority which they tend to placate. They cannot take seriously the ability of the masses to change the situation, but they may partially participate in the revolution at a certain stage.

The middle peasant: The percentage of this section of the peasantry is on the increase. They now form about 20 per cent of the rural population. The increase in their numbers is due to the emigration of poor peasants, which causes shortages of labour and forces the landlords to sell some of their land. Some of these peasants who leave the country then come back with their savings and buy land. The middle peasant generally derives his income from his own labour. He toils very hard in order to avoid borrowing from usurers. He is self-supporting, selling the produce of his land, cattle and poultry. Sometimes he sells part of his own labour — that happens when a middle peasant does not own enough land of his own to satisfy his living requirements. Some of the middle peasants practise exploitation and usury to a very small extent.

Their economic situation is precarious, as their crops are subject to blight and natural disasters, lack of proper crop protection, pressures exerted upon them and heavy taxation. The middle peasants are badly exploited and oppressed by imperialism, the landlords and the bourgeoisie. The comprador bourgeoisie exploit them directly through their control of agricultural machinery and requirements. Being exploited and oppressed, the middle class peasantry are an important motive force of the revolution.

The poor peasant: The poor peasants in Oman form approximately 60 per cent of the rural population. They lead a harsh life because of feudal exploitation and low wages which they receive for selling their labour. To make ends meet, a poor peasant is often compelled to work on more than one farm. They work all day long and are often compelled to borrow from landlords especially in winter. This is because Oman depends a great deal on the date crop, which is usually harvested in summer. So in winter large numbers of poor peasantry emigrate in search of a livelihood. They return just before the beginning of the summer season. In the meantime, a relative is usually left in charge of the small plot of land or else a small fee is paid to some other person to look after it. In some regions date-palms are left unattended because the owner cannot afford such a fee. The poor peasants in general depend on selling part of their labour power. The meagre wages they receive vary from one region to another. In some areas wages do not exceed 250 rials (Qatar-Dubai) per annum. That is why they have to sell their labour to more than one master while working on their own little plots. This is what the peasant would get in the mountainous region. In the east a peasant would get for his labour a bunch of dates from each date-palm plus the crop of two or three palms per annum. This sort of reward does not in most cases equal a quarter of the harvest for a year's toil. In certain areas a peasant might get his wages equivalent to one third of the produce and in very exceptional circumstances he would get the equivalent of half the crop. Generally the poor peasants are wretched and ruthlessly exploited and oppressed.

Their production does not allow for an annual surplus. Often they are short of the basic necessities and are threatened with starvation and displacement. Their position is made even worse by the high prices of imported goods which the compradors monopolize and by the lower prices they get for their own produce which often finds no market e.g. the annual date crop. In order to supplement a meagre income all the members of the family have to toil and take on any job that comes their way.

Thus oppressed and exploited and deprived of any human rights, the poor peasants are yearning for change. They are the main contingent of the revolutionary forces.

The farm labourers: These form about 15 per cent of the rural population. Naturally they do not own any means of production and depend on selling their labour power, though they might raise poultry or cattle to supplement their incomes. Their wages are similar to those of the poor peasants and their position is not much different from theirs. Unlike the poor peasants, however, they do not own any land and far larger numbers of this section emigrate in search of work abroad. The farm labourer has been oppressed throughout the ages, and feudalism has reduced him to the status of serf. This has come about as a result of his need to borrow and the practice of usury. Opportunities for work abroad have given this section of the peasantry a welcome outlet. They have emigrated in large numbers and this has reduced their numbers. Their position has improved comparatively and they have been able to shake off some of the shackles imposed upon them by feudalism. This development has come as result of:

1 Opportunities for work in other regions of the Gulf, and of late in Omani territory, e.g. 'Abū Dhabi and Dubai.
2 The deterioration of agriculture in many areas.
3 The need of feudalism for more labour.
4 The feudalists are no longer wholly dependent on land, but rather on the concessions given to them by imperialist monopolies as they represent the supporting pillars of these monopolies.

Amongst the various sections of the peasantry, this is the most receptive to revolutionary propaganda. They are more than any others conscious of their class problems. In spite of their relatively small numerical strength they constitute the major force for widening and deepening the class conflict in rural Oman. This is because they have been deprived of owning any means of production and have been, and are still, subjected to all kinds of humiliation and servitude. By virtue of their class status they are the closest section to the proletariat.

The proletariat: To speak about the proletariat in our Omani society is practically the most difficult part of analysing this society, since our society is no different from any other backward society, and even more backward than others. This is due to the autocratic imperialist policy which dominates our country. Making use of its vast past experience, imperialism is trying to prevent the emergence and growth of a working class in our country, because the growth of such a class is diametrically opposed to its exploitive presence here. To prevent the emergence of the proletariat as a class, imperialism devised two policies. First, it has tied our economy to its own by turning our country into a consumer market after destroying our national economy. Second, it opened the gates of our country to an influx of foreigners whose presence was to prevent the growth of a local proletariat. These foreigners provide cheap labour, on the one hand, and enjoy better living conditions than they would have done in their countries of origin, on the other. The effect of this on the Omani working class is that it is unsettled and lacking in cohesion. Many of its members have emigrated because of the constraints imposed upon them from all directions – political, social and economic. This has been advantageous to the imperialists and their policies. Individuals working for the same establishments have found it difficult to come together. This is because of the divergence between them and the foreign workers who have always humiliated them and failed their just claims. But in spite of all the imperialist policies and pressures, the Omani proletariat has come into existence. Although newly emergent and numerically weak, the nucleus is there.

The Omani proletariat is formed of: workers employed by foreign and national companies, workers employed by the oil companies, building workers, maritime and ship workers, shop workers, workers employed by the public and private sector organisations, agricultural labourers in the rural areas and vehicle drivers. Because of the lack of official statistics we cannot estimate the numerical strength of the Omani working class. The absence of a proper and cohesive working class in Oman is due to the absence of a national bourgeois class and to the fact that it is not tied to a developed national economy. And, in addition to its recent origin, numerical weakness, lack of concentration in the country, low political consciousness, detachment from a developed national economy, lack of organisation into trade unions and inexperience, it is, like the proletariat the world over, deprived of any access to ownership of the means of production. Like the proletariat the world over it is against exploitation and has its roots in the peasantry. This will facilitate close co-operation between the emergent proletariat and the peasantry. Its members have been forced to emigrate but all the plotting by the trilogy will not stop the revolutionary progress of the working class. The Omani proletariat is most brutally oppressed by international imperialism, feudalism, and the comprador bourgeoisie. Whatever negative aspects our proletariat might have, these will not detract it from its combative role and the inevitability of its leading the revolution. As such it is under the leadership of the Party, the principal motive force of the revolution. Without the leadership of the proletariat the revolution is doomed to failure. The experience of other peoples and that of Arab peoples in particular confirms this. A striking example is what happened on 5 June 1967, because the proletariat and its revolutionary party was not there to lead the struggle. The Arab revolution is still wavering and that is because of its petty bourgeois leadership.

Hence, the Omani proletariat should understand its responsibilities towards the revolution. It must unite with the peasantry which is its firm ally and without whose support the revolution cannot be victorious. The proletariat must also fully understand the different stages and varying circumstances of the struggle, and on the basis of such understanding enter into alliance with all the classes and strata which can take part in the revolution and form a united front. Among these classes the petty bourgeoisie, which is a reliable ally, is included.

The objectives of the Omani revolution: After it has become clear to us who the enemies of the Omani revolution are, we have to define its objectives. So what are these objectives?

On account of the oppression and brutal exploitation to which imperialism and feudalism subject our people, thus hindering their progress and development, we must eliminate these two enemies together with the third enemy, the big comprador bourgeoisie, the appendage of international imperialism and the mainstay of the colonialist presence on our soil. Dependence on the imperialist economy is the highest form of dependence that the imperialists recognise. This class is an agent for the continuation of the imperialist and feudalist oppression and exploitation of the Omani people.

The elimination of imperialism is a fundamental objective if we want to curb oppression and exploitation. The feudalist and the comprador classes must also be destroyed because they are the two main supports of imperialism, as imperialism is their main support. But if we fail to destroy imperialism we cannot destroy these classes. And if we do not destroy these classes we cannot defeat imperialism and build a people's army. The peasantry is the major force of the revolution. If the revolution does not make it its task to liberate them, it will not be able to realise anything for our society. The liberation of our society cannot be attained by peaceful struggle. This is what our history confirms and so do the experiences of other societies.

Ending fragmentation and unifying the country: International imperialism aims at keeping the economies of under-developed countries tied to the wheels of its own, realising that the growth and development of these economies will come at the expense of its own. To ensure this, imperialism is always planning and plotting to create situations which will guarantee the flow of wealth from these countries into its own coffers. The victories that the revolutionary peoples of the world have scored against imperialism have taught the imperialists some lessons which they have begun to make use of against those who are still striving for independence and liberation. So they resorted to the creation of weak structures in these countries in order to keep their economies tied to their own and turn them into consumer markets for their products. To achieve this they followed the policy of trying to divide and fragment every country that they colonised, so that it would not be able to oppose their policies or achieve any revolutionary objective along the road to socialism.

Many countries have been divided into small and helpless units which lack the strength to stand in the face of imperialism or any reactionary move. This is because such divided territories have no economic integration. Historical and living examples of such situations abound. The Arab homeland has been divided by the imperialists and the feudalist governments into more than 20 parts each of which has been further divided into yet smaller fragments. South Yemen is a good example of this process. This region was divided into 20 states while in fact South Yemen is itself part of a part of the Arab homeland which is Yemen. In other parts of the world we find that Vietnam, Korea and the Congo were also divided. Even European countries did not escape this fate. Germany and Ireland suffer from territorial divisions. As for Oman, it has been divided into eight parts, each considered an independent political unit. All criminal means and methods were resorted to in order to maintain and uphold these divisions. The recent moves to establish the so-called Union of the Emirates are meant to put the final seal on this fragmentation and thus realise great gains for British imperialism and its strategies, which we have previously explained. Omani territory has suffered from this fragmentation, which has played a great part in shattering its national unity and retarding its economic development. The rejection of this division and the unification of our country is one of our revolutionary objectives in the national democratic stage. We can, by doing so, slam the door in the face of the imperialists. All the revolutionary forces in Oman must regard the unification of the country as a fundamental objective of the national democratic revolution. In order to create the new Oman a solid, broad base which embraces all its people and all its territories and plays its part in realising an Arab unity with a scientific socialist content — to do this, we must strive relentlessly against the division of our country.

What is the character of our revolution and what are its prospects? From our preliminary analysis of the Omani society — which is colonial and feudal — and from our definition of the anti-revolutionary forces and the first objectives of the revolution, it has become clear to us that the Omani revolution belongs to the national democratic revolutions which have been and are still fought by all the struggling peoples of the world under the leadership of the proletariat with the oppressed and exploited classes comprising the workers, peasants, the petty bourgeoisie, revolutionary intellectuals and all those who stand up against imperialism, feudalism and traitors.

Those oppressed forces have suffered and are still suffering the worst kinds of oppression and exploitation to which they are subjected by imperialism, feudalism and the compradors.

To define our revolution as a national democratic revolution means that its aim is not directed, at the present stage, against private property but that its tasks are to overthrow imperialism, feudalism as represented by the rulers and the Suļtans and the comprador class. These three are the mortal enemies of the national democratic revolution at the present stage.

The character of our revolution is, then, national and democratic, and it does not purport to eliminate private property. It is a national democratic revolution with a united front which comprises all the forces striving under the leadership of the proletariat to overthrow imperialism and feudalism. All those who are true to its principles have the right to participate in its strife and shoulder its patriotic and revolutionary responsibilities.

It should be mentioned here that the Omani revolution is organically bound with the Arab revolution which emerged in the fifties but has remained wavering and vacillating on account of the hopes and dreams of the petty bourgeoisie, who did not fully grasp the real meaning of revolution, nor did they put their revolutionary concepts to any practical application towards changing the old situation which was created by imperialism and the forces of feudalism, and towards the emergence of a new society based on the principles of non-exploitation. The Arab revolution did not go about achieving the targets of the national democratic revolution in the correct manner because it was not founded on a sound scientific ideology. It was also remote from the masses. Matters were treated in a bureaucratic manner and there was a great deal of rhetoric and empty slogans. But after the defeat of June 1967 things started to change. The Arab masses realised that the regimes which incurred defeat could not be depended upon to deal with revolutionary questions. From that point in time the masses, under the leadership of their revolutionary vanguard, began to tackle the first tasks of the revolution. The escalation of the struggle in the occupied Arab territories is a true reflection of this fact. The rallying of the Arab masses to the Palestinian cause is a true expression of their aspiration to realise Arab unity in a practical manner.

The Omani revolution is not isolated from what is happening in the outside world, as it has international affiliations with other revolutions fighting against the forces of oppression, with the US at their head. The Omani revolution is staged in an international situation in which the struggle of the oppressed peoples has revealed clearly the extent of imperialist oppression and exploitation. It also reveals the organic bond between the bourgeoisie the world over as an oppressor of the toiling masses. Hence the democratic revolution in Oman will undoubtedly be a preparation for the socialist revolution, which is founded on a scientific basis. It will firmly oppose imperialism and its appendages. In the economic and political fields it will be directed against imperialist projects and capital, which will be the property of the masses. This revolution is going to be a progressive alliance of all forces which oppose imperialism, feudalism and the compradors. It would operate within a broad front composed of all the progressive forces under the leadership of the proletariat.

There is no doubt that a revolution, in which the struggle will be between the revolutionary forces and the counter-revolutionary forces led by America, is going to take place. The aim of this revolution will be to abolish exploitation and oppression, establish brotherly co-operation between men, throw overboard the exploitative relations of production and replace them with economic relations based on collective ownership. This revolution would follow a socialist line, based on the elimination of exploitation and oppression of all human beings, and prepare the way for a really democratic socialist society of the masses. It will pave the way for the emergence of a totally different Oman which would assume its revolutionary role in the Arab world and internationally, and deal stunning blows to the imperialists and their appendages. It would form a true unity with the progressive revolutions of the world.

The British colonized our country for about two centuries during which they oppressed our people and exploited our resources. They kept our people in ignorance and isolation from the outside world. Our people are now taking a definite stand concerning the imperialist nightmare, and the revolution is socialist-orientated. All the experiences of the peoples opposing imperialism have proved that if the national democratic revolution does not take the road to scientific socialism it will only be an instrument serving the oppressors and exploiters to oppress the exploited classes. We will stand firmly against such a revolution and support the national democratic revolution which aims at liberating the oppressed classes and completely overthrowing imperialism, feudalism and their appendages.

From the experience of the Arab revolution we have come to learn that without the effective participation of the broad masses the revolution will be weak and susceptible to collapse. At the same time we would say that the present situation in the Arab world is conducive to transition from the democratic revolution to the socialist revolution within an alliance of all the Arab revolutionary forces, based on a strategy which would serve the Arab masses and put all the Arab potential at the service of this strategy. In this case, and if the revolutionary forces opposing imperialism join hands, the achievement of Arab unity will no longer be impossible or difficult. Undoubtedly the forces that are going to carry on the struggle for the democratic revolution will be the same forces as those of the socialist revolution. This will no doubt facilitate the development of the democratic revolution into the socialist revolution. This will be conditioned by the particular character of our country which has suffered feudalist and capitalist exploitation. This revolution will without doubt take the road to socialism.

Appendix 3

PFLOAG: internal directives

Introductory note

The publication of this document coincides with the early period of the third phase of the PFLO's historical development. The timing of this publication is significant in so far as the three sections of the document point out the internal crisis PFLOAG was encountering after Qabus's accession to power, the creation of the United Arab Emirates, and shortly before Iranian intervention in the Omani war. The first section is the most important, as it was published less than two years after the September 1970 internal upheaval. It is noteworthy that the document draws its important references on internal organisational issues from Mao's analysis of guerrilla warfare, and little or no attention is given to other 'theoreticians' on the subject.

On correcting mistakes

Revolution is a long and tedious process which must necessarily face passivism, and many mistakes and minor contradictions. As the revolution develops and advances every year, more difficulties, duties and tasks are placed on it. It is thus our duty, in the course of the advancement and development of the revolution, to increase our alertness, be firm in confronting errors and enhance the zeal and enthusiasm of each individual at all levels.

We fully realise that mistakes and passivism will continue to exist in our work, just as it does in any other revolution in the world, and that contradictions will continue to exist during this and the coming stages of our revolution. The only correct method to confront mistakes and eliminate contradictions in our work is criticism, self-criticism and revolutionary accountability at all levels. Likewise, we realise that each individual in this front simply does make mistakes and has some harmful habits, whether consciously or unconsciously, and this makes regular daily criticism of the utmost importance in our work in order to prevent our mistakes from accumulating (just as dust neglected in a house). When mistakes do accumulate, if they are not corrected immediately they will develop into more complex bigger mistakes which will affect our work in a negative and serious way. Since everyone of us is liable to make mistakes, and this applies to any sector, committee or administration, every member of this revolution must be subject to the laws of criticism, self-criticism, accountability and control, whether he be in a military base, a leader or in administration. Such laws are meant to develop and correct every member of this revolution in order to make him capable of performing his duties and to embody the revolutionary attitudes in daily life better. Mistakes are an integral part of any work or revolution and they all, without exception, have a damaging effect on the interests of the revolution and the people. Accordingly they must be avoided and rectified.

An attitude of lack of criticism, control and correction implies the accumulation of elements acting against the revolution and the public; this attitude will conflict with the principles for which we are making sacrifices and will harm the cause for which hundreds of our comrades have given their souls and blood. Criticism and self-criticism are the first stage of the accountability process for mistakes, a rule to which all members of this front are subject. Any comrade whom we do not criticise will definitely be liable to conceit, ostentation and superiority, which are the worst diseases that afflict the fighter and are most dangerous to his commitment as a revolutionary.

Cause of revolt

Errors which remain uncorrected despite criticisms should be treated by other kinds of punishment in addition to criticism which should continue despite all difficulties. Criticism and self-criticism are not only the right of every fighter but a duty which he should exercise. In other words, the fighter is not only given freedom to criticise sincerely and seriously any error, and to call the person concerned to account when necessary, but to give any views he considers to be in the interests of the revolution and the people. Further, it is the duty of the fighter to criticise himself and to sincerely try to correct his own mistakes and not to repeat them. By doing this the fighter participates in the development of the revolution since by practising self-criticism he develops himself as an element of the revolution. In the same way the fighter participates in the development of the revolution by criticising his comrades in a positive and revolutionary way which serves the development of such comrades as well as the revolution.

The combatant may not develop without criticism which applies to the Front, which is a large collection of combatants who also may not develop without constantly daily criticism and self-criticism. Criticism and accountability result in the correction, or at least the gradual correction, of our errors. It is not shameful to make a mistake, this is natural in any job, but it is shameful to keep silent about mistakes without correcting them.

We as revolutionaries are not afraid of admitting our mistakes. We tackle them with revolutionary frankness. It is only reactionary institutions, imperialists and petty bourgeois organisations who are afraid of admitting their mistakes and fear criticism and self-criticism. As for us, we are not afraid of disclosing our mistakes, whether to each other, to the bases, leaders or the public, considering that we are all concerned about the soundness of our work, the necessity of development, rectification and protection which are all in the interests of the people.

Unlike imperialists and reactionaries, the revolution has taught us scientific method and we have learned that criticism is the correct way of solving contradictions and errors in revolutionary work, and we have learned how to respect the will and thoughts of the masses. Political work at different levels and bases of the revolution has shown us that criticism and self-criticism is the basic difference between our revolution and institutions and bourgeois institutions, and also between revolutionary armies and traditional regular armies. It is a basic factor of strength which always gives us the edge on enemies, whatever their military power.

Should political work, including criticism and self-criticism, be reduced among revolutionary circles, there will remain no big difference between our army, for example, and the enemy's or between our institutions and theirs. In fact there is no big difference between the soldier of any reactionary traditional army and a fighter who does not clearly understand his cause, or who does not consider the practice of criticism and self-criticism as a right and duty. While we emphasise the importance of both criticism and self-criticism (considering that they are daily bread without which we can never survive) we should be very careful not to practise criticism incorrectly, and to clarify to every individual the negative methods which one should avoid in criticism, so that we may all avoid liberalism and opportunism in practising criticism or dealing with errors and passivism.

There are two types of criticism: one is opportunist liberal and the other is constructive revolutionary. The revolutionary is the one who avoids liberal criticism and sticks firmly to revolutionary criticism, and constantly applies it to himself, his comrades, and work policies in general. He who applies criticism in an opportunist way is classified as an opportunist and those who never apply criticism in any way whatsoever are opportunist whether they realise this or not. Each one of us can avoid both these problems by trying hard: he will neither give up his right and duty to criticise, nor apply criticism incorrectly or in an opportunist way. There are many reasons why incorrect and opportunist forms of criticism may occur in our practice of criticism, and this gives vital importance to the criticism of criticism in order to correct both the concept of criticism and that of self-criticism and to maintain and develop them in a positive way.

In this circular, we wish to disclose a number of negative and incorrect aspects which have emerged in our work, and which we must now quickly and continuously criticise and correct. These aspects are:

The first negative aspect: The question of criticising behind someone's back: we all have, through political guidance, learnt the types of opportunism, and realised that criticism behind someone's back is one form of opportunism. A number of comrades still apply this form of criticism by slandering and criticising their friends behind their backs and being silent about their criticism when meeting their friends; they go further and pretend to be contented and in agreement with their friends in their presence. Also when a certain subject is put down for discussion at a session, you may find some comrades keeping silent without expressing their views, then, after the session is over, they start gossiping behind the back and thus lack revolutionary frankness and practise an opportunist method of criticism. They also lack courage and bravery in expressing their views and criticism or calling for discussions or accountability thereof. Such behaviour is undesirable in work and is not of our nature as revolutionaries; on the contrary it represents the character of the bourgeoisie and their mercenaries. The revolutionary does not need to practise courtesy nor does he adopt a cowardly attitude in his criticism or in expressing his views to his comrades. Comrades who adopt this behaviour, whether consciously or unconsciously, whether they are aware of its danger or not, and whatever level they may be at, cause much harm to the internal relations of the front and to the interests of the revolution and the people. The problem under discussion in all its forms should be criticised seriously, opposed, and tackled by guidance.

The second negative aspect: This is silence about mistakes, not discussing them either person to person, or behind someone's back. There are comrades who adopt this opportunist attitude towards our mistakes, who, despite the fact that they see and realise their wrong attitudes, and understand that this harms our work, abstain from criticising or mentioning mistakes on the pretext that they don't want to arouse susceptibilities, problems and complications. This conduct shows a peculiar understanding of matters as we should not conceal our mistakes, be afraid to tackle them, and thus let them develop and recur on the pretext that we do not want to cause problems. We wonder what is the experience or theory such comrades know which makes them believe that silence about mistakes will lead to solving and correcting them? On the other hand, we want to ask those comrades whether our mistakes are not the cause of many susceptibilities, problems and complications. (If we all take that attitude we will be like the patient who refuses to be operated on on the pretext that he wants to be sick). The comrade who sees a mistake and remains silent about it lacks a sense of responsibility towards our work, because we are all responsible for our work and the correction of mistakes, and that includes those of us in the bases, the administration, or in leadership committees. We may be silent about minor mistakes which do not affect our work or activities or internal relations, but any other mistakes should be criticised or corrected. Mistakes are ultimately against the interests of the revolution and the people, and hence we should not remain silent about them, conceal them, or allow them to recur. Comrades who under any pretext adopt a position of spectator towards mistakes suffer from the opportunist disease of courtesy or indifference which is one aspect of individualism. No matter what the position of these comrades is, they must get rid of their disease. Courtesy and indifference in revolutionary work are attitudes which are bad for the revolutionary; the revolutionary should be deeply concerned with the soundness of work and be keen to improve the standard of his comrades, he is not supposed to be courteous in matters which conflict with our interests.

The third negative aspect: This is the reduction of political activities, when comrades pay no attention to attending political sessions and give unacceptable justification and excuses for their absence. This may be ascribed to mere negligence and indolence on the part of the administration and instructors. What could be the excuse for any group which fails to hold a weekly, bi-weekly or at least a monthly meeting?

Comrades give excuses like the need for military mobilisation, patrols, and incomplete number of groups or the shortage of instructors; this type of excuse does not justify stopping political sessions for such long periods. Even at times of intense military activities or on the front, it is possible to hold a meeting for an hour a day or every two or three days, or at least once a week in order to discuss problems related to the revolution, review our experience, give the fighter the opportunity to criticise or give his views on a certain question, and also to hear regularly and continuously the base's opinion on any aspect of our activities.

Should a patrol group move, it is not necessary to stop the sessions of another stationary group, and even the patrol which is moving can hold short sessions while on duty in order to review their experience and do the necessary criticism and self-criticism. When there is no instructor in a group a meeting can still be held by selecting one of the group's members to conduct a particular session and the group may select the subject of discussion so that any comrade may give his views and criticise any subject, improper action, or passive attitude in the work. Even in the most difficult situations and at the busiest times when we cannot hold long sessions lasting an hour or more, it would be sufficient to hold short sessions of a quarter or half an hour at most in order to criticise and practise self-criticism. Without this procedure it would definitely be possible for us to gradually transform ourselves, after a short time, into a traditional army where the soldier does not criticise anything, discuss anything, or give any opinion. The fighter in the popular liberation army differs from the mercenary and the traditional soldier because we need his opinion, criticism and remarks, and we want to make him into a good fighter as well as a good politician.

This also applies to the popular militia as the revolution wants to build its bases not only militarily but as a complete revolutionary education; the revolution needs the opinion of the base by regularly holding meetings, developing revolutionary democracy and encouraging the spirit of criticism and self-criticism in each comrade. Those who abuse or repress these principles in any way, or neglect them for any reason, abuse fundamental and basic principles in our work; they unconsciously weaken the factors on which our strength, survival and supremacy over the enemy are based. We do not want our base to be led by administrators as if they were blind, nor do we want bases which do not criticise, make proposals or raise points for discussion. Consequently we want the political sessions to continue at regular intervals so that criticism and self-criticism may continue and flourish positively in all fields and at all levels; failing this there would be no revolutionary leadership or base and in effect the revolution will cease. Our revolution will not allow such a thing to take place, and even if it did, the bases would oppose it and the people would combat it.

The fourth negative aspect: This is the spread of arbitrary evaluation and rash classification of people, and the expression of individual opinions without sound reasoning investigation. In most cases we find that such classifications and opinions arise from personal feelings, old disputes, differences of opinion, and sometimes even from ostentation and the defamation of their comrades. Criticism and evaluation in such cases deviate from their revolutionary course to follow the path of inflaming, defaming and revenge. All these forms represent ugly liberal tendencies which we practise while boasting of revolution, loyalty, truth and good manners. Comrades who adopt such attitudes are far from loyalty, truth or sincerity to their comrades. Such comrades are also far from the revolution, regardless of their theoretical education or role in fighting. Revolution, loyalty and truth are not mere words, they represent a combination of daily acts, morals and attitudes, and a person is judged by others, not by what he thinks of himself; thus a person is assessed by his behaviour, manners and attitude. The revolutionary must be honest and always truthful even if it shows up his failings. He is loyal in his work and to his comrades and does not try to ruin any other comrade or defame his role in the revolution for any reason whatsoever. The revolutionary must have a pure soul and not harbour malice for any comrade, nor should he pay attention to susceptibilities and differences. In brief, he combines revolutionary talk and revolutionary practice. Arbitrary valuation, rash classifications and the passing of judgement against comrades chaotically like, for example, describing a comrade as a coward, another as opportunist or hopeless, etc. are acts which do not benefit the fighter and should not emanate from a comrade who cares about correct work and unity of the bases of the revolution. Comrades who pursue such bad habits do great service to the enemy and sow the seeds of dissent and disintegration in our ranks. Even if their judgement were correct, it would be their duty as revolutionaries to assist other comrades to rectify their mistakes and co-operate in improving the comrades' attitude instead of using methods of destruction and defamation to worsen their position. Criticism by the use of improper words or by inflaming or slandering is a method applied only by opportunists.

Passing judgement arbitrarily and making decisions on the basis of insufficient information are forms of individualism. Opportunist, chaotic and individualistic tendencies are malignant diseases which can affect our day to day progress. Thus our regular duty, which we must do today more than at any time before, is to hasten the process of rectification.

Our comrades who suffer from the above-mentioned mistakes and passivism should be subjected to regular violent criticism and instruction. Meanwhile we should follow the example of those comrades who are free from these diseases and passivism. The history of our revolution has witnessed a number of martyrs who gave good examples as revolutionaries and from them we have much to learn; we should learn their modesty, purity of soul, and the way they used to treat other comrades as well as their love for their brother comrades and the people. In addition we should learn how brave, well-disciplined and loyal those martyrs were. All this will help us continue our mission until we have realised all the objectives for which our martyrs have sacrificed their lives and our people have suffered and sacrificed much. We have already had hard times, so let us look for more experience, rectification and victories.

Dhofar Province, 5 April 1972

On desertion — statement to all members and individuals

Desertion from the ranks of the revolution is something which cannot be totally avoided in the history of any revolution. All revolutions in the world have experienced the withdrawal of some members; this is natural and cannot be prevented since the abilities, inclinations and mental attitudes of people are different. Individual people's class, origin, consciousness and mentality are not the same and these factors mean that we must not expect that all comrades will be able to continue the revolution until complete victory. Some people get tired and bored and their efficiency gets exhausted a quarter way or half way through, depending on their ability, inclination, expectation, mental attitude or class position.

Desertion is more noticeable in national wars because of the presence of a variety of allied groups, but national revolutions accept in their ranks any nationalist element whatever his class origin, capability or personal inclinations. The revolution should give a chance to all such individuals to join its ranks and have national trust in them until their ability reduces or weakens in another way, either by their withdrawal to the ranks of the enemy or by their return to their normal position as good citizens, thus leaving the revolution to the true revolutionaries. This applies particularly to national revolutions pursuing a strategy of long-term popular war which does not end in one, two or five years. Consequently the type of fighters we need are those who are endowed with long-term fighting ability and revolutionary perseverance. Thus the question of desertion and abandonment of the principle of struggle is something natural. According to Mao-Tse tung protracted popular warfare requires bravery in fighting, sacrifices, tolerance of toil and overwork, and endurance in struggle until complete victory. Such character may not be found in everyone who joins the revolution and consequently it is not strange to see many people leaving the revolution's ranks at various periods. Desertion from the revolution can take place among some poor elements who are uneducated or lack the spirit of sacrifice and the ability to toil continuously, and it can also take place among a few bourgeois elements who are still unable to free themselves of vacillation and selfishness. Anyone entertaining the idea of deserting and abandoning the revolution will no doubt find many excuses to justify his attitude, such as the presence of mistakes and the existence of passivism and defects. It is true that such people, during the period of their participation in the revolution, may have encountered many problems and wrong susceptibilities, or have been liable to criticism and accountability which they may use as an excuse for giving up the revolution. In our opinion these excuses can only apply to people who have a weak faith in the revolution or in themselves or to people whose morale has collapsed because of violent struggles or who have lost the ability to endure work, exhaustion and fighting. The same excuses can be made by people who harbour malice for certain elements of the revolution itself or to others whose tribal feeling prevails over national feeling, and begin to place their private and family interests above those of the revolution. Deserters can also include people who failed to realise certain ambitions and aspirations through the revolution. If anyone decides to quit the ranks of the revolution and join those of the enemy to be a traitor to the revolution, or decides to abandon the gun of the revolution and the struggle, his comrades will, as we have said, find many excuses to justify his acts, including the above-mentioned ones. In this respect, we wish to mention the names of the following deserters and traitors:

1. Ghāzy 'Abdullah,   2. Muḥad Sa'īd Hadhūf,   3. Abū Bakr Salem,
4. Salem Ahmad 'Akīl,   5. Tamān Muḥad,   6. 'Azād Muḥammad,
7. Bakhīt Suhail Zafīnān.

We have heard that these people have deserted the revolution to become agents of imperialism and reaction. Their withdrawal was not by chance and it must have been premeditated and based on primary and secondary motives. However this withdrawal took place behind a cloud of heavy dust of nonsensical revolutionary talks, slogans and expressions. Before deserting, these traitors have tried to create chaos and much noise, just like a besieged soldier who explodes a smoke bomb to camouflage his withdrawal. Desertion came after the following series of improper acts and movements on the part of these traitors:

1 The creation of a state of instability among the troops of the liberation army by requesting frequent leave of absence, misunderstandings with the administration, or passivism on the part of the administration.
2 Unofficial social visits to some houses at night, and staying there until late hours as if they were not in a war situation.
3 Criticising comrades and responsible authorities behind their backs either in their own meetings or among the people.
4 Discussing many internal situations and secrets of the revolution in contravention of the revolution's regulations.
5 Looking for mistakes in the management of the troops or in any other element they disliked among the troops; listing such mistakes, enlarging them and circulating them improperly in order to create chaos and not to correct the mistakes or develop the work.
6 Noncompliance with the discipline of the revolution; violating the regulations of official sessions held to discuss their mistakes and call them to account; these sessions were usually opened in the name of the revolution and martyrs. Meanwhile the said traitors used to boast widely about the martyrs and pretend that they were the only supporters of the revolution.
7 Disdaining or humiliating any comrade or citizen who criticised them or drew their attention to their mistakes, while getting together and defending each other even in their most obvious mistakes.

These are the most conspicuous incorrect attitudes and acts of this group, carried out before leaving the forces of the revolution. Of course each one of them played a different role in such actions and therefore we cannot convict them at the same level. During the meetings of accountability it became clear that the most guilty among that group were Ghāzy 'Abdullah, Abū Bakr Salem and Tamān Muḥad. During the accountability meetings, these members tried to obstruct discussion and make them fail, but they did not succeed. The principal conspirators were Muḥad Hadḥūf and Ghāzy 'Abdullah. Muḥad Hadḥūf's role in those movements was not apparent as he did not leave his house during that period, nor did he attend the accountability meetings of other elements; but we discovered later that he had secret contacts with other elements through other prominent members. The military committee and the unit administration held lengthy sessions with those elements to listen to their views and investigate criticism raised by the base, the administration and the citizens and also to check the errors attributed to them. The main elements tried their best to complicate the meetings and evade the points laid down for discussions, while other elements adopted an attitude of fanaticism and fanatic defence of their mistakes. Before the group left, some of its members were interrogated, while investigations were being carried out. In fact the idea of desertion did not occur to us, at least in relation to the majority of these elements who dishonoured the confidence which their comrades placed in them and began to prepare for the role of desertion as a final step in their treacherous plan. As we have already pointed out, desertion can affect some elements of the poor classes who lack consciousness or the spirit of sacrifice and hard work, as well as some bourgeois elements who cannot get rid of their vacillation and selfishness.

As for comrades Khalid Salem, Sa'īd Djīnshān and Sa'īd Ahmad Ḥūr, they had co-operated with the group we have discussed, and participated in some errors and movements, but their mistakes were less serious than those of the others. These people were not aware of the intentions of the other elements and in particular their plan to desert. In the last meeting these three criticised themselves for their previous attitudes and co-operation with the other elements and claimed that they were misled. The decisions taken against these three were confined to the following:

1 Comrade Khalid Salem: suspension of membership for two months.
2 Comrade Sa'īd Djīnshān: suspension of membership for two months.
3 Comrade Sa'īd Ahmad Ḥūr: suspension of membership for one month.

We hope that these members will benefit from this experience and be careful about intrigue, and return to the service of the revolution actively and with a spirit of self-sacrifice, unless their connection with the revolution is based on personal grounds, in which case they are free to do what they wish.

Finally we wish to remind our comrades and noble citizens that every revolution includes various categories of fighters, some of whom have a morale which can be described like that of tree leaves which get burnt by the sun and fall down with the wind, while others have the morale of a tree itself which remains steadfast in the earth despite the strong wind. There are also others whose morale is high and firm like the top of our 'Arām mountain, and these are the majority in the revolution, and they will continue their mission until final victory.

Dhofar Province

On cliques

A comprehensive operation of rectification and development must take many forms and pass through many stages, starting with circulars, then educational and criticism meetings, both closed and open, and finally accountability and legal action. In order to be properly conducted, such operations should not be confined to executive instructions and measure from the top, but should be open to the participation of the base in order to demonstrate their positions and initiatives in the form of dialogue, criticism and general rectification. Talk about cliques has become widespread and complaints about them are discussed by almost everyone, despite the fact that few people understand cliques or their forms, or realise how dangerous they are, or can distinguish them from other problems. The state of ambiguity involving cliques is one of the factors which allow their continuation and prevent us from putting an end to them despite numerous remarks, complaints and nonsensical criticism. If words are not followed by action, they tend to be nonsense and if criticism is not connected with correction and practical action it will tend to be nonsense. Many of our comrades have, for a long time, criticised the tendency of cliques at work and complain about it, while they themselves practise it either consciously or unconsciously. Cliques can take numerous forms. We will first mention the factors which assist their development at work.

What are the causes contributing to the emergence of cliques?

1 The low standard of bourgeois class consciousness: the firmer class consciousness is, the weaker bourgeois reactionary consciousness is, and in as much as revolutionary thoughts become dominant in the

human mind, backward thoughts become accordingly weak. Consolidation of proletarian culture does not mean learning a number of revolutionary phrases and repeating them brainlessly, since a conscious proletarian is not one who reads a large collection of good books and stops at that. Proletarian education is achieved through class struggle, practice, action and widespread contact with the masses or, in short, by connecting revolutionary theory with practice, and it is the only correct method to develop a real proletarian; in as much as we succeed in this we shall succeed in preventing the emergence of wrong thoughts, expectations and conduct, including cliques.

2   Badly-organised relations among front members concerning the existing regulations of the front; such relations must be strengthened and must govern everyone in the front. Democratic centralism based on strict discipline, criticism and self-criticism, control, accountability, respect of the senior by the junior and democratic elections are the best means to consolidate sound relations within the framework of the revolution. Weakly-organised relations imply the development of wrong relations such as cliques.

Everyone in the front, whether he is an executive, a member of a certain committee or in the base, should be accustomed to the strict discipline, criticism, accountability and obedience to the senior. These attitudes must become part of our daily life and penetrate our feelings and conduct. The training of members in democratic centralism and the introduction of such a system in our daily life is the strongest weapon which we have against cliques or any other wrong habits which are practised. We should all fight to strengthen and organise relations as they are outlined in our regulations and every one of us must comply with and obey the centralised democratic system.

3   Remnants of individualism which the revolution has inherited from its society of origin. We came to the revolution from a backward society, affected by corrupt thoughts and destructive trends which we carried with us to the revolution, such as individualist mentality arising from petty bourgeois communities and small production whether in the country or the town. Individualism takes various forms and types, such as placing personal interest above general interest, the individual preferring himself to the group, his concern with himself and his problems rather than with others and their problems, the tendency to seek high positions, sometimes even by unacceptable means, and the desire to hear oneself praised and spoken well of.

These are some forms of individualist mentality which form a good soil for the development of cliques. He who places his private interests above those of the people can be described as forming a clique by himself, and the same can be said about one who places the interest of the individual above that of the group, one who concerns himself with his private matters more than with the problems of others, one who likes to reach a senior position, one who is fond of ostentation, or one who wishes to see others praising him. All these types of people have no right to speak of the revolution until they become real revolutionaries by giving up selfishness and subjugating their own interests and affairs to those of the revolution. In order to combat cliques we should fight the remnants of individualism and substitute collective thinking for individual thinking and the collective spirit for individualist spirit.

What are the forms of cliques and what are their manifestations?

1   Intimacy: there are small groups of comrades who do not feel content or happy unless they are with a certain group; these members are always found sitting together, visiting together, and they do not discuss anything except when they are with each other; they even sleep in the same place. Such groups consist of four or five persons or more and they consider themselves to be a group of friends who feel close to each other and understand each other. Such groups still understand friendship in the old sense which they inherited from the corrupt society and they reflect this in the new relations created by the revolution. Their behaviour reveals that they place private relations of friendship above the comradely relationship which connects them to all fighters. While members of such groups have very close relations with each other, their relations with other comrades are formal and irregular. These groups must stop preferring themselves to others and must deal with all friends with the same degree of familiarity and understanding. They should subject private relations to popular ones, and realise that the relations they have with the liberation army or the popular militia are more important and of a higher level than relations of traditional friendship.

2   The second form involves defending a certain group, finding justifications for its mistakes and speaking well of it. Such cliques try to defend certain elements even if they are wrong or find justification for the passive behaviour of other elements and incorrectly enlarge their positive features. By this type of behaviour they try to show their friends that they look after their interests and are faithful to them, even when they are wrong. This fault is found in various circles, among

the troops of the popular liberation army, the administration, committees, or individuals in the bases. When comrades consistently defend a certain group and try to justify its passivism and errors, they do it to show their comrades how good they are in order to win them over as supporters and followers. In this way groups cannot build good working relations or strengthen the revolution, they only build a group of members lacking consciousness. Such groups suffer from ostentation and by this behaviour they deepen the effect of their mistakes and passivism instead of applying the necessary criticism and correction; in this way they harm the interest both of their friends and of the revolution.

3   The third form is overlooking the mistakes of a certain group, circle or element, keeping silent about them and launching criticism campaigns against other groups, circles or elements. Criticism and in particular self-criticism are vital in our work, but when they are based on bias and overlook the mistakes of elements whom we favour while attacking others merely because they are not from our team, we are practising opportunism itself. The revolutionary must be honest with himself and his friends and should not overlook mistakes in his unit or scope of work to launch a campaign of criticism on other elements or groups. The revolutionary should not favour certain elements or groups because of companionship or association with them, and attack others out of bias or lack of association, or as a result of old hatred. If I feel close to, and like, a group of comrades, I should not be lenient towards them and thus overlook their mistakes or direct blame away from them; on the contrary I should be more frank with them and consider the interests of the revolution and its laws as more important than my liking for these people. Similarly if old misunderstandings have existed in the past between two parties they should not be allowed to develop, nor should they be a cause of hatred towards the comrades concerned or of expanding their mistakes. Anyone who is biased towards a certain group and attacks and criticises others is a former of cliques.

4   This form of clique is apparent in discriminatory treatment of fighters concerning, for example, rations, leave or duty. The misunderstanding of the meaning of friendship is reflected in the conduct of some comrades who are in responsible positions when they try to relieve certain comrades from work or give them more privileges than others. This shows a serious mentality of favouritism which is, in fact, a type of opportunism aimed at winning the affection and confidence of certain comrades in a wrong way. The confidence and respect of the base cannot be obtained by such bad methods unless there are ignorant elements who assess people according to their own personal interests.

Confidence of the base should be won through revolutionary principles and not by flattery and bribery. Although this form of discriminatory treatment between comrades is not yet very common it constitutes the most dangerous form of clique in so far as political trends are concerned.

5   This is seen when friendship is given a chance to prevail over regulations, for example in employment, which should be subject to the principles of qualifications and ability, as well as the presence of certain qualities such as firmness, consciousness and modesty in the candidate. Personal friendship, inclinations and sympathies should be set aside when deciding to recruit someone or give him an assignment. Regulations, principles and the interests of the revolution should always be above personal sympathies, inclinations and friendship. Comradely association and friendship are not rejected in the revolution, provided that they do not lead to wrong favouritism and sympathies in recruitment. Thus we should not be influenced by friendship or personal tendencies when we review the names of some people to elect or appoint them for certain posts.

6   This is found in larger groups when some comrades insist on remaining or ask for transfers to another unit despite the fact that work circumstances do not allow this. A member of the popular liberation army should be ready to work with any unit at any place. The interests of the work must come first and personal desires and pleasures second. In this respect we are not talking about comrades asking transfers for family reasons, which is something natural. We only mean those who insist on remaining in a certain unit or moving to another on the grounds that they have stayed with such a unit for a long time and can get on better with its members. By taking such an attitude we forget the requirements of work and revolutionary obligations, and we leave the final word to intimacy, mood and personal desires. Such attitudes are attributed to clique mentality which dominates such comrades without them realising its presence, as is evident from their behaviour when their desires are not met; then they live for a long time in an extraordinary psychological state and do not show the usual interest in work.

7   This is marked by a tendency to boast and be vainglorious, and is found mainly when comrades participate in violent battles on any line or in any area. This tendency first appeared under the name 'the Line heroes' when the battles were violent on the Red Line. This was accompanied by vanity and pure military boasting which some comrades expressed by contempt for others involved in different fronts. When

the Red Line became quiet and violent battles moved to the eastern region in October, we began to hear the title 'October heroes' and vanity and military boasting was repeated by some comrades who took part in the October campaign. When that campaign was finished and the eastern area became quiet the battle moved to Hoshi paths and we began to hear the phrase of 'Path heroes'. These days it would not be strange to hear new phrases of praise in the Sarfit area. This tendency to boast and be vain reminds us of the tribal attitudes, when one tribe used to pride itself by comparison with the other and this tendency shows evidence of the existence of the tribal mentality among most of us. The popular liberation army is one army and its units are the same and enjoy the same fighting ability and high morale, which is evident from the splendid heroic acts which resulted in the defeat of the enemy, be it on the Red Line, in the October campaign or in the Hoshi paths. A member of the liberation army should not claim priority and excellence over his colleagues in any unit. The real revolutionary does not boast or take pride in himself, or deprecate the ability of others, nor does he get conceited over victories or boast of them. This tendency not only reveals tribal mentality but also indicates a tendency to cliques among those who suffer from it.

What we have discussed represents the most important forms of cliques as well as the dangers and bad influence they cause. They may be summarised as follows:

1 Cliques weaken discipline and subject the policy and aims of the revolution to personal disposition and whim which will result in weakening the power to fight or to execute plans.

2 Cliques lead to strengthening individualist mentality and bourgeois thinking and to consolidating old habits from the pre-revolution period. They are thus considered to be a stumbling block in the path of the development of revolutionary thinking and the widening of proletarian culture.

3 Cliques affect friendly relations among comrades as they encourage the development of susceptibilities, suspicion and lack of confidence. They thus weaken the strong revolutionary links and internal unity among comrades. They also weaken comrades' ability to withstand hardship and achieve victories. Susceptibilities, suspicion and lack of confidence are aspects which cannot be avoided when cliques exist.

4 Cliques assist the emergence of a number of detestable tendencies such as conceit, ostentation, selfishness and individualist thinking which impede the development of comradeship and deepen passivism, while at the same time preventing positive moves.

5   Cliques cover mistakes, defend them and follow wrong methods of criticism, such as inflaming and slander. They thus obstruct the operation of correction and distort the purpose both of criticism and self-criticism and deprive them of their essential and positive meanings.

6   As a by-product of cliques, many work secrets leak out and a number of serious internal problems leak to the wrong places; this results in much passivism and even serious consequences. Cliques are thus against the secrecy of work which is one of the fundamental rules essential to the safety of both the revolution and its members.

7   Cliques lead to blocking and at best obstructing the development of many abilities. Revolutionary cadres emerge only from the heart of the struggle and not automatically from within themselves. However they need care, encouragement of positive initiatives and must be given the chance to develop their abilities; these things cannot be achieved unless we behave in a revolutionary way, free from the effects of personal friendships or hatred.

The development of various types of cliques at various levels is something inevitable in any revolution or organisation, and ultimately it does not constitute a serious danger to the struggle of any organisation; if it is watched from the very beginning and treated carefully and seriously and it is not ignored, then it cannot develop into more serious problems.

Towards furthering revolutionary consciousness, revolutionary determination and revolutionary honesty, without which nothing can be corrected.

Dhofar Province

Appendix 4

Minutes of talks

Between Chou En-lai and Muḥammad al-'Adsānī, Kuwait Minister of Trade, Peking, 5 December 1972

al-'Adsānī: I am honoured to have met the Premier in Cairo.

Chou: Yes, in 1965. Kuwait and Egypt are brotherly states.

al-'Adsānī: We are part of the Arab world.

Chou: There are only few Arab states left with whom we do not have [diplomatic] relations. Your neighbour, Saudi Arabia, is one example.

al-'Adsānī: We are pleased to see China represented in the Arab world.

Chou: According to our expectation, this is not a distant goal.

al-'Adsānī: Especially when China supports Arab causes without restrictions.

Chou: This is our duty. We have to thank you for your support for China's admission to the United Nations, last year.

al-'Adsānī: In point of fact, China's representation in the United Nations gives added support for freedom. The United Nations without China suffers a large vacuum.

Chou: We thank you for this support. But we are still learning at the United Nations; the tasks are not finished.

al-'Adsānī: If the Premier allows me: we know about China and follow its resistance to colonialism everywhere in the world. We also know of China's humanistic message which the world needs. When we came to China, we were surprised to notice the honesty, dedication and faithfulness of the Chinese people in their discipline.

Chou: We thank you for these compliments. But as Chairman Mao says, there is a good side, and a bad one too. There are bad Chinese [elements] who abhor discipline.

320

al-'Adsānī: This is a normal occurrence in a population of 800 million.

Chou: Because of this, we must exert more effort.

al-'Adsānī: If the Premier allows me to give a small example. I and my friends stayed at Shanghai. Usually I lock my suitcases. But there and in Peking, we neither locked our suitcases nor our doors.

Chou: Generally speaking this is the way things are in China. Things are safe. But other hotels have witnessed thefts. Lately a few thefts have occurred, but we have quickly captured the thieves. I particularly recommend the Peking Hotel and the workers there. But they must not hear this compliment or they will become complacent. We have signed a chemical agreement with your chemical company. Though our diplomatic relations have been established recently, our trade relations date back to 1955. Our Vice-Trade Minister has visited your country. I asked him about the needs of the Kuwaiti market for Chinese products, but he gave me no satisfactory answers. This is our weakness, we lack the spirit to serve all the peoples' needs in different nations. We must export the best we have to you so that we benefit mutually. Whenever I ask them [Chinese Ministry of Trade] they do not give satisfactory answers to help the furthering of our co-operation. Japanese companies are more careful in this field. I told them we must not compete with brotherly Arab states on the Kuwaiti market. We take this fact into consideration over every product we sell you. Profit is not the first consideration, but friendship is.

al-'Adsānī: We believe in free enterprise. Our market is open to the East and the West. It all depends on the quality of the products and price competitivity. All world products are available in Kuwait. I recall that the Kuwaiti agent for Chinese meat complains about the lack of quality of Chinese products.

Chou: Canned or frozen ones?

al-'Adsānī: Canned.

Chou: I do not know the reason for that. Perhaps they are not of good quality.

al-'Adsānī: The quality is good.

Chou: I do not know. We have to ask other [opinions].

al-'Adsānī: It is excellent.

Chou: This is a compliment.

al'Adsānī: One further point. The trade balance between us is favour-
               able to China. Our imports [from China] are approximately
               thirty million dollars whereas China's imports from
               Kuwait are approximately twelve million dollars. We are
               trying to close the gap. This is possible by purchasing
               more chemicals and petroleum products. We hope we can
               negotiate this.

Chou: We buy chemicals from you.

al-'Adsānī: You do indeed.

Chou: I heard that your petroleum products do not fill our
               buying capacity.

al-'Adsānī: We concentrate on petroleum products in our production.
               We have still not received any answer to our offer, and
               moreover the negotiations are lengthy.

Chou: Because in China, we are self-sufficient in petroleum. If
               you have chemicals, we are ready to buy from you. Now
               we buy from Japan. And we do not want to depend on
               one country only for our purchases. What quantity of
               sulphur do you have available?

al-'Adsānī: The quantity that has been negotiated with you is twenty
               thousand tons.

Chou: Is it possible to supply it?

al-'Adsānī: Yes, in the future.

Chou: You want to buy products for a paper industry.

al-'Adsānī: We do not have a paper industry. We thought, perhaps,
               that the two friendly states could co-operate in this field.
               We are thinking of a joint effort. Our conditions are that
               Kuwait law allows 51 per cent for the Kuwaiti side and
               49 per cent to the foreign side.

Chou: We do not operate on this basis. We do not invest in other
               countries for the sake of profit. We can export the
               machinery and the experts, and when their job is finished
               they will leave. What type of paper do you want to
               produce?

al'Adsānī: Our production will not be confined to the Kuwaiti
               market. Our needs include those for newspapers and other
               items.

Chou: What type of newspapers?

al-'Adsānī: We need all types of paper. We mostly import from
               Europe.

Chou: Then you need wood-paper products. Since the [Kuwaiti] Ambassador is present, we will instruct our Foreign Trade Ministry to contact him and make the necessary arrangements.

al-'Adsānī: Our experience has taught us that when a foreigner invests with his money he feels the burden of loss and gain and thus becomes more serious in the investment.

Chou: Perhaps. We in China do not indulge in such deals, for our system does not allow us to do so. We have announced eight principles in our dealings with foreign countries in the United Nations and Chile.

al-'Adsānī: If you will excuse me, Mr Premier, the person in charge in your Foreign Trade Ministry has informed me that China lacks expertise in this field.

Chou: No longer so. We can send you our experts or you can send Kuwaitis for training here. We will consult with the Kuwaiti Ambassador on this matter. I gather that because of the large numbers of ships navigating through the [Arabian] Gulf, there is a noticeable problem of pollution there.

al-'Adsānī: We are seriously looking into the matter. A conference will be called to discuss pollution problems among Gulf states.

Chou: I hear that you drink desalinated water from the Gulf, and the Gulf has large fish resources. Doesn't pollution pose a problem?

al-'Adsānī: We have felt the danger.

Chou: I asked some Japanese friends about this matter. They said they are thinking of separating water from petroleum.

al-'Adsānī: It is forbidden for ships to discharge their waters in the Gulf. If a ship violates this law, it is liable to a fine of eight thousand dinars.

Chou: There are Japanese companies who have plans to erect separate petroleum and water tanks in the ship itself. If they do not do this, the Japanese coast will be highly polluted.

al-'Adsānī: We have felt the danger.

Chou: You have strong relations with Japan. Perhaps because of the oil trade.

al-'Adsānī: I thank your Excellency for this meeting.

Chou: We have learned from you. Please convey my regards to

> the Emir, Prince Ṣabah al-Salim al-Ṣabah, and to the
> Crown Prince and Prime Minister, Prince Jabir al-'Aḥmad
> al-Ṣabah.

al-'Adsānī: His Highness the Emir and Crown Prince and Prime
Minister have asked me to convey their regards to Chairman Mao Tse-tung and to your Excellency personally.

Between Li Hsien-nien and Taiysīr Ḳuba'h, PFLP, Peking, October 1974

Li: Welcome. You have come from the land of struggle.

Ḳuba'h: We come to China to learn from your experiences. As you
know our struggle suffers from great hardship, but
ultimately we will win. We will win because of our
determination, and because revolutionary consciousness
is high among Arab and Palestinian Arab masses.

Li: Your [Arab] nation is located in a strategic position. It is
the crossroad to three continents. And that is why they
[imperialists] want to control the area.

Ḳuba'h: People are stronger than imperialists. They cannot control
the three continents from our area, because our time is
the era of people's war.
Naturally, we are not alone in our struggle. Many fronts
come to our aid; and our friends are increasingly supporting us, primarily China and its people under the leadership
of the Great Chairman.

Li: We must support you in your struggle against the imperialists and world hegemonism. We support the Palestinian
Liberation Organisation, as well as you, in your [joint]
struggle against imperialism and the Soviet Union. Both
of them are in a race to appease and control you. It is
because of this that your conditions are hard. Moreover,
it is they who created Zionism, claiming, at the time, that
they were numerically inferior. How many Jews are in
Israel?

Ḳuba'h: Approximately three millions. The problem does not rest
with the Jews alone, we Arabs are one hundred million.
Israel is the base of imperialism. That is why we claim that
imperialism is our number one enemy. They created this
base to act as an impediment to Arab technological
superiority. That is why we undertook the path of

protracted people's war. Our victory is assured, but currently we are lacking the correct political line.

Li: Perhaps your relations with Hussein are not good?

Kuba'h: Hussein is an ally of the enemy. We do not differentiate between him and an Israeli like Rabin.

Li: We do not have amicable relations with him [Hussein]. Israel constantly approaches us to establish relations. It voted for China's rightful admission to the UN. It even sent us a congratulatory telegram. We refused to accept it, and it was returned.

Kuba'h: This is a fact. One must realise that the Zionist State is illegal. We are not against Jews, but Zionists. Zionism is another imperialist mask. We are against Israel as a state. And our struggle aims at creating a democratic society in Palestine, whereby all religions could be practised freely. Former [Arab] leadership regimes distorted the true nature of our cause. It presented our struggle in a religious form; Muslims against Jews. Our struggle has two basic characteristics, a national struggle and, in the meantime, a class struggle. It is because of this that reactionaries and imperialists fear our struggle.

Li: Reactionaries exist in every nation. In China, there was Chiang Kai-shek, but he escaped to Taiwan. The day will come when we liberate Taiwan.

Kuba'h: You follow an anti-hegemony policy.

Li: We warned our friends and our people that the day when China reaches this stage, they must rise and struggle against Chinese leaders who are in power. That is why we pay a great deal of attention in educating our people. We educate our younger generation on this basis so that in the future they will not rule others. We are still poor, and told our youngsters that when they become rich they must not seek hegemony in the world. They must stress the concept of mutual benefit among nations.

In the past, many states interfered in China's internal affairs, Britain, France, Italy, USA and Japan, and even small states like Belgium and Holland. They all came to China to slice it into pieces and they call them their 'domains'. But they failed. Several wars ensued. The Chinese fought each other; alas, behind every [reactionary] faction there was a foreign element. It is because of this that we uphold the concept of

non-interference in other nations. Those who seek world
hegemony better leave China alone. The Chinese are peace-
loving people, we advocate equality among nations. If they
oppose us, then we will mount a struggle. In your area, it
was American imperialism which created Israel. Your war is
a just one. We wholeheartedly support you.

It is unpermissible that they [Zionists] bring millions of
people to inhabit your land. Your cause is a just one. But
only through unity can the enemy be defeated. Is this a fair
judgement?

Ḳuba'h: Indeed. We have studied several experiences. Historically, the
Palestinian masses are oppressed and enslaved people. In the
beginning came the Turks and then the British. Of course,
our people rose in revolt against the Zionist settlers. They
came in batches just like in Rhodesia. When they arrived
they exploited Arab backwardness. They were backed by
British colonialists and Arab lackeys. 1948 was the year of
Arab awakening. Many changes occurred in Egypt, Syria and
Iraq; Arab masses began to question matters.

Even now, there is a move to legitimise the existence of the
State of Israel in the area. In return, for our recognition of
Israel they offered us pieces of land in Gaza and the West
Bank. Actually, that is one-quarter of the land of Palestine.
The imperialists and colonialists recognise the importance of
our revolution, consequently they seek to terminate it. They
have recognised that Israel cannot last for ever. Since they
have failed to terminate our revolution militarily, they are
seeking to do it politically.

We are not totally against negotiations, there are few which
could be beneficial to our revolution. We think that the
Geneva Conference scheme, which is led by Kissinger, is a
step towards a political solution. There are many international and Arab forces who seek such a solution. Our
masses, who underwent many hardships, can ignite another
revolution. Our primary task now is to educate our masses
in order to reject such a reactionary plan. We as a Front are
sure of our drive.

Li: Is there any disagreement amongst you [the Palestine
Resistance Movement]?

Ḳuba'h: Regrettably, yes.

Li: We cannot present our view on this. All we can hope is that you continue your fight in a unified form. Your cause is a just one. To give judgement is like interfering in your internal affairs.

Ḳuba'h: I am sure you are against this [political] solution. You always express your desire for our unity. We have studied your experiences in national unity. Our political line stresses two things: to defeat this political solution and to present to our masses a Marxist-Leninist Front. If there is a unified national front our struggle must be among the masses and not among leaders. We are sure that China supports our political line. We have studied Chairman Mao's instructions on people's war. However, I would like to stress to my comrade that we support a unified national front.

Li: Unity among Arab people. Reactionaries have no choice but defeat. Your nation is historically old. The peoples of the Third World must unite. Your disagreements amongst Arab people must be different from your disagreements with Israel. Because against Israel one must carry a gun.

Ḳuba'h: It is true there are disagreements [amongst Arabs]. But these are found not amongst Arab people, but leaders. The Saudis and Jordanians are oppressed masses, Arab rulers fear armed struggle. But we cannot negotiate with our enemy [Israel].

Li: You cannot argue with your enemy. For example, if we tell Chaing Kai-shek to leave Taiwan peacefully, of course he will refuse. How is it that the population of Israel is multiplying? Perhaps it is a combination of Soviet, European and socialist countries' encouragement of Jewish immigration to Israel!

Ḳuba'h: You call these socialist countries! Their socialism is only verbal. Lenin once said that we must differentiate between those who voice socialism and at the same time practise imperialism.

Li: Is Isaac Rabin an immigrant?

Ḳuba'h: No, he was born in Jerusalem. So was Moshe Dayan. But their families emigrated to Palestine.

Li: There were some Jews in China; but now they have been integrated with the rest of the society.

Ḳuba'h: There are many Jews who struggle for our cause; but they are oppressed ones.

Li: Do the Arabs have a unified language?

Ḳuba'h: Yes, but there are different dialects. In writing it, we proceed from right to left.

Li: Have you visited the Great Wall? The Emperor who built it
             was instrumental in unifying the Chinese language.
Ḳuba'h: We have a proverb that says: Seek knowledge even in China.*
Li: The silk road extended to Iran, then to your area.
Ḳuba'h: We have a minority called *al-Duruz*, which believes that after
             death souls rest at the Great Wall.
Li: The Chinese people, like the Arabs, are conservative people.
             We hope that you will be victorious and united.

* This is one of the Prophet Muhḥamed's sayings (Had<u>ith</u>).

Appendix 5[1]

Sino-Arab delegation exchanges, 1956–75[2]

Section A: Arab delegations to People's Republic of China

Type	*Date*
Egyptian Trade Delegation	February 1956
Egyptian Trade Delegation	April 1956
Egyptian Historian Cultural Delegation	April 1956
Syrian Jurists' Delegation	April 1956
Prime Minister of Sudan	May 1956
Sudanese Cultural Delegation	May 1956
Sudanese Trade Union Delegation	May 1956
Sudanese Member of Parliament	May 1956
Lebanese Archbishop	June 1956
Egyptian Students' Delegation	June 1956
Moroccan and Syrian Students' Delegation	June 1956
Egyptian Professor	July 1956
Syrian Governmental Delegation	August 1956
Sudanese Women's Delegation	September 1956
Syrian Mission	September 1956
Egyptian Artists' Delegation	September 1956
Arab Workers' Delegation (not specified)	October 1956
Egyptian Artists' Delegation	October 1956
Syrian Members of Parliament's Delegation	November 1956
Egyptian Cultural Delegation	October 1957
Egyptian Trade Delegation	November 1957
Egyptian Medical Delegation	December 1957
Sudanese Trade Delegation	December 1957
Yemeni Crown Prince	December 1957
Arab and Algerian Delegation (not specified)	March 1958
Arab Trade Union Delegation (not specified)	April 1958
Algerian Students' Delegation	September 1958

Type	*Date*
Iraqi Cultural Delegation	December 1958
Iraqi Peace Delegation	December 1958
UAR Teachers' Delegation	December 1958
Deputy 'Imām of Oman	January 1959
Algerian Military Delegation	April 1959
Iraqi Women's Delegation	June 1959
Iraqi Special Representative	July 1959
Iraqi Student Delegation	July 1959
Iraqi Medical Delegation	August 1959
Iraqi Teachers' Delegation	August 1959
Moroccan Trade Delegation	September 1959
Tunisia-China Association Delegation	September 1959
Iraqi Communist Party Delegation	September 1959
Algerian Communist Party Delegation	September 1959
Sudanese Journalists' Delegation	September 1959
Israeli Communist Party Delegation	September 1959
Jordanian Communist Party Delegation	September 1959
Lebanese Communist Party Delegation	September 1959
Sudanese Cultural Delegation	September 1959
Syrian Communist Party Delegation	September 1959
Algerian Provisional Government Delegation	September 1959
Moroccan Delegation	September 1959
Yemeni Government Delegation	October 1959
Former Moroccan Prime Minister	November 1959
Sudanese Women's Delegation	November 1959
Algerian Youth Delegation	April 1960
Algerian Trade Union Delegation	April 1960
Iraqi Cultural Delegation	April 1960
Algerian Provisional Government Delegation (headed by Vice Premier Belkacem)	April 1960
Iraqi Trade Delegation	May 1960
Moroccan Youth Delegation	May 1960
Sudanese Students' Delegation	July 1960
Sudanese Trade Delegation	August 1960
President of Iraqi General Union of Students	August 1960
Algerian Premier Abbas	September 1960
Iraqi Military Goodwill Mission	September 1960
Moroccan Lawyers	September 1960
Assad al Mokadam, Chief Editor of Lebanese Paper	September 1960

Type	*Date*
Moroccan Journalist	September 1960
Delegation of Neo-Destour of Tunisia	September 1960
Moroccan Cultural Delegation	September 1960
Yemeni Journalists' Delegation	September 1960
UAR Guests	September 1960
Iraqi Minister, Faisal al-Samir	October 1960
Tunisian Delegate of Sino-Tunisian Friendship Association	October 1960
Iraqi Educational Delegation	October 1960
Yemeni Moslem Delegation	November 1960
Iraqi Engineers' Delegation	December 1960
Sudanese Cultural Delegation	January 1961
Israeli Woman Writer, Rosel Wuhl	May 1961
Algerian Diplomatic Mission	May 1961
Sudanese Guest	June 1961
Tunisian Goodwill and Friendship Delegation	July 1961
Sudanese Medical Delegation	September 1961
Algerian Writers	March 1962
UAR Trade Delegation	May 1962
Sudanese Trade and Cotton Delegation	May 1962
Iraqi Education Delegation	August 1962
UAR Agricultural Delegation	August 1962
Syrian Economic Delegation	February 1963
Algerian Journalists	March 1963
Moroccan Trade Unionists	March 1963
Algerian Heroine	March 1963
Moroccan Government Trade Delegation	March 1963
Sudanese President Abboud	April 1963
UAR 'Ali Ṣabrī	April 1963
Algerian Women's Delegation	April 1963
Algerian Guests (non-specified)	May 1963
Algerian Trade Union Delegation	May 1963
Sudan Cotton Trading Delegation	May 1963
Moroccan Guests (non-specified)	May 1963
Algerian Journalists' Delegation	August 1963
Yemeni Guests (non-specified)	August 1963
Algerian Minister of State with Governmental Delegation	September 1963
Syrian Journalist	September 1963
Algerian Trade Union Delegation	September 1963

Type	Date
Algerian Military Delegation	September 1963
Iraqi Radio and Television Delegation	September 1963
Yemeni Party Leader	September 1963
UAR Educational Delegation	October 1963
Algerian Jurists' Delegation	January 1964
Àlgerian Guest	January 1964
Algerian Cultural Delegation	April 1964
Yemeni Governmental Trade Delegation	May 1964
Sudanese President Ibrahim Abboud	May 1964
Iraqi Cultural Delegation	May 1964
UAR Women's Delegation	May 1964
Yemeni President and Delegation	June 1964
UAR Correspondent	June 1964
Iraqi Delegation (for Peking Symposium)	August 1964
Algerian Scientific Delegation (for Peking Symposium)	August 1964
Algerian Orphans	August 1964
Algerian Guests (non-specified)	August 1964
UAR Scientific Delegation (for Peking Symposium)	August 1964
Algerian President	August 1964
Sudanese Islamic Scholar	September 1964
Algerian Government Economic Delegation	September 1964
Iraqi Government Trade Delegation	September 1964
Moroccan Guest (non-specified)	September 1964
Yemeni Journalists' Delegation	September 1964
Moroccan Prince	September 1964
Sudanese Guest (non-specified)	September 1964
Algerian Trade Unionists	September 1964
Delegation of the Kingdom of Morocco	September 1964
UAR National Assembly Member	September 1964
Algerian Party and Government Delegation	October 1964
Algerian Trade Delegation	October 1964
President of Algerian National Assembly	November 1964
Syrian Leading Journalist	November 1964
UAR Minister	November 1964
Algerian Minister	December 1964
Moroccan Guest (non-specified)	December 1964
Algerian Militia Delegation	December 1964
UAR Deputy Prime Minister	December 1964

Type	*Date*
Moroccan Guest (non-specified)	January 1965
Lebanese Parliamentary Delegation (Kamal Junblat)	February 1965
Moroccan Communist Party Delegation	February 1965
Kuwait Friendship Delegation (Finance Minister)	February 1965
UAR Educational Delegation	March 1965
Syrian Friendship Delegation (Syrian Foreign Minister)	March 1965
UAR President's Advisor, Mr Husain Ṣabrī	April 1965
UAR Civil Aviation Delegation	April 1965
UAR Journalist	April 1965
Yemeni Cultural Delegation	April 1965
UAR Film Delegation	May 1965
Secretary of Pan-Arab Journalists Association	May 1965
Algerian Health Delegation	May 1965
Algerian Trade Union Delegation	May 1965
Algerian Military Delegation	June 1965
UAR Industrial Delegation	July 1965
Syrian Teachers' Delegation	July 1965
Syrian Historian	July 1965
Algerian Government Delegation	August 1965
UAR Journalists	August 1965
Sudanese Journalists	September 1965
Syrian Trade Union Delegation	September 1965
Lebanese Journalist	September 1965
Sudanese Jurists' Delegation	October 1965
Delegation of the Sudanese Peasants' General Federation	October 1965
Kuwait Assistant Under Secretary	October 1965
UAR Health Delegation	October 1965
Syrian Military Delegation	October 1965
Syrian Guest	October 1965
Tunisian Students' Delegation	October 1965
UAR Mme 'Ali Ṣabrī	October 1965
Lebanese MP Delegation	December 1965
Algerian and Syrian Trade Union Delegation	April 1966
Syrian Cotton Trade Delegation	April 1966
Iraqi Guests (non-specified)	April 1966
Algerian Journalists' Delegation	May 1966
Sudanese Guest (non-specified)	May 1966

Appendix 5

Type	*Date*
Yemeni Trade Unionists	May 1966
Sudan Teachers' Delegation	May 1966
Arab Lawyers' Federation Delegation	June 1966
Sudan Cotton Delegation	July 1966
Lebanese MP	July 1966
Visiting group of Algerian College Students	August 1966
Sudanese Guest (non-specified)	September 1966
Moroccan Guests (non-specified)	September 1966
Director of Iraqi Newspaper	September 1966
Algerian Trade Delegation	November 1966
Moroccan Special Envoy of Presidency	November 1966
Delegation of Sudan-China Friendship	May 1967
Association	April 1967
UAR Government Trade Delegation	May 1967
Dhofar Liberation Front Delegation	June 1967
Syrian Guests (non-specified)	August 1967
Delegation of Sudanese-Chinese Friendship	
Association	September 1967
Syrian Song and Dance Ensemble	March 1968
Yemeni Guests (non-specified)	May 1968
Delegation from People's Republic of South	
Yemen	September 1968
UAR Government Trade Delegation	February 1969
Military Delegation from Syrian Arab Republic	May 1969
Democratic People's Republic of Algeria	
Government Delegation	September 1969
Iraqi Civil Aviation Delegation	November 1969
Delegation from People's Front for Liberation	
of Occupied Arab Gulf	March 1970
People's Republic of South Yemen, Salem Rubic	
'Alī, Chairman of Presidential Council	July 1970
Sudanese President Nimerī and Government	
Friendship Delegation	August 1970
Iraqi Teachers' Union Delegation	September 1970
UAR Goodwill Delegation	January 1971
UAR Dr Hussni al Sayad Hidjazi	March 1971
Sudanese Friendship Delegation	April 1971
Arab Journalists (visit and cover 'Palestine	
International Week')	May 1971
Sudanese Government Delegation	June 1971

Type	*Date*
Iraqi Economic and Technical Delegation	June 1971
UAR Sports Delegation	July 1971
UAR Government Trade Delegation	July 1971
Delegation of Preparatory Committee of National Congress of Socialist League of Sudan	July 1971
Jordanian Guest	July 1971
Minister of Interior of People's Republic of Yemen	July 1971
Ahmed Ḥaïder, Yemeni Under Secretary of State for Foreign Affairs	August 1971
President of Jordanian Economists' Association	August 1971
3 Jordanian Friends (Sulaiman Nabulsī, former P.M.; Shafik 'Arsh̲īdat, Secretary-General of Arab Lawyers' Federation; Maruan al-Hamūd)	September 1971
Libyan Journalists' Delegation	October 1971
Kuwaiti Table Tennis Delegation	November 1971
Syrian Guests (non-specified)	November 1971
Sudan High-level Government Delegation (Deputy President Abbas)	December 1971
Iraqi Government Delegation	December 1971
Peasants' Delegation from People's Democratic Republic of Yemen	March 1972
Egyptian Government Delegation	March 1972
Director of Sudan News Agency	April 1972
Syrian Women's Delegation	April 1972
Syrian Sports Federation Delegation	May 1972
Syrian Government Delegation	May 1972
Tunisian Trade Delegation	May 1972
Iraqi Table Tennis Association Delegation	May 1972
Kuwait Table Tennis Federation Delegation	May 1972
Representative of Lebanese Table Tennis Federation	May 1972
Lebanese Delegation of Commerce and Industry	May 1972
Lebanese Writer	May 1972
Kuwaiti Member of Parliament	May 1972
Sudanese Youth Delegation	June 1972
Peasants' Delegation from People's Democratic Republic of Yemen	June 1972
Government Delegation from People's Republic of Yemen	July 1972

Type	*Date*
Yemen Arab Republic — Prime Minister	July 1972
Kuwaiti Parliamentary Delegation	July 1972
Egyptian Government Industrial Delegation	August 1972
Algerian College Students' Football Delegation	August 1972
Algerian Friendly Personage	August 1972
Algerian Health Delegation	August 1972
Sudanese Rural Cadres	August 1972
Kuwaiti Table Tennis Delegation	August 1972
Tunisian Government Delegation (Tunisian Foreign Minister)	August 1972
Egyptian Anaesthetists' Association Delegation	September 1972
Algerian Insurance Delegation	October 1972
Algerian Government Delegation	October 1972
Youth Delegation of Party of National Liberation Front of Algeria	October 1972
Syrian Professor and wife	October 1972
Syrian People's Army Delegation	October 1972
Egyptian Health Delegation	November 1972
Lebanese Foreign Minister	November 1972
Egyptian Journalist	December 1972
Kuwaiti Governmental Trade and Economic Delegation	December 1972
Egyptian President and Chief Editor of *Al 'Ahram*	January 1973
Egyptian Foreign Minister and his Party	March 1973
Secretary General of Kuwait Table Tennis Federation	March 1973
Sudanese Delegation	April 1973
Algerian Delegation	May 1973
Journalists' Delegation from People's Democratic Republic of Yemen	May 1973
Workers' and Womens' Delegation from People's Democratic Republic of Yemen	May 1973
Iraqi Health Delegation	June 1973
Sudanese Governmental Economic and Trade Delegation	June 1973
Algerian Health Delegation	July 1973
Kuwaiti Medical Delegation	July 1973
Lebanese Racing-Club Football Delegation	July 1973

Type	*Date*
Director and Chief Editor of Sudanese Paper *Al Saafa*	August 1973
Journalists' Delegation from Yemen Arab Republic	August 1973
Medical Delegation from Morocco	August 1973
Lebanese Friend (non-specified)	August 1973
Egyptian Vice-President and Goodwill Delegation	September 1973
Sudan National Men's Basketball Team	October 1973
Sudan Friendship Delegation	October 1973
Egyptian Pharmaceutical Study Group	November 1973
Education Delegation from People's Democratic Republic of Yemen	December 1973
Syrian Government Civil Aviation Delegation	January 1974
President Boumedienne and Distinguished Algerian Guests	February 1974
Kuwait Olympic Committee President and National Men's Volley-ball Team	February 1974
Iraq Economic Delegation	February 1974
Kuwait National Assembly Speaker	March 1974
Syrian Delegation of Federation of Revolutionary Youth and National Union of Students	March 1974
Iraq Youth Delegation	March 1974
Algerian Delegation	April 1974
Sudan Acrobatics Trainees' Delegation	April 1974
Public Health Delegation from Yemen Arab Republic	April 1974
Yemen Arab Republic Consultative Assembly Delegation	April 1974
Egypt Anti-Epidemic and Public Health Delegation	May 1974
Moroccan Princess Lamia and Other Distinguished Guests	May 1974
Kuwaiti Gymnastic Team	June 1974
Syrian Minister of Industry	June 1974
Egypt Gymnasts Delegation	July 1974
Algerian Friends (non-specified)	July 1974
Special Envoy of Moroccan King	July 1974
Tunisian Minister of External Affairs Ḥabib Chatti	July 1974
Iraq Trade Union Delegation	July 1974

Type	*Date*
People's Democratic Republic of Yemen Football Team	July 1974
People's Democratic Republic of Yemen Delegation	July 1974
Algerian Teachers' and Students' Friendship Delegation	August 1974
Sudan 'Gezira' Football Team	August 1974
Sudanese Medical Delegation	August 1974
Moroccan Track and Field Delegation	August 1974
Sudanese Educational Delegation	September 1974
Yemen Arab Republic Commander of 'Giant' Forces	September 1974
Friends from United Arab Emirates	September 1974
Egypt Men's Basketball Delegation	September 1974
Delegation of Bahrain Chamber of Commerce and Industry	November 1974
Delegation of Algerian Ministry of Agriculture and Agrarian Reform	November 1974
Chairman Rubic 'Ali, Head of People's Democratic Republic of Yemen	November 1974
Distinguished Egyptian Guests	December 1974
Moroccan Minister of State, Dr Ahmed Laraki	March 1975
Algerian Track and Field Team	April 1975
Algerian Minister of Agriculture	April 1975
UAR Deputy Commander-in-Chief	April 1975
Kuwaiti National Assembly Delegation	April 1975
Tunisian Prime Minister	April 1975
Egyptian Special National Council Delegation	May 1975
Egyptian Academics' Study Group	May 1975
Egyptian Trade Delegation	May 1975
General Federation of Syrian Trade Unions Delegation	May 1975
Iraqi News Agency Director	June 1975
Egyptian Ministry of Tourism Delegation	July 1975
Egyptian Men's Volley-ball Team	July 1975
Egyptian People's Assembly Delegation	July 1975
Algerian Scientific Delegation	July 1975
Tunisian Volley-ball Team	July 1975
Tunis Afrique Press Delegation	July 1975
Iraqi Vice-President Taha Marouf	July 1975

Type	*Date*
Lebanese Lawyers' Delegation	July 1975
Sudanese Men's Volley-ball Team	August 1975
Sudanese Women's Delegation	September 1975
Mayor of Baghdad	September 1975
Iraqi Journalists' Delegation	September 1975
Sudanese High Ranking Military Delegation	September 1975
President of Kuwaiti National Football Association	September 1975
Editor of Hilal Publishing House (Egypt)	November 1975
Iraqi Education Delegation	October 1975
Bahrain Trade Delegation	November 1975

Section B: Chinese delegations despatched to the Arab World 1956–75

Type	*State*	*Date*
Trade Mission	Saudi Arabia	January 1956
Trade Mission	Egypt	January 1956
Cultural Delegation	Egypt	February 1956
Trade Mission	Egypt	March 1956
Trade Mission	Sudan	April 1956
Trade Mission	Lebanon	April 1956
Cultural Delegation	Sudan	April 1956
Cultural Delegation	Syria	May 1956
Cultural Delegation	Lebanon	June 1956
Youth Delegation	Egypt	July 1956
Pilgrimage Mission	Saudi Arabia	July 1956
Youth Delegation	Sudan	August 1956
Trade Delegation (Damascus Fair)	Syria	August 1956
(Religious) Cultural Delegation	Yemen	August 1956
Trade Representative	Lebanon	August 1956
Youth Delegation	Lebanon	August 1956
Religious Delegation	Syria	August 1956
Pilgrimage Mission	Syria	August 1956
Pilgrimage Mission	Jordan	August 1956
Trade Delegation	Egypt	September 1956
Trade Representative	Lebanon	September 1956
Trade Delegation	Tunisia	October 1956
Trade Delegation	Morocco	December 1956
Journalist Delegation	Egypt	December 1956

Type	*State*	*Date*
Student Delegation	Syria	November 1957
Law Delegation	Syria	November 1957
Cultural Delegation	Egypt	December 1957
Acrobatic Delegation	Tunisia	January 1958
Artists' Delegation	Morocco	February 1958
Youth Delegation	Egypt	February 1958
Military Mission	UAR (United Arab Republic: Egypt-Syria)	March 1958
Minister (non-specified)	Yemen	April 1958
Trade Delegation	Tunisia	September 1958
Artists' Delegation	UAR (Egypt-Syria)	September 1958
Trade Delegation	Morocco	October 1958
Trade Delegation	UAR (Egypt-Syria)	October 1958
Trade Delegation	Iraq	December 1958
Youth Delegation	UAR (Egypt-Syria)	January 1959
Peace Delegation	Iraq	March 1959
Artists' Delegation	Iraq	July 1959
Experts	Morocco	December 1959
Pilgrimage Mission	Saudi Arabia	June 1960
Student Leader	Morocco	July 1960
Moslem Pilgrim Delegation	UAR (Egypt-Syria)	August 1960
Moslem Pilgrim Delegation	Yemen	September 1960
Military Goodwill Delegation	UAR (Egypt-Syria)	September 1960
Professor	Morocco	October 1960
Women Delegates	UAR (Egypt-Syria)	January 1961
Delegation	Sudan	January 1961
Delegation for Afro-Asian Solidarity	UAR (Egypt-Syria)	January 1961
Delegate for Student Congress	UAR (Egypt-Syria)	February 1961
Delegation	Morocco	March 1961
Observers for 3rd All African People's Conference	UAR (Egypt-Syria)	March 1961
Vice-Minister of Agriculture	UAR (Egypt-Syria)	March 1961
Delegation Leader	Sudan	April 1961
Vice-Minister of Foreign Trade	Morocco	May 1961

Type	*State*	*Date*
Women Delegates	Algeria	May 1961
Ambassador to Morocco	Tunisia	October 1961
Government Delegation	Yemen	January 1962
Leader of Writers' Delegation	UAR	February 1962
Writers	Morocco	April 1962
International Trade Council Leader	UAR (Egypt-Syria)	May 1962
Table Tennis Team	UAR (Egypt)	May 1962
Ministry of Communication Delegation	UAR (Egypt)	May 1962
Engineers	Sudan	June 1962
Table Tennis Team	Sudan	June 1962
Moslem Pilgrims	Saudi Arabia	June 1962
Moslem Pilgrim Delegation	UAR (Egypt)	June 1962
Trade Union Representative	Morocco	June 1962
Government, Military Delegation	Iraq	July 1962
Red Cross Delegation	Morocco	October 1962
Student Leader	UAR (Gaza) (Egypt)	October 1962
Government Delegation (for National Day Celebration)	Algeria	October 1962
Trade Union and Women Delegates	Algeria	October 1962
Delegation (non-specified)	Iraq	November 1962
Cultural Delegation	UAR (Egypt)	November 1962
Cultural Delegation	Sudan	December 1962
Trade Union Delegation (for Avockees Congress)	Algeria	January 1963
Trade Union Delegation	Morocco	January 1963
Cultural and Goodwill Delegation	UAR (Egypt)	January 1963
Health Delegation	Algeria	March 1963
Medical Team	Algeria	April 1963
Trade Union Delegation	Morocco	April 1963
Health Delegation	Morocco	April 1963
Second Group Medical Team	Algeria	June 1963
Government Delegation	UAR (Egypt)	July 1963
Trade Delegation	UAR	July 1963
Student Delegation	Morocco	August 1963

Appendix 5

Type	*State*	*Date*
Television Delegation	UAR (Egypt)	August 1963
Cultural Delegation	Algeria	September 1963
Government Delegation	Yemen	September 1963
Cultural Delegation	Morocco	September 1963
Expert Team	Algeria	October 1963
Communist Party Delegation	Algeria	October 1963
Government Delegation	Algeria	October 1963
Military Delegation	Algeria	October 1963
Womens Delegation	Algeria	October 1963
Youth Delegation	Algeria	October 1963
Premier Chou En-Lai & Vice Premier Chen-Yi	Algeria	December 1963
Premier Chou En-Lai & Vice Premier Chen Yi	UAR (Egypt)	December 1963
Premier Chou En-Lai & Vice Premier Chen Yi	Morocco	December 1963
Water Conservation Delegation	Egypt	December 1963
Premier Chou En-Lai & his Party	Tunisia	Jan 1964
Premier Chou En-Lai & his Party	Sudan	January 1964
Trade Union Leader	UAR (Egypt)	January 1964
Delegation for Afro-Asian Solidarity Council Meeting	Algeria	March 1964
Railway Delegation	UAR (Egypt)	March 1964
Petroleum Research Delegation	Algeria	April 1964
Haj Delegation	Saudi Arabia	April 1964
Educationalists Delegation	Algeria	April 1964
Film Delegation	Algeria	April 1964
Envoy	Tunisia	April 1964
Journalist Delegation	Algeria	April 1964
Delegate for Fair	Morocco	April 1964
Educationalists	UAR (Egypt)	April 1964
Education Trade Union Leader	UAR (Egypt)	April 1964
Women Delegation	UAR (Egypt)	April 1964
Assistant Minister of Foreign Trade	Morocco	April 1964

Type	*State*	*Date*
Moslem Delegation	Syria	April 1964
Scientific Delegation	Morocco	May 1964
Experts Group	Syria	May 1964
Scientific Delegation	Algeria	May 1964
Tung Fang-Song and Dance Ensemble	Algeria	June 1964
Building Delegation	UAR (Egypt)	June 1964
Building Delegation	Algeria	July 1964
Youth Delegation	Algeria	August 1964
Experts	Yemen	September 1964
Trade Union Leader	Algeria	September 1964
Vice Minister of Light Industry	Algeria	September 1964
Medical Team	Algeria	October 1964
Medical Delegation	UAR (Egypt)	October 1964
Party and Government Delegation	Algeria	October 1964
Youth Delegation and Trade Union Delegation	Algeria	October 1964
Scientific and Technological Delegation	Algeria	December 1964
Government Delegation	UAR (Egypt)	December 1964
Scientific & Technological Delegation	UAR	December 1964
Government Scientific Delegation	UAR (Egypt)	January 1965
Delegation for Afro-Asian Economic Seminar	Algeria	February 1965
Journalist Delegation	UAR (Egypt)	March 1965
Trade Union Delegation	Algeria	March 1965
Representative of Peking Jen-Min Jir-Pao	Syria	March 1965
Premier Chou En-Lai	UAR (Egypt)	April 1965
Trade Union Delegation	UAR (Egypt)	April 1965
Delegation to Casablanca Fair	Morocco	April 1965
Teachers Delegation	Algeria	April 1965
Trade Union Delegation	Syria	April 1965
Highway Experts	UAR (Egypt)	May 1965
Journalist Delegation	Algeria	May 1965
Vice Foreign Minister	Morocco	May 1965

Type	*State*	*Date*
Premier Chou En-Lai and Vice Premier Ch'en Yi (Government Delegation)	UAR (Egypt)	June 1965
Ch'en Yi Government Delegation	Algeria	June 1965
Premier Chou En-Lai	Sudan	June 1965
Friendship Delegation	Kuwait	June 1965
Premier Chou En-Lai and Government Delegation	Syria	June 1965
Premier Chou En-Lai and Delegation	Iraq	June 1965
Student Delegation	UAR	July 1965
Television Delegation	UAR (Egypt)	August 1965
Exhibition Delegation for International Fair	Algeria	September 1965
Vice Premier Ch'en Yi	Algeria	September 1965
Government Delegation	Yemen	September 1965
Radio-Television Delegation	Syria	September 1965
First Medical Team	Algeria	October 1965
Lawyers Delegation	Sudan	October 1965
Radio-Television Delegation	Iraq	October 1965
Military Delegation	Algeria	October 1965
Trade Union Delegation	Algeria	November 1965
Scientific Delegation	Iraq	November 1965
Second Medical Team	Algeria	December 1965
Hydro-geologists	UAR (Egypt)	December 1965
Scientific Delegation	Syria	December 1965
Cinema Delegation	UAR (Egypt)	December 1965
Youth Delegation	UAR (Egypt)	February 1966
Education Delegation	UAR (Egypt)	March 1966
Amity Delegation	UAR (Egypt)	March 1966
Trade Union Delegation	Syria	March 1966
Government Trade Delegation	UAR (Egypt)	April 1966
Educational Workers	Yemen	April 1966
Educational Workers Trade Union Delegation	Syria	April 1966
Government Cultural Delegation	Syria	April 1966
Women Delegation	Syria	April 1966

Type	*State*	*Date*
Trade Union Delegation	UAR (Egypt)	April 1966
Sport Delegation (Shanghai Football Team)	Kuwait	April 1966
Government Cultural Delegation	UAR (Egypt)	May 1966
Experts	UAR (Egypt)	May 1966
Government Cultural and Friendship Delegation	Yemen	May 1966
Moslem Goodwill Delegation	Sudan	May 1966
Writers Delegation	Sudan	May 1966
Moslem Goodwill Delegation	Iraq	May 1966
Government Cultural and Friendship Delegation	Iraq	May 1966
Government Civil Aviation Delegation	UAR (Egypt)	June 1966
Moslem Goodwill Delegation	Syria	June 1966
Moslem Delegation	Kuwait	June 1966
Government Civil Aviation Delegation	Syria	June 1966
Moslem Goodwill Delegation	Lebanon	June 1966
Government Civil Aviation Delegation	Iraq	June 1966
Medical Team	Yemen	July 1966
Experts in Schistosomiasis	UAR (Egypt)	August 1966
Trade Union Delegation	Algeria	October 1966
Agriculture-Forestry Trade Union Delegation	Syria	December 1966
Economic and Trade Exhibition Delegation	Kuwait	January 1967
Trade Union Delegation	Syria	January 1967
Artistic Delegation	Iraq	November 1967
Medical Team	Yemen	March 1968
Government Military Delegation	Algeria	October 1969
Economic and Technical Investigation Team	Yemen	February 1970
Medical Team	Yemen	February 1970
Government Trade Delegation	UAR (Egypt)	March 1970
Government Delegation	Iraq	July 1970

Type	*State*	*Date*
Vice Minister of Foreign Trade Chi Peng-fei	Algeria	September 1970
Vice Minister of Foreign Trade Chi Peng-fei	Syria	September 1970
Gymnastic Team	Algeria	December 1970
Survey Team	Sudan	December 1970
Vice Minister of Light Industry	UAR (Egypt)	February 1971
Medical Team	Sudan	April 1971
Table Tennis Team	UAR (Egypt)	August 1971
Government Delegation for Opening Ceremony of 8th International Fair	Algeria	August 1971
Government Delegation led by Minister of Foreign Trade, Pai Hsiang-kuo	Algeria	October 1971
Table Tennis Delegation	Sudan	November 1971
Government Trade Delegation	Egypt	March 1972
Table Tennis Delegation	Kuwait	April 1972
Table Tennis Team	Syria	April 1972
Table Tennis Team	Iraq	April 1972
Government Delegation	Sudan	May 1972
Government Trade Delegation	Kuwait	May 1972
Football Team Delegation	Syria	May 1972
Football Team Delegation	Yemen	May 1972
Table Tennis Delegation	Tunisia	June 1972
Men's Basketball Delegation	Algeria	June 1972
Men's Basketball Delegation	Egypt	July 1972
Men's Basketball Delegation	Sudan	July 1972
Government and Military Delegation	Algeria	July 1972
Youth Representative	Algeria	Jyly 1972
Public Health and Friendship Delegation	Algeria	July 1972
Table Tennis Delegation	Morocco	July 1972
Government Delegation	Arab Republic of Yemen	September 1972
Youth Table Tennis Delegation	Arab Republic of Yemen	September 1972

Type	*State*	*Date*
Youth Table Tennis Delegation	Egypt	October 1972
Youth Table Tennis Delegation	Lebanon	October 1972
Government Delegation	People's Democratic Republic of Yemen	October 1972
Youth Table Tennis Delegation	People's Democratic Republic of Yemen	October 1972
Delegation of the Bank of China	Algeria	November 1972
Football Team	Kuwait	November 1972
Inspection Group	Syria	November 1972
Economic and Trade Exhibition Group	Lebanon	November 1972
Economic and Trade Exhibition Group	Kuwait	November 1972
Peking Acrobatic Troupe	Algeria	December 1972
Volley-ball Team	Kuwait	December 1972
Acrobatic Troupe	Sudan	December 1972
Acrobatic Troupe	Egypt	February 1973
Acrobatic Troupe	Tunisia	February 1973
Exhibition Group	Yemen	February 1973
Gymnastic Team	Egypt	March 1973
Gymnastic Team	Kueait	March 1973
Shanghai Men's Basketball Team	Syria	April 1973
Shanghai Men's Basketball Team	Lebanon	April 1973
Shanghai Men's Basketball Team	Iraq	April 1973
Director of Pavillion at 25th Casablanca Fair	Morocco	April 1973
Medical Delegation	Kuwait	April 1973
Gymnastic Team	Libya	April 1973
Kwantung Men's Volley-ball Team	Sudan	May 1973
Head of Pavillion at Tunis International Fair	Tunisia	May 1973

Type	*State*	*Date*
Peking Men and Women Volley-ball Team	Syria	June 1973
Delegation of Bank of China and Insurance Company	Lebanon	June 1973
Peking Men and Women Volley-ball Team	Lebanon	July 1973
Peking Physical and Culture Institute Football Team	Morocco	July 1973
Peking Men's Basketball Team	Tunisia	July 1973
Medical Delegation	Tunisia	July 1973
Agriculture Study Group	Egypt	September 1973
Youth Delegation	Algeria	November 1973
Red Cross Delegation	Algeria	November 1973
Liaoning Provincial Football Team	Sudan	January 1974
Trade Delegation	Tunisia	February 1974
Peking Football Team	Syria	March 1974
Teachers' Friendship Delegation	Iraq	April 1974
Medical Delegation	Egypt	May 1974
Gymnastic Team	Morocco	May 1974
Gymnastic Team	Tunisia	May 1974
Gymnastic Team	Iraq	May 1974
Medical Delegation	Syria	July 1974
Head of Pavillion of Damascus International Fair	Syria	July 1974
Government Delegation	Iraq	July 1974
Gymnastic Team	Lebanon	July 1974
Table Tennis (1st International TT Tournament)	Tunisia	August 1974
Liaoning Men's Volley-ball Team	Egypt	September 1974
Government Trade Delegation	Iraq	September 1974
Government Trade Delegation	Kuwait	September 1974
Government Trade Delegation	Syria	September 1974

Type	*State*	*Date*
Militia Delegation	Syria	September 1974
Peking Opera Troupe	Algeria	October 1974
Government and Military Goodwill Delegation	Algeria	October 1974
Men's Basketball Team	Algeria	October 1974
Medical Delegation	Lebanon	October 1974
Medical Delegation	Syria	December 1974
Youth Football Team	Kuwait	March 1975
Track Delegation	Bahrain; United Arab Emirates	April 1975
Architects Delegation	Algeria	April 1975
Youth Football Delegation	Syria	April 1975
Volley-ball Team	Iraq	April 1975
Military Friendship Delegation	Sudan	May 1975
General Manager of China Ocean Shipping Company	Egypt	June 1975
Medical Delegation	Algeria	July 1975
Athletics Team	Sudan	July 1975
PLA Delegation	Algeria	August 1975
Government Shipping Delegation	Algeria	October 1975
Posts and Telecommunications Delegation	Algeria	October 1975
Wushu Delegation	Egypt	October 1975
First Chinese Medical Team	Tunisia	October 1975
Football Team	PDRY	November 1975
Public Health Delegation	Algeria	November 1975
Wushu Delegation	Algeria	November 1975
Football Team	UAR	November 1975

Appendix 6

Sino-Arab trade, cultural, and friendship treaties and agreements 1955–75

The Arab world, considered as one political entity here, occupies an important place in China's treaties and agreements with foreign countries. The total of 144 treaties and agreements, and their distribution in the Arab world, are as follows (indicating the various Arab states' positions in China's foreign policy in the area): Egypt 32; Algeria 20; Iraq 17; Syria 16; PDRY (South Yemen) 15; Sudan 13; Yemen Arab Republic (North Yemen) (YAR) 12; Morocco 9; Tunisia 8; Lebanon 2. Of the total, Sino-Arab Cultural Agreements amount to 14: Iraq 5; Yemen Arab Republic 4; Algeria 3; Egypt 2. Of all the Arab states that established diplomatic relations with China until the end of 1975, only Kuwait had not signed any such treaty and/or agreement.

Trade agreements have constantly been used by China as a first step towards the establishment of diplomatic relations. This happened with Egypt, Syria and Sudan. The longest periods between signing a treaty and/or an agreement and establishing diplomatic relations with an Arab state were in the cases of Lebanon and then Tunisia. All forms of Treaty of Friendship are of a political nature. The two Sino-YAR Friendship Treaties, signed in 1958 and 1964 respectively, are typical (the Sino-Algerian one of 1964 is of minor importance politically). The 1958 Treaty, for example, was signed by al-Badr, son of the feudal ruler 'Imām 'Aḥmad. By 1956, 'Imām 'Aḥmad's relations with the British reached its lowest ebb, and, besides seeking closer ties with the communist bloc, the 'Imām followed the Egyptian line in paying lip-service to Arab nationalism headed by Naṣir. al-Badr's visit to China in December 1957–January 1958 was fruitful in gaining the latter's unequivocal support for Yemen's side in the dispute with the British.

Algeria

Name of Document	*Date*
Sino-Algerian Cultural Co-operation Agreement	11 September 1963
Sino-Algerian Agreement on Economic and Technical Co-operation	28 October 1963
*1964 Executive Plan for Sino-Algerian Cultural Co-operation Agreement	14 April 1964
*Sino-Algerian Radio and TV Co-operation Agreement	14 April 1964
Agreement of Friendship and Co-operation between New China News Agency and Algerian Press Service	15 July 1964
*Sino-Algerian Trade Agreement	19 September 1964
* ” ” Payments Agreement	19 September 1964
*Protocol on Sino-Algerian Economic and Technical Co-operation Agreement	19 September 1964
Sino-Algerian Scientific and Technical Co-operation Agreement	25 December 1964
Sino-Algerian Protocol for Supply of Gratis Equipment by China for Algerian Militia	11 February 1965
Executive Plan of Sino-Algerian Cultural Co-operation Agreement for 1965	3 June 1965
Sino-Algerian Protocol on Medical Co-operation	17 March 1970
*Agreement on Economic and Technical Co-operation between China and Algeria	27 July 1971
Long-term Trade Agreement between China and Algeria	27 October 1971
*Trade Protocol for 1973 between China and Algeria	6 November 1972
*Documents on Implementation of the Sino-Algerian Agreement on Economic and Technical Co-operation	6 November 1972
Agreement on Reinsurance for Maritime Goods within the Framework of Trade between China and Algeria	4 May 1973
Trade Protocol between China and Algeria for 1974	23 February 1974

Algeria cont'd.....

Name of Document	*Date*
*Trade Protocol for 1975 between China and Algeria	29 November 1974
Shipping Agreement between China and Algeria	20 October 1975

Egypt

Name of Document	*Date*
*Sino-Egyptian Trade Agreement	22 August 1955
* " " Protocol on the First Fiscal Year of the Trade Agreement	22 August 1955
Sino-Egyptian Agreement on Cultural Co-operation	15 April 1956
Sino-Egyptian Payments Agreement	22 October 1956
" " Protocol on the Second Fiscal Year of the Trade Agreement	22 October 1956
*Sino-Egyptian Protocol on the Third Year of the Trade Agreement	21 December 1957
*Sino-Egyptian Exchange of Notes on Article 3 of the 1957 Payments Agreement	21 December 1957
*Sino-UAR Postal Agreement	25 August 1958
" " Trade and Payments Agreement and its First Year's Protocol	15 December 1958
*Sino-UAR Protocol to Trade Agreement for Second Agreement Year	24 February 1960
China-UAR Trade Protocol for 1961	15 February 1961
* " " Trade Agreement	17 March 1962
* " " Payments Agreement	17 March 1962
* " " Trade Protocol for 1962	17 March 1962
* " " Telecommunications Agreement 1963	5 January 1963
1963 Protocol for China-UAR Trade Agreement	14 July 1963
Executive Programme of China-UAR Cultural Co-operation Agreement	11 April 1964
*China-UAR Economic and Technical Co-operation Agreement	21 December 1964
China-UAR Agreement on Scientific and Technical Co-operation	13 January 1965

Name of Document	*Date*
China-UAR Air Services Agreement	2 May 1965
” ” Trade Protocol for 1966	4 May 1966
Executive Programme for 1966/67 for China-UAR Cultural Co-operation Agreement	7 May 1966
*China-UAR Trade Protocol for 1967	15 May 1967
China-UAR Trade Protocol for 1968	4 July 1968
*China-UAR Trade Protocol for 1969	5 March 1969
Protocol for China-UAR Trade Agreement 1970	19 March 1970
*Exchange of Instruments for Extension of the Trade Agreement and the Payments Agreement between China and the UAR	2 August 1971
*Protocol for 1971 on the Trade Agreement between China and UAR	2 August 1971
China-Egypt Trade Protocol for 1972	18 March 1972
Minutes of Talks on Building a Sand-Brick Factory for Egypt with Chinese Assistance	26 June 1973
*Letters on Extension of the Trade Agreement and Payments Agreement between China and Egypt from 1 January 1974 to 31 December 1976	31 May 1975
*Protocol to the Trade Agreement for 1975 between China and Egypt	31 May 1975

Iraq

Name of Document	*Date*
Sino-Iraq Trade and Payments Agreement	3 January 1959
” ” Agreement on Cultural Co-operation	4 April 1959
*Sino-Iraq Trade and Payments Agreement	25 May 1960
” ” Trade Agreement	18 October 1961
1961/62 Executive Plan for Sino-Iraqi Cultural Co-operation Agreement	25 November 1961
Accord for Renewal of Sino-Iraqi Trade Agreement Concluded in 1960	10 January 1963
*1964–1965 Executive Plan of Sino-Iraqi Cultural Co-operation Agreement	25 May 1964
*Sino-Iraqi Trade Agreement	23 September 1964

Iraq cont'd.....

Name of Document	*Date*
1966/67 Executive Plan of Sino-Iraqi Cultural Co-operation Agreement	3 June 1966
Sino-Iraqi Broadcasting and TV Co-operation Protocol	3 June 1966
*Accord Renewal of Sino-Iraqi Cultural Co-operation Agreement	25 May 1967
Sino-Iraqi Agreement on Economic and Technical Co-operation	21 June 1971
Protocol on Development of Economic and Technical Co-operation between China and Iraq	20 December 1972
Minutes of Talks between China and Iraq on Building Mosul Bridge	25 November 1973
*Minutes of Trade Talks between China and Iraq	16 February 1974
*Two Documents on Development of Trade and Economic and Technical Co-operation between China and Iraq	6 July 1975
Protocol on Amending the Trade Agreement between China and Iraq	30 November 1975

Lebanon

Name of Document	*Date*
Sino-Lebanese Trade Agreement	31 December 1955
*Trade Agreement between China and Lebanon	29 November 1972

Morocco

Name of Document	*Date*
*Sino-Moroccan Trade Agreement for 1959/60	30 September 1959
” ” ” ” ” 1960/61	10 November 1960
” ” Payments Agreement	27 October 1961
* ” ” Trade Agreement	30 March 1963
Additional Protocol of Sino-Moroccan Trade Agreement	20 May 1966
1971 Trade Protocol between China and Morocco	26 April 1971

Name of Document	*Date*
*Chinese-Moroccan Agreement on Co-operation Constructing a Sports Complex in Morocco	19 March 1975
*Protocol on China's Sending a Medical Team to Morocco	19 March 1975
*Chinese-Moroccan Agreement on Long-term Trade	19 March 1975

People's Democratic Republic of Yemen (South Yemen)

Name of Document	*Date*
China-PDRY Protocol on Dispatching of Chinese Medical Team to PDRY	4 December 1969
Protocol to China-PDRY Agreement on Economic and Technical Co-operation	30 July 1970
Letters of Exchange on Dispatch of Chinese Engineering and Technical Personnel by Chinese Government to PDRY	30 July 1970
*China-PDRY Agreement on Economic and Technical Co-operation	7 August 1970
Minutes of talks on Establishment of the Yemen Cotton Textile Printing-Dyeing Combined Enterprise between China and PDRY	6 July 1971
Minutes of talks between China and PDRY on Reconstruction of the Khormaksar Salt Works	6 July 1971
Minutes of talks between China and PDRY on Construction of a Road from Ain to Mahfidh	14 August 1971
Minutes of talks between China and PDRY on Construction of Zinjibar Bridge	14 August 1971
Minutes of talks between China and PDRY on Drilling Wells	14 August 1971
Minutes of talks between China and PDRY on Building of Small Agricultural Implements and Hardware with China's Assistance	13 January 1972
*Agreement on Economic and Technical Co-operation between China and PDRY	12 July 1972

PDRY *cont.*

Name of Document	*Date*
*Agreement on Economic and Technical Co-operation between China and PDRY	12 July 1972
Minutes of talks between China and PDRY on Construction of Malifid-Mukallā Road	24 March 1973
*China-PDRY Economic and Technical Co-operation Agreement	13 November 1974
Notes on Construction of Shi'r-Sayhūt Road in PDRY with Chinese Assistance	8 May 1975

Sudan

Name of Document	*Date*
Sino-Sudanese Exchange of Notes on Trade Relations	12 April 1956
*Communiqué on the Sino-Sudanese Trade Conference	30 December 1957
*Sino-Sudanese Trade Agreement	23 May 1962
*China-Sudan Trade Protocol for 1967	27 July 1966
” ” ” ” ” 1968	20 June 1968
” ” ” ” ” 1969	1 April 1969
” ” ” ” ” 1970	21 May 1970
” ” Protocol on Dispatching Chinese Medical Team to Sudan	14 December 1970
*Sino-Sudan Economic and Technical Co-operation Agreement	20 December 1971
China-Sudan Trade Protocol for 1972	27 May 1972
Notes on Talks between China and Sudan on Construction of Factories in Sudan	15 January 1973
*China-Sudan Trade Protocol for 1973	4 July 1973

Syria

Name of Document	*Date*
Sino-Syrian Trade Agreement	20 November 1955
” ” Payments Agreement	30 November 1955
” ” Agreement on Cultural Co-operation	12 June 1956
Sino-Syrian Protocol on the Revision of the 'Trade and Payments Agreements'	3 July 1957

Name of Document	*Date*
*Agreement on Sino-Syrian Trade	21 February 1963
*Sino-Syrian Agreement on Payments	21 February 1963
*Sino-Syrian Agreement on Economic and Technical Co-operation	21 February 1963
*Sino-Syrian Cultural Co-operation Agreement	18 March 1965
1965 Plan for Sino-Syrian Cultural Co-operation Agreement	18 March 1965
Sino-Syrian Protocol for Co-operation in Broadcasting and TV	6 October 1965
1966/67 Executive Plan for Sino-Syrian Cultural Co-operation Agreement	20 April 1966
Agreement on News Co-operation between New China News Agency and Syrian Arab News Agency	6 April 1968
Agreement on China's Assistance to Syria in Construction of a Spinning Mill	13 December 1971
*China-Syrian Agreement on Economic and Technical Co-operation	24 May 1972
*China-Syrian Agreement on Broadcasting and TV Co-operation	22 September 1975
China-Syrian Agreement on Civil Air Transport	10 November 1975

Tunisia

Name of Document	*Date*
Sino-Tunisian Trade Agreement	25 September 1958
Sino-Tunisian Trade Agreement for 1960/61	30 November 1960
*Protocol on Supplement to China-Tunisia Trade Agreement	19 May 1972
*Agreement on Economic and Technical Co-operation between China and Tunisia	5 August 1972
Protocol on Sending of a Chinese Medical Team to Tunisia	5 June 1973
Additional Protocol to the Trade Agreement between China and Tunisia	8 February 1974
*Protocol to Chinese-Tunisian Economic and Technical Co-operation Agreement	14 July 1974

Tunisia *cont.*
Name of Document   *Date*
  Exchange Notes for Local Expenditure of
    China-Tunisia Economic and Technical
    Co-operation Agreement   7 December 1974

Yemen Arab Republic (North Yemen)

Name of Document   *Date*
*Sino-Yemeni Treaty of Friendship   12 January 1958
*   ”   ”   ”   ” Commerce   12 January 1958
*   ”   ”   Agreement on Scientific,
    Technical and Cultural Co-operation   12 January 1958
  China-Yemeni Protocol for Maintenance of
    Sana'a-Hūdaidh Highway   18 March 1962
*Sino-Yemeni Treaty of Friendship   9 June 1964
*Sino-Yemeni Cultural Co-operation
    Agreement   9 June 1964
*Sino-Yemeni Economic and Technical
      Co-operation Agreement   9 June 1964
  China-Yemeni Protocol on Building Sana'a
    Textile Factory   23 March 1965
*1965 Executive Plan for Sino-Yemeni
      Cultural Co-operation Agreement   3 May 1965
  Executive Plan for 1966/67 of Sino-Yemeni
    Cultural Co-operation Agreement   23 May 1966
  Minutes of Talks between China and ARY
    on building the Taĭz Hospital for ARY   16 March 1972
*Agreement on Economic and Technical
      Co-operation between China and AR
      Yemen   21 July 1972

*Indicates Treaty and/or Agreement signed in Peking

Notes

1 China and the Arab World

1 For documents related to the conference see Kenneth T. Young, *The 1954 Geneva Conference – Indo-China and Korea*, New York, reprinted 1968.
2 A. Yodfat and M. Abir, *In the Direction of the Gulf*, (London, 1977), p. 30.
3 Chinese Ministry of Information, Comp., *China Handbook, 1937–1945*, New York, 1947, p. 181.
4 Ibid., p. 182.
5 Chu Jung-fu, 'Foreign relations of new China during the past five years', *Current Background*, no. 307, (6 December 1954), pp. 2–3.
6 Ibid., p. 4.
7 Ibid., p. 5.
8 Ibid., p. 6. For further discussions on the 'capitalist camps' relations in international relations see So Ying, 'A discussion: growing contradictions between capitalist nations', *Selection of China Mainland Magazine*, no. 63, (31 December 1956), pp. 26–30.
9 Ibid., p. 8.
10 John Gittings, *The World and China, 1922–1972*, (London, 1974), p. 211.
11 See, for example, *People's Daily* editorial concerning Soviet support for Arab causes, 'The best friend of national liberation', in *Peking Review*, vol. 1, no. 23, (5 August 1958).
12 Nan Han-chen, 'For the economic emancipation of Afro-Asian peoples', *Peking Review*, vol. 7, no. 10, (5 March 1965), pp. 16–26.
13 Ibid., p. 17.
14 Ibid., pp. 18–20.
15 Ibid., p. 21.
16 Ibid., pp. 23–6.
17 *Peking Review*, vol. 3, no. 42, (18 October 1968), pp. 16–17.
18 The first time after the Cultural Revolution when the Chinese view of the division of the world was stated, was by Teng Hsiao-peng in

Special Session of United Nations General Assembly, 10 April 1974. For full text see *Peking Review*, vol. 17, no. 16, (19 April 1974), pp. 6–11.

19 The *People's Daily*, 'Chairman Mao's theory of the differentiation of the Three Worlds is a major contribution to Marxism-Leninism' in *Peking Review*, vol. 20, no. 45, (4 November 1977), pp. 10–41.

20 Ibid., p. 11.

21 Ibid., p. 12.

22 Ibid., p. 16.

23 Ibid., p. 20.

24 Ibid., p. 21.

25 Ibid., p. 23.

26 Ibid., p. 30.

27 See Gérard Challand, *Revolution in the Third World: Myths and Prospects*, London 1977, and Robert L. Rothstein, *The Weak in the World of the Strong*, (New York, 1977).

28 *Peking Review*, op. cit., p. 24.

29 Ibid., p. 25.

30 Ibid., p. 27.

31 Ibid., p. 28.

32 See Wolfgang Bartke, *China's Economic Aid*, (New York, 1975), Table 8, p. 23.

33 Ibid., Table 2, p. 13. I have drawn this figure from the above mentioned table which was drawn on a geographical basis.

34 See Janos Howath, *Chinese Technology Transfer to the Third World*, (New York, 1976).

2 Sino-Palestinian relations 1955–66

1 Participants were Afghanistan, Burma, Cambodia, Ceylon, Egypt, Ethiopia, Gold Coast, India, Indonesia, Iran, Iraq, Japan, Laos, Lebanon, Libya, Nepal, Pakistan, People's Republic of China, Philippines, Saudi Arabia, Sudan, Syria, Thailand, Turkey, Democratic Republic of Vietnam, State of Vietnam, Yemen; and one state declined to attend: Central African Federation.

2 George M. Kahin, *Asian-African Conference*, p. 3.

3 Through the Arab league, Arab regimes were authorised to encourage relations with the Afro-Asian states with the primary object of advocating the Palestinian cause internationally, see M. Khalil, *The Arab States and the Arab League*, vol. 2, pp. 150–1. On origins and early development of the Arab League see the interesting study by A. Gom'aa, *The Foundations of the League of Arab States*.

4 *'Arba'ūn 'am*, pp. 379–88.

5 *New York Times*, 21 April 1955.

6 *NCNA (New China News Agency)*, 25 April 1955.

7 *NCNA*, Supplement no. 226, pp. 3–4.

8 For full text of the Agreement, see *NCNA*, 14 October 1955.

9 For the allegations see *The Daily Telegraph*, 21 October 1955; for its denial see *NCNA*, 23 October 1955.

10 M. Nasser-Eddine, *Arab-Chinese Relations*, Beirut, n.d., p. 84.

11 For Chou's supplementary speech see G. M. Kahin, op. cit., pp. 52–6.

12 See, for example, the speech broadcast through Peking Radio: 'Chinese Moslem Leader Joseph Ua addresses foreign Moslems on Asian-African Conference', *Survey of China Mainland Press*, no. 1035, (April 1955, p. 10).

13 In Belgrade, 1961; Cairo 1964; Lusaka, Zambia 1970; Algiers 1973 and Lima 1975.

14 *NCNA*, 1 November 1955.

15 *NCNA*, 16 November 1955.

16 *NCNA*, 20 April 1956.

17 *SCMP* (Survey of China Mainland Press), no. 1355, p. 30.

18 Y. Ro'i, *From Encroachment*, (Jerusalem, 1974), p. 189.

19 C. Neuhauser, *Third World Politics*, (Cambridge, Mass., 1968), p. 14.

20 *Egyptian Gazette*, 29 December 1957; see also *NCNA*'s reference to the proposed visit, 29 December 1957.

21 *NCNA*, 15 October 1960.

22 For full text see *NCNA*, 14 December 1963.

23 *NCNA*, 20 December 1963.

24 *NCNA*, 22 December 1963.

25 *New York Herald Tribune*, 27 December 1963.

26 *NCNA*, 29 December 1963. See also Sino-Tunisian joint communiqué, *NCNA*, 11 January 1964; Sino-Sudanese joint communiqué, *NCNA*, 13 January 1964; and Chou En-lai's press conference in Somalia, *NCNA*, 6 February 1964.

27 *SCMP*, no. 923, (4 November 1954), p. 6; no. 979, (31 January 1955), p. 9.

28 *SCMP*, no. 2108, (27 September 1949), p. 48.

29 It was an invitation extended to 'all' Communist parties in the world, especially from the Third World, to attend an international meeting to celebrate the tenth anniversary of the founding of the PRC. It should be stressed that the Israeli C.P. took an anti-western stand against the Israeli government, opposed Israel's stand on the Korean war, and was closely linked with the Soviet Union.

30 See M. Brecher: *Israel, the Korean War and China*, (Jerusalem, 1974), p. 16.

31 M. Nahumi, 'China and Israel', *New Outlook*, vol. 9, no. 6, (July 1966), pp. 45–6.

32 M. Brecher, op. cit., pp. 72–3.

33 J. Cooley, 'China and the Palestinians', p. 21.

34 Jacob Landau, *The Arabs in Israel: A Political Study*, (Oxford, 1969).

35　*NCNA*, 2 March 1959.

36　*NCNA*, 18 March 1960.

37　*NCNA*, 21 January 1960.

38　*NCNA*, 15 March 1960.

39　*NCNA*, 19 April 1960.

40　*NCNA*, 18 April 1960.

41　*NCNA*, 15 August 1960.

42　*NCNA*, Ibid.

43　*NCNA*, 26 August 1960.

44　*NCNA*, 11 August 1960.

45　*NCNA*, 21 March 1961.

46　*NCNA*, 14 April 1961.

47　*NCNA*, 15 May 1961.

48　*NCNA*, 5 February 1961.

49　*NCNA*, 8 April 1961.

50　*NCNA*, 8 April 1961.

51　Gene T. Hsiao, *The Foreign Trade of China: Policy, Law and Practices*, (University of California, 1977), Table 9, p. 28.

52　The Arab Nationalist Movement (ANM) — National Conference, created, in May 1964, a new branch under George Habash's command, called the National Front for the Liberation of Palestine. This branch of ANM, unlike that of Fataḥ, was not based on the idea of mobilising the Palestinians to wage independently a 'war of liberation' but rather on the principle of 'official Arab involvement'. The major political and military objective of NFLP was to act merely as a catalyst which would detonate a conventional war between the Arab states, led by the UAR, and Israel. Walid Kazziha, *Revolutionary Transformation in the Arab World*, (London, 1975), p. 84.

53　Interview data with Fataḥ leaders; Beirut and Damascus, February 1978. Among current Fataḥ leaders Abu Djhad remains the most authoritative on Sino-Palestinian relations.

54　Author's interview with 'Abū al-'Abid, Damascus, February 1978.

55　Thomas Kiernan, the only writer so far who has doubts on this first visit in his *Yasir 'Arafat*, (London, 1975), relates this episode in the most fashionable 'journalistic gossip recollections' ever written about Abū 'Amar and the emergence of Fataḥ. The lengthy quotation is included because of its inaccuracies. These are obvious in the main text:

> In April of 1963 [wrong date] word came to Yasir from
> Algiers that the Chinese would welcome a visit from two
> representatives of Fataḥ. A hurried meeting of the founders
> was called in Beirut. Khalid al-Ḥassan was unable to get there
> from Germany in time, but the other seven [founders of Fataḥ]
> met, again at the Dekwaneh [refugee] camp, to vote on who

should go. There was no question that one member of the
delegation should be Khalil al-Wazir; he, after all, had initiated
Algerian interest in Fataḥ and was still the group's primary
link to FLN [National Liberation Front]. Al-Ḥassan had
indicated by mail that he would like to be the other member,
since his interest in Chinese revolutionism preceded that of
the other founders of Fataḥ. But Yasir, who continued to
think of <u>Kh</u>alid as an intellectual rather than a potential
guerrilla fighter, lobbied against al-Ḥassan's selection and
declared that he should go. He argued that as the moving
force behind *Our Palestine* he would be able to print his
observations of China, and that such observations would be
more valuable to the cause than anything al-Ḥassan could
contribute. Yasir got the vote. He and Khalil immediately
flew to Algiers. There they joined a delegation of second-
string FLNists — mostly Algerian college teachers being sent
to China on a cultural exchange programme — and took off
for Peking. They were dismayed at the reception they
received on their arrival. They were met by functionaries
of the Chinese cultural programme who mistook them for
members of the FLN. Thereafter during their two weeks
stay they had little to do but attend lectures on the
communist revolution in China and visit agricultural
communes. None of their guides understood Arabic and
their scholarly Algerian travelling companions, who did,
had scant interest in Palestinian matters. They finally
managed to convince their guides that they were in China
on business other than that having to do with Algerian-
Chinese relations. They demanded interviews with Mao Tse-
tung and Chou En-lai and other leaders of the revolution,
threatening to expose the Chinese affront to the Palestinian
Revolution on their return to the Middle East if such interviews
were not granted. They got to see none of the leaders but
were eventually ushered into the presence of the Chinese
army officer who had gained some fame as a guerrilla fighter
during the revolution. Through an interpreter he regaled them
with tales of Chinese guerrilla exploits. They made little
sense to the two Palestinians, and they left China bitterly
disillusioned by the indifferent reception they had received.
They were determined not to let the nature of their stay in
China become known, however. On returning to Beirut in
May of 1963 Yasir began to publish articles in *Our Palestine*
glorifying China and claiming that in secret interviews with
Mao, Chou and others China had given its official support
and approval of the Fataḥ cause. Drawing more on conventional

revolutionary literature than on anything he had learned in his non-existent audiences with the Chinese leaders, he wrote that the Chinese had laid out for him and Khalil a vital revolutionary scenario, called first for the establishment of a consolidated leadership which, Yasir claimed, the revolution already possessed in the form of the collectively operating founders of Fatah. The next step was for the leadership to win the Palestinian people's confidence in it, to enlighten the people about their oppression and to inspire and incite them to 'revenge'. The third step was to gain control of all the organisations and institutions that served the people so as to create a national discipline and organisation. The climatic step was to organise and arm the people, and to begin the military struggle against the oppressor — in this case Israel, primarily, but also against anyone else who might stand in the way.

The key to the implementation of the scenario, Yasir claimed he was told by Mao, would be the occurrence of an imperialist event that would enable the revolutionary leadership to invoke the national emotions necessary to commence the process of revolutionary revenge. He was unaware of it, but such an event was then in its germination stages, and it would provide the motive powers for Yasir's and Fatah's leap into prominence in the Arab world.

(pp. 187–9.)

56 *Dawn*, 28 March 1964.
57 *NCNA*, 20 March 1964.
58 Ibid.
59 *NCNA*, 21 March 1964.
60 *NCNA*, 23 March 1964.
61 This is not an uncommon practice in China's relations with world liberation movements.
62 *NCNA*, 3 April 1964.
63 *Dawn*, op. cit.
64 Author's interviews with 'Abū al-'Abid, Damascus, February 1978.
65 Author's interview with 'Abū al'Amīn, Kuwait, January 1978.
66 For the background of the plan see Georgiana Stevens, *Jordan River Partition*, (Stanford, 1965).
67 Naṣir's aims in calling an Arab Summit Conference were four: 'The war in Yemen — Royalists v Republicans, with Egypt backing the latter dragged on for a much longer period than was expected and thus cost the UAR Treasury more than it could afford. This led to pressing internal economic problems which threatened the effectiveness and development plans of the regime in the UAR. Besides, the revolutionary elements in the Arab world were accusing Naṣir of having neglected the Palestine problem. The fourth reason

was Naṣir's need for a respite in order to strengthen his position and deal with the pressing problems, both internal and external. In other words he wanted a sort of period of truce with his Arab opponents so he could catch his breath, review past achievements and consolidate his gains in preparation for the coming battle'. Leila S. Kadi, *Arab Summit Conferences and the Palestine Problem*, (Beirut, 1966), p. 94.

68 Ibid., p. 101.

69 Ibid., p. 105. Objections to selecting the Council's representatives, whom al-Shuḳairy appointed according to geographical distribution, was another reason. Such geographical distribution-representation neglected the importance of the political nature of the organisation, and, therefore, the power of the distributed areas over-lapped giving an unhealthy balance of power. For geographical distribution of the representatives by area see Table I in Rashīd Hamid, 'What is the PLO?', *Journal of Palestine Studies*, vol. 4, no. 4 (Summer 1975), p. 95.

70 Nine committees elected from the PLO-NC were entrusted with carrying out the working of the organisation: Political, Financial, Education and Indoctrination, Information, Legal, Refugee Affairs, the National Organisation, the National Charter and the Suggestions and Nomination committees. And 'on 2 June the Palestine National Congress held its final plenary session, during which it approved the recommendations put forward by its nine committees which were in the form of "Resolutions of the Palestine National Congress"'. Leila S. Kadi, op. cit., p. 107.

71 *NCNA*, 27 May 1964.

72 Rashīd Hamid, *Mukararat al-madjlis al-watani al-filistini, 1964–1974*, (Beirut, 1975), p. 45.

73 *Soviet News*, 2 June 1964.

74 *NCNA*, 7 June 1964.

75 *NCNA*, 27 August 1964.

76 *NCNA*, 4 September 1964.

77 *Egyptian Gazette*, 7 February 1965. See also Vice-Premier Chen Yi's declaration of support on the occasion of visiting Syrian Friendship Delegation, headed by Foreign Minister Hassan Hura'ad, *NCNA*, 15 and 16 March 1965 respectively.

78 *Min al-quma ila al-hazima ma'al-muluk wa al-ru'asa*, (Beirut, 1971), pp. 214–65.

79 *NCNA*, 8 February 1964.

80 *NCNA*, 16 March 1965.

81 *NCNA*, 17 March 1965.

82 A. al-Shuḳairy, op. cit., pp. 229–32.

83 *New York Times*, 7 July 1971.

84 For background on this subject see Arnold Krammer, 'Soviet Motives in the Partition of Palestine 1947–8', *Journal of Palestine*

Studies, vol. 2, no. 2, (winter 1973), pp. 102–19; George J. Tomeh, ed., *United Nations Resolutions on Palestine and the Arab-Israeli Conflict, 1947–1974*, (Beirut, 1975), pp. 4–14; and Yaacov Ro'i, *From Encroachment to Involvement*, (Jerusalem, 1974), pp. 48–51.

85 A. al-Shuḳairy, op. cit., pp. 214–16.

86 George J. Tomeh, ed., op. cit., p. 14.

87 A. al-Shuḳairy, op. cit., pp. 233–5.

88 *NCNA*, 18 March 1965.

89 A. al-Shuḳairy, op. cit., pp. 237–8.

90 *NCNA*, 19 March 1965.

91 A. al-Shuḳairy, op. cit., p. 252.

92 *NCNA*, 23 March 1965.

93 A. al-Shuḳairy, op. cit., pp. 257–8.

94 *NCNA*, 24 March 1965.

95 *NCNA*, 26 March 1965.

96 A. al-Shuḳairy, op. cit., pp. 259–60.

97 Ibid., p. 260.

98 *Egyptian Gazette*, 1 April 1965.

99 A. al-Shuḳairy, op. cit., p. 270.

100 See *Egyptian Gazette*, 8 May 1965, for al-Shuḳairy's announcement; and *NCNA*, 13 and 24 May and 1 June, 1965, respectively.

101 *Daily Star*, 20 May 1965.

102 *al-Muḥru*, 13 May 1965.

103 *NCNA*, 4 June 1965.

104 *NCNA*, 14 May 1965.

105 *NCNA*, 15 May 1965.

106 As quoted in *New York Times*, 4 June 1965. See also: Chou's statement at Baghdad, Iraq, *al-'Anwar*, 5 June 1965; Chen Yi's speech at Egyptian Embassy in Peking, *NCNA*, 23 July 1965.

107 *al-Kifaḥ*, 1 May 1965.

108 *Egyptian Gazette*, 27 March 1966. Meanwhile al-Shuḳairy kept constant contacts with China's ambassador to Egypt, Huang Hua; see *NCNA*, 11 May, 1966; *al-Yumiyat al-filistinya*, vol. 3, (11 May 1966), p. 164.

109 *NCNA*, 14 May 1966.

110 al-Shuḳairy stated that Kosygin informed him during their discussion on 18 May 1966 in Cairo that Tashkent Spirit 'does not apply to the Palestine question'. *al-Yumiyat al-filistinya*, vol. 3, (20 May 1966), p. 181.

111 Ibid., p. 184.

112 *NCNA*, 20 May 1966.

113 *NCNA*, 21 May 1966.

114 *'Akhbar Filistin*, 30 May 1966.

115 *al-Fadjr al-Djadid*, 22 May 1966.

116 Rashid Hamid, op. cit., p. 94.

117 Charles Neuhauser, op. cit., p. 67.
118 *al-Watha'ik al-filistinya al-'arabiya al-Saniwiya lil-'am 1966*, (Beirut, 1967), pp. 305–6.
119 *NCNA*, 22 October 1966.
120 *al-Yumiyat al-filistinya*, vols. 4 and 5, (4 November 1966), p. 200.
121 *NCNA*, 29 November 1966.
122 *al-Watha'ik*, op. cit., p. 614.

3 The 1967 June War and its aftermath: developments in the Palestinian Resistance Movement

1 W. Kazziha, *Revolutionary Transformation in the Arab World*, London, 1975, p. 84.
2 Author's interview data, 'Abū al-'Abid, Damascus, January 1978. However, Fatah's first military trip to China occurred immediately after the June 1967 war.
3 Leila S. Kadi, *Basic Political Documents*, Beirut, 1969, p. 26.
4 Rashīd Hamid, op. cit., p. 31.
5 *NCNA*, 26 May 1967; see also the *People's Daily* commentary on the events in *NCNA*, 25 May 1967.
6 *NCNA*, 25 May 1967.
7 *NCNA*, 27 May 1967.
8 Ibid.
9 *NCNA*, 30 May 1967.
10 *NCNA*, 3 June 1967.
11 *NCNA*, 4 June 1967.
12 *NCNA*, 12 May 1967.
13 See the *People's Daily* commentary, 29 May 1967; *NCNA*'s extensive article on Arab-Israeli conflict, 31 May 1967; and *NCNA*'s condemnation of USSR's role, 3 June 1967.
14 See John Cooley's commentary on Sino-Soviet polemics during this crucial week of May in *The Christian Science Monitor*, 5 June 1967.
15 *Sunday Times*, 4 June 1967.
16 *NCNA*, 6 June 1967.
17 Ibid.
18 *NCNA*, 8 June 1967.
19 *NCNA*, 9 June 1967.
20 See *NCNA*, 7, 8 and 9 June 1967 respectively.
21 *NCNA*, 10 June 1967.
22 Fred J. Khouri, *Arab-Israeli Dilemma*, Syracuse, 1968, p. 265.
23 *Nasir wa al-'alām*, Beirut, 1972, pp. 424–5.
24 *NCNA*, 11 June 1967.
25 *NCNA*, 15 June 1967.
26 *NCNA*, 22 June 1967.

27   As quoted in *The Japan Times*, 3 July 1967.

28   *NCNA*, 23 August 1967, pp. 1–13.

29   Ibid., p. 9.

30   Ibid., p. 10.

31   Ibid., p. 11.

32   The unanimously adopted resolution was to become the basis for Arab-Israeli point of departure for peaceful co-existence in the area. For the text see George J. Tomeh, *United Nations Resolutions on Palestine and the Arab-Israeli Conflict, 1947–1974*, Beirut, 1975, p. 143.

33   See the *People's Daily* commentary in *NCNA*, 25 November 1967.

34   See, for example, Li Hsien-nien's comments cited in *NCNA*, 27 November 1967.

35   *The Christian Science Monitor*, 22 March 1968.

36   See, for example, *Sunday Telegraph*, 24 March 1968, when Israeli forces captured al-'Asifa weapons of Chinese make.

37   See the *People's Daily* and *Liberation Army Daily* articles in *NCNA*, 15 May 1968.

38   'US-Soviet design to strangle Arab people's anti-imperialist struggle', 5 June 1967.

39   Ibid., p. 3.

40   George J. Tomeh, op. cit., pp. 143–5.

41   *NCNA*, 'Raging storm of Arab people's struggle against US imperialism', 5 June 1968. For further vehement attacks on US and Israel, especially on Jewish immigration from US and Europe to Israel, see *NCNA* correspondent's article 'Israel, tool of US imperialist aggression, faces innumerable difficulties', 7 June 1968.

42   *NCNA*, 11 July 1968.

43   Rashīd Hamid, op. cit., p. 112. It was reported that, at his stormy PLO-NC meeting, the USSR attempted to hamper Fatah's leadership of the PLO, whether through upgrading other Palestinian fronts or supporting Arab communist parties. John Cooley reported that: 'During the Palestinian council meeting in Cairo, Soviet and perhaps Egyptian influence was directed at strengthening two guerrilla groups, the Palestine Liberation Organisation (PLO) and the Popular Front for the Liberation of Palestine, at the expense of al-Fatah, militarily the best of the three . . . [and] The anti-guerrilla views of Arab Communists were aired in a long manifesto issued after July's secret communist meeting, held in an unspecified place. The Beirut weekly *al Akhbar* (The News), close to leaders of the banned Lebanese Communist Party, published them. The document urges Arabs to struggle for implementation of last November's 1967 UN Security Council resolution, for a political settlement, and to fight anti-communism. The manifesto is entitled "Pressing missions facing the Arab national liberation movement

for elimination of the consequences of the Israeli imperialist aggression". It is listed "two dangerous courses taken by the Arab national liberation movement" since the Arab-Israeli war of 1967. The first was "the adventurous and sentimental course of ... upholding only one pathway for national struggle, a course encouraged by the Mao Tse-tung clique". Analysts here were certain the "one pathway" is guerrilla warfare, as urged by Peking'. *Christian Science Monitor*, 22 August 1968.

44 *NCNA*, 'US imperialism, Soviet revisionism speed up counter-revolutionary collusion in Middle East', 31 December 1968; see also the *People's Daily* editorial in *NCNA*, 6 January 1969.

45 *NCNA*, 'US imperialism, Soviet revisionism step up conspiracy of 'political solution' of Middle East question', 25 January 1969.

46 *NCNA*, 'Another glaring exposure of Soviet revisionists' sham support for, real betrayal of Arab people', 2 February 1969. See also message sent by CCAAS on greeting the convening of PLO-NC meeting at Cairo, *NCNA*, 3 February 1969.

47 Rashīd Hamid, op. cit., p. 136.

48 *NCNA*, 'Soviet revisionists' hideous performance at international Conference betraying Arab people', 5 February 1969; see also *NCNA* 'Soviet revisionist "5-point plan" on Middle East question betrays Arab people's interests', 4 February 1969.

49 John Cooley, *Christian Science Monitor*, 1 March 1969; see also the *Daily Telegraph*, 5 April 1969.

50 *NCNA*, 13 May 1969.

51 *NCNA*, 17 May 1969.

52 *NCNA*, 20 May 1969.

53 *NCNA*, 16 May 1969.

54 John Cooley, *Christian Science Monitor*, 17 May 1969.

55 *al-'Ahram*, 14 June 1969. For the Chinese view see *NCNA*, 11 July 1969.

56 *al-Yumīyat*, vol. 10, (3 July 1969), p. 15.

57 John Cooley, *Christian Science Monitor*, 12 July 1969.

58 *New York Times*, 6 August 1969.

59 Rashīd Hamid, op. cit., p. 153.

60 Ibid.

61 *NCNA*, 8 September 1969.

62 *NCNA*, 'Palestinian guerrilla fighters ardently study Chairman Mao's works', 19 September 1969.

63 Ibid.

64 *NCNA*, 27 September 1969.

65 *NCNA*, 28 September 1969.

66 *NCNA*, 29 September 1969.

67 'Revolutionary Palestinian people claim Mao Tse-tung Thought as powerful ideological weapon for vanquishing enemy', *NCNA*, 30 September 1969.

68 Ibid.

69 *NCNA*, 5 October 1969.

70 *NCNA*, 'Palestinian nationalist organisations and Arab public opinion oppose imperialist plot of Arab-Israeli "indirect talks"', 15 October 1969; see also *NCNA*, 'Armed struggle of Palestinian people, anti-imperialist movement of Arab people develop vigorously', 23 October 1969.

71 See *Tass*'s statement of 25 October 1969 in *Soviet News*, 28 October 1969. The Soviet Foreign Ministry, in a press conference on 31 October 1969, attacked Israel's policies of aggression, terrorising the Arab population in occupied Arab land since the 1967 war, and stated its support for 'progressive Arab regimes', but without mentioning the Palestinian role at all. *Soviet News*, 4 November 1969. See also, Warsaw Pact 'statement on situation in Middle East', *Soviet News*, 2 December 1969.

72 See, for example, 'Arafat's press conference as cited in *NCNA*, 28 October 1969.

73 *NCNA*, 29 October 1969.

74 *Soviet News*, 16 December 1969.

4 Black September and its aftermath

1 See Chien Feng: 'Persevering in armed struggle means victory', *NCNA*, 1 January 1970; *NCNA*, 'We want armed struggle not "political solution"', 1 January 1970; and the *People's Daily*, 'Armed struggle of the Palestinian people is forging ahead in victory', in *NCNA*, 7 January 1970.

2 *NCNA*, 2 February 1970.

3 *NCNA*, 17 February 1970.

4 *al-'Ahram*, for example, quoting a correspondent of Voice of Palestine radio, who accompanied the delegation, gave no names of 'high ranking' Soviet leaders whom the delegation was said to have met.

5 *NCNA*, 17 March 1970; see also the *People's Daily* article on this issue in *NCNA*, 20 March 1970.

6 *NCNA*, 21 March 1970.

7 *NCNA*, 21 March 1970.

8 *NCNA*, 23 March 1970.

9 *NCNA*, 27 March 1970.

10 *NCNA*, 22 March 1970.

11 *NCNA*, 28 March 1970.

12 The following account is drawn from the analysis by a Palestinian participant in the battle. 'Adib 'abū Kamel, 'Observations of a Fedayee in al-'Arķūb battle', *Dirāsāt 'Arabiya* no. 9 (July 1970), pp. 91–7.

13 Ibid., p. 96.

14 *NCNA*, 27 May 1970.

15 *NCNA*, 'Arab people's anti-US revolutionary struggle is sure to win', 5 June 1970.

16 Ibid., pp. 1–2.

17 Ibid., p. 2–3.

18 See, for PLO-NC 7th Session's resolutions and declarations, Rashīd Hamid, op. cit., pp. 159–68.

19 For communiqué issued at the end of the Meeting, see *International Documents on Palestine, 1970*, Beirut, 1973, p. 756.

20 *NCNA*, op. cit., p. 4.

21 Ibid., p. 5.

22 *International Documents on Palestine, 1970*, op. cit., p. 829.

23 See *NCNA*, 7 and 9 June respectively.

24 *al-Yumīyat*, vol. 3, (4 June 1970), p. 483.

25 *NCNA*, 14 June 1970. See also the *People's Daily* editorial in *NCNA*, 2 June 1970.

26 *al-Yumīyat*, vol. 12, (5 July 1970), p. 34.

27 *al-Yumīyat*, vol. 12, (21 August 1970), p. 224.

28 *al-Yumīyat*, vol. 12, (20 August 1970), and *NCNA*, 20 August 1970.

29 *NCNA*, 6 September 1970.

30 Author's interviews with PLO members, Peking, April 1974 and Beirut, February 1978. *Daily Star*, quoting PFLP's *al-Hadaf*, reported that Habash was in China, on 15 September, after ending a visit to North Korea; but the stay in China was cut off after news of his front's infamous aircraft hi-jackings. *Daily Star*, 18 October 1970. See also *Christian Science Monitor*, 1 October 1970.

31 *NCNA*, 6 September 1970. *NCNA*'s reference to Habash's interview appeared four days after it was published in *Jeune Afrique*, and, moreover, it was selective in its references to the content of Habash's talks. See, for comparison, *al-Yumīyat*, vol. 12 (2 September 1970), p. 260.

32 Rashīd Hamid, op. cit., p. 171.

33 *Soviet News*, 22 September 1970.

34 See the *People's Daily* editorials in *NCNA*, 19 and 24 September 1970 respectively and *NCNA*'s commentary, 20 and 24 September 1970 respectively.

35 *NCNA*, 21 September 1970.

36 Author's interview with Abū al-'Abid, Damascus, January 1978.

37 See *al-Yumīyat*, vol. 11, (25–28 June 1970), pp. 579–92; and *Fatah* 24 July 1970.

38 *NCNA*, 'Rogers' "political initiative" on Middle East further exposed', 7 August 1970. In contrast the USSR was willing to participate further and back Naṣir's efforts in following a 'peaceful political

solution' to the Arab-Israeli conflict. See press releases during and after Naṣir's visit to the USSR, in late July 1970, and Egypt-East German joint communiqué in *Soviet News*, 21 July and 4 August respectively.

39 *NCNA*, 26 January 1971.

40 Two days later, 28 January, the Egyptian delegation held a meeting with Premier Chou En-lai. Present were Kuo Mo-jo, Vice Chairman of the Standing Committee of the National People's Congress, and Chiu Hui-tso, Deputy Chief of the General Staff of the Chinese People's Liberation Army (*NCNA*, 28 January 1971). Chiu's presence is significant, for he not only was consistently present at all PLO and other Arab military delegations to China, but was also a close protégé of Lin Piao, whose militant stand on China's foreign policy — especially aid to world liberation movements — is well recognised. Chiu also held the Directorship of the General Rear Services Department, whose basic duties covered the Chinese PLA's logistical support, pay and medical services. Chiu disappeared in September 1971 after the alleged death of Lin Piao and the subsequent purges of his associates.

41 *NCNA*, 28 January 1971.

42 Ibid.

43 *Egyptian Gazette*, 17 February 1971.

44 Rashīd Hamid, op. cit., p. 177.

45 *Soviet News*, 16 March 1971.

46 *NCNA*, 3 May 1971.

47 *NCNA*, 4 May 1971.

48 *NCNA*, 4 May 1971.

49 *NCNA*, 4 May 1971.

50 *NCNA*, 5 May 1971.

51 *NCNA*, 4 May 1971.

52 *NCNA*, 4 May 1971.

53 *NCNA*, 10 May 1971 and *al-Yumiyat*, vol. 13, (10 May 1971), p. 524.

54 *al-Kifaḥ*, 10 May 1971.

55 *NCNA*, 24 May 1971.

56 Author's interview data, Damascus and Beirut, January–February 1971.

57 *al-Kitab al-Sanawi lil-Ḳadya al-Filisṭinya lil-'am 1971*, Beirut, 1975, p. 462.

58 *NCNA*, 28 June 1971.

59 *al-Yumiyat*, vol. 14, (26 July 1971), pp. 121–2.

60 Ibid., p. 124.

61 *The Daily Telegraph*, 5 July, *The Guardian* and *International Herald Tribune*, July 1971. The author has been unable to establish whether this shipment was allowed through or not.

62 The 9th NC session acknowledged in its resolutions PLO's appreciation of the 'socialist states, which support the Palestine revolution, spearheaded by the People's Republic of China and the USSR'. Rashīd Hamid, op. cit., p. 188.
63 *NCNA*, 24 July 1971.
64 *al-Yumiyat*, vol. 14, (18 September 1971), p. 344.
65 *NCNA*, 20 September 1971.
66 *NCNA*, 22 September 1971.
67 *NCNA*, 23 September 1971.
68 *NCNA*, 28 September 1971.
69 *al-Yumiyat*, vol. 14, (21 October 1971), p. 450.
70 *al-Yumiyat*, vol. 14, (30 October 1971), p. 474.
71 *The Egyptian Gazette*, 11 November 1971.
72 *Soviet News*, 2 November 1971.
73 Data collected from George J. Tomeh, op. cit., pp. 125–55.
74 One of the immediate results of China's UN admission was Lebanon's recognition of China and exchange of ambassadors; this left Saudi Arabia, Jordan, Oman, Qatar, Bahrain and later the newly-created United Arab Emirates, who still recognised Taiwan.
75 *Peking Review*, 19 November 1971, no. 47, p. 8.
76 *al-Yumiyat*, vol. 14, (1 November 1971), p. 480.
77 *al-Yumiyat*, vol. 14, (22 November 1971), p. 555.
78 George J. Tomeh, op. cit., pp. 88–9.
79 *al-Nahar*, 2 December 1971.
80 George J. Tomeh, op. cit., pp. 90–1.
81 *al-Yumiyat*, vol. 14, (9 December 1971), p. 629.
82 See Fu Hau's speech at the General Assembly's Special Political Committee, *NCNA*, 3 December 1971.

5 Turning point in Sino-Palestinian relations

1 *NCNA*, 'Persist in fighting till victory', 1 January 1972.
2 *al-Yumiyat*, vol. 15, (16 January 1972), p. 62.
3 *NCNA*, 16 February 1972.
4 *NCNA*, 21 March 1972.
5 *Soviet News*, 8 February 1972.
6 *al-Yumiyat*, vol. 15, (15 March 1972), p. 283–4.
7 *NCNA*, 18 March 1972.
8 *NCNA*, 18 March 1972.
9 *NCNA*, 30 March 1972.
10 *NCNA*, 30 March 1972.
11 *NCNA*, 31 March 1972.
12 *NCNA*, 1 April 1972.
13 *NCNA*, 2 April 1972.
14 *NCNA*, 4 April 1972.

15 *NCNA*, 4 April 1972.

16 *NCNA*, 12 April 1972.

17 See Rashīd Hamid, op. cit., pp. 195–224.

18 *NCNA*, 8 April 1972.

19 *al-Yumīyat*, vol. 15, (14 April 1972), p. 405.

20 The *People's Daily*, 'New achievements of the Palestinian people's revolutionary cause', in *NCNA*, 14 April 1972.

21 *al-Yumīyat*, vol. 15, (4 April 1972), p. 373.

22 *The Road to Ramadan*, London, 1976, p. 164–84.

23 Ibid., p. 171.

24 *Egyptian Gazette*, 1 August 1972.

25 *NCNA*, 25 August 1972.

26 *Soviet News*, 25 September 1972.

27 *Soviet News*, 26 September 1972.

28 *New York Times*, 22 September and *Daily Telegraph*, 28 September 1972.

29 *Soviet News*, 19 September 1972.

30 *NCNA*, 13 September 1972.

31 *NCNA*, 7 December 1972.

32 George J. Tomeh, op. cit., pp. 91–2.

33 *NCNA*, 2 March 1972.

34 *Palestine Revolution* reported that 'a Palestinian military delegation headed by 'Abū Mahr, Member of General Command of al-'Asifa forces, is visiting China to strengthen the continuous support that China extends towards the Palestinian revolution'. *al-Yumīyat*, vol. 17, (14 March 1973), pp. 225–6.

35 *NCNA*, 25 June 1973.

36 See, for example, I. Alexandrov's article in *Pravda*, 'Concerning certain principles of the foreign policy of the Chinese leadership' in *Soviet News*, 4 September 1973.

37 *NCNA*, 'Sham friend unmasked', 6 September 1973.

38 For a fuller account of the military dimensions of the October war, see the valuable study by 'As'ad Abdul Raḥmān, ed., *al-Ḥarab al-'arabiya al-'Israi'liya al-rabi'ah*, Beirut, 1974.

39 The first Soviet Government official statement appeared on 7 October. It declared, among other things, that: 'True to its principled policy of support for the people striving for freedom and independence, the Soviet Union consistently comes out as a reliable friend of the Arab states. Condemning the expansionist policy of Israel, the Soviet Union resolutely supports the legitimate demands of the Arab states for the relinquishing of all Arab territories occupied by Israel in 1967', *Soviet News*, 9 October 1973.

40 *NCNA*, 9 October 1973. The Chinese ambassador to Lebanon declared his government's support for the Arab side. See *The Times*, 8 October 1973.

41 *NCNA*, 8 October 1973.

42 *NCNA*, 12 October 1973.

43 *NCNA*, 12 October 1973.

44 *Soviet News*, 16 October 1973.

45 Egyptian and Syrian accounts of this affair differ, and confusion remains especially after peace negotiations started between Egypt and Israel, through Kissinger. See M. Heikal, *The Road to Ramadan*, London, 1976, Ch. 4, pp. 206–41; also Sadat's interview with *al-Nahar*, 29 March 1973.

46 George J. Tomeh, op. cit., p. 151.

47 Heikal alleges that 'the Chinese, persuaded by the Americans and some other delegates, had agreed to abstain in the voting, so Russia's fear that they might be tempted to use their veto was removed', op. cit., p. 248. It is most likely that because of the Arab bloc's desire and acceptance of a cease-fire that China did not use its veto power; for its condemnation of the USA during debates at the Security Council was evident enough to dispel any of Heikal's assumptions.

48 *NCNA*, 25 October 1973.

49 For detailed explanations of the antagonists' military positions see 'As'ad Abdul Raḥmān, ed., op. cit., pp. 107–10.

50 *Egyptian Mail*, 24 November 1973.

51 As quoted in *Egyptian Mail*, 1 December 1973.

52 *Soviet News*, 27 November 1973.

53 *Soviet News*, 29 January 1974.

54 *Financial Times*, 9 March 1974.

55 *Soviet News*, 23 April 1974.

56 *al-Safir*, 29 April 1974.

57 *NCNA*, 19 May 1974.

58 Rashīd Hamid, op. cit., p. 248. Chou En-lai sent a congratulatory message to 'Arafat on convening the meeting, *NCNA*, 2 June 1974.

59 Ibid., p. 251.

60 Heikal describes Ponomaryev as the 'ideologue of the Soviet party. . . . Indeed, he and his assistant, Olinovsky Ulyanovsky had developed a well-known theory of the "non-capitalist way of development in the Third World"', op. cit., p. 141. Moreover, some of Ulyanovsky's writings had been translated into Arabic. See P. Ulyanovsky and B. Pavlov, *Bisadad Madmūn al-takadum al-'adjtimā'i fi al-marhalh al-intikalia*, (On Social Progress in the Transitional Period), Moscow, 1975.

61 *Soviet News*, 6 August 1974.

62 Ibid.

63 *The Times*, 3 August 1974.

64 *NCNA*, 30 August 1974.

65 *NCNA*, 5 September 1974.

66 Hanī al-Ḥasan, prior to his visit, declared at Damascus that the 'delegation might be received by Mao Tse-tung, though no final arrangements were made', thus giving the visit certain importance. *al-Safīr*, 28 August 1974.

67 *NCNA*, 19 September 1974.

68 *NCNA*, 12 October 1974.

69 *al-Nahar*, 19 September 1974.

70 *NCNA*, 3 October 1974.

71 *NCNA*, 12 October 1974.

72 *NCNA*, 17 October 1974.

73 *NCNA*, 18 October 1974.

74 According to *al-Safīr*, 5 November 1974, a 'responsible member of the Chinese embassy at Damascus informed the PLO leadership of the result of the talks' between Chinese leaders and PFLP delegation, and that China still stands by its 'firm belief in PRM unity'. It is worth noting that O. Muḥtar, Assistant to the Head of the PLO Mission in Peking, was present at the Li-Ḳuba'h talks *only*, but not when the delegation had talks with Ho Ying during which, most likely, concrete issues were discussed.

75 George J. Tomeh, op. cit., p. 109.

76 *NCNA*, 27 October 1974. See, however, Huang Hua's address at the General Assembly Plenary Session, explaining China's support for the Palestinian cause. *NCNA*, 20 November 1974.

77 *NCNA*, 19 November 1974.

78 George J. Tomeh, op. cit., p. 111.

79 *NCNA*, 28 October 1974.

80 *NCNA*, 27 October 1974.

81 *Soviet News*, 3 December 1974. See also, for USSR's strong support of PLO cause, *Soviet News*, 10 December 1974.

82 *The Egyptian Gazette*, 8 January 1975.

83 *Soviet News*, 4 February 1975.

84 *The Egyptian Gazette*, 5 February 1975.

85 *al-Hadaf*, 29 February 1975.

86 *al-'Ahram*, 1 March 1975.

87 *al-Nahar*, 2 April 1975.

88 *NCNA*, 9 April 1975.

89 *Soviet News*, 6 May 1975.

90 *The Egyptian Gazette*, 4 May 1975.

91 *NCNA*, 16 May 1975.

92 *al-Nahar*, 9 June 1975.

93 *NCNA*, 21 June 1975.

94 *International Herald Tribune*, 23 June 1975.

95 Ibid., p. 6.

96 *NCNA*, 18 July 1975.

97 *NCNA*, 19 July 1975.

 98 *NCNA*, 22 July 1975.
 99 *NCNA*, 24 July 1975.
100 *al-Safīr*, 12 August 1975.
101 *al-Nahar*, 14 August 1975.
102 *NCNA*, 8 September 1975.
103 *NCNA*, 13 September 1975.
104 *NCNA*, 17 September 1975.
105 *al-Hurriyāh*, 6 October 1975.
106 See, for example, *NCNA*, 4, 15, 28 May, 10 June, 14 and 26 July. In all accounts Chinese reports give more prominence to the role played by the 'Lebanese army' in repulsing Israeli attacks.
107 *NCNA*, 10 November 1975 and *Soviet News*, 18 November 1975.
108 *Egyptian Gazette*, 21 December 1975.

6 Brief history of the Liberation Movement in Oman

 1 It is beyond the scope of this study to trace the historical significance of tribal allegiances vis-à-vis the Sultan. However, the most significant political development up to 1955 was the signing of the Treaty of al-Sib, 1920. This treaty ended hostilities between the Sultanate and the 'Imāmate. The central question was whether the Sultan did exercise authority, as a sovereign, on the 'Imāmate of Oman; and, consequently, whether, according to the Treaty, the 'Imāmate did or did not constitute an independent state.

Between 1919 and 1921 Major R. E. L. Wingate, Britain's political agent in Muscat, was instrumental in mediating and finalising the Treaty.

Nevertheless, the 'treaty is vague in several instances. For example, the exact nature of the Sultan's rights of sovereignty in Oman is not detailed nor is the 'Imām specifically granted independence. Nothing was said concerning the right of the 'Imām to carry on relations with foreign powers, although one authority mentions a secret pact that forbade any requests for foreign intervention. Yet much was set down concerning the extradition of criminals and free exchange of peoples and goods between the territories controlled by the two governments. In summary, the two signatories seem to have recognised each other's mutual autonomy within their respective spheres and avoided specific mention of the thorny question of sovereignty and precedence'. R. G. Landen, *Oman since 1856*, Princeton, 1967, p. 404. The full text of the Treaty is published variously; see, for example, in ibid., pp. 403–4. For further discussions on the subject see: J. B. Kelly, *Sultanate and Imamate of Oman*, Oxford, 1959, pp. 7–10, and J. E. Peterson, 'The Revival of the Ibadi Imamate in Oman', in *Arabian Studies* III, London, 1976, pp. 165–87.

2 R. G. Landen, *Oman Since 1856*, Princeton, 1967, p. 418.

3 The application of the 'Imāmate for admission to the Arab League as an independent state was given due consideration; though no meaningful steps were taken toward the creation of a state. A good account is given in M. Khalil, *The Arab States and the Arab League*, Beirut, 1962, vol. 2, p. 177.

4 For a later interpretation of 'Imām Ghalib's failure, see Tisa Yuniya 9 June study, *The Oman War, 1957–1959; A Critical History*, Trans. Gulf Committee, London, 1972, pp. 32–43.

5 For opposite point of view see W. Phillips, *Oman: A History*, London, 1971, p. 216.

6 See in particular, *The role of the workers in the struggle of British occupied Arabia*, n.d., n.p.

7 A. R. Buzwak *et al.*, *'uman fi al-mahafil al-dwaliya* (Oman in the International Arena), Cairo, 1977, pp. 352–4.

8 The Council consisted of the following: 'Imām Ghalib, President; Talib bib 'Alī; Shaikh Sulaiman bin Ḥimyer; Shaikh bin 'Isa, and Shaikh Muḥammad bin 'Abdullah al-Salami.

9 See in particular, *Report of the Special Representative of the Secretary General on his visit to Oman*, UN Document A/5562. And subsequent report: A/C.4/604/add.1, 2 October 1963.

10 Buzwak *et al.*, op. cit., pp. 352–4.

11 *al-Watha'k al-Arabiya*, Cairo, 1962, p. 687.

12 Buzwak *et al.*, op. cit., p. 11.

13 Author's interview with Sa'id Masoud, Popular Front for the Liberation of Oman's spokesman, January, 1977, Aden.

14 T. Y. Ismael, *The Arab Left*, Syracuse, 1976, pp. 63–4.

15 W. Kazziha, *Revolutionary Transformation in the Arab World*, London, 1975, p. 87.

16 PFLOAG, *Documents*, p. 45. See also F. Halliday: *Arabia without Sultans*, London, 1974, p. 315. It is worth noting that the Dhofar Liberation Front did not begin operating in an organised way in 1962, but at the end of 1964; and, moreover, there seems to be a confusion about the creation of the Dhofar Charitable Association.

17 Author's interview with a former prominent member of the Dhofar Soldiers' Organisation, Kuwait, August 1974.

18 Yūsif 'Alawī was one of its most prominent leaders. When the DLF was created, he was put in charge of the Front's office in Cairo. Later, when Ḳabūs came to power in 1970, Yūsif offered his services to the new Sultan. Subsequently he was appointed Under-Secretary at the Ministry of Foreign Affairs in the Sultanate.

19 For a translated version of the DLF's 'declaration on the launching of armed struggle, June 1965', see Gulf Committee, *Documents of the National Struggle in Oman and the Arabian Gulf*, London, 1974, pp. 7–9.

20 This unique tropical land lies on the southern coast of the Arabian peninsula half-way between Aden at the south-west and Muscat at the north-east. On one side it is flanked by the Mahra province of South Yemen, now the Sixth Governorate of the PDRY, and on the other it is separated from Oman by the 500-mile wide Jaddat al-Harasī desert. The area of Dhofar is approximately 38,000 square miles, with a 200-mile coastline that stretches from the Kuria Muria Bay to Ras Darbat Alī, on the Yemeni border. A coastal mountain range rises to 4,500 feet and catches the monsoon rains between May and September. Annual rainfall in Dhofar is thirty inches; however, towards either side of the area the average rainfall for the year is only three inches.

Dhofar's relatively heavy rainfall produces in the mountains a tropical forest and creates an area of vegetation extending up to 40 miles inland before the mountains taper off into the barren desert that stretches away to Saudi Arabia. The population of Dhofar, estimated at 150,000, inhabits this green strip, the mountains and the coastal plains. The most important of these is the Jurbaib Plain, in the middle of Dhofar, forty miles long and up to ten miles wide. The capital, Salala, is sited here, with the Sultan's adjacent villages of al-Husn, site of the prison and the Sultan's palace, and Umm al-Qawarif, the military base, to which is attached an RAF airfield. Farther to the east lie the towns of Mirbat, Taqa and Sadh, while to the west are situated Raysut, the only natural port in Dhofar, and the town of Rakhyut. Halliday, op. cit., pp. 305–6.

21 PFLOAG, op. cit., p. 46.

22 PFLOAG, op. cit., p. 46.

23 A prominent member of the Popular Front for the Liberation of Oman informed this author that it was well known that Hawātma claimed, publicly, that his Front exerted a 'great influence' on PFLO's ideology and decision-making; this lasted until 1973. Author's interview, Aden, July 1973.

24 Kazziha, op. cit., pp. 89–90.

25 Prominent among this faction within the ANM was Muḥsin 'Ibrahim. His newly-created *Organisation of Lebanese Socialists* (OLS) argued, generally, that because of the ANM's class structure, especially in the 1950s, the Movement was not able to carry out its 'proper historical role' in enhancing revolution.

26 Britain decided, when the PDRY was about to be declared independent, to cede the two small, but militarily significant, Kuria Muria islands to Ṣuḷtan Sa'id bin Taimūr. Prior to the date of cession, 15 November 1967, the islands were under the jurisdiction of the Protectorate of Aden. These islands are forty miles off the Dhofari shore; the PDRY claimed its right of ownership over the islands.

However, on 30 November, the day they were formally ceded to the Sultanate, the UN trusteeship committee passed a resolution stating them to be part of the territory of the new state and sent a recommendation to that effect to the General Assembly. Goronwy Roberts, a Minister of State at the Foreign Office, told a questioner in the House of Commons on 11 December that the wish of the people of the Kuria Muria Islands to revert to the Sultanate of Muscat and Oman 'was expressed as unanimous'. The islands' 78 inhabitants were divided into five families and consultations with them were conducted by an Arabic-speaking member of the Aden High Commission staff on 28 and 29 October, he said. *Arab Report and Record*, no. 22, 1–15 December 1967, p. 374. For terms of cession of the islands between Ṣulṭan Sa'id and the UK Government, see Cmd. 3505, Treaty Series no. 8 (1968).

27 The exact date of this Conference is difficult to determine. PFLOAG, *Documents*, op. cit., p. 53 state that it was held in August 1968. While Kazziha, op. cit., p. 90, argues that it was convened between 19 and 21 July 1968. Kazziha's date seems more likely.

28 Kazziha, op. cit., pp. 90–1.

29 PFLOAG, *Documents*, p. 53.

30 Gulf Committee, *Documents*, London, 1974, p. 10.

31 *Saūt al-Thawra*, no. 157, n.d., p. 5.

32 Author's interview with Sa'id Mas'ūd, PFLO Office, Aden, January 1977.

33 Ibid.

34 For first-hand information of the Front's experience in the field see Halliday, op. cit., pp. 376–81; and contrast this with P. A. Lienhardt: 'Some social aspects of the Trucial States' in D. Hopwood, ed., *The Arabian Peninsula*, London, 1972, Ch. 10.

35 Author's interview with a member of the six-man Political Bureau, Kuwait, August 1975.

36 Halliday, op. cit., p. 324.

37 D. L. Price, 'Oman: Insurgency and Development', *Conflict Studies*, no. 53 (January 1975), pp. 3–19, confuses the *emergence* of NDFLOAG with that of its *components*. Moreover, he states that 'most of the NDFLOAG members had received guerrilla training in Iraq, or China, or with the Palestine Liberation Organisation (PLO) at its refugee camps near Amman'. *Oman*, London, 1975, p. 5. No NDFLOAG member was ever sent to China for either military or political training. Moreover, it seems highly unlikely, given the Front's background, i.e. its historical development out of the ANM — that any of its members were trained by the PLO; for the PLO is dominated by al-Fataḥ rather than any other Palestinian organisation. Lastly, NDFLOAG's document 'On the launching of Armed Struggle', 12 June 1970 (see Gulf Committee *Documents*,

pp. 11–20) states that: 'The NDFLOAG was set up from the following organisations:

   a) *The People's Revolutionary Movement in Oman and the
      Arabian Gulf*
   b) *The Revolutionary Students' Vanguard in Oman and the
      Arab Gulf*
   c) *The Patriotic Soldiers' Association of Oman*
   d) Various tribal organisations in Oman.'

This is completely misleading and deserves some notice: Price took
for granted that this formula was authentic. First, NDFLOAG
originated from the ANM's splinter group in the Gulf. Second, the
organisers of NDFLOAG's first conference, announcing its birth,
inserted the name *The Revolutionary Students' Vanguard in Oman
and the Arab Gulf* without consulting it. The latter is an organisation of Bahraini students, scattered in Beirut and Baghdad, who
never operated actively in Oman. Third, throughout the whole
history of the Omani war, there *never* existed an organisation such
as c). None of the persons concerned whom the writer interviewed
had ever heard of it, let alone its operations in either Oman or the
Gulf. Fourth, d) is stated in such a way that it would lead a reader
to presume beforehand that there were 'tribal organisations' in
actual existence. The terms 'tribal' and 'organisations' are, in their
intrinsic political meanings, in direct contradiction to each other.
In the final analysis, from all accounts presented above, it seems
that NDFLOAG's creation by the mother organisation had one
significant aim in mind: after the June 12 uprising, the Front went
underground, and ceased military operations; it *hoped* thus to give
the newly-formed and announced Front a political significance and
weight in the area, and that the Front would continue operations
despite earlier developments.

38 J. D. Anthony, *Arab States of the Lower Gulf*, Washington D.C.,
    1975, p. 5.
39 D. Holden, 'The Persian Gulf: After the British Raj', *Foreign Affairs*,
    vol. 49, no. 4, July 1971, pp. 724–5.
40 For earlier stages of UAE development see M. Sadik and W. Snavely,
    Bahrain, Qatar and the United Arab Emirates, Lexington, 1972,
    Ch. 6.
41 J. D. Anthony, 'The Union of Arab Emirates', *Middle East Journal*,
    vol. 26, no. 3, Summer 1972, p. 274. For extensive description of
    the UAE's political development see Anthony's op. cit.
42 For a description of boundary disputes in the Gulf see M. R. al-Fil
    'The Boundary Disputes', *Journal of the Gulf and Arabian Peninsula
    Studies*, vol. 2, no. 8, October 1976, pp. 25–64.
43 S. Chubin and S. Zabih, *The Foreign Relations of Iran*, Berkeley,
    1974, p. 245. See also D. R. Tahtinen, *Arms in the Persian Gulf*,

Washington D.C., 1974, from which this evaluation of Iran's military capabilities is largely drawn.

44 S. Chubin and S. Zabih, op. cit., p. 227.

45 J. Townsend, *Oman: The Making of the Modern State*, London, 1977, pp. 74–5. Ch. 5 of this study is significant in recounting the moribund rule of Sultan Sa'id and his total dependence on British advisers.

46 R. Fiennes, *Where Soldiers Fear to Tread*, London, 1975, p. 152. Andrew Wilson, of the *Observer*, reported that: 'there is little doubt that officials close to Sir Alec Douglas-Home were told in advance of this week's coup in Muscat and Oman by Ḳabūs bin Said against his father, Sultan Said bin Taimur, who is now recovering from gunshot wounds in an RAF hospital at Swindon. Ḳabūs, trained at Sandhurst, disclosed his plans to British officers seconded, or contracted, to the Sultan's armed forces. Word is believed to have been passed to Sir Stewart Crawford, the British Political Resident here (Bahrain), who in turn advised Whitehall. Sir Stewart returned to Britain yesterday (1 August 1970) at the end of his tour of duty. The smooth coup in Muscat is said to have been 'the most satisfactory send-off that he could possibly have wished'. The phrase recalls the elation of an earlier Resident, Sir William Luce – now Sir Alec's special representative for Gulf affairs – at the overthrow of the Ruler of Abu Dhabi in 1966. Both Sultans were autocrats with large oil revenues and kept their peoples in feudal subjection. Muscat is important to British interests for two reasons. First, peace within the Sultanate, and between Muscat and its neighbours, is vital to hopes of leaving the Gulf stable when British forces depart. . . . Secondly, the Sultanate owns Masira Island, which serves as an alternative to Bahrain in the string of RAF staging-posts carrying supplies to the Far East. If Bahrain ceased to be usable for political reasons, the small and sparsely populated island of Masira could become very important indeed. 'On both scores, the young Sultan's coup has improved British prospects'. *Observer*, 2 August 1970; see also *Financial Times*, 28 August 1970.

47 This faction must not be confused with earlier PLF members – i.e. those who left the movement after the Ḥimrin Conference – who disassociated themselves from PFLOAG programmes.

48 Author's interview with a prominent member of the PFLOAG-General Command, June 1975, Kuwait. This interviewee was condemned to death by the Front for taking part in the uprising, but was released after an investigation into the matter. He was subsequently stripped of all his responsibilities. He left the PFLOAG and resides in self-exile in the Gulf.

49 Ibid.

50 In analysing this period of PFLOAG history, F. Halliday gives a

number of unfounded reasons for the upheaval by stating that 'The British aim was to use the narrow social base for counter-revolution within Dhofar society to confuse the revolutionary forces. In the eastern sector they set about organising a conspiracy. The east was the most populated part of the country, but had seen the least fighting; it was therefore the area where the traditional tribal system and the social forces of pro-imperialism were strongest. Furthermore, the new Sultan's mother was from a tribe in the East of Dhofar, and this gave the British a link with a number of Shaikhs. Since the Second Congress of 1968 some Shaikhs had crossed over to the British side where they were well rewarded with money, and the British hoped that the same manoeuvre would work in 1970.' Op. cit., pp. 334–5.

D. L. Price states the date wrongly, and also argues the reasons misleadingly. 'The failure to open a northern front created a crisis within the movement over strategy and tactics. Its disarray was worsened on 10 October (1970) when a counter-revolution began in the eastern part of the jabal in protest at such practices as forced collectivisation, torture and execution'. op. cit., p. 5.

51 *9 June*, no. 7, (December 1970), pp. 6–7.
52 *Saūt al-Thawra*, no. 157, (n.d.), p. 6.
53 For the full text of the declaration see Gulf Committee, *Documents*, pp. 20–4.
54 The two states had agreed to exchange envoys on 26 August 1971. See op. cit., no. 16, (16–31 August 1971), p. 435.
55 For Sulṭan Kabūs's attempt to modernise Oman see J. Townsend, op. cit., Chs. 7–8.
56 3 January, 1972. Robert Stephens, of *The Observer*, reported that during an interview with Sa'id Masūd at PFLOAG's office at Aden, Sa'id 'claimed that increasing numbers of British troops were being used in Oman against the Dhofar rebels. He produced two documents said to have been found in an armoured car in which a British captain was killed last year. One was a kind of log book, or operational diary. The other was a folder... marked 'Ministry of Defence, March 1969' and 'Restricted Army Code no. 70511' and was entitled 'Company and Combat Team Commanders' Aide Memoire'. There was no doubt of their authenticity'. 4 January 1972.

During the author's first field trip to Aden, August 1972, these documents were presented. The more important was the 'aide memoire'. It point out clearly the popularity and strength of PFLOAG at the time among the people. It pointed out that the officer himself and several of his colleagues believed that the use of helicopters in hit-and-run operations is imperative, since the Americans were using this method successfully in the Vietnam war. In discussing this both Sa'id and Abdullah abdul al-Hafidh acknowledged the importance of helicopters in the Omani war; but went on to note that 'steps are being taken to learn from the Vietnamese in combating such methods in guerrilla warfare'.

57 *The Sunday Times*, 25 June 1972.

58 *Financial Times*, 15 November 1972.

59 Author's interview, July 1973, Kuwait.

60 Sulṭan Ḳabūs, prior to this Jordanian military delegation, paid a three-day state visit to Jordan seeking military assistance. *ARR*, no. 12, 16–30 June 1972, p. 310.

61 Chubin and Zabih, op. cit., p. 311; also Tahtinen, op. cit., pp. 18–19; *The Times*, 12 January 1974; and *The Daily Telegraph*, 7 February 1974, for Shah's interview.

62 *The Middle East Journal*, 'Documents', vol. 28, no. 3, p. 303; see also *Oman*, 9 March 1974.

63 Gulf Committee, *Documents*, p. 92.

64 Ibid., p. 99.

65 Author's interview, PFLO Office, Aden, January 1977.

66 *Oman*, 23 November 1975.

67 Author's interview with Sa'id Mas'ūd, Aden, January 1977.

68 *Saūt al-Sha't*, no. 16, 1 December 1969, p. 11.

69 One of the most important articles written in the USSR press is that of *Pravda* correspondent A. Vasiliev in September 1969. He sent back from Dhofar enthusiastic articles on the popularity and efficient organisation of the People's Liberation Army and on the brutality of the British, using napalm on defenceless villages and setting up an economic blockade on the coast to prevent the Dhofaris from buying vitally needed food. He also described the joy with which they received Lenin and Kremlin badges which they wore as 'battle decorations'. See S. Page, *The USSR and Arabia*, (London 1971), p. 16.

During the author's several field trips on the subject, all PFLOAG members who were interviewed pointed out that the Russian reporter was not at ease in picturing PLA men; for all of them wore Mao badges. The reporter left Dhofar with 'strong impressions that the Front was totally pro-Chinese'.

70 Ibid.

71 For PFLOAG delegations to the USSR and Eastern Europe and Cuba bloc see: *Saūt al-Thawra*, no. 42 (10 March 1973), p. 3; no. 63, (4 August 1973), p. 2; no. 64, (11 August 1973), p. 8; no. 75, (27 October 1973), p. 6; no. 161, (12 July 1975), p. 1, and no. 129, (9 November 1974), p. 1.

72 See *Political Commentary*, no. 46, (7 April 1973), pp. 7–8.

73 *An-Nahar Arab Report*, vol. 7, no. 6, (9 February 1976).

74 This argument is advanced by Sulṭan Ḳabūs.

7 **China's attitudes, involvement in, and withdrawal from, the Omani War, 1955–75**

1 *NCNA*, 3 November 1955.
2 *NCNA*, 17 July 1957.
3 *NCNA*, 6 August 1957.
4 See for example *NCNA*, 9 August 1957.
5 *NCNA*, 10 August 1957.
6 *NCNA*, 14 August 1957.
7 *NCNA*, 22 August 1957.
8 *NCNA*, 23 August 1957.
9 *NCNA*, 23 August 1957.
10 Chou En-lai, 'The present international situation and China's foreign policy' in *Current Background* no. 492, (14 February 1958), p. 4.
11 *NCNA*, 1 December 1958.
12 *NCNA*, 30 January 1959.
13 *NCNA*, 6 February 1959.
14 *NCNA*, 8 February 1959.
15 *NCNA*, 9 February 1959.
16 *NCNA*, 10 February 1959.
17 Author's interviews with Khalid 'Amīn, PFLO Office, Aden, January 1977.
18 *NCNA*, 20 February 1959.
19 For summary of the speech, see *NCNA*, 21 February 1959.
20 In John K. Fairbank and Robert R. Bowie, *Communist China, 1955–1959: Policy Documents with Analysis*, Oxford, 1971, p. 525.
21 *NCNA*, 18 July 1959.
22 Quoted in C. Neuhauser, *Third World Politics*, Harvard, 1970, pp. 27–8.
23 See the exclusive interview given by Ṣaliḥ bin 'Isa al-Harithī to *NCNA* reporter at Damascus, 17 April 1960.
24 *NCNA*, 17 July 1960.
25 *NCNA*, 17 July 1960.
26 For example, *NCNA* reported on 13 August 1961 on the subject from Cairo that: 'Imām Ghalib bin 'Alī of Oman, has ordered the formation of 'Consultative Council of State of the 'Imāmate of Oman' according to a statement issued by the Omani Office here today. The Consultative Council will be headed by the 'Imām and composed of leaders of the Omani struggle. The Council will supervise political and military affairs of Oman and pass resolutions in this respect. Its headquarters will be in a place where the 'Imām resides. [Saudi Arabia].
27 *NCNA*, 18 July 1963.
28 M. Nasser-Eddine, *Arab-Chinese Relations, 1950–1971*, Beirut, n.d., p. 1971.

Notes

29 *al-Watha'ik al-'Arabiya, 1963*, Beirut, 1964, p. 826.
30 *Peking Review*, vol. 6, no. 52, (27 December 1963), p. 11.
31 *NCNA*, 23 December 1963.
32 *NCNA*, 19 August 1965.
33 Author's interview with former member of DLF, Kuwait, June 1976.
34 Author's interview with Khalid Amin, PFLO Office, Aden, January 1977.
35 Ibid.
36 *NCNA*, 27 June 1967.
37 All information is drawn from the author's various interviews with Sa'id Masūd and Khalid 'Amin, PFLO Office, Aden, January 1977, and with other members who left the PFLO and are now residing in Arabian Gulf countries.
38 Author's interview with Khalid 'Amin, PFLO Office, Aden, January 1977.
39 Ibid.
40 Ibid.
41 *NCNA*, 6 November 1969.
42 Ibid.
43 Ibid. A resumé of these articles appeared in *Peking Review*, vol. 12, no. 49, (5 December 1969), pp. 29–30.
44 *NCNA*, 17 October 1969.
45 For full text see *Saūt al-Thawra*, no. 3, (9 May 1969), pp. 4–9.
46 PFLOAG, *al-Watha'ik*, p. 29.
47 Ibid., p. 32, and Fred Halliday's *Arabia without Sultans*, London, 1974, pp. 373–5.
48 *NCNA*, 1 March 1970.
49 *Peking Review*, vol. 13, no. 15, (10 April 1970), p. 38.
50 Author's interview with Khalid 'Amin, PFLO Office, Aden, January 1977.
51 *NCNA*, 16 April 1970.
52 *NCNA*, 12 June 1970. Li was later appointed (15 December 1970) as the first Chinese Ambassador Extraordinary and Plenipotentiary to the PDRY.
53 Ibid.
54 In *NCNA*, 10 June 1970.
55 *NCNA*, 13 June 1970.
56 *NCNA*, 25 July 1970.
57 *NCNA*, 2 August 1970.
58 *NCNA*, 14 August 1970.
59 *NCNA*, 14 December 1970.
60 *NCNA*, 9 June 1971.
61 *Arab Report and Record*, no. 14, (16–31 July 1972), p. 358.
62 Author's interview with Khalid 'Amin and Yusuf Ṭahr, PFLO Office, Aden, January 1977.

63 Speech by Abdul al-Fataḥ 'Isma'īl, 9 July 1972 (in Arabic). The
   author is grateful to the Kuwait Embassy in Peking for supplying
   the entire speech.
64 Ibid.
65 *NCNA*, 18 July 1972.
66 Author's interview with Khalid 'Amīn, PFLO Office, Aden, January
   1977. According to a former PFLO member who was included in
   the delegation, its members 'were surprised to meet new faces and
   different emphasis was put by the Chinese on their foreign policy
   priorities in the area; and in contrast to earlier Chinese statements
   and vehement support, the Chinese seemed totally unsympathetic
   to our cause'. Author's interview data, Kuwait, March 1977.
67 *Arab Report and Record*, no. 7, (1–15 April 1973), p. 163.
68 See *Saūt al-Thawra* issues for September–October 1973.
69 *Saūt al-Thawra*, no. 72, (6 September 1973), p. 6.
70 *Oman*, 15 September 1973, p. 5.
71 See, e.g. *Saūt al-Thawra*, 'Czechoslovakia wa-al-Yemen al-demoḵraṭi',
   no. 38, (10 February 1973), pp. 2–3.
72 Text in Arabic; given to the author by Kuwait Embassy in Peking.
73 Ibid.
74 *B.B.C.D.S.W.B.* (*Middle East and North Africa*), no. 5029, (10
   October 1975).
75 *Peking Review*, vol. 18, no. 31, (1 August 1975), pp. 13–14.

8 China and Kuwait

1 For an interesting study of this period see Nadjah A. al-Jasim, *al-
   tatawur al-siyasī wa al-iḵtṣadi lil-Kuwait 1914–1939*, Cairo, 1973.
2 A. H. T. Chisholm, *The first Kuwait oil concession*, London, 1975,
   p. 3; and for the text of this Agreement see no. 55, pp. 242–6.
3 *Financial Times*, 26 April 1957.
4 For terms of the Kuwaiti-AOC agreement, see B. A. al-Ḥuṣūsī,
   Dirāsat fī tarīkh al-Kuwait, Kuwait, 1972, pp. 366–77.
5 *The Japan Times*, 13 April 1958.
6 *NCNA*, 10 August 1958. The first Chinese Ambassador arrived in
   Baghdad on 29 August 1958; see *NCNA*, 30 August 1958.
7 *NCNA*, 29 July 1958.
8 See Appendix 5, Sections A and B.
9 *NCNA*, 21 May 1959.
10 *NCNA*, 18 February and 21 February 1960 respectively.
11 Kuwaiti authorities abhor the terminology of independence, but
   prefer to call 19 June a national day; the implication being, though
   its arguments are not satisfactory, that Kuwait had always exer-
   cised internal self-rule.
12 Martha Dūkas, *'Azmat al-Kuwait*, Beirut, 1973, p. 23.

13   Ibid., p. 75.
14   *NCNA*, 29 June 1961.
15   *NCNA*, 30 June 1961.
16   *NCNA*, 10 April 1961.
17   *NCNA*, 23 June 1961.
18   *NCNA*, 3 July 1961.
19   *NCNA*, 6 July 1961.
20   *NCNA*, 6 July 1961.
21   *NCNA*, 5 July 1961.
22   *NCNA*, 7 July 1961.
23   *NCNA*, 6 July 1961.
24   *NCNA*, 7 July 1961. See also *NCNA*, 9 July 1961 for further UN Security Council discussions on Kuwait.
25   *NCNA*, 15 July 1961.
26   Majid Khadduri, *Republican Iraq*, London, 1969, p. 171.
27   *NCNA*, 28 July 1961.
28   *NCNA*, 27 and 29 July 1961.
29   *NCNA*, 16 September 1961.
30   *NCNA*, 11 October 1961.
31   *NCNA*, 27 February 1962; see also *NCNA*, 27 April 1962; and for further claims by Ḳasim for Kuwait's annexation in *NCNA*, 8 March 1962.
32   Abdul Amir Kubbah, *OPEC: past and present*, Vienna, 1974, p. 12.
33   *NCNA*, 3 April 1962. The same analogy was drawn about Saudi Arabia's oil production. See *NCNA*, 'ARAMCO: an octopus in Saudi Arabia', 21 June 1962.
34   *The Sudan Daily*, 29 June 1962.
35   *NCNA* referred to this delegation in the briefest way possible, 19 May 1963.
36   *NCNA*, 19 June 1963.
37   Martha Dūkas, op. cit., p. 68.
38   See *NCNA* reporting on Kuwait National Assembly and Shaikh Ṣabah al-Salim, Foreign Minister, condemnation of British actions in Yemen, 2 and 3 April 1964; and on oil production in Kuwait, *NCNA*, 21 July 1964.
39   *NCNA*, 12 February 1965.
40   *NCNA*, 13 February 1965.
41   *NCNA*, 14 February 1965.
42   *NCNA*, 18 February 1965.
43   *NCNA*, 6 June 1965.
44   *NCNA*, 8 June 1965.
45   *NCNA*, 9 June 1965.
46   *The Egyptian Gazette*, 8 June 1965.
47   *NCNA*, 11 June 1965.
48   *NCNA*, 27 November 1965.

49 *NCNA*, 6 December 1965. See also messages of greetings from Chairman Lin Shao-chi and Chou En-lai to their respective Kuwaiti counterparts in *NCNA*, 25 February 1966. After S͟haik͟h Ṣabaḥ al-Salim's accession to power Kuwait's national day date was changed to 25 February.

50 *NCNA*, 10 October 1965.

51 *al-Kuwaiti*, 11 June 1966.

52 *NCNA*, 20 January 1967.

53 *NCNA*, 21 January 1967.

54 *NCNA*, 20 January 1967.

55 *Madjalh Ghoifh al-Tadjarh war Ṣana'h al-Kuwait*, 18 February 1968.

56 *al-Kuwaiti*, 8 March 1968.

57 *al-Ṭalī'a* (Kuwait), 9 October 1968.

58 For an earlier study of fertilisers in the Chinese economy, see Jung-chao liu, *China's fertilizer economy*, Edinburgh, 1971.

59 'Support the petroleum exporting countries' just struggle' in *NCNA*, 13 February 1971.

60 *NCNA*, 30 March 1971.

61 Ibid.

62 *al-Ra'i al-'Ām*, 2 March 1971.

63 Ibid., 14 March 1971.

64 *NCNA*, 30 March 1971.

65 *al-Hadaf*, 25 March 1971.

66 *Kuo Chi Chih Shih*, no. 2, December 1971, pp. 34–5.

67 Ibid., pp. 45–6.

68 *NCNA*, 31 March 1971.

69 *NCNA*, 25 August 1971.

70 *al-Risallah*, 8 August 1971.

71 *NCNA*, 8 December 1971.

72 *Kuo Chi Chih Shih*, no. 3, December 1971, p. 60.

73 S. F. Zabih, *The Communist Movement in Iran*, Berkeley and Los Angeles, 1966, p. 199.

74 *Current Background*, no. 621, 27 June 1961.

75 *NCNA*, 18 May 1961.

76 See for example *NCNA*, 8 May 1961 and 22 July 1962 respectively.

77 *NCNA*, 15 December 1961, and throughout the remaining years until the Cultural Revolution, for support to Tudeh.

78 A. P. Pouyan and M. Māni, *Iran, three essays on: imperialism, the revolutionary left, and the guerrilla movement*, Florence, Italy, n.d., p. 80. The flourishing Iranian splinter groups had published several pro-Chinese studies, though blind pro-Chinese propaganda is most evident among intellectuals living in Europe and the USA. See, e.g. *Iraninform*, no. 1, n.d., n.p., and Iranian Student Association, *On the alliance of the October League (M-L) with the Shah of Iran*, Houston and Berkeley, n.d., n.p.

79   For full text see Anon., *Mu'tamar al-'Ahzab al-Shuy u'iya wa al-'umaliya al-'alamī*, Moscow, 1969, Prague 1969, pp. 717–27.

80   *NCNA*, 4 October 1970. See also *NCNA*, 15 March 1970, for quoting unnamed sources on the 'determination of Iranian revolutionaries to advance revolution under great red banner of Marxism-Leninism-Mao Tse-tung Thought'.

81   *Dawn*, 13 December 1970.

82   *NCNA*, 15 April 1971.

83   *NCNA*, 15 April 1971.

84   *NCNA*, 15 April 1971.

85   *NCNA*, 15 April 1971.

86   *NCNA*, 20 April 1971.

87   *NCNA*, 1 May 1971.

88   *NCNA*, 13 May 1971.

89   *NCNA*, 26 May 1971.

90   *NCNA*, 18 August 1971.

91   *NCNA*, 18 September 1972.

92   China signed with Iran a trade and payments agreement on 18 April 1973 upon the latter's despatch of a delegation to Peking. See *NCNA*, 9 April 1973 and further detail see *Khayan International*, 14 April 1973, p. 6.

93   *NCNA*, 2 June 1973.

94   *NCNA*, 29 September 1973.

95   *NCNA*, 15 June 1973.

96   *NCNA*, 16 June 1973.

97   John K. Cooley, 'Peking swings support to Iran', *Christian Science Monitor*, 19 June 1973.

98   During the author's attendance at the Canton Trade Fair, Spring 1975, several Arab merchants from the Gulf and Saudi Arabia were concluding contracts for various commodities for export to the area. With the exception of Kuwait, the Gulf Arab states and Saudi Arabia have no diplomatic relations with China.

99   *NCNA*, 15 July 1972.

100   *NCNA*, 16 July 1972.

101   The author was asked not to quote directly from this minute of the talks with Chou En-lai, but was permitted to refer to the main contents. The author is grateful to certain members of the delegation who assisted by providing the minutes.

102   The report was privately handed to the author by the National Assembly President's office, Kuwait, December 1976.

103   *NCNA*, 3 December 1972. On the same day a Chinese economic and trade exhibition opened in Kuwait, see *NCNA*, 4 December 1972.

104   *NCNA*, 6 December 1972.

105   The author is unable to corroborate this, the major obstacle being that there is no statistical material available in Kuwait.

106 *NCNA*, 10 December 1972.

107 *Peking Review*, 'Energy crisis and scramble for energy resources', vol. 16, no. 39, 28 September 1973.

108 See, for example, *NCNA*, 'The Arab countries are advancing in militant solidarity', 9 October 1973.

109 See *NCNA*, 'The Middle East people struggle for the defence of oil resources and sovereignty', 21 October 1973.

110 Tschen Shen-chen, 'A-la-po kuo chia shih yu tou cheng ti ch'ien ch'ien hou hou' (On the recent oil strife of the Arab states), *Hsiieh Shsi I p'i p'an* (Study and Criticism), February 1975, pp. 85–91.

111 Ibid., p. 86.

112 Ibid., p. 87.

113 Ibid., p. 88.

114 Ibid., p. 91. For further theoretical and less lucid discussion on the issue see Ch'ang Ch'ien, 'Behind the so-called "energy crisis"', *Hung Ch'i* (Red Flag), in *Survey of Mainland China Press*, nos. 769–70, (25 February–4 March 1974), pp. 96–100; *People's Daily*, 'False friend with honey in mouth and dagger in heart', in *NCNA*, 26 May 1974; Jen Ku-ping, 'What is behind the "petrodollar" rush?', *Peking Review*, vol. 17, no. 42, (18 October 1974), pp. 18–19; and *NCNA*, 'Using oil as weapon, historic pioneering action in struggle against imperialism, hegemonism', 27 December 1974.

115 The information gathered here is from the author's interview with Khalid al-Sana', Treasurer of the Olympic Committee of Kuwait and President of the Volleyball Association of Kuwait, 20 July 1975. The author is grateful for these interviews.

116 Ibid.

117 *NCNA*, 17 February 1974.

118 Author's interview with Khalid al-Sana', *supra*.

119 Ibid.

120 *NCNA*, 10 March 1974.

121 According to the Speaker's report to the Kuwait National Assembly, his meetings and talks with Chinese leaders did not include any substantial discussions between the two parties. The report was given to the author privately with the Speaker's consent. Kuwait, August 1975.

122 The 'Secret Report' of the Kuwait Embassy was given to the author by members of the Kuwait Foreign Ministry. The 'Secret Report' was addressed, as usual, to the Under-Secretary, and dated 19 March 1974.

123 Ibid.

124 *NCNA*, 15 March 1974.

125 *NCNA*, 5 July 1975.

Appendix 1   Fataḥ military study on China

1 Popular Front for the Liberation of Palestine, *'A la Tarik al-thawra al-filistinyiā*, Beirut, 1970, pp. 32–3.
2 Ibid., pp. 80–6.
3 Ibid., pp. 53–9.
4 Ibid., pp. 70–80. For further discussion of the PFLP's doctrine for the Palestinian war of liberation and Mao's influence, see the following: Anon, *al-mukawama al-filistinyā: al-wā'ak wā al-tawuka'āt*, Beirut, 1971, pp. 113–47; Nadji Allūsh, *Munakashat hawal al-thawra al-filistinyā*, Beirut, 1970, pp. 80–172.
5 See for example, Na'if Ḥawātma, *Hawal'azmat ḥarakat al-mukawama al-filistiniyā*, Beirut, 1970; and Nadjī 'Allūsh, op. cit., pp. 173–264, especially p. 186.
6 al thawra al-filistinyiā wā al-maūkaf min al-ḥalāf fi al-ḥarakah al-shūū'ya al-'alamīya, *Dirasat 'Arabiya*, no. 1, November 1975, pp. 47–54.
7 Ibid.
8 Nadjī 'Allūsh, *al Khat al-'almī al-thawrī wa al-thawrah al-kamiya al-dimukratya*, Beirut, 1976.
9 Author's interview with Munīr Shafīk, Beirut, February 1978. For Shafīk's writings see bibliography. His writings remain one of the most interesting and valuable Palestinian analyses on the political development of the Palestinian Resistance Movement.

Appendix 2   Arab Labour Party of Oman's study on the historical development of Oman

1 All un-sourced historical accounts of ALPO are drawn from various interviews conducted by the author in the Gulf, 1972–7. It is obvious that those who agreed to reveal their information preferred to remain anonymous.
2 F. Halliday states such confusion as follows:

> The PFLOAG Third Congress led to other ties with Gulf groups and to the broadening of the Front's political appeal. In November 1972 PFLOAG held talks with another Omani anti-imperialist group, the Arab Workers' Party in Oman [ALPO]. This had been the Omani branch of the MEN right wing and had confined itself to the Sultanate. After the 1972 meeting the two Fronts also agreed to coordinate on the basis of the national democratic working plan. F. Halliday, *Arabia Without Sultans*, p. 388.

Moreover, in a note on the above quoted paragraph, F. Halliday continues to argue confusingly the origins of ALPO:

In 1970 the Popular Front for the Liberation of Palestine,
led by Dr George Ḥabbash, began to build up a pan-Arab party,
the Arab Workers' Party . . . . On the Omani section of the
Arab Workers' Party, see the interview with one of their
representatives in *al-Ittihad*, Kuwait, no. 53, October 1972.
op. cit., p. 392.

Perhaps the confusion of the origins of the ALPO originates from the two almost identically-named parties: Dr Ḥaba_sh_'s party was called Arab Socialist Labour Party (ASLP) by contrast with ALPO, which is widely referred to in the Arab world as the Arab Labour Party. Furthermore, the literature of the two Parties is strikingly different in tone though much less so in substance. Dr Ḥaba_sh_'s party published a short-lived periodical called *Tarik al-Thawra* (Road to Revolution) as its mouthpiece, and its entire political literature fails to mention the Party's role in either Oman or the Gulf. It is clear that Halliday is unaware of the existence of two different parties, and that he assumes that ALPO and ASLP are a single party, which he calls AWP [Arab Workers' Party]. Finally, when checking Halliday's reference to *al-Ittihad* magazine one notices, contrary to expectation, that no organisational or historical links between the two Parties are mentioned.

3 See the interview referred to in note 2.
4 See 'Documents', *Dirasat 'Arabiya*, no. 2, (December 1971), pp. 144–52.
5 Gulf Committee, *Documents*, p. 66.
6 Gulf Committee, Trans., London 1964.

Appendix 5   Sino Arab delegation exchanges 1956–75

1 Deleted from Section A is Palestinian Resistance Movement delegations to China.
2 Information gathered here is from *Survey of China Mainland Press* for years concerned.

Bibliography

Articles

'Abdullah, M. Morsy, 'Development in Culture on Coast of Oman Between 1900–1940', *Arabian Studies*, ed. Serjeant, R. B. and Bidwell, R. L., London, no. 11 (1975), pp. 167–8.

'Abdullah, Nawaf, 'ḥawal al-azma al-lubnaniya: 'arad wa taḳyim lil-masar al-syasi lil al-ahda<u>th</u> wa <u>kh</u>uṭuṭ sayr al-ḳiṭal' (On the Lebanese Crisis: An Exposé and Evaluation of Political Events and Military Operations), *Sh'un filisṭiniya* (Palestine Affairs), no. 57 (May 1976), pp. 87–105.

Abu al-Namil, Hussain, 'al-ṭa'ifiya al-siyasiya wa al-ḥaḳa'iḳ al-iḳtiṣadiya fi lubnan' (Political and Economic Reality in Lebanon), *Shu'un filisṭiniya* (Palestine Affairs), no. 50–1 (October–November 1975), pp. 41–7.

*Abu Kamal, Adib, 'mulaḥaẓat fida'i fi ma'rakat al-'arḳub' (Notes of a Fida'i in the Battle of Al-'arkub), *Dirasat 'arabiya* (Arab Studies), no. 9 (July 1970), pp. 91–7.

*Abu Nidhal, Nazih, 'al-<u>th</u>awra al-filisṭiniya wa al-mauḳif min ḳaḍaya al-<u>kh</u>ilaf fi al-ḥaraka al-shuyu'iya al-'alamiya' (Palestinian Revolution and the Stand on the International Communist Movement Issues), *Dirasat 'arabiya* (Arab Studies), no. 1 (November 1975), pp. 47–54.

Adie, W. A. C., 'China's Foreign Policy I; II', *World Today*, vol. 24, no. 3 (March 1968), pp. 111–20, vol. 24, no. 6 (June 1968), pp. 257–68.

Adie, W. A. C., 'China's Middle East Strategy', *World Today*, vol. 23, no. 8 (August 1967), pp. 317–26.

Adie, W. A. C., 'The Middle East: Sino-Soviet Discord', *Survey* (London), no. 42 (June 1962), pp. 132–47.

Adie, W. A. C., 'Peking's Revised Line', *Problems of Communism*, vol. 21, no. 5 (September–October 1972), pp. 54–68.

Adie, W. A. C., 'Some Chinese Attitudes', *International Affairs* (London), vol. 42, no. 2 (April 1966), pp. 241–52.

Al-'afif, Al-akhdar, 'min kumunat baris ila madjazarat 'amman' (From the Paris Commune to the Amman Massacre), *Dirāsāt 'Arabiya* (Arab Studies), no. 7 (May 1971), pp. 3–6.

Al-afif, Al-akhdar, 'mulaḥaẓat ḥawla: al-muḳawama, al-ḥarb al-thauriya wa'l waḍ' al-rahin' (Notes on: the Resistance, Revolutionary War and the Present Situation), *Dirāsāt 'Arabiya* (Arab Studies), no. 9 (July 1971), pp. 2–13.

Agwani, M. S., 'The Reactions of West Asia and the U.A.R.', *International Studies*, vol. 5, nos. 1, 2 (July–October 1963), pp. 75–9.

Agwani, M. S., 'The Soviet Union, China and West Asia', *International Studies*, vol. 6, no. 4 (April 1965), pp. 345–66.

Akins, James E., 'The Oil Crisis: this Time the Wolf is Here', *Foreign Affairs*, vol. 51, no. 3 (April 1975), pp. 462–90.

Alexeyev, I., 'Anti-Sovietism in Peking's Strategy', *International Affairs* (Moscow), (July 1973), pp. 21–6.

Alexeyev, I. and Apalin, G., 'Peking Ideological Subversion', *International Affairs* (Moscow), (October 1975), pp. 42–54.

Ali, Iman Ghalib ibn, 'The Role of the Workers in the Struggle of British-Occupied Arabia', n.d., n.p.

'Allūsh, Nadjī, ed., 'nahwa istratidjiya djadida lil thawra al-filisṭiniya' (Towards a New Strategy for the Palestinian Revolution), *Dirāsāt 'Arabiya* (Arab Studies), no. 4 (February 1971), pp. 9–16.

'Allūsh, Nadjī, ed., 'naḳd taḳrir al-djebha as-sha'biya al-dimuḳraṭiya hawla hamlat aylul' (Critique of the PDFLP Report on the September Campaign), *Dirāsāt 'Arabiya* (Arab Studies), no. 5 (March 1971), pp. 5–16.

Amuzegar, Jahangir, 'Ideology and Economic Growth in the Middle East', *The Middle East Journal*, vol. 28, no. 1 (Winter 1974), pp. 1–9.

Anon., 'Arab Petroleum Congress Espouses OPEC Programme', *World Petroleum*, vol. 34, no. 13 (December 1963), pp. 462–90.

Anon., 'New Oil Agreements in the Middle East', *World Today*, vol. 14, no. 4 (April 1958), pp. 135–43.

Anon., 'A New Pattern in Soviet Middle East Studies', *World Today*, vol. 14, no. 2 (February 1958), pp. 71–80.

Anon., 'Offshore Production to Reach One Million Barrels Daily in Persian Gulf this Year', *World Petroleum*, vol. 35, no. 7 (July 1964), pp. 28–31.

Anon., 'Oil and Bahrain', *World Today*, vol. 7, no. 2 (February 1951), pp. 76–83.

Anon., 'Oil in the Persian Gulf', *World Today*, vol. 20, no. 7 (July 1964), pp. 305–13.

Anon., 'Petrochemicals for the Developing Nations', *World Petroleum*, vol. 36, no. 1 (January 1965), pp. 50–5.

Anon., 'Petrochemical Plants for Developing Countries Require Careful Study', *World Petroleum*, vol. 35, no. 5 (May 1964), pp. 39–40.

Anthony, John Duke, 'The Union of Arab Emirates', *The Middle East Journal*, vol. 26, no. 3 (Summer 1972), pp. 271–87.

Apalin, G., 'The Anti-Socialist Substance of Peking's Foreign Policy', *International Affairs* (Moscow), (December 1971), pp. 23–31.

Apalin, G., 'Peking and the Third World', *International Affairs* (Moscow), (December 1972), pp. 28–34.

Apalin, G., 'Peking's Provocation', *New Times* (Moscow), (1973), nos. 45–6, pp. 28–30.

Ashbar, Riad, 'The Syrian and the Egyptian Campaigns', *Journal of Palestine Studies*, vol. 3, no. 2 (Winter 1974), pp. 15–33.

Bauer, P. T., 'Price Control in Underdeveloped Countries', *Journal of Development Studies*, vol. 2, no. 1 (October 1965), pp. 19–37.

Ben-Dak, Joseph D., 'China in the Arab World', *Current History*, vol. 59, no. 349 (September 1970), pp. 147–52.

Ben-Dak, Joseph D., 'China and Peace in the Middle East; a Proposal for Conflict Resolution', *Middle East Information Series*, vol. 18, (April 1972), pp. 30–5.

Ben Shahar, Haim, 'Capital Formation and Government Capital Policy in Developing Countries', *Journal of Development Studies*, vol. 4, no. 1 (October 1967), pp. 86–96.

*Berkir, R. N., 'On Marxian Thought and the problem of International Relations', *World Politics*, vol. 24 no. 1 (October 1971), pp. 80–105.

Bernstein, Marver H., 'The Appeal of Communism in Arab Countries', *World Politics*, vol. 9, no. 4 (July 1957), pp. 623–9.

Berrehy, Jean-Jacques, 'Oil in the Orient: Growing Oil Needs Influence Soviet Policy', *New Middle East* (London), no. 15 (December 1969), pp. 44–5.

Berrehy, Jean-Jacques, 'Oil in the Orient: Re-Colonisation – a Soviet Timetable', *New Middle East* (London), no. 16 (January 1970), pp. 11–12.

Berrehy, Jean-Jacques, 'Oil in the Orient: The Limits of American-Soviet Entente', *New Middle East* (London), no. 26 (November 1970), pp. 24–7.

Berry, John A., 'Oil and Soviet Policy in the Middle East', *The Middle East Journal*, vol. 26, no. 2 (Spring 1972), pp. 149–60.

Bill, James A., 'Class Analysis and the Dialectics of Modernisation in the Middle East', *International Journal of Middle East Studies*, vol. 3, no. 4 (October 1972), pp. 417–34.

Al-Bitar, Salah al-Din, 'The Implications of the October War for the Arab World', *Journal of Palestine Studies*, vol. 3, no. 2 (Winter 1974), pp. 34–45.

*Bondrevsky, G. L., 'The Continuing Western Interest in Oman – As Seen from Moscow', *New Middle East* (London), no. 35 (August 1971), pp. 11–15.

Borisov, O. and Koloskov, B., 'Peking's Foreign Policy After the Tenth

Congress of CPC', *International Affairs* (Moscow), (July 1974), pp. 32–44.

Brewer, William D., 'Yesterday and Tomorrow in the Persian Gulf', *The Middle East Journal*, vol. 23, no. 2 (Spring 1969), pp. 149–58.

Brown, Neville, 'Communist China's Strategic Weakness', *New Middle East* (London), no. 27 (December 1970), pp. 41–2.

Bull, Hedley, 'Order v. Justice in the International Society', *Political Studies*, vol. 19, no. 3 (September 1971), pp. 269–83.

Burrell, R. M., 'The Gulf Pot Begins to Bubble Once More', *New Middle East*, no. 56 (May 1973), pp. 37–8.

Burrell, R. M., 'The Gulf Where Britannia Once Ruled', *New Middle East* (London), no. 51 (December 1972), pp. 32–6.

Burrell, R. M., 'Iranian Foreign Policy During the Last Decade', *Asian Affairs*, vol. 61, no. 1 (February 1974), pp. 7–15.

Bush, Briton Cooper, 'Britain and the Status of Kuwait, 1896–1899', *The Middle East Journal*, vol. 21, no. 2 (Spring 1967), pp. 187–98.

Bustani, Emile, 'The Arab World and Britain', *International Affairs* (London), vol. 35, no. 4 (October 1959), pp. 427–37.

Calvert, P. A. R., 'Revolution: The Politics of Violence', *Political Studies*, vol. 15, no. 1 (February 1967), pp. 1–11.

Campbell, John C., 'The Communist Powers and the Middle East; Moscow's Purposes', *Problems of Communism*, vol. 21, (September–October 1972), pp. 40–53.

Campbell, John C., 'Middle East Oil: American Policy and Super-Power Interaction', *Survival*, vol. 15 (September–October 1973), pp. 210–17.

Carlson, S., 'China's Urgent Need for Stability in the Middle East', *New Middle East*, no. 36 (September 1971), pp. 25–31.

Carlson, S., 'The Explosion of a Myth: China, the Soviet Union and the Middle East', *New Middle East* (London), no. 27 (December 1970), pp. 32–40.

Chandler, Geoffrey, 'The Myth of Oil Power: International Groups and National Sovereignty', *International Affairs* (London), vol. 46, no. 4 (October 1970), pp. 710–18.

Chao, Kang, 'The Production and Application of Chemical Fertilizers in China', *China Quarterly*, no. 64 (December 1975), pp. 712–29.

Clemens, Jr., Walter C., 'China's Nuclear Tests: Trends and Portents', *China Quarterly*, no. 32 (October–December 1967), pp. 111–31.

Conant, Melvin A., 'Oil: Co-operation or Conflict', *Survival*, vol. 15, no. 1 (January–February 1973), pp. 8–14.

Cooley, John, 'China and the Palestinians', *Journal of Palestine Studies*, vol. 1, no. 2 (Winter 1972), pp. 19–34.

Cooley, John, 'The Shifting Sands of Arab Communism', *Problems of Communism*, no. 24 (March–April 1975), pp. 22–42.

Cooper, John Franklin, 'Chinese Objectives in the Middle East', *China Report* (New Delhi), no. 5 (January–February 1969), pp. 8–13.

Bibliography

Cranmer-Byng, John, 'The Chinese View of their Place in the World: An Historical Perspective', *China Quarterly*, no. 53 (January–March 1973), pp. 67–79.

Crozier, Brian, 'The Struggle for the Third World', *International Affairs*, vol. 40, no. 3 (July 1964), pp. 440–50.

Dai, Shen-yu, 'Peking and the Third World', *Current History*, vol. 49, no. 289 (September 1965), pp. 142–9.

Deighton, H. S., 'The Arab Middle East and the Modern World', *International Affairs* (London), vol. 22, no. 4 (October 1946), pp. 511–20.

Deutsch, Karl W., 'Imperialism and Neo-Colonialism', *Peace Science Society*, vol. 23 (November 1973), pp. 1–26.

*Dinestein, Herbert, 'Rivalry in Underdeveloped Areas', *Problems of Communism*, no. 13 (March–April 1964), pp. 64–72.

Disney, Nigel, 'China and the Middle East', *Middle East Research and Information Project*, no. 63, pp. 3–18.

Dutt, Gargi, 'China and the Shift in Super-power Relations', *International Studies*, vol. 13, no. 4 (October–December 1974), pp. 635–62.

Dymov, G., 'Persian Gulf Countries at the Crossroads', *International Affairs* (Moscow), (March 1973), pp. 53–9.

Emerson, Rupert, 'The Fate of Human Rights in the Third World', *World Politics*, vol. 27, no. 2 (January 1975), pp. 201–26.

Emminger, Otmar, 'International Financial Markets and the Re-Cycling of Petro-Dollars', *World Today*, vol. 31, no. 3 (March 1975), pp. 95–102.

Enders, Thomas C., 'OPEC and the Industrial Countries: the Next Ten Years', *Foreign Affairs*, vol. 53, no. 4 (July 1975), pp. 625–37.

Eyal, E., 'Israeli Ping-Pong with Peking', *Ma'ariv* (23 April 1971).

Farmanfarmaian, Khodadad, *et al.*, 'How can the World Afford OPEC Oil?, *Foreign Affairs*, vol. 53, no. 2 (January 1975), pp. 201–22.

Farra, Randa, 'The Chinese People's Republic and the Arab World', *Middle East Forum*, vol. 42, no. 1 (Winter 1966), pp. 43–50.

Al-fil, Mohammed Rashid, 'mushkelat al-ḥudud bayna emarat al-khalidj al-'arab' (The Boundary Disputes Between the Emirates of the United Arab Emirates and her Neighbours), *Journal of the Gulf and Arabian Peninsula Studies*, vol. 2, no. 8 (October 1976), pp. 25–64.

Finnie, David, 'Recruitment and Training of Labour: The Middle East Oil Industry', *Middle East Journal*, vol. 12, no. 2 (Spring 1958), pp. 127–43.

Frandjie, Samir, 'al-azma wa'l-badil' (The Crisis and the Alternative), *Shu'un filistiniya* (Palestine Affairs), nos. 50–51 (October–November 1975), pp. 17–20.

Gafurov, B., 'The Soviet Union and the National Liberation Movement', *International Affairs* (Moscow), (July 1971), pp. 17–21.

Gasteyyer, Kurt, 'Moscow and the Mediterranean', *Foreign Affairs*, vol. 46, no. 4 (July 1968), pp. 676–87.

398

Geller, Harry, 'Nuclear Weapons and Chinese Policy', *Adelphi Paper*, no. 99 (1973).

Germin, Ernest, 'The Industrialisation of Backward Countries', *Marxist Studies* (London), vol. 2, no. 1 (Winter 1969–70), pp. 31–44.

Ghareeb, Edmund, 'The U.S. Arms Supply to Israel During the October War', *Journal of Palestine Studies*, vol. 3, no. 2 (Winter 1972), pp. 114–21.

Gittings, John, 'Co-operation and Conflict in Sino-Soviet Relations', *International Affairs* (London), vol. 4, no. 1 (January 1964), pp. 60–75.

Gittings, John, 'The Great Power Triangle and Chinese Foreign Policy', *China Quarterly*, no. 39 (July–September 1969), pp. 41–54.

Gittings, John, 'New Light on Mao: His View of the World', *China Quarterly*, no. 60 (October–December 1974), pp. 750–66.

Goldman, Marshall I., 'Communist Foreign Aid: Successes and Short-comings', *Current History*, vol. 51, no. 300 (August 1966), pp. 78–87.

Gottlieb, G., 'China and the Middle East', *Middle East Information Series*, vol. 18 (April 1972), pp. 2–10.

Gozzano, Francesco, 'China's Stand on the Middle East', *New Outlook* (Tel Aviv), vol. 5, no. 1 (January 1972), pp. 39–42.

*Gray, Collin S., 'The Practice of Theory in International Relations', *Political Studies*, vol. 22, no. 2 (June 1974), pp. 129–46.

Gurtov, Melvin, 'The Foreign Ministry and Foreign Affairs During the Cultural Revolution', *China Quarterly*, no. 40 (October–December 1974), pp. 750–66.

Haddad, George, 'al-muḵawama amam marḥala a'la min taṭawuriya' (The Resistance Movement Facing a Higher Stage of its Evolution), *Dirasat 'arabiya* (Arab Studies), no. 7 (May 1971), pp. 7–12.

Halpern, M., 'Towards Further Modernisation of the Study of the New Nations', *World Politics*, vol. 17, no. 1 (October 1964), pp. 157–81.

Hamdan, Yousef, 'isra'il wa'l-azma al-lubnaniya' (Israel and the Lebanese Crisis), *Shu'un filisṭiniya* (Palestine Affairs), nos. 53–4 (January–February 1976), pp. 6–21.

Hamīd, Rashid, 'What is the P.L.O.?', *Journal of Palestine Studies*, vol. 4, no. 4 (Summer 1975), pp. 90–109.

Harris, Lillian Graig, 'China's Relations with the P.L.O.', *Journal of Palestine Studies*, vol. 7, no. 1 (Autumn 1977), Issue 25, pp. 123–54.

Hartshorn, J. E., 'Oil Diplomacy: The New Approach', *World Today*, vol. 29, no. 7 (July 1973), pp. 281–90.

*Hasan, Sa'dat, 'filisṭin fi al-umam al-mutaḥida: ḵararat tarikhiya wa khalfiyat' (Palestine in the United Nations: Historical Decisions and Background), *Shu'un filisṭiniya* (Palestine Affairs), nos. 53–4, (January–February 1976), pp. 6–21.

Hay, Rupert, 'Great Britain's Relations with Yemen and Oman', *Middle Eastern Affairs*, vol. 2, no. 5 (May 1960), pp. 142–9.

Hay, Rupert, 'The Impact of the Oil Industry on the Persian Gulf Shaykhdoms', *The Middle East Journal*, vol. 9, no. 4 (Autumn 1955), pp. 361–72.

Heard Bey, Franke, 'The Gulf States and Oman in Transition', *Asian Affairs*, vol. 59, no. 1 (February 1972), pp. 14–22.

Heard Bay, Franke, 'Social Changes in the Gulf States and Oman', *Asian Affairs*, vol. 59, no. 3 (October 1972), pp. 309–16.

Heilleiner, G. K., 'The Less Developed Countries and the International Monetary System', *Journal of Development Studies*, vol. 10, nos. 3, 4 (April–July 1974), pp. 347–73.

Heller, C. A., 'Kuwait Prepares for Mammoth Tankers', *World Petroleum*, vol. 39, no. 7 (July 1968), pp. 26–8.

Heller, C. A., 'Oil for the Lamps of China and Russia', *World Petroleum*, vol. 33, no. 13 (December 1962), pp. 58–64.

Heller, C. A., 'The Role of Oil in Middle East Economy, 1961–1963', *World Petroleum*, vol. 25, no. 1 (October 1964), pp. 82–4.

Hendryx, Frank, 'It's time for a New Approach to Arab Concession Negotiations', *World Petroleum*, vol. 37, no. 10 (September 1966), pp. 58–62.

Herbert, Paul, 'First All-Hydrogen Refinery Now Operating in Kuwait', *World Petroleum*, vol. 39, no. 9 (August 1968), pp. 32–6.

Hirsch, Fred, 'The Oil-Financing Conundrum', *World Today*, vol. 31, no. 3 (March 1975), pp. 103–13.

Holden, David, 'The Persian Gulf: After the British Raj', *Foreign Affairs*, vol. 49, no. 4 (July 1971), pp. 721–35.

Hook, Brian, 'Historical Perspective on China's New Diplomacy', *Asian Affairs*, vol. 61, no. 2 (June 1974), pp. 135–43.

Hopkins, Harry, 'Can Oil Save the Arab Revolution', *New Middle East* (London), no. 7 (April 1969), p. 21.

Hotlinger, Arnold, 'The Depth of Arab Radicalism', *Foreign Affairs*, vol. 51, no. 3 (April 1973), pp. 491–504.

Hourani, Albert, 'The Decline of the West in the Middle East; I, II', *International Affairs* (London), vol. 29, no. 1 (January 1953), pp. 22–42, vol. 29, no. 2 (April 1953), pp. 156–83.

Hudson, Geoffrey, 'Paper Tigers and Nuclear Teeth', *China Quarterly*, no. 39 (July–September 1969), pp. 64–75.

Hudson, Michael C., 'Development and Setbacks in the Palestine Resistance Movement, 1967–1971', *Journal of Palestine Studies*, vol. 2, no. 2 (Winter 1973), pp. 79–101.

Ibrahim, Sa'd al-din, 'kisindjir wa ḥarb tashrin' (Kissinger and the October War), *Dirasat 'arabiya* (Arab Studies), no. 4 (February 1975), pp. 3–21.

Isawi, Charles, 'Economic and Social Foundations of Democracy in the Middle East', *International Affairs*, vol. 32, no. 1 (January 1956), pp. 27–42.

Isawi, Charles, 'Growth and Structural Change in the Middle East', *Middle East Journal*, vol. 25, no. 3 (Summer 1971), pp. 309–24.

Ismael, Tarek Y., 'al-ṣin al-sha'biya wa al-ḳaḍiya al-filisṭiniya' (People's Republic of China and the Palestinian Question), *Shu'un filisṭiniya* (Palestine Affairs), no. 36 (August 1974), pp. 179–82.

Itayim, Fuad, 'Arab Oil – The Political Dimension', *Journal of Palestine Studies*, vol. 3, no. 2 (Winter 1974), pp. 84–97.

Ivanov, A., 'Soviet Imports from Developing Countries', *Foreign Trade* (Moscow), no. 9 (September 1974), pp. 38–43.

Ivry, Isaac, 'Can Israeli-Chinese Relations Improve?', *American Zionist*, (October 1971), pp. 35–8.

Jaber, Fuad, 'The Arab Regimes and the Palestinian Revolution, 1967–1971', *Journal of Palestine Studies*, vol. 2, no. 2 (Winter 1973), pp. 79–101.

Jabir, Khalid, 'al-sulṭah wa al-tawazun fi lubnan' (The Superstructure and the Balance of Power in Lebanon), *Shu'un filisṭiniya* (Palestine Affairs), nos. 50, 51 (October–November 1975), pp. 25–40.

Kambara, Tatsu, 'The Petroleum Industry in China', *China Quarterly*, no. 60 (October–December 1974), pp. 699–719.

Kapchenko, N., 'Maoism's Foreign Policy Platform', *International Affairs* (Moscow), (February 1972), pp. 35–41.

Katz, Ze'ev, 'China's Role in the Middle East', *Asian Analyst* (July 1967), pp. 10–12.

Katz, Ze'ev, 'The Sino-Soviet Conflict and the Arabs', *New Outlook*, vol. 7, no. 4 (1964), pp. 35–7.

Kelly, J. B., 'The British Position in the Persian Gulf', *World Today*, vol. 20, no. 6 (June 1964), pp. 238–49.

Kelly, J. B., 'Hadramut, Oman, Dhofar: The Experience of Revolution', *Middle Eastern Studies*, vol. 12, no. 2 (May 1970), pp. 213–30.

Kelly, J. B., 'Muscat and Oman', *St. Anthony's Papers* (Lecture), (16 September 1957).

Kelly, J. B., 'The Persian Claims to Bahrain', *International Affairs*, vol. 33, no. 1 (January 1957), pp. 51–70.

Kelly, J. B., 'Sovereignty and Jurisdiction in Eastern Arabia', *International Affairs*, vol. 34, no. 1 (January 1958), pp. 16–24.

Kennedy, Edward M., 'The Persian Gulf: Arms Race or Arms Control?', *Foreign Affairs*, vol. 51, no. 1 (October 1975), pp. 14–35.

Kent, George, 'Foreign Policy Analysis: Middle East', *Peace Research Society*, vol. 14, (1969), pp. 95–112.

Kergan, J. L., 'Social and Economic Changes in the Gulf Countries', *Asian Affairs*, vol. 62, no. 3 (October 1975), pp. 282–9.

Khadduri, Majid, 'Political Trends in Iraq and Kuwait', *Current History*, vol. 52, no. 306 (February 1967), pp. 84–9.

Khalil, Ahmed Khalil, 'djanub lubnan: bayna al-dawla wa al-thawra (South Lebanon: Between the State and the Revolution), *Dirasat 'arabiya* (Arab Studies), no. 4 (February 1975), pp. 22–3.

Bibliography

Khalil, J.E., 'Communist China and the United Arab Republic', *Asian Survey*, no. 10 (April 1970), pp. 308–19.

Khalil, J.E., 'Sino-Arab Relations', *Asian Survey*, vol. 8, no. 8 (August 1968), pp. 678–90.

Kimbe, Jon, 'The Soviet-Arab Scenario', *Midstream*, vol. 30, no. 10 (December 1973), pp. 9–22.

Krammer, Arnold, 'Soviet Motives in the Partition of Palestine 1947–48', *Journal of Palestine Studies*, vol. 2, no. 2 (Winter 1973), pp. 102–19.

Landau, Jacob M., 'Soviet Studies on Workers' Movements in the Middle East', *Middle Eastern Studies*, vol. 6, no. 3 (October 1970), pp. 346–9.

Landis, Lincoln, 'Soviet Interest in the Middle East Oil', *New Middle East* (London), no. 3 (December 1968), pp. 16–20.

Laqueur, Walter Z., 'The Appeal of Communism in the Middle East', *The Middle East Journal*, vol. 9, no. 1 (Winter 1955), pp. 17–27.

Laqueor, Walter Z., 'The National Bourgeoisie: A Soviet Dilemma in the Middle East', *International Affairs* (London), vol. 35, no. 3 (July 1959), pp. 324–31.

Larkin, Bruce D., 'China and the Third World', *Current History*, vol. 69, no. 408 (September 1965), pp. 75–9.

Lenczowski, George, 'Arab Bloc Realignment', *Current History*, vol. 53, no. 316 (December 1967), pp. 346–51.

Levy, Walter, J., 'Oil Power', *Foreign Affairs*, vol. 49, no. 4 (July 1971), pp. 652–68.

Lewis, Bernard, 'Communism and Islam', *International Affairs*, vol. 30, no. 1 (January 1954), pp. 1–12.

Lieberthal, Kenneth, 'The Foreign Policy Debate in Peking as seen through Allegorical Articles 1973–1976', *China Quarterly*, no. 71 (September 1977), pp. 528–54.

Liebesny, Herbert J., 'Administrative and Legal Development in Arabia: The Persian Gulf Principalities', *The Middle East Journal*, vol. 10, no. 1 (Winter 1956), pp. 33–42.

Liebesny, Herbert J., 'British Jurisdiction in the States of the Persian Gulf', *The Middle East Journal*, vol. 2, no. 1 (July 1949), pp. 330–2.

Lienhart, Peter A., 'The Authority of Shaykhs in the Gulf: An Essay in Nineteenth Century History', in Serjeant, R.B. and Bidwell, R.L., eds., *Arabian Studies*, 11, London, (1975), pp. 61–75.

Loftus, John A., 'Middle East Oil: The Pattern of Control?', *The Middle East Journal*, vol. 2, no. 1 (January 1948), pp. 17–32.

Longrigg, S.H., 'The Decline of the West in the Middle East: An Alternative View', *International Affairs*, vol. 29, no. 3 (July 1953), pp. 326–39.

Lowenthal, Richard, 'Russia, the One-Party System and the Third World', *Survey*, no. 58 (January 1966), pp. 41–58.

El-Iozi, Salim, 'Oman: Problems On All Sides', *Events* (October 15, 1976), pp. 13–16.

Luttwak, Edward, 'The Containment of Russia: China's New Policy', *New Middle East* (London), nos. 42–3 (March–April 1972), pp. 49–50.

Mabro, Robert and Elizabeth Monroe, 'Arab Wealth from Oil: Problems of its Investment', *International Affairs* (London), vol. 50, no. 1 (January 1974), pp. 15–27.

MacFarquhar, Roderick, 'The Chinese Model and the Underdeveloped World', *International Affairs* (London), vol. 39, no. 3 (July 1963), pp. 372–85.

Macintyre, Ronald R., 'The Palestine Liberation Organization: Tactics, Strategies and Options Towards the Geneva Conference', *Journal of Palestine Studies*, vol. 4, no. 4 (Summer 1975), pp. 65–89.

Magnus, Ralph, H., 'Middle East Oil', *Current History*, vol. 68, no. 402 (February 1975), pp. 49–53.

Maksud, Klufis, 'karar 'idanat al-sahiuniya bi al-'unsuriya: madha ya'ni 'ala al-sa'id al-'amali?' (Resolution Condemning Zionism of Racism: What Does it Mean Practically?), *Shu'un filistiniya* (Palestine Affairs), no. 52 (December 1975), pp. 5–11.

El-Mallakh, Regaei, 'The Challenge of Affluence: Abu Dhabi', *The Middle East Journal*, vol. 24, no. 2 (Spring 1970), pp. 135–45.

El-Mallakh, Regaei, 'Economic Development Through Co-operation: The Kuwait Fund', *The Middle East Journal*, vol. 18, no. 4 (Autumn 1964), pp. 405–20.

El-Mallakh, Regaei, 'Economic Requirements for Developments, Oman', *The Middle East Journal*, vol. 26, no. 3 (Autumn 1972), pp. 415–27.

El-Mallakh, Regaei, 'Kuwait's Economic Development and her Foreign Aid Programmes', *World Today*, vol. 22, no. 1 (January 1966), pp. 13–22.

El-Mallakh, Regaei, 'Oil and the OPEC Members', *Current History*, vol. 69, no. 407 (July–August 1975), pp. 6–9.

Mallison, Jr. W. T. and Mallison, S. V., 'The Juridical Characteristics of the Palestine Resistance: An Appraisal in International Law', *Journal of Palestine Studies*, vol. 2, no. 2 (Winter 1973), pp. 49–78.

March, James, G., 'An Introduction to the Theory and Measurement of Influence', *American Political Science Review*, vol. 49, no. 2 (June 1955), pp. 431–51.

Masannat, G. A., 'Sino-Arab Relations', *Asian Survey*, vol. 6, no. 5 (April 1966), pp. 216–25.

Mates, Leo, 'Non-Alignment and the Great Powers', *Foreign Affairs*, vol. 48, no. 3 (April 1970), pp. 525–36.

Mazrui, Ali A., 'Consent, Colonialism and Sovereignty', *Political Studies*, vol. 11, no. 1 (February 1963), pp. 36–55.

Medzin, Meron, 'Israel and China, A Missed Opportunity', *Weiner Library Bulletin*, vol. 25, nos. 1, 2 (1971), pp. 33–42.

Bibliography

Medzin, Meron, 'Reflections on Israel's Asian Policy', *Midstream*, vol. 18, no. 6 (June–July 1972), pp. 25–35.

Medzini, R., 'China and the Palestinians – A Developing Relationship?', *New Middle East*, no. 32 (May 1971), pp. 34–40.

Medzini, R., 'Chinese Penetration in the Middle East', *New Outlook*, vol. 6, no. 9 (November–December 1973), pp. 16–28.

Medzini, R., 'Peking and the Middle East: Ideology vs. Expediency', *Issues and Studies*, vol. 7, no. 2 (1971), pp. 24–9.

Melamid, Alexander, 'Political Geography of Trucial Oman and Qatar', *Geographical Review*, no. 20 (1953), pp. 194–206.

Millar, T. B., 'Soviet Policies South and East of Suez', *Foreign Affairs*, vol. 49, no. 1 (October 1970), pp. 70–80.

Moes, John E. and Bottomley, Anthony, 'Wage Rate Determination with Limited Supplies of Labour in Developing Countries', *Journal of Development Studies*, vol. 4, no. 3 (April 1968), pp. 380–5.

Monroe, Elizabeth, 'British Bases in the Middle East: Assets or Liabilities?', *International Affairs* (London), vol. 42, no. 1 (January 1966), pp. 24–34.

Monroe, Elizabeth, 'British Interests in the Middle East', *The Middle East Journal*, vol. 2, no. 2 (April 1948), pp. 129–46.

Monroe, Elizabeth, 'Kuwait and Aden: A contrast in British Policies', *The Middle East Journal*, vol. 18, no. 1 (Winter 1964), pp. 63–74.

Monroe, Elizabeth, 'The Shaikhdom of Kuwait', *International Affairs* (London), vol. 30, no. 3 (July 1954), pp. 271–84.

Mosley, Philip, 'The Kremlin and the Third World', *Foreign Affairs*, vol. 46, no. 1 (October 1967), pp. 64–77.

My telka, Lynn Krieger, 'The Salience of Gains in Third-World Integrative Systems', *World Politics*, vol. 25, no. 2 (January 1973), pp. 236–50.

Nahumi, Mordechai, 'China and Israel', *New Outlook*, vol. 9, no. 6 (July–August 1966), pp. 40–8.

Nelson, Joan, 'The Urban Poor: Disruption or Political Integration in Third World Cities?', *World Politics*, vol. 22, no. 3 (April 1970), pp. 393–414.

Nikolayev, L. and Mikhailov, Y., 'China's Foreign Economic Policy', *International Affairs* (Moscow), (September 1973), pp. 44–51.

Obminsky, E., 'International Monopolies in the Third World', *International Affairs* (Moscow), (September 1975), pp. 55–63.

O'Leary, Greg, 'Chinese Foreign Policy – From "Anti-Imperialism" to "Anti-Hegemonism"', in Bill Brugger, ed., *China: The Impact of the Cultural Revolution* (London), (1978), pp. 203–52.

Owen, R. P., 'The British Withdrawal From the Persian Gulf', *World Today*, vol. 28, no. 2 (February 1972), pp. 75–81.

Owen, R. P., 'Development in the Sultanate of Muscat and Oman', *World Today*, vol. 26, no. 9 (September 1970), pp. 379–82.

404

Owen, R. P., 'Rebellion in Dhofar: A Threat to Western Interests in the Gulf', *World Today*, vol. 29, no. 6 (June 1973), pp. 266–72.

Pennar, Joan, 'The Arabs, Marxism and Moscow: An Historical Survey', *The Middle East Journal*, vol. 22, no. 4 (Autumn 1968), pp. 433–47.

Penrose, Edith, 'Vertical Integration with Joint Control Raw-Material Production of Crude Oil in the Middle East', *Journal of Development Studies*, vol. 1, no. 3 (April 1965), pp. 251–68.

Peretz, Don, 'Arab Palestine: Phoenix or Phantom?', *Foreign Affairs*, vol. 48, no. 2 (January 1970), pp. 322–33.

Peterson, John E., 'The Revival of the Ibadi Imamate in Oman and the threat to Muscat 1913–1920', *Arabian Studies* III, (London 1976), pp. 165–87.

Petrov, Y., 'Industrialisation Problems of the Developing States', *International Affairs* (Moscow), (September 1975), pp. 64–71.

Preston, Lee E., 'Market Control in Developing Economics', *Journal of Development Studies*, vol. 4, no. 4 (July 1968), pp. 481–96.

Price, D. L., 'Oman: Insurgency and Development', *Conflict Studies*, no. 53 (January 1975), pp. 3–19.

Prybyla, Jan S., 'Foreign Aid: The Chinese Are Coming', *Current History*, vol. 61, no. 361 (September 1971), pp. 142–7.

Ramazani, Rouhollah, K., 'Iran's Changing Foreign Policy: A preliminary Discussion', *The Middle East Journal*, vol. 24, no. 4 (Autumn 1970), pp. 421–37.

Rhee, T., 'The Sino-Soviet Conflict and the Middle East', *New Outlook*, vol. 13, no. 7 (September 1970), pp. 20–4.

Richardson, John P., 'Arab Civilians and the October War', *Journal of Palestine Studies*, vol. 3, no. 2 (Winter 1974), pp. 122–9.

Ridker, Ronald G., 'The Economic Determinants of Discontent: An Empirical Investigation', *Journal of Development Studies*, vol. 4, no. 2 (January 1968), pp. 174–219.

Roucek, J., 'Communist China's Penetration of the Middle East', *Ukrainian Quarterly*, no. 26 (Summer 1970), pp. 149–63.

Rouleau, Eric, 'The Palestinian Quest', *Foreign Affairs*, vol. 53, no. 2 (January 1975), pp. 264–83.

Rubin, Barry, 'U.S. Policy, January–October 1973', *Journal of Palestine Studies*, vol. 3, no. 2 (Winter 1974), pp. 98–113.

Sam'o, E., 'The Arab States and China's U.N. Representation', *Middle East Forum*, vol. 48, no. 2 (Summer 1972), pp. 43–54.

Sayigh, Yusuf, 'Arab Oil Policies: Self-Interest Versus International Responsibility', *Journal of Palestine Studies*, vol. 4, no. 3 (Spring 1975), pp. 59–73.

Sayigh, Yusuf, 'Problems and Prospects of Development in the Arabian Peninsula', *International Journal of Middle East Studies*, vol. 2, no. 1 (January 1971), pp. 40–58.

Schwarz, Henry G., 'The Ts'an-K'ao Hsiao-hsi: How Well Informed Are Chinese Officials About The Outside World', *China Quarterly*, no. 27 (July–September 1966), pp. 54–83.

Seigman, Henry, 'Arab Unity and Disunity', *The Middle East Journal*, vol. 16, no. 1 (Winter 1962), pp. 48–59.

Sharabi, Hisham, 'Liberation or Settlement?', *Journal of Palestine Studies*, vol. 2, no. 2 (Winter 1973), pp. 33–48.

Sharabi, Hisham, 'The Transformation of Ideology in the Arab World', *The Middle East Journal*, vol. 19, no. 4 (Autumn 1965), pp. 471–86.

Sharif, Walid, 'Soviet Marxism and Zionism', *Journal of Palestine Studies*, vol. 6, no. 3 (Spring 1977), pp. 77–97.

Shils, Edward, 'The Concentration and Dispersion of Charisma: Their Bearing on Economic Policy in Underdeveloped Countries', *World Politics*, vol. 11, no. 1 (October 1958), pp. 1–19.

Shinn, Jr., William T., 'The National Democratic State: A Communist Programme for Less Developed Areas', *World Politics*, vol. 15, no. 3 (April 1963), pp. 377–89.

Shmelev, N.P., 'A Critique of Bourgeois Theories of Economic Development', *Journal of Development Studies*, vol. 1, no. 1 (October 1964), pp. 71–92.

Shoufani, Elias, 'Israeli Reactions to the War', *Journal of Palestine Studies*, vol. 3, no. 2 (Winter 1974), pp. 46–64.

Shwadran, Benjamin, 'Middle East Oil', *Current History*, vol. 66, no. 390 (February 1974), pp. 79–83.

Sigler, John H., 'Co-operation and Conflict in U.S.-Soviet-Chinese Relations, 1966–71: A Quantitative Analysis', *Peace Research Society*, vol. 19 (1972), pp. 107–28.

Sirc, L., 'Changes in Communist Advice to Developing Countries', *World Today*, vol. 22, no. 8 (August 1966), pp. 326–35.

Smirnov, V. and Matyukhin, I., 'USSR and The Arab East', *International Affairs* (Moscow), no. 9 (September 1972), pp. 83–7.

Standish, J.F., 'British Maritime Policy in the Persian Gulf', *Middle East Studies*, vol. 3, no. 4 (July 1967), pp. 324–54.

Stevens, Georgiana G., 'Arab Neutralism and Bandung', *The Middle East Journal*, vol. 2, no. 2 (Spring 1957), pp. 139–52.

Stevens, Harley, C., 'Some Reflections on the First Arab Petroleum Congress', *The Middle East Journal*, vol. 13, no. 2 (Spring 1959), pp. 273–80.

Suo, Ibrahim, 'Western Europe and the October War', *Journal of Palestine Studies*, vol. 3, no. 2 (Winter 1974), pp. 65–83.

Thoman, Roy E., 'Iraq and the Persian Gulf Region', *Current History*, vol. 64, no. 377 (January 1973), pp. 21–5.

Thoman, Roy E., 'The Persian Gulf Region', *Current History*, vol. 60, no. 353 (January 1971), pp. 38–45.

Thomas, Bertram, 'Arab Rule Under the Al Bu Sa'id Dynasty of Oman, 1741-1937', *Proceedings of the British Academy*, vol. 24 (January 1938), pp. 2-29.

Thomas, Bertram, 'The Musanadam Peninsula and its People the Shihuh', *Journal of the Central Asian Society*, vol. 15 (1928), pp. 1-16.

Thweat, William O., 'Economic Development with Limited Supplies of Labour', *Journal of Developing Areas*, vol. 2, no. 3 (April 1968), pp. 343-62.

Todaro, Michael P., 'A Theoretical Note on Labour As An "Inferior" Factor in Less Developed Countries', *The Journal of Development Studies*, vol. 5, no. 4 (July 1969), pp. 252-9.

Ṭrabulsī, Fawaz, 'The Liberation of Dhufar', *Merip Report*, no. 6, (January 1972).

Tretiak, Daniel, 'The Canton Fair: An Academic Perspective', *China Quarterly*, no. 56 (October–November 1973), pp. 740-8.

Tschen Shen-chen, 'A-la-Po Kuo chia shih yu tou cheng ti ch'ien ch'ien hou hou' (On the Recent Oil Strife of the Arab States), *Hsuch Hsi i P'i P'an*, February (1975), pp. 85-91.

Tsou, Tang and Halperin, Morton H., 'Maoism at Home and Abroad', *Problems of Communism*, vol. 14 (July–August 1965), pp. 1-12.

Tueni, Ghassan, 'After October: Military Conflict and Political Change in the Middle East', *Journal of Palestine Studies*, vol. 3, no. 4 (Summer 1974), pp. 114-30.

Tu'ma, George, 'al-ḳaḍiya al-filisṭiniya wa'l-ṣira' al-'arabi al-isra'ili fi'l-'umam al-mutaḥida' (The Palestinian Problem and the Arab-Israeli Conflict in the United Nations), *Shu'un filisṭiniya* (Palestine Affairs), vol. 41, no. 42 (June–July 1975), pp. 119-38.

Twitchett, Kenneth, 'Colonialism: An Attempt at Understanding Imperial, Colonial and Neo-Colonial Relationship', *Political Studies*, vol. 13, no. 3 (October 1965), pp. 300-23.

Ukraintsev, M., 'Maoist Ideology and Peking's Foreign Policy', *International Affairs* (Moscow), (May 1975), pp. 32-44.

Valkenier, Elisabeth K., 'New Trends in Soviet Economic Relations with the Third World', *World Politics*, vol. 22, no. 3 (April 1970), pp. 415-32.

Valkenier, Elisabeth K., 'Sino-Soviet Rivalry in the Third World', *Current History*, vol. 57, no. 338 (October 1969), pp. 201-6.

Van Ness, Peter, 'China and the Third World', *Current History*, vol. 67, no. 397 (September 1974), pp. 106-9.

Van Ness, Peter, 'Mao Tse-tung and Revolutionary "Self-Reliance"', *Problem of Communism*, vol. 20 (January–April 1971), pp. 68-71.

Volsky, D., 'Middle East Schemes of Peking', *New Times* (Moscow), no. 3 (22 January 1969), pp. 15-16.

Volsky, D., 'Soviet-American Relations and the Third World', *New Times* (Moscow), no. 36 (1973), pp. 4-6.

Vostokov, D., 'The Foreign Policy of the People's Republic of China Since the 9th Congress of the CCP', *International Affairs* (Moscow), (January 1972), pp. 23–32.

Ward, Richard J., 'The Long-Run Employment Prospect for Middle East Labour', *The Middle East Journal*, vol. 24, no. 2 (Spring 1970), pp. 147–62.

Watt, D. C., 'The Arabs, The Heath Government and the Future of the Gulf', *New Middle East* (London), no. 30 (March 1971), pp. 25–7.

Watt, D. C., 'Britain and the Future of the Persian Gulf', *World Today*, vol. 20, no. 2 (November 1964), pp. 488–96.

Watt, D. C., 'Old Promises and New Dangers: The Gulf on the Eve of British Withdrawal', *New Middle East* (London), no. 39 (December 1971), pp. 8–9.

Watt, D. C., 'The Persian Gulf – Cradle of Conflict?', *Problems of Communism*, vol. 21 (May–June 1972), pp. 32–40.

Watt, D. C., 'The Soviet Presence in the Mediterranean: A Study in the Application of Political Influence', *New Middle East* (London), no. 1 (October 1968), pp. 14–19.

Wells, Michael J., 'New Concessions and New Strikes Spotlight the Arab Gulf', *World Petroleum*, vol. 36, no. 7 (July 1965), pp. 22–7.

Wells, Michael J., 'Oil Production Brings Oman to an Uncertain Future', *World Petroleum*, vol. 38, no. 7 (July 1967), pp. 22–4.

Wheeler, Geoffrey, 'Russia and the Arabs', *World Today*, vol. 17, no. 7 (July 1961), pp. 317–18.

Wheeler, Geoffrey, 'Russia and the Middle East', *International Affairs*, vol. 35, no. 3 (July 1959), pp. 295–304.

Wheeler, Geoffrey, 'Soviet and Chinese Policies in the Middle East', *World Today*, vol. 22, no. 2 (January 1966), pp. 64–78.

Whetter, Lawrence J., 'Changing Soviet Attitudes Towards Arab Radical Movements', *New Middle East* (London), no. 18 (March 1970), pp. 20–7.

Whiting, Allen S., *et al.*, 'China's New Diplomacy: A Symposium 1, 2', *Problems of Communism*, vol. 20 (November–December 1971), pp. 1–32, vol. 21 (January–February 1972), pp. 48–70.

Wilkinson, J. C., 'Bio-Bibliographical Background to the Crisis Period in the Ibadi Imamate of Oman', in Serjeant, R. B. and Bidwell, R. L., *Arabian Studies* 3, (London 1976), pp. 137–64.

Wilkinson, J. C., 'The Oman Question: The Background to the Political Geography of South East Arabia', *Geographical Society*, vol. 137, no. 3 (September 1971), pp. 361–71.

Williams, Maurice, 'The Aid Programmes of the OPEC Countries', *Foreign Affairs*, vol. 54, no. 2 (January 1976), pp. 308–24.

Windsor, Philip, 'The Middle East and the World Balance', *World Today*, vol. 23, no. 7 (July 1967), pp. 279–85.

Woodhouse, Edward J., 'Re-visioning the Future of the Third World:

An Ecological Perspective of Development', *World Politics*, vol. 25, no. 1 (October 1972), pp. 1–33.

Wooley, C. M., and Tarnpoll, M., 'Why developing Nations Buy Technical Services', *World Petroleum*, vol. 37, no. 13 (December 1966), pp. 42–8.

Wright, Denis, 'The Changed Balance of Power in the Persian Gulf', *Asian Affairs*, vol. 60, no. 3 (October 1973), pp. 255–62.

Wu, Yuan-li, 'China's Energy Resources and Prospects', *Current History*, vol. 69, no. 407 (July–August 1975), pp. 25–7.

Yahuda, Michael B., 'Chinese Foreign Policy After 1963: The Maoist Phases', *China Quarterly*, no. 36 (October–December 1968), pp. 93–113.

Yodfat, A., 'The USSR and the Arab Communist Parties', *New Middle East* (London), no. 32 (May 1971), pp. 29–33.

Zabih, Sepehr, 'Change and Continuity in Iran's Foreign Policy in Modern Times', *World Politics*, vol. 23, no. 3 (April 1971), pp. 522–43.

Zyzniewski, Stanley J., 'The Soviet Bloc and the Underdeveloped Countries: Some Economic Factors', *World Politics*, vol. 11, no. 3 (April 1959), pp. 378–98.

Books

Abdul Wahab, Abdul Muhs'in, *al-naft bayna al syasa wa al-iḵtiṣad* (Oil Between Politics and Economics), Kuwait, n.d.

*Abdul Raḥmān, 'As'ad, ed., *al-ḥarab al-'arabiya al-isra'iliya al-rabi'a: waka'a wa tafa'ulat* (The Fourth Arab-Israeli War), Beirut, 1974.

Abū Djaber, Kamal S., *The Arab Ba'th Socialist Party: History, Ideology and Organisation*, New York, 1966.

Afifi, Mohammed el-Hadi, *The Arabs and the United Nations*, London, 1964.

Agwani, M. S., *Communism in the Arab East*, London, 1969.

Ali, Sheikh Rustrum, *Saudi Arabia and Oil Diplomacy*, New York, 1976.

Allen, George C. and Domithorne, Audrey, G., *Western Enterprise in Far Eastern Economic Development*, London, 1954.

Allfree, P. S., *Warlords of Oman*, London, 1967.

Allūsh, Nadjī, ed., *al-masyra ila filistin* (March to Palestine), Beirut, 1964.

*Allūsh, Nadjī, ed., *munakashat ḥawal al-thawra al-filistiniya* (Discussions on the Palestinian Revolution), Beirut, 1970.

Amin, Abdul Amir, *British Interests in the Persian Gulf*, Leiden, 1967.

Amirie, Abbas, ed., *The Persian Gulf and Indian Ocean in International Politics*, Tehran, 1975.

Anon., *The Gulf: Implications for British Withdrawal*, Washington D.C., 1969.

Anon., *al-khalidj al-'arabi fi muwadjahat al-tahaddiyat* (Arabian Gulf in Facing Challenges), Kuwait, 1972.

Anon., *Insurrection in Oman*, n.p., n.d.

Anon., *al-mukawama al-filistiniya: al-wā'ak wā al-tawaka'at* (Palestinian Resistance: Reality and Expectations), Beirut, 1971.

Anon., *mu'tamar al-'ahzeb al-shuyu'iya al-'umaliya al-'alami, Moscow 1969* (Communist Workers Conference), Prague, 1969.

Anthony, John Duke, *Arab States of the Lower Gulf: People, Politics, Petroleum*, Washington, D.C., 1975.

Bartke, Wolfgang, *China's Economic Aid*, New York, 1975.

Bartke, Wolfgang, *Oil in the People's Republic of China: Industry, Structure, Production, Exports*, Institute of Asian Affairs, Hamburg, 1977.

Baylis, John, Boothe, Ken, Garnett, John and Williams, Paul, *Contemporary Strategy: Theories and Policies*, London, 1975.

Becker, Abraham S., Hansen, B. and Kerr, Malcolm H., *The Economics and Politics of the Middle East*, New York, 1975.

Bell, David V. J., *Power, Influence and Authority: An Essay in Political Linguistics*, Oxford, 1975.

Belling, Willard A., ed., *The Middle East Quest for an American Policy*, New York, 1973.

Belling, Willard A., ed., *Pan-Arabism and Labour*, Cambridge, Mass., 1960.

Bent, M. V. A., *Southern Arabia*, London, 1900.

Bidwell, Robin, ed., *The Affairs of Kuwait*, London, 1971, 4 vols.

Binder, Leonard, *Factors Influencing Iran's International Role*, Rand Monograph, (October) 1969.

Binder, Leonard, *The Ideological Revolution in the Middle East*, New York, 1964.

Black, Cyril E. and Thornton, Thomas P., eds., *Communism and Revolution: The Strategic Uses of Political Violence*, Princeton, 1964.

Blandford, Linda, *Oil Sheikhs*, London, 1976.

Bowie, Robert R. and Fairbank, John K., *Communist China 1955–59: Policy Documents With Analysis*, Cambridge, Mass., 1971.

Brecher, Michael, *Decisions in Israel's Foreign Policy*, London, 1974.

*Brecher, Michael, *Israel, The Korean War and China: Images, Decisions and Consequences*, Jerusalem, 1974.

Buchan, Alastair, ed., *China and the Peace of Asia*, London, 1965.

Burrell, R. M., *The Persian Gulf*, New York, 1972.

Busch, Briton Cooper, *Britain and the Persian Gulf 1894–1914*, Berkeley and Los Angeles, 1967.

Butwell, Richard, ed., *Foreign Policy and the Developing Nations*, Lexington, 1969.

Buzwak, Abdul Rahman, *et al.*, *'uman fi al-mahafil al-dwaliya* (Oman in the International Arena), Cairo, 1977.

Chai, Winberg, ed., *The Foreign Relations of the People's Republic of China*, New York, 1972.

Cheng, Chu-yuan, *China's Petroleum Industry: Output, Growth and Export Potential*, New York, 1976.

*Chevalier, Jean-Marie, *The New Oil Stakes* (trans. Ian Rock), London, 1975.

Chibwe, E. C., *Arab Dollars for Africa*, London, 1976.

Chinese Ministry of Information, Comp., *China Handbook, 1937–1945, A Comprehensive Survey of Major Developments in China in Eight Years of War*, New York, 1947, reprinted 1975.

Chisholm, A. H. T., *The First Kuwait Oil Concession: A Record of the Negotiations for the 1934 Agreement*, London, 1975.

*Chubin, Shahram and Zabih, Sepehr, *The Foreign Relations of Iran: A Developing State in a Zone of Great Power Conflict*, Berkeley, 1974.

Churba, Joseph, *Conflict and Tension Among the States of the Persian Gulf: Oman and South Arabia*, Maxwell Airforce Base, Ala., Air University Documentary Research Study (AV – 204 – 71 – 1PD), December 1971.

*Cooper, John Franklin, *China's Foreign Aid: An Instrument of Peking's Foreign Policy*, Mass., 1976.

Cremeans, Charles D., *The Arabs and the World: Nasser's Arab Nationalist Policy*, New York, 1963.

Czudnowski, Moshe M. and Landau, Jacob M., *The Israeli Communist Party and the Election of the Fifth Knesset, 1961*, Stanford, 1965.

Dagan, Avigdor, *Moscow and Jerusalem*, New York, 1970.

Davis, Uri, Mack, Andrew and Yuval, Nina, eds., *Israel and the Palestinians*, London, 1975.

Demir, Soliman, *The Kuwait Fund and the Political Economy of the Arab Regional Development*, New York, 1976.

Dickson, H. R. P., *The Arab of the Desert: A Glimpse into the Bedouin Life in Kuwait and Sau'di Arabia*, London, 1949.

Dickson, H. R. P., *Kuwait and her Neighbours*, London, 1968.

Ducan, Raymond, W., ed., *Soviet Policy Toward Developing Countries*, Waltham, Mass., 1970.

*Dūkas, Martha, *'azmat al-kuwait: al-'alakat al-kuwaitiya al-'irakiya, 1961–1963* (Kuwait Crisis: Kuwait-Iraqi Relations, 1961–1963), Beirut, 1973.

Eid, Nimr, *The Legal Aspects of Marketing Behaviour in Lebanon and Kuwait*, Beirut, 1970.

Ekstein, Alexander, *China's Economic Revolution*, Cambridge, 1977.

Ekstein, Alexander, *Communist China's Economic Growth and Foreign Trade*, New York, 1966.

Ekstein, Alexander, Galenson, Walter and Liu, Ta-chung, eds., *Economic Trends in Communist China*, New York, 1968.

Evron, Yair, *The Middle East: Nations, Super-Powers and Wars*, London, 1973.

Fallon, Nicholas, *Middle East Oil Money and its Future Expenditure*, London, 1975.

Fawzi, Ahmed, *betrol wa dukhan: kasim wa al Kuwait* (Oil and Smoke: Kassim and Kuwait), Cairo, 1961.

Fayaz, Ali, *harb al-sha'b fi 'uman: wa yantasir al-hufat* (People's War in Oman: The Barefooted Will Triumph), Beirut, 1975.

Field, Michael, *A Hundred Million Dollars a Day*, London, 1975.

Fiennes, Ranulf, *Where Soldiers Fear to Tread*, London, 1975.

Fisher, S. N., ed., *The Military in the Middle East: Problems in Society and Government*, New York, 1963.

Fisher, S. N., ed., *Social Forces in the Middle East*, New York, 1968.

Frankel, Joseph, *National Interest*, London, 1970.

Freedman, Robert O., *Economic Warfare in the Soviet Bloc: A Study of Soviet Economic Pressure Against Yugoslavia, Albania and Communist China*, New York, 1970.

Freeth, Zahra, *A New Look at Kuwait*, London, 1972.

German Association for East Asian Studies, ed., *China in the Seventies*, Wiesbaden, 1975.

Giritli, Ismet, *Super-Powers in the Middle East*, Istanbul, 1972.

Golan, Galia, *Yom Kippur and After: The Soviet Union and the Middle East Crisis*, Cambridge, 1977.

Gom'aa, Ahmad, M., *The Foundations of the League of Arab States: Wartime Diplomacy and Inter-Arab Politics, 1941–1945*, London, 1977.

Grunwald, K. and Ronall, J.D., *Industrialisation in the Middle East*, New York, 1960.

Haddad, George, *Revolutions and Military Rule in the Middle East: The Arab States*, 11, New York, 1971.

Haim, S. G., ed., *Arab Nationalism: An Anthology*, Berkeley, 1962.

Halliday, F., *Arabia Without Sultans*, London, 1974.

Halliday, F., *Mercenaries: 'Counter-Insurgency' in the Gulf*, London, 1977.

Halpern, A.M., ed., *Policies Towards China: Views from Six Continents*, New York, 1965.

Halpern, M., *The Politics of Social Change in the Middle East and North Africa*, Princeton, 1963.

*Hamid, Rashid, ed., *mukararat al-madilis al-watani al-filistini, 1964–1974* (Resolutions of the Palestine National Assembly, 1964–1974), Beirut, 1975.

Hanna, Sami A. and Gardner, G.H., *Arab Socialism: A Documentary Survey*, Leiden, 1969.

Hanreider, Wolfram, *Comparative Foreign Policy: Theoretical Essays*, New York, 1970.

Harkabi, Yehoshafat, *Arab Strategies and Israel's Response*, New York, 1977.

*Harrison, Selig S., *China, Oil and Asia: Conflict Ahead*, New York, 1977.

Hassouna, Hussein A., *The League of Arab States and Regional Disputes: A Study of Middle East Conflicts*, New York, 1975.

Al-hasusi, Bader al-din 'Abas, *dirasat fi tarikh al-kuwait al-idjtima'i wa al-iḳtiṣadi, 1913–1961* (Studies in the Social and Economic History of Kuwait 1913–1961), Kuwait, 1972.

Al-hatrash, Futuh Abdul Mohsin, *tarikh al-'alaḳat al-syasiya al-britaniya al-kuwaitiya 1880–1921* (History of Anglo-Kuwaiti Relations 1880–1921), Kuwait, 1974.

*Ḥawātma, N., *ḥarakat al-mukawama al-filisṭiniya fi waḳi'ha al-rahin* (The Palestinian Resistance Movement at Present), Beirut, 1970.

*Ḥawātma, N., *ḥawal azmat ḥarakat al-mukawama al-filisṭiniya* (On the Crisis of the Palestinian Resistance Movement), Beirut, 1970.

Hay, Rupert, *The Persian Gulf States*, Washington, D.C., 1959.

Heikal, M. H., *Naṣir wa al-'alam* (Nasser and the World), Beirut, 1972.

Heikal, M. H., *The Road to Ramadan*, London, 1976.

Hershlag, Z. Y., *Introduction to the Modern Economic History of the Middle East*, Leiden, 1964.

Hinton, Harold C., *China's Turbulent Quest: An Analysis of China's Foreign Relations Since 1949*, Indiana, 1970.

Hirst, David, *Oil and Public Opinion in the Middle East*, London, 1966.

Hopwood, Derek, ed., *The Arabian Peninsula: Society and Politics*, London, 1972.

Hourani, Albert, *Arabic Thought in the Liberal Age, 1798–1939*, Oxford, 1962.

*Howath, Janos, *Chinese Technology Transfer to the Third World: A Grants Economy Analysis*, New York, 1976.

Hsiao, Gene T., *The Foreign Trade of China: Policy, Law and Practices*, University of California, 1977.

Hsiung, James Chieh, *Law and Policy in China's Foreign Relations: A Study of Attitudes and Practice*, New York, 1972.

Hsiung, James Chieh, ed., *The Logic of Maoism: Critique and Explication*, New York, 1974.

Hsueh, Chun-tu, ed., *Dimensions of China's Foreign Relations*, New York, 1977.

Hudson, Michael, C., *Arab Politics: The Search for Legitimacy*, New Haven, 1977.

Hurewitz, J. C., *Middle East Politics: The Military Dimension*, London, 1969.

Al-ibrahim, Hassan Ali, *al-kuwait: dirasa siyasiya* (Kuwait: A Political Study), Beirut, 1972.

International Bank for Reconstruction and Development, *The Economic Development of Kuwait*, Baltimore, 1965.

Iranian Student Association, *On the Alliance of the October League (M-L) with the Shah of Iran*, Houston and Berkeley, n.d., n.p.

Ismael, Tarek Y., *The Arab Left*, Syracuse, 1976.

Ismael, Tarek Y., ed., *The Middle East in World Politics: A Study in Contemporary International Relations*, Syracuse, 1974.

Al-Jahani, Sa'id Ahmed, *kunto fi dhofar: mushahadat fi arḍ al-thawra* (I Was in Dhofar: Observations in the Land of Revolution), Beirut, 1974.

Al-Jasim, Nadjah A., *al-taṭawur al-siyaṣi wa as-iḵtiṣadi lil-kuwait, 1914–1939* (The Political and Economic Development of Kuwait, 1914–1939), Cairo, 1973.

Johnson, Chalmers, *Autopsy on People's War*, Berkeley, 1973.

Johnson, J.J., ed., *The Role of the Military in Underdeveloped Countries*, Princeton, 1962.

Joshua, W. and Gilbert, Stephen P., *Arms for the Third World: Soviet Military Aid Diplomacy*, Baltimore, 1970.

*Kadi, Leila S., *Arab Summit Conferences and the Palestine Problem, 1936-1950 and 1964-1966*, Beirut, 1966.

*Kadi, Leila S., *Basic Political Documents of the Armed Palestinian Resistance Movement*, Beirut, 1969.

*Kahin, George McTurnan, *Asian-African Conference, Bandung, Indonesia. April 1955*, Washington, 1956.

Kantsky, John H., ed., *Political Change in Underdeveloped Countries: Nationalism and Communism*, New York, 1962.

Karpat, Kemal H., *Political and Social Thought in Contemporary Middle East*, London, 1968.

Kaushik, Devendra, *China and the Third World*, New Delhi, 1975.

Kay, Geoffrey, *Development and Underdevelopment: A Marxist Analysis*, London, 1975.

*Kazziha, Walid, *Revolutionary Transformation in the Arab World: Habash and his Comrades From Nationalism to Marxism*, London, 1975.

Kelly, J. B., *Britain and the Persian Gulf, 1795-1880*, Oxford, 1968.

Kelly, J. B., *Eastern Arabian Frontiers*, London, 1964.

Kelly, J. B., *Sultanate and Imamate of Oman*, Oxford, 1959.

Khadduri, Jill and Walid, Khalidi, eds., *Palestine and the Arab-Israeli Conflict*, Beirut, 1974.

Khadduri, Madjid, *Political Trends in the Arab World: The Role of Ideas and Ideals in Politics*, Baltimore, 1970.

Khadduri, Madjid, *Republican Iraq: A Study in the Iraqi Politics Since the Revolution of 1958*, London, 1969.

Khalil Mohammed, *The Arab States and the Arab League: A Documentary Record*, 2 vols., Beirut, 1962.

*Khalili, J. E., *Communist China's Interaction with the Arab National-ists Since the Bandung Conference*, New York, 1970.

Khouri, Fred J., *The Arab-Israeli Dilemma*, Syracuse, 1968.

Kiernan, Thomas, *Yasir 'Arafat, the Man and the Myth*, London, 1975.

King, R. and Stevens, J. H., *A Bibliography of Oman, 1900-1970*, London, 1973.

Klieman, Aaron S., *Soviet Russia and the Middle East*, Baltimore, 1970.

Korany, Bahgat, *Social Change and International Behaviour: Toward a Theory of Foreign Policy-Making in the Third World*, Leiden, 1976.

Landau, Jacob, *The Arabs in Israel: A Political Study*, Oxford, 1969.

Landen, Robert Geran, *Oman Since 1856, Disruptive Modernisation in a Traditional Arab Society*, Princeton, 1967.

Landis, Lincoln, *Politics and Oil: Moscow in the Middle East*, New York, 1973.

Laqueur, Walter, Z., *Communism and Nationalism in the Middle East*, London, 1956.

Laqueur, Walter Z., *Confrontation: The Middle East War and World Politics*, London, 1974.

Laqueur, Walter Z., ed., *The Middle East in Transition*, London, 1958.

Laqueur, Walter Z., ed., *The Soviet Union and the Middle East*, New York, 1959.

Laqueur, Walter Z., ed., *The Struggle for the Middle East: The Soviet Union in the Mediterranean, 1958-1968*, London, 1969.

Larkin, Bruce, *China and Africa 1949-1970: The Foreign Policy of the People's Republic of China*, Berkeley, 1971.

Lederer, Ivo J. and Vucinich, Wayne S., *The Soviet Union and the Middle East*, Stanford, 1973.

Lenczowski, George, *Soviet Advances in the Middle East*, Washington D.C., 1971.

Lerner, D., *The Passing of Traditional Society: Modernising the Middle East*, London, 1958.

Lewin, Pauline, *The Foreign Trade of Communist China: Its Impact on the Free World*, New York, 1964.

Liu, Jung-chao, *China's Fertilizer Economy*, Edinburgh, 1971.

Longrigg, S. H., *Oil in the Middle East: Its Discovery and Development*, Oxford, 1968.

Lorimer, J. G., *Gazettes of the Persian Gulf, Oman and Central Arabia*, 5 vols., London, 1970.

Lutfi, Ashraf, *OPEC Oil*, Beirut, 1968.

Mabro, Robert and Monroe, Elizabeth, *Oil Producers and Consumers: Conflict or Co-operation*, New York, 1974.

MacDonald, Robert W., *The League of Arab States: A Study in the Dynamics of Regional Organization*, Princeton, 1965.

McLane, Charles B., *Soviet Middle East Relations*, vol. 1, London, 1973.

Macridis, R. C., ed., *Foreign Policy in World Politics*, New Jersey, 1972.

Bibliography

Mah, Feng-hwa, *The Foreign Trade of Mainland China*, Edinburgh, 1972.

El-Mallakh, Regaei, *Economic Development and Regional Co-operation: Kuwait*, Chicago, 1968.

Mao Tse-tung, *Selected Works of Mao Tse-tung*, 3 vols. Foreign Language Press, Peking, 1967.

Maoz, M., *Soviet and Chinese Relations with the Palestinian Guerilla Organizations*, Jerusalem, 1974.

Marlowe, John, *The Persian Gulf in the Twentieth Century*, New York, 1972.

Mashvenieradze, Vladimir, *Anti-Communism Today*, Moscow, 1974.

Mason, Edward, *Foreign Aid and Foreign Policy*, New York, 1964.

Mikdashi, Zuhayr, *A Financial Analysis of Middle Eastern Oil Concessions, 1901–1965*, New York, 1966.

Monroe, Elizabeth, *The Changing Balance of Power in the Persian Gulf*, New York, 1972.

Morris, James, *Sultan in Oman*, London, 1957.

Mozinggo, David, *China's Foreign Policy and the Cultural Revolution*, New York, 1970.

Mueller, Kurt, *The Foreign Aid Programme of the Soviet Bloc and Communist China*, New York, 1967.

*munazamat al-ishtrakiyin al-lubnaniyin, *limadha munazamat al-ishtrakiyin al-lubnaniyin? (harakat al-kawmiyin al-'arab min al-fashiya ila al-nasiriya)* (Why the Lebanese Socialist Organization? Arab Nationalist Movement from Fascism to Nasserism), Beirut, 1970.

munazzamat mudjahidi al-sha'b al-irani, *ihtizar imbratoriat al-dular wa mukhtetat al-imbryaliya al-amrikiya*, n.p., 1974.

munazzamat mudjahidi al-sha'b al-irani, *watha'ik siyasiya-'askariya*, (Military-Documents), n.p., n.d.

Musa, Shahada, *'alakat isra'il ma'a duwal al-'alam, 1967–1970* (Israeli International Relations, 1967–1970), Beirut, 1971.

Nabil, Zakaria, *Bu'rat al-khatar fi al-khalidj al-'arabi* (Centre of Danger in the Arabian Gulf), Cairo, 1974.

Nahas, Dunia, *The Israeli Communist Party*, London, 1976.

Nakhleh, Emile A., *Arab-American Relations in the Persian Gulf*, Washington D.C., 1975.

Nasser-Eddine, Mon'im, *Arab-Chinese Relations, 1950–1971, With Special Emphasis on Egyptian-Chinese Relations*, Beirut, n.d.

Neilan, Edward and Smith, Charles R., *The Future of the China Market: Prospects for Sino-American Trade*, Stanford, 1975.

*Neuhauser, Charles, *Third World Politics, China and the Afro-Asian People's Solidarity Organization, 1957–1967*, Cambridge, Mass., 1968.

Newens, Stan, ed., *Third World: Change or Chaos?* London, 1977.

North, Robert, C., *The Foreign Relations of China*, Belmont, 1969.

Northege, F. S., ed., *The Foreign Policies of the Powers*, London, 1968.

Al-Nufisi, Abdullah Fahad, *tathmin al-ṣira' fi Dhofar* (Evaluation of the Struggle in Dhofar), n.p., n.d.

Nurske, Ragner, *Problems of Capital Formation in Underdeveloped Countries*, Oxford, 1953.

Nuseibeh, Hazem Zaki, *The Ideas of Arab Nationalism*, New York, 1956.

Odell, Peter R., *Oil and World Power: Background to the Oil Crisis*, London, 4th edition, 1975.

Ogunsanwo, Alba, *China's Policy in Africa, 1958-1971*, Cambridge, 1974.

Ojha, Ishwar C., *Chinese Foreign Policy in an Age of Transition: the Diplomacy of Cultural Despair*, Boston, 1969.

O'Shea, Raymond, *The Sand Kings of Oman*, London, 1947.

Page, Stephen, *The USSR and Arabia: The Development of Soviet Policies and Attitudes Towards the Countries of the Arabian Peninsula*, London, 1971.

Paust, Jordan J. and Blaustein, Albert P., *The Arab Oil Weapon*, New York, 1977.

Pennar, Joan, *The USSR and the Arabs: The Ideological Dimension, 1917-1972*, London, 1973.

Penrose, Edith, *The Growth of Firms: Middle East Oil and other Essays*, London, 1971.

Penrose, Edith, *The Large International Firms in Developing Countries: The International Petroleum Industry*, London, 1968.

Phillips, Wendell, *Oman: A History*, London, 1971.

Phillips, Wendell, *Unknown Oman*, London, 1971.

Pouyan, A.P., *dururat al-kifah al-musalah wa dahd nazariyat al-baka'* (The Necessity of Armed Struggle and the Refutation of the Theory of Survival), n.p., 1976.

Pouyan, A.P. and Māni, M., *Iran, Three Essays on: Imperialism, The Revolutionary Left and the Guerrilla Movement*, Florence, n.d.

*Quandt, William B., *Palestinian Nationalism: Its Political and Military Dimensions*, Rand Corporation Report, California, November 1971.

*Quandt, William B., Jabber, Fuad and Leach, Ann Mosely, *The Politics of Palestinian Nationalism*, Berkeley and Los Angeles, 1973.

Ra'anan, Uri, *The USSR Arms and the Third World*, Cambridge, Mass., 1969.

Rabi'a, Hamed, *silah al-betrol wa al-ṣira' al-'arabi al-isra'ili* (Oil Weapon amid the Arab-Israeli Struggle), Beirut, 1974.

Ramazani, Rouhollah K., *Iran's Foreign Policy, 1941-1973: A Study of Foreign Policy in Modernizing Nations*, Charlottesville, 1975.

Ramazani, Rouhollah K., *The Persian Gulf: Iran's Role*, Charlottesville, 1972.

El-Rayyes, Riad and Nahas Dunia, *Guerillas for Palestine*, London, 1976.

Bibliography

Reich, Bernard, *Quest for Peace: United States-Israel Relations and the Arab-Israeli conflict*, New Jersey, 1977.

Remer, G. F., ed., *Three Essays on the International Economics of Communist China*, New York, 1959, reprinted in 1969.

The Revolutionary Organisation of Tudeh Party Abroad, *History of the Iranian Communist Movement*, Roma, n.d.

Rida, Adil, *'uman wa al-khalidj: kadiya wa munakashat* (Oman and the Gulf: Issues and Discussions), Cairo, 1969.

*Ro'i, Yaacov, *From Encroachment to Involvement: A Documentary Study of Soviet Policy in the Middle East, 1945–1973*, Jerusalem, 1974.

Rosenau, James N., *The Scientific Study of Foreign Policy*, New York, 1971.

Rosenau, James N., ed., *International Politics and Foreign Policy: A Reader in Research and Theory*, New York, 1969.

*Rothstein, Robert L., *The Weak in the World of the Strong: The Developing Countries in the International System*, New York, 1977.

Rouhani, Fuad, *A History of OPEC*, New York, 1971.

Rubinstein, Alvin Z., ed., *Soviet and Chinese Influence in the Third World*, New York, 1975.

Al-Rumyahi, Mohammed Ghanim, *al-betrol wa al-taghir al-idjtima'i fi al-khalidj al-'arabi* (Oil and Social Change in the Arabian Gulf), Cairo, 1975.

Rybczynski, T. M., ed., *The Economics of the Oil Crisis*, London, 1976.

Sadik, T. Muhammad and Snavely, William P., *Bahrain, Qatar and the United Arab Emirates: Colonial Past, Present Problems and Future Prospects*, Lexington, Mass., 1972.

Safa'i, Farahani A. A., *hawal al-wihda al-wataniya al-filistiniya* (On the Palestinian National Unity), Beirut, 1976.

Safa'i, Farahani, A. A., *ma yadjib an ya'rifuhu al-thawri* (What a Revolutionary Should Know), n.p., 1976.

Safa'i, Farahani A. A., *mudhuk'at tadjrubat al-thawra al-filistiniya* (Issues from Palestinian Revolution Experience), Beirut, 1974.

Safa'i, Farahani A. A., *munakashat 'ara' hawla al-thawra al-filistiniya* (Discussions of Views on the Palestinian Revolution), Beirut, 1977.

*Safa'i, Farahani A. A., *nazra fi tanakudat al-wad' al-'arabi al-'am* (A View on the Contradictions in the General Arab Condition), Beirut, 1975.

Safa'i, Farahani, A. A., *al-thawra al-filistiniya bayna al-nakd wa al-tahtim* (Palestinian Revolution Between Criticism and Destruction), Beirut, 1973.

Safran, Nadav, *Israel: The Embattled Ally*, Cambridge, Mass., 1978.

Said, Abdel Moghny, *Arab Socialism*, London, 1972.

Sampson, Anthony, *The Seven Sisters: The Great Oil Companies and the World They Made*, London, 1975.

418

Sanger, Richard, *The Arabian Peninsula*, New York, 1954.

Sayegh, Fayez A., ed., *The Dynamics of Neutralism in the Arab World: A Symposium*, San Francisco, 1964.

Sayegh, Kamal, S., *Oil and Arab Regional Development*, New York, 1968.

Schou, August, and Brundtland, Arne Olar, eds., *Small States in International Relations*, New York, 1971.

Shafik, Munir, *ba'd al-kawanin al-'askariya fi al-thawra al-filistiniya* (Some Military Rules in the Palestinian Revolution), Beirut, 1976.

*Shafik, Munir, *Hawal al-tanakud wa al-mumarasa fi al-thawra al-filistiniya* (On Contradiction and Practice in the Palestinian Revolution), Beirut, 1971.

Shafik, Munir, *al-hazima al-kubra* (The Great Defeat), 2 vols., Beirut, 1973.

Shafik, Munir, *hiwar wa asrar ma'a'l-muluk wa'l-ru'asa'* (Dialogue and Secret Dealings with Kings and Heads of States), Beirut, n.d.

Sharabi, Hisham, *Palestine Guerillas: Their Credibility and Effectiveness*, Beirut, 1970.

El-Sheikh, Riad, *Kuwait: Economic Growth of the Oil State: Problems and Policies*, Kuwait, 1973.

*Al-Shukairy, Ahmad, *arba'un 'am fi'l-hayat al-'arabiya wa'l-dowliya* (Forty Years on the Arab Political Scene), Beirut, 1959.

Shwadran, Benjamin, *The Middle East Oil and the Great Powers*, New York, 1974 edition.

Sigmond, P.E., ed., *The Ideologies of the Developing Nations*, New York, 1963.

Skeet, Ian, *Muscat and Oman: The End of an Era*, London, 1974.

Skorov, G.E., ed., *Science, Technology and Economic Growth in Developing Countries*, London, 1978.

Smil, Vadav, *China's Energy: Achievements, Problems, Prospects*, New York, 1976.

Smiley, David, *Arabian Assignment*, London, 1975.

Stahnke, Arthur A., ed., *China's Trade With the West: A Political and Economic Analysis*, New York, 1971.

Stevens, Georgiana, *Jordan River Partition*, Stanford, 1965.

Sua'udi, Muhammad, *al-watan al-'arabi: dirasa li-ma'alimihi al-djughrafiya* (The Arab World: A Study of its Geography), Beirut, n.d.

Tahtinen, Dale R., *Arms in the Persian Gulf*, Washington D.C., 1974.

Thomas, Bertram, *Arabia Felix: Across the Empty Quarter of Arabia*, London, 1932.

*Tomeh, George J., ed., *United Nations Resolutions on Palestine and the Arab-Israeli Conflict, 1947–1974*, Beirut, 1975.

Townsend, John, *Oman: The Making of the Modern State*, London, 1977.

Turki, Fawaz, *The Disinherited: Journal of a Palestinian Exile*, New York, 1972.

*US Congress, House of Representatives, Committee on International Relations, *The Soviet Union and the Third World: A Watershed in Great Power Policy*, Washington D.C., 1977.
US Department of State, *Background Notes: Muskat and Oman*, Washington D.C., April 1968.
*US Department of State, *The Sino-Soviet Economic Offensive in the Less Developed Countries*, New York, 1958, reprinted 1969.
*Van Ess, Peter, *Revolution and Chinese Foreign Policy: Peking's Support for Wars of National Liberation*, Berkeley, 1970.
Vital, David, *The Survival of the Small States: Studies in Small Power-Great Power Conflict*, Oxford, 1971.
Weng-Byron, S. J., *Peking's U.N. Policy, Continuity and Change*, New York, 1972.
Wilson, Sir Arnold T., *The Persian Gulf: An Historical Sketch from the Earliest Times to the Beginning of the Twentieth Century*, London, 1959.
Whitson, William W., ed., *Doing Business with China: American Trade Opportunities*, New York, 1974.
Young, Cuyler T., ed., *Middle East Focus: The Persian Gulf*, Princeton, 1968.
Young, Kenneth T., *The 1954 Geneva Conference – Indo-China and Korea*, New York, reprinted 1968.
Zeine, Zeine N., *The Emergence of Arab Nationalism: With a Background Study of Arab-Turkish Relations in the Near East*, Beirut, 1958.

Periodicals and documents

Non-Arabic sources

*Arab Report and Record (ARR)
Christian Science Monitor
*Current Background
Daily Star
Daily Telegraph, The
Dawn
Egyptian Gazette
Financial Times
Guardian, The
*Hong Chi
*International Documents on Palestine
International Herald Tribune
Iraninform
Japan Times, The
Jerusalem Post

Jerusalem Star
Khayhan International
Kuo Chi Chih Shih (International Knowledge)
Kuo Chi Chih Shih (Current Affairs)
An-Nahar Arab Report
*New China News Agency (Hsinhua)
New York Herald Tribune (European Edition)
New York Times
Observer, The
Observer Foreign News Service
Oman
*Peking Review
*People's Daily
Political Commentary
*Selection of China Mainland Magazine (SCMM)
South China Morning Star
Soviet News
Sudan Daily, The
Summary of World Broadcasts (Middle East and North Africa)
Sunday Telegraph
Sunday Times, The
*Survey of China Mainland Press (SCMP)
*Ta Kung Pao
Tass
Times, The (London)
Training Course (Lectures) For the Diplomats of the Ministry of
    Foreign Affairs, Ministry of Foreign Affairs, State of Kuwait
Washington Post
World Petroleum
Yearly and Monthly Bulletin of Foreign Trade Statistics, Planning
    Board, State of Kuwait

Arabic sources

*akhbar filistin
al-'akida
al-'alam (Morocco)
al-dastour (Jordan)
*dirāsāt 'arabiya
al-fadjr al-djadid (Syria)
filistin
*filistinyna (Our Palestine)
*al-hadaf
al-hayah (Lebanon)
*al-hurriya

*al-khat al-ahmar
al-kifah
*al-kitab al-sanawī lil-ḳaḍya al-filisṭinya lil-'am
al-liwa'
madjalat ghurfat tidjarat wa ṣina'at al-kuwait
al-manar
Ministry of Information, Yemen Arab Republic '*al-sadakatu al-yemeniya*'
    (Sino-Yemen Friendship) Ṣan'a, 1972
al-muharir
al-nahar
PFLOAG (watha'ik)
al-ra'i al-'ām
al-safīr
saūt al-thawra
saūt al-'uruba
al-ṣayyad (Lebanon)
al-siyasa
al-ṭali'a (Egypt)
al-ṭalī'a (Kuwait)
al-thawra (Syria)
Tis'a yuniya (9 June)
*Wafa
al-watha'iḳ al-'arabiya
*al-watha'iḳ al-filisṭiniya al-'arabiya
*al-yumiyat al-filistiniya (Palestine Diaries, 14 vols.)

Index